Computer Networks

Protocols, Standards, and Interfaces

Second Edition

Uyless Black
Bell Atlantic Education Services

PTR PRENTICE HALL
Englewood Cliffs, New Jersey 07632

Black, Uyless D.
Computer networks: protocols, standards, and interfaces/Uyless Black. -- 2nd ed.
p.   cm.
Includes bibliographical references and index.
ISBN 0-13-175605-2
1. Computer networks.   I. Title.
TK5105.5.B56   1993
004.6--dc20   92-41469

Prentice Hall Computer Communications Series
Wushow Chou, *Advisor*
Editorial/production supervision: *The Wheetley Company*
Buyer: *Mary Elizabeth McCartney*
Acquisitions editor: *Michael Hays*

©1993 by PTR Prentice-Hall, Inc.
A Simon & Schuster Company
Englewood Cliffs, New Jersey 07632

The publisher offers discounts on this book when ordered in bulk quantities.
For more information, contact:

> Corporate Sales Department
> PTR Prentice Hall
> 113 Sylvan Avenue
> Englewood Cliffs, New Jersey 07632
>
> Phone: 201-592-2863
> Fax: 201-592-2249

Printed in the United States of America
10 9 8 7 6 5 4 3 2 1

ISBN 0-13-175605-2

Prentice-Hall International (UK) Limited, *London*
Prentice-Hall of Australia Pty. Limited, *Sydney*
Prentice-Hall Canada Inc., *Toronto*
Prentice-Hall Hispanoamericana, S.A., *Mexico*
Prentice Hall of India Private Limited, *New Delhi*
Prentice-Hall of Japan, Inc., *Tokyo*
Simon & Schuster Asia Pts. Ltd., *Singapore*
Editora Prentice-Hall do Brasil, Ltda, *Rio de Janeiro*

This is dedicated to the readers of my books . . . thank you, you keep me going.

Contents

Preface, ix

Organization of this Book, xi

Acknowledgments, xii

Chapter One   *Introduction to Computer Networks*

Introduction, 1   Advantages of Networks, 1   Structure of the
Communications Network, 2   *Point-to-point and Multidrop
Circuits*, 4   *Data Flow and Physical Circuits*, 4   Network
Topologies, 6   *Topologies and Design Goals, 6   Hierarchical
Topology, 7   Horizontal Topology (Bus), 9   Star Topology, 9
Ring Topology, 9   Mesh Topology, 9*   The Telephone Network, 10
Switched and Nonswitched Options, 12   Fundamentals of
Communications Theory, 13   *Channel Speed and Bit Rate, 13
Voice Communications and Analog Waveforms, 14   Bandwidth and
the Frequency Spectrum*, 14   Connecting the Analog and Digital
Worlds, 18   *Digital Signals, 18   The Modem*, 18   Synchronizing
Network Components, 19   *Synchronization Codes, 20
Asynchronous and Synchronous Transmission, 22*   Message
Formats, 24   The Communications Port, 24   Additional Network
Components, 25   Summary, 27

Chapter Two   *Communications Between and Among
Computers and Terminals*, 28

Introduction, 28   Traffic Control and Accountability, 28   *Checking
for Errors*, 30   Wide Area and Local Networks, 30   Connection-
oriented and Connectionless Networks, 34   Classification of
Communications Protocols, 36   Polling/Selection Systems, 38
*Selective and Group Polling, 40   Stop-and-Wait Polling/Selection,
41   Continuous ARQ (Sliding Windows), 43*   Nonpolling Systems,
46   *Request to Send/Clear to Send, 47   Xon/Xoff, 47   Time
Division Multiple Access (TDMA), 48*   Peer-to-Peer Nonpriority
Systems, 49   *Time Division Multiplexing (TDM) or Slot, 49
Register Insertion, 50   Carrier Sense (Collision) Systems, 50
Token Passing, 52*   Peer-to-Peer Priority Systems, 54   *Priority
Slot, 54   Carrier Sense (Collision-free) Systems, 54   Token-passing
(Priority) Systems*, 55   Summary, 55

Chapter Three   *Layered Protocols, Networks, and the OSI Model*, 56

Introduction, 56   Goals of Layered Protocols, 56   Network Design Problems, 57   Communication Between Layers, 58   A Pragmatic Illustration, 61   Introduction to Standards Organizations and the OSI Model, 63   *Standards Organizations, 63*   *The Layers of OSI, 64*   *OSI Status, 66*   GOSIP, 67   *GOSIP, Version 1, 68*   *GOSIP, Version 2, 71*   Summary, 71

Chapter Four   *Polling/Selection Protocols,* 72

Introduction, 72   Character and Bit Protocols, 72   Binary Synchronous Control (BSC), 73   *BSC Formats and Control Codes, 73*   *Line Modes, 74*   *Line Control, 75*   *Problems with BSC, 76*   HDLC, 76   *HDLC Options, 77*   *HDLC Frame Format, 79*   *Code Transparency and Synchronization, 81*   *HDLC Control Field, 83*   *Commands and Responses, 85*   *The HDLC Transmission Process, 89*   *HDLC Subsets, 95*   SDLC, 97   Protocol Conversion, 100   Summary, 100

Chapter Five   *Satellite Networks,* 101

Introduction, 101   Satellite Components, 101   *Pros and Cons of Satellite Networks, 102*   *Brief History, 103*   Using Satellites to Communicate, 104   *Conventional Multiplexing*, 104   *Polling/Selection*, 105   *Nonpolling Peer/Peer Systems, 108*   *Nonpolling Primary/Secondary Systems, 111*   Satellite Delay Units (SDUs), 114   The Teleport, 115   Summary, 116

Chapter Six   *Local Area Networks,* 117

Introduction, 117   Way LANs?, 117   Primary Attributes of a LAN, 118   *Broadband and Baseband LANs, 118*   IEEE LAN Standards, 119   *Relationship of the 802 Standards to the ISO/CCITT Model, 120*   *Connection Options with LANs, 120*   *LLC and MAC Protocol Data Units, 123*   *LAN Topologies and Protocols, 125*   *CSMA/CD and IEEE 802.3, 125*   *Token Ring (Priority), 130*   *Token Bus and IEEE 802.4, 134*   *Metropolitan Area Networks (MANs), 137*   *Summary of the 802 Specifications, 137*   Other Systems, 138   *AT&T Information System Network (ISN), 138*   *IBM Token Ring, 139*   *ANSI Fiber Distributed Data Interface, 145*   Summary, 148

Chapter Seven   *Switching and Routing in Networks,* 149

Introduction, 149   Telephone Switching Systems, 149   *Electromechanical Systems, 152*   *Stored Program Control Systems, 153*   Message Switching, 156   Packet Switching, 157   *When and When Not to Use Packet Switching, 159*   *Packet Routing, 161*   Packet-Switching Support to Circuit-Switching Networks, 170   Summary, 172

Chapter Eight

The X.25 Network and Supporting Protocols, 173

Introduction, 173   Features of X.25, 173   Why X.25?, 175
Layers of X.25, 175   *X.25 and the Physical Layer,* 175   *X.25 and the Data Link Layer,* 176   *Companion Standards to X.25,* 177
Features of X.25, 178   *X.25 Channel Options,* 178   Flow-Control
Principles, 182   Other Packet Types, 182   X.25 Logical Channel
States, 186   Timeouts and Time Limits, 187   Packet Formats, 188
The D Bit, 192   *The M Bit,* 192   *A and B Packets*, 193   *The Q Bit,*
193   *The A Bit,* 194   Flow Control and Windows, 194   X.25
Facilities, 195   Other Standards and Layers, 198   *The Pad,* 198
PAD: Packet Formats and Packet Flow, 204   *The Transport Layer,*
204   Internetworking, 209   Connectionless-mode Networks, 211
X.75, 211   Communications between the Layers, 214   Frame
Relay and X.25, 224   *The Frame Relay and X.25 Stacks,* 225
International X.25 Networks, 226   *Does a Standard Assure
Compatibility?,* 226   Summary, 227

Chapter Nine

Digital Networks, 228

Introduction, 228   Advantages of Digital Systems, 228   Signal
Conversion, 230   Digital Carrier Systems, 232   Channel and Data
Service Units, 234   Analog-to-Digital Techniques, 234   *Waveform
Analysis,* 234   *Parameter Coding (Vocoders),* 237   Future Digital
Systems, 238   Integrated Digital Networks, 239   *SBS Integrated
Network,* 239   *The Integrated Services Digital Network (ISDN),* 241
Digital Switching, 255   Voice Transmission by Packet, 257   Bell
Labs' Packet-Switched Voice-Data Patent, 260   Summary, 260

Chapter Ten

TCP/IP, 261

Introduction, 261   TCP/IP and Internetworking, 261   Example of
TCP/IP Operations, 263   Related Protocols 264   Ports and Sockets,
264   The IP Address Structure, 265   Major Features of IP, 265   *IP
Datagram,* 267   Major IP Services, 269   *IP Source Routing,* 269
Route-Recording Option, 271   *The Timestamp Option,* 271   *ICMP,*
271   *ICMP Message Format,* 271   *ICMP Error- and Status-
Reporting Procedures,* 272   Value of the Transport Layer, 273
TCP, 274   *Major Features of TCP,* 274   *Passive and Active Opens,*
276   *The Transmission Control Block (TCB),* 277   The TCP
Segment, 277   User Datagram Protocol (UDP), 279   *Format of the
UDP Message,* 279   Route Discovery Protocols, 280   *Examples of
Route Discovery Protocols,* 282   *The Application Layer Protocols,*
285   Summary, 285

Chapter Eleven

Personal Computer Networks, 287

Personal Computer Introduction, 287   Growth in the Personal
Computer Industry, 287   Personal Computer Communications
Characteristics, 288   *Error Handling,* 289   Using the Personal
Computer as a Server, 291   Linking the Personal Computer to
Mainframe Computers, 292   File Transfer on Personal Computers,

294   Personal Computers and Local Area Networks, 298   Network Operating Systems (NOSs), 300   Common IBM PC LAN Protocol Stacks, 301   AppleTalk and EtherTalk, 303   Summary, 305

Chapter Twelve

The PBX and Data Communications Networks, 306
Introduction, 306   Why Use a PBX in Data Communications?, 306 Evolution of the PBX, 307   Issue of Voice/Data Integration, 310 Issue of Using a PBX in a LAN, 311   *Wiring Costs*, 312   The Fourth-Generation PBX, 313   Examples of Modern PBXs, 314 The Digital Multiplexed Interface (DMI) and Computer-to-PBX Interface (CPI) Proposals, 315   Summary, 318

Chapter Thirteen

Upper-Layer Protocols, 319
Introduction, 319   Network Security, 319   *Encryption with Private Keys*, 321   *The Data Encryption Standard (DES)*, 323   *Encryption with Public Keys*, 326   *ISO Security Recommendations*, 328   The Session Layer, 328   *Session Layer Operations*, 329   *The Graceful Close*, 329   *Synchronization Services*, 329   *Session Layer Activities*, 331   The Presentation Layer, 331   ASN.1, 331   *ASN.1 Coding Rules*, 333   Some Examples of ASN.1 Coding, 333 *Transfer Syntax*, 337   The Application Layer, 338   ACSE, 340 RTSE, 340   ROSE, 342   CCR, 344   Terminal Systems and Protocols, 346   *Telematics*, 346   *Teletex*, 347   Electronic Mail, 348   X.400, 349   X.500 Directory Services, 353   Protocols for File Management, 353   FTAM, 356   Virtual Terminal Protocols, 360   Distributed Transaction Processing, 363   RDA, 364   EDI, 365   Summary, 365   Final Thoughts, 366

Appendix A A Data Communications Tutorial, 367
Appendix B Translation Tables, 380
Appendix C Physical Level Interfaces, 383
Appendix D Commonly Used Standards, 400
Appendix E Supporting Standards to X.25/X.75 Networks, 412

Index, 425

Preface

In my role as a consultant and lecturer in the field of data communications, I am often asked the following question: "How do computers and terminals actually communicate with each other?" Upon further probing, usually I find the person is actually seeking answers to a more difficult question: "How can I understand the many parts of a communications network and how they fit together?" This is not an easy question to answer, since there are many parts of a communications system. Computer networks can now consist of satellite systems, packet switches, personal computers, private branch exchanges (PBXs), local area networks (LANs), digital systems, and a myriad of other complex technologies.

My goal in writing this book is to provide answers to the questions posed above, and to do so with simple prose rather than with pages upon pages of arcane formulas. Although books based on mathematical concepts and algorithms obviously are quite important, they rarely satisfy the practitioner whose primary concern is with nontheoretical problems, and it is the practitioner for whom this book is intended. Nevertheless, any book on the subject of computer networks must be somewhat technical and detailed if it is to adequately address the subject. Although a background in electronic engineering or a mathematics degree is not required to understand this book, the reader will need to delve into the chapters with some patience and care. If this premise is accepted, then the book should be useful.

This book is written for individuals with varying levels of knowledge and experience, from the beginner who needs an overview to the more advanced data communications professional who needs to fill some information gaps in specific areas. The beginner should read Appendices A and B before moving into Chapter One. After reading Chapter One, Appendix C is available if the reader wishes more information on physical-level interfaces. The more advanced reader can browse through these appendices and then delve into any of the chapters. The book guides the reader to (or around) sections that go into more technical detail. Readers wishing only an overview may choose to skip those sections or chapters.

The chapters have been written to be as self-contained as possible, but each chapter assumes the reader understands the previous chapters and Appendices A, B, and C. Appendices D and E have been included for ease of reference to some of the more important international standards. Each chapter contains suggested readings and, where applicable, notes regarding information sources.

This book is organized around the International Organization for Standardization's Open Systems Interconnection (OSI) layered protocol model, described in Chapter Three. Emphasis is placed on the first four layers of the model, since most of the communications functions reside in those layers. However, information is also provided on some of the more important aspects of the upper three layers.

The book is also structured around the Protocol Classification Tree. The classification tree is not intended to be all-inclusive, but serves as a method to describe some of the more important functions of computer networks.

This book is the second edition of *Computer Networks*. It reflects the changes that have occurred in the industry since the original edition (1987). The major changes reflected in this edition include descriptions of the emerging technologies, such as Frame Relay and ATM. Of course, the material on outdated technologies has been eliminated.

Organization of this Book

This book has been designed to be as modular as possible. The chapters are relatively self-contained, as each chapter is devoted to a specific aspect of data communications networking or an analysis of a specific type of network.

It is recommended, however, that readers new to the subject of data communications networks read Chapter 1 first, followed by Chapter 2. All readers are encouraged to read Chapter 3, since layered protocols and the OSI Model form the basis for many networks today. The only other recommendation concerning the order in which chapters are read is to review the HDLC material in Chapter 4. HDLC serves as the foundation for a wide variety of important protocols such as link access procedure for the D channel (LAPD), the logical link control (LLC), and so on.

Following this review, the chapters can be read in the order best suited to the information needs of the reader.

Acknowledgments

I would like to thank several people and organizations who have helped me during the writing of this book. Several ideas about the explanations on internetworking are the result of contract work I did through the Bell Atlantic Education Services (BAES) with several clients. These endeavors once again reinforced the age-old truism that one learns by teaching.

One program was with the U.S. Army 7th Signal Command, located at Ft. Ritchie, Maryland. Forty-five personnel at Ft. Ritchie went through an intensive training program on data communications and computer networks. These individuals gave me several wonderful ideas on how to present some of the material that is reflected in this book. To those forty-five people: thank you and congratulations on completing an arduous curriculum. I would like to recognize Colonel Michael Yokom, David Hughes, and Chris McKinney for their foresight that led to this program, and thank them for their trust and patience during the development of the course modules.

Another program was instituted through BAES with Ascom Timeplex. Again, I learned much from my students. The engineers at Ascom Timeplex gave me many ideas about how to present descriptions about bridges and routers. I want to thank Jeff Mandel and Bill Challis for their support for this training program.

1

Introduction to
Computer Networks

INTRODUCTION

Due to the tremendous impact of computers and computer networks on society during the past decade, this period in history has come to be called the "information age." The productivity and profitability of both organizations and individuals have been enhanced significantly by these revolutionary tools. Individuals use computer networks almost daily to conduct personal and professional business. This trend is accelerating as more people discover the power of computers and communications networks both for businesses and for homes. The day-to-day transactions at department stores, banks, reservation counters, and other businesses are all dependent upon computer networks. The information age is equally dependent on the computer *and* the computer network.

What is a computer network? Several definitions are accepted in the industry. Perhaps the simplest is the following: a computer network is a number of computers (and usually terminals) interconnected by one or more transmission paths. The transmission path often is the telephone line, due to its convenience and universal presence. The network exists to meet one goal: the transfer and exchange of data between the computers and terminals. This data exchange provides for the many computer-based services we often take for granted in our daily lives, such as bank teller machines, point-of-sale terminals, check-verification devices, and even the guidance of the space shuttle.

ADVANTAGES OF NETWORKS

Computer networks provide several important advantages to enterprises and individuals.

1. Modern organizations today are widely dispersed, with offices located in diverse parts of a country and the world. Many of the computers and terminals at the sites need to exchange information and data, often daily. A network provides the means to exchange data among these computers and to make programs and data available to the people of the enterprise.

2. The networking of computers permits the sharing of resources. For instance, if a computer becomes saturated with too much work at one site, the work can be reloaded through the network onto another computer in the network. Such load sharing permits a better, more even utilization of resources.

3. Networking also supports the critical function of backup. In the event a computer fails, its counterpart can assume its functions and workload. Backup capability is especially important in systems such as those used for air traffic control. In the event a computer malfunctions, backup computers rapidly take over and assume control of operations without endangering air travelers.

4. The use of networking allows a very flexible working environment. Employees can work at home by using terminals tied through networks into the computer at the office. Many employees now carry terminals or portable personal computers on trips and connect into their networks through hotel room telephones. Other employees travel to remote offices and use telephones and networks to transmit and receive critical sales, administrative, and research data from computers at company headquarters.

The information age is aptly named, for our society now relies on information to reduce the costs to produce our goods as well as to improve the overall quality of our lives. Communications systems and computer networks provide for rapid exchange of information among computers throughout a country.

STRUCTURE OF THE COMMUNICATIONS NETWORK

Before proceeding further, it will be helpful to define some terms. Figure 1-1 illustrates a simple data communications system. The *application process* (AP) is the end-user application. It usually consists of software such as a computer program. Typical examples are an accounts receivable program, a payroll program, an airline reservation system, an inventory control package, or a personnel system.

In Figure 1-1, site A could execute an application process (AP_{A1}) in the form of a software program to access an application process at site B (which is, in this case, a program [AP_{B1}] and a data base). Figure 1-1 also shows a site B program (AP_{B2}) accessing a file at site A through an application program (AP_{A2}). (This book uses the term *application process* to describe end-user applications, unless otherwise noted.)

The application resides in the *data terminal equipment,* or DTE. DTE is a generic term used to describe the end-user machine, which is usually a computer or terminal. The DTE could be a large mainframe computer, such as a large IBM or ICL machine, or it could be a smaller machine, such as a terminal or a personal computer. The DTE takes many forms in the industry. Here are several examples:

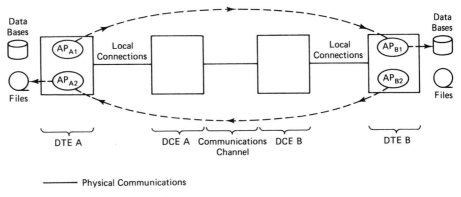

—————— Physical Communications

— — — Logical Communications

Figure 1-1.　A Communications System

- a work station for an air traffic controller
- an automated teller machine in a bank
- a point-of-sale terminal in a department store
- a sampling device to measure the quality of air
- a computer used to automate the manufacturing process in a factory
- an electronic mail computer or terminal
- a personal computer in the home or office.

　　The function of a communications network is to interconnect DTEs so they can share resources, exchange data, provide backup for each other, and allow employees and individuals to perform their work from any location.

　　Figure 1-1 shows that a network provides *logical* and *physical* communications for the computers and terminals to be connected. The applications and files use the physical channel to effect logical communications. Logical, in this context, means the DTEs are not concerned with the physical aspects of the communications process. Application A1 need only issue a logical *Read* request with an identification of the data. In turn, the communications system is responsible for sending the *Read* request across the physical channels to application B1.

　　Figure 1-1 also shows the *data circuit-terminating equipment,* or DCE (also called data communications equipment). Its function is to connect the DTEs into the communication line or channel. The DCEs designed in the 1960s and 1970s were strictly communications devices. However, in the last decade the DCEs have incorporated more user functions, and today some DCEs contain a portion of an application process. Notwithstanding, the primary function of the DCE remains to provide an *interface* of the DTE into the communications network. The familiar modem is an example of a DCE.

　　The interfaces are specified and established through *protocols.* Protocols are agreements on how communications components and DTEs are to communicate with each other. They may include actual regulations which stipulate a required or recommended convention or technique. Typically, several levels of interfaces and protocols are required to support an end-user application.

Today, many organizations are adapting common interfaces and protocols as a result of worldwide efforts to publish recommended *standards* that are vendor- and product-independent. Our goal is to gain an understanding of these valuable protocols, standards, and interfaces.

Point-to-point and Multidrop Circuits

DCEs and DTEs are connected in one of two ways. As illustrated in Figure 1-1, they are connected in a point-to-point configuration in which only two DTE devices are on the line or channel. Illustrated in Figure 1-2 is another approach called a multidrop configuration. In this configuration, more than two devices are connected to the same channel.

Data Flow and Physical Circuits

The DTEs and DCEs send communications traffic to each other in one of three methods:

Simplex: Transmission in one direction only

Half-Duplex: Transmission in both directions, but only one direction at a time (also called two-way alternate [TWA])

Full-Duplex (or Duplex): Transmission simultaneously in both directions (also called two-way simultaneous [TWS]).

Simplex transmission is common in television and commercial radio. It is not as common in data communications because of the one-way nature of the process, but simplex systems are found in some applications, such as telemetry. Half-duplex transmission is found in many systems, such as inquiry/response applications wherein a DTE sends a query to another DTE and waits for the applications process to access and/or compute the answer and transmit the response back. Terminal-based systems (keyboard terminals and terminals with CRT screens) often use half-duplex techniques. Full-duplex (or simply duplex) provides for simultaneous two-

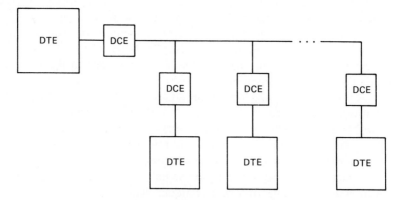

Figure 1-2. Multidrop Circuits

way transmission, without the intervening stop-and-wait aspect of half-duplex. Full-duplex is widely used in applications requiring continuous channel usage, high throughput, and fast response time.

Thus far, the terms *half-duplex* and *full-duplex* (duplex) have been used to describe how data move across the circuit. We have focused on these terms as they are used in the data communications industry. Figure 1-3 shows the physical circuit itself, without regard to how data moves. Some people in the industry use half-duplex and full-duplex to describe data flow *and* the physical circuit itself (an unfortunate mixing of these terms). The following discussion explains the physical circuit.

In telephone communications, the terms *two-wire* and *four-wire* circuits are used to describe the channel. One wire is for the transmission of data and the other is for the return circuit. (See Appendix A for a discussion of return circuits.) In a four-wire circuit, two pairs of two wires exist—two for the data and two for the return circuits. The telephone company usually configures a two-wire circuit as a switched dial-up circuit and a four-wire circuit as a leased, nonswitched circuit. However, exceptions exist and the reader is encouraged to check with the specific telephone company. The tradeoffs of switched and nonswitched circuits are discussed later in the chapter.

The advantages cited earlier concerning communications networks cannot be realized without the addition of an important component to the system. This component is the *data switching equipment,* or DSE. Figure 1-4 illustrates the use of the DSE in conjunction with the DTE and DCE. As the name implies, the major function of the DSE is to switch or route traffic (user data) through the network to the final destination. The DSE provides the vital functions of network routing around failed or busy devices and channels. The DSE may also route the data to the final destination through intermediate components, perhaps other switches.

Figure 1-4 illustrates a simple arrangement of the DCE, DTE, and DSE in the network. Later discussions will reveal that the configurations can be considerably more complex.

(a) Two-wire Circuit

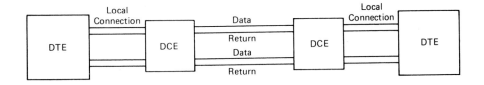

(b) Four-wire Circuit

Figure 1-3. Two-Wire and Four-Wire Circuits

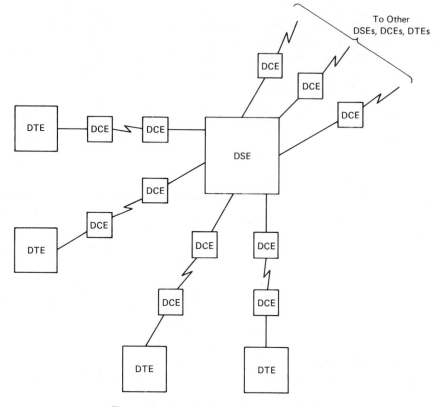

Figure 1-4. Data Switching Equipment (DSE)

NETWORK TOPOLOGIES

Topologies and Design Goals

A network configuration is also called a *network topology.* A network topology is the shape (or the physical connectivity) of the network. The term *topology* is borrowed from geometry to describe the form of something. The network designer has three major goals when establishing the topology of a network:

- provide maximum possible reliability to assure proper receipt of all traffic (alternate routing)
- route the traffic across the least-cost path within the network between the sending and receiving DTEs (although the least-cost route may not be chosen if other factors, such as reliability, are more important)
- give the end user the best possible response time and throughput.

Network reliability refers to the ability to deliver user data correctly (without errors) from one DTE to another DTE. It entails the ability to recover from errors or lost data in the network, including channel, DTE, DCE, or DSE failure. Reliability also refers to the maintenance of the system, which includes day-to-day testing; relieving faulty or failing components of their tasks; and fault isolation in the event of problems. When a component creates problems, the network diagnostic system should pinpoint the error readily, isolate the fault, and perhaps isolate the component from the network.

The second major goal in establishing a topology for the network is to provide the least-cost path between the application processes residing on the DTEs. This involves:

1. minimizing the actual length of the channel between the components, which usually entails routing the traffic through the fewest number of intermediate components;
2. providing the least expensive channel option for a particular application; for instance, transmitting low-priority data over a relatively inexpensive dial-up, low-speed telephone line, in contrast to transmitting the same data over an expensive high-speed satellite channel.

The third major goal in establishing a topology is to provide the best possible response time and throughput. Short response time entails minimizing delay between the transmission and the receipt of the data between the DTEs, and is especially important for interactive sessions between user applications. Throughput entails the transmission of the maximum amount of end-user data in a given period.

The more common network topologies are depicted in Figure 1-5:

- the hierarchical topology (tree)
- the horizontal topology (bus)
- the star topology
- the ring topology (hub)
- the mesh topology.

Hierarchical Topology

The hierarchical topology is one of the more common networks found today. The software to control the network is relatively simple and the topology provides a concentration point for control and error resolution. In most cases, the DTE at the highest order of the hierarchy is in control of the network. In Figure 1-5(a), traffic flow among and between the DTEs is initiated by DTE A. Many vendors implement a distributed aspect to the hierarchical network by providing methods for the subordinate DTEs to directly control the DTEs below them in the hierarchy. This reduces the workload of the central host at site A.

While the hierarchical topology is attractive from the standpoint of simplicity of control, it presents significant potential bottleneck problems. In some instances, the uppermost DTE, typically a large-scale mainframe computer, controls all traffic between DTEs. Not only can this create bottlenecks, it also presents reliability problems. In the event the upper-level machine fails, the network capabilities are lost

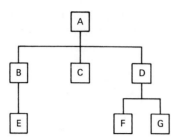

(a) Hierarchical or Tree Topology

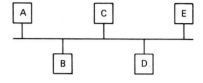

(b) Horizontal Topology

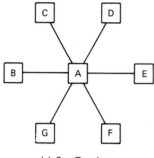

(c) Star Topology

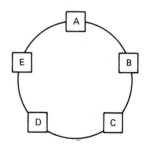

(d) Ring Topology

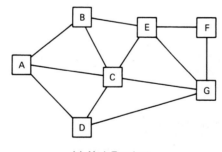

(e) Mesh Topology

Figure 1-5. Network Topologies

completely if this DTE is not fully backed up by another computer. Nonetheless, hierarchical topologies have been used widely in the past and will continue to be used in the future. They permit a graceful evolution toward a more complex network, because subordinate DTEs can be added relatively easily.

The hierarchical topology is also called a "vertical network" or a "tree network." The word "tree" is appropriate because a hierarchical network often resembles a tree with branches stemming from the top of the tree down to the lower level. You might pause at this point and determine if you could draw a tree-type network topology relating to one of your daily activities. One common example is the organizational chart hanging in your office. Indeed, the advantages and disadvantages of a vertical data communications network are much the same as those of a hierarchically structured business—clear lines of authority with frequent bottlenecks at the upper levels and often insufficient delegation of responsibility.

Horizontal Topology (Bus)

The horizontal topology or bus topology is illustrated in Figure 1-5(b). This arrangement is quite popular in local area networks (discussed in Chapter Six). It is relatively simple to control traffic flow between and among the DTEs because the bus permits all stations to receive every transmission. That is, a single station *broadcasts* to multiple stations. The main drawback of a horizontal topology stems from the fact that usually only one communications channel exists to service all the devices on the network. Consequently, in the event of a failure of the communications channel, the entire network is lost. Some vendors provide for fully redundant channels in the event of the loss of a primary channel. Others provide bypass switches around failed nodes. Another problem with this particular configuration is the difficulty in isolating faults to any one particular component tied into the bus. The absence of concentration points makes problem resolution difficult.

Star Topology

The star topology is another widely used structure for data communications systems. One of the major reasons for its continued use is based on historical precedence. The star network was used in the 1960s and early 1970s because it was easy to control—the software is not complex and the traffic flow is simple. All traffic emanates from the hub of the star, the central site in Figure 1-5(c), labeled A. Site A, typically a computer, is in complete control of the DTEs attached to it. Consequently, it is quite similar to the hierarchical topology, except that the star topology has limited distributed processing capabilities.

Site A is responsible for routing traffic to the other components; it is responsible for fault isolation as well. Fault isolation is relatively simple in a star network because the lines can be isolated to identify the problem. However, like the hierarchical structure, the star network is subject to potential bottleneck and failure problems at the central site. Several star networks built in the 1970s experienced serious reliability problems because of the centralized aspect of the network. Other systems established a redundant backup of the hub node, which provided considerably more reliability to the system.

Ring Topology

The ring topology is another popular approach to network configuration. As illustrated in Figure 1-5(d), the ring topology is so named because of the circular aspect of the data flow. In most instances, data flow in one direction only, with one single station receiving the signal and relaying it to the next station on the ring. The ring topology is attractive because bottlenecks, such as those found in the hierarchical or star systems, are very uncommon. Moreover, the logic to implement a ring network is relatively simple. Each component is tasked with a straightforward job of accepting the data, sending it to the DTE attached to it, or sending it out on the ring to the next intermediate component. However, like all networks, the ring network does have its deficiencies. The primary problem is the one channel tying in all the components in the ring. If a channel between two nodes fails, then the entire network is lost. Consequently, some vendors have established designs which provide for backup channels in the event a channel is lost. In other instances, vendors build switches which automatically route the data around the failed node to the next node on the ring to prevent the failure from bringing down the entire network. Yet another solution is the use of dual rings in which the network remains operational as long as one ring is operational.

Mesh Topology

The mesh topology has been used somewhat in the last few years (Figure 1-5(e)). Its attraction is its relative immunity to bottleneck and failure problems. Due to the multiplicity of paths from the DTEs and DSEs, traffic can be routed around failed components or busy nodes. Even though this approach is an expensive undertaking, some users prefer the reliability of the mesh network to that of the others (especially for networks with only a few nodes that need to be connected).

THE TELEPHONE NETWORK

Since many DCEs, DTEs, and DSEs are connected by a telephone channel, it should prove useful to examine the telephone system. Figure 1-6 illustrates the telephone network structure. The components are arranged in a hierarchy starting with the customer location at the bottom of the hierarchy. The customers, either in homes or offices, connect through the telephone system into the class 5 office, which is also called the *central office* (CO), local exchange, or end office. Thousands of these offices may be installed around a country (over 18,000 are installed in the United States). Connection is provided to the CO through a pair of wires (or four wires) called the *local loop* or *subscriber loop.*

Connections between COs are also provided by a facility called a *tandem center* (also called a tandem switch or toll center). The tandem center interconnects COs that do not have direct connections with each other. Four classes of tandem centers exist in the U.S. and Canada: toll centers, primary centers, sectional centers, and regional centers. The regional center (ten in the U.S.) has the largest area to serve, with each lesser class serving a smaller area.

The system is designed for each switching center to be connected to an office of a higher level, except at the highest level. The top-level offices are completely interconnected. The structure ensures that a path exists from each switch in the network to any other switch.

The CO is responsible for relaying a dialed telephone number to a local loop across to another CO or tandem office. The design philosophy is to route the call through the most economical path, which is usually the shortest path and/or the fewest number of switches. This design approach reduces the delay of establishing

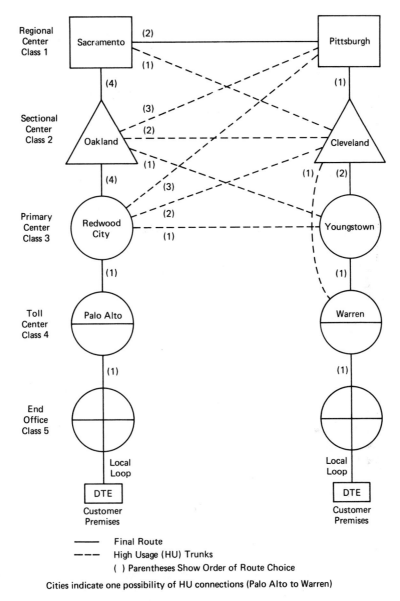

Figure 1-6. The Telephone Network

the connection with the other DTE, and the fewer number of intermediate switches reduces the expense to the telephone company. As the tandem path becomes longer, it must go through more components, incurring more delay and additional expense.

The system is built around *high-usage trunks* (or high-volume trunks), which carry the bulk of the traffic. High-usage trunks are established when the volume of calls warrants the installation of high-capacity channels between two offices. Consequently, trunk configurations vary depending on traffic volume between centers. The system attempts to switch the call down into the hierarchy, across the hierarchy, or, as a last resort, up into the hierarchy. Routing the call up usually entails more intermediate switching, thereby increasing the connection delay and the telephone company's cost to obtain the connection.

Figure 1-6 provides an example of the routing. Assume a connection is desired from a terminal in Palo Alto, California, to a computer in Warren, Ohio. The connection would be made from the Palo Alto central office to its tandem office (the toll center in Redwood City). If high-usage trunks did not exist, the path would follow the final trunk route. However, a high-usage trunk connects Redwood City to Warren's toll center, Youngstown. If a trunk (channel) is free, the route follows this path. If all trunks were busy on the Redwood City–Youngstown group, the next choice would be to the sectional center serving Warren, which is Cleveland, Ohio. If all possible routes are occupied, the call is blocked, resulting in a busy signal.

The long distance carriers now implement a routing concept called *dynamic nonhierarchical routing* (DNHR). This new technology is not constrained by a fixed hierarchical structure, but allows a *choice of path* based on heavy overflow traffic from the fixed topology. Major portions of DNHR have replaced much of the hierarchical network. DNHR means fewer busy signals and faster connections to the end user.

Switched and Nonswitched Options

A telephone customer may choose to acquire a leased or private line, through which the customer has a permanent connection in the telephone network from one site to another. (Private lines can also be switched through private switches.) A private, nonswitched line is often very useful when users cannot afford the delay of a connection or the actual blockage of a call when all circuits are busy. Moreover, users that have traffic with several hours of connection time per day can save money by using a leased line. The major tradeoffs between switched, dial-up circuits and nonswitched, leased circuits are as follows:

Switched *Advantages*
Flexible
Inexpensive for low volume
Disadvantages
Slow response
Blocking possible (busy signals)
Low quality
Expensive for high volume

Nonswitched *Advantages*
Supports higher volume
Higher quality possible
No blockage (busy signals)
Disadvantages
Expensive for low volume
Lack of flexibility when line is inoperable

The next section provides an explanation of communications theory. The reader who does not wish this detail should skip to the section on analog and digital signals.

FUNDAMENTALS OF COMMUNICATIONS THEORY

Channel Speed and Bit Rate

Appendix A describes how data are transmitted from one computer or terminal to another in binary images—1s and 0s. For example, the binary number 1001 represents the number 9 in base 10. (Appendix B also is provided to assist the reader with terms used in this section of the book.)

The most elementary method a device uses to send a binary number on a communications path is to switch the signal on and off electrically, or to provide high or low voltages on the line to represent the 1s and 0s. Regardless of how the data are represented on the path—in the form of on/off states, levels of voltage, or directions of current flow—the communications channel is described by its capacity in the number of *bits per second* transmitted. Abbreviations for bits per second are *bit/s, bps,* or *bs.* When one speaks of a 4800 bit/s line, it means a device sends 4800 bits per second through the channel. A bit is simply the representation of the electrical, optical, or electromagnetic state of the line: voltages, current, or some form of radio or optical signal. Seven or eight bits usually comprise a user-coded character, or byte (see Appendix A).

A data communications channel utilizing conventional telephone lines is very slow. Below are some examples. For purposes of comparison, a channel is classified by categories of low speed, medium speed, and high speed:

Low Speed: 0–600 bits per second
Medium Speed: 600–4800 bits per second
High Speed: 4800–9600 bits per second.

Only recently, in the last few years, has the industry successfully moved to 9.6 kilobits per second (kbit/s) on telephone channels. The typical speeds found beyond 9600 bits per second are 14,400, 19,200, 56,000, and 64,000 bit/s, and 1.544 megabit/s (1,544,000 bits per second) and 2.048 Mbit/s in Europe. (Chapter Nine explains the basis for these data rates.) The 1.544 megabits per second channel is the well-known T1 carrier. This offering is prevalent in transmissions such as high-speed digital channels and digital switches.

The idea of a high-speed channel operating at 9.6 kbit/s is rapidly changing. With the proliferation of optical fiber technology, mbit speeds are becoming commonplace. Notwithstanding, the focus of this section is to describe the communications capability from the end-user device, which remains in the kilobit range.

One might reasonably ask, why the slow speed? The answer is that DTEs and DCEs usually communicate through the telephone line. It was the most convenient and readily available path when the industry developed computers and began to interface them with terminals and other computers in the 1960s. The telephone channel is not designed for fast transmission between high-speed computers, but for voice transmission between people, which does not require the speed associated with data transmission.

Moreover, the majority of DTEs remaining today are connected through the telephone line with an interface called EIA-232-D. This rather ancient interface is still the most pervasive way of connecting DTEs and DCEs to the telephone lines. The EIA-232-D is constrained to bit rates up to 20 kbit/s.

Voice Communications and Analog Waveforms

Voice communications generate acoustical waveforms which propagate through the air. In effect, voice communications are physical energy. When one speaks, oscillating waveforms of high and low air pressure are created. These waveforms are called *analog* waveforms. They are so named because they exhibit a continuous, repeating occurrence and they are nondiscrete, gradually changing from high to low pressure. Of course, one cannot see waveforms in the air because the voice transmissions are air pressure variations.

The telephone handset translates the physical oscillations of the air to electrical energy with similar waveform characteristics. The waveform exhibits three primary characteristics that are very important to data communications: *amplitude, frequency,* and *phase.* Figure 1-7 shows these components. The amplitude of the signal is a measurement in relation to its voltage, which can be zero or a plus or minus value. Notice the analog aspect of the signal—it gradually increases in positive voltage, then traverses the zero voltage to the negative voltage, and returns to zero again. This complete oscillation is called a *cycle.* Figure 1-7 also illustrates the second major aspect of the signal, its frequency. The frequency describes the number of complete cycles per second or the number of oscillations per second. The number of oscillations per second or frequency is also called Hertz (Hz). Hertz describes the number of complete waveforms that pass a reference point in a second.

The term *baud* refers to the rate of signal change on the channel, regardless of the information content of those signals. For example, an 1800 Hz signal can be changed at 1200 times per second. The 1800 Hz signal describes the "carrier" frequency and the 1200 changes describe the baud. Many people use the term "baud rate," which is actually redundant, since baud implies a rate.

The third major component of the analog signal is also shown in Figure 1-7. The phase of the signal represents the point the signal has reached in the cycle. As illustrated in the figure, when the cycle has gone one-fourth of its phase at point A, it is said to have traversed through 90 percent of its cycle, just as traversing one-fourth the way around a circle represents a distance of 90 degrees. We will examine amplitude, frequency, and phase later in this chapter to explain one of the functions of certain DCEs.

Bandwidth and the Frequency Spectrum

A voice transmission consists of waveforms containing many different frequencies. The particular meld of these frequencies determines the pitch and sound of a per-

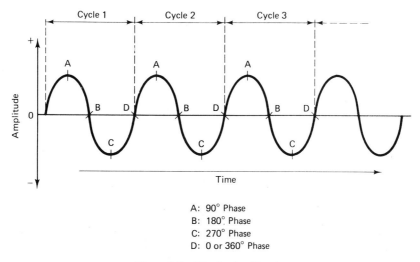

A: 90° Phase
B: 180° Phase
C: 270° Phase
D: 0 or 360° Phase

Figure 1-7. The Analog Signal

son's voice. A human voice occupies the frequencies of approximately 200 Hz to 15,000 Hz. The human ear can detect frequencies over a broader range, from around 40 Hz to 18,000 Hz. The range of frequencies (for example, those comprising the human voice spectrum) is called the *bandwidth,* a term also used in computer networks. Bandwidth refers to the range of transmission frequencies that are carried on a communications line. Bandwidth is a critical aspect in networks because the capacity of a channel (its bit rate) is directly related to its bandwidth.

Most physical phenomena with which we are familiar manifest themselves in some form of frequencies. These frequencies range from the audio frequencies to the extremely high frequencies found in the x-ray and gamma ray spectrum. Figure 1-8 illustrates the frequency spectrum. The spectrum ranges from the relatively limited bandwidth of the audio frequency, such as voice, through the high frequencies found in coaxial cable, microwave broadcasting, and the very high frequency range where visible light exists.

The idea of bandwidth is sometimes confusing, but its effect can readily be seen by some graphic illustrations. First, bandwidth is actually computed by subtracting the lowest frequency found in the signal, such as a telephone channel or a voice transmission, from the highest frequency found in the signal. A telephone channel in North America typically occupies a band ranging from 3300 Hz down to 300 Hz. (The band is actually slightly larger than this range, but we round it to this figure for convenience.) Consequently, subtracting the lower band from the upper band yields a bandwidth of 3000 Hz or 3 kHz. The European telephone bandwidth ranges from 300 Hz to 3400 Hz. These composite frequencies are used by the human voice and by data communications components to transmit an analog or a digital signal through the circuit.

Figure 1-8 shows that the bandwidth between the frequency spectrum of 10^3 to 10^4 is 9000 Hz. If a telephone channel occupies 3 kHz of band, then this bandwidth is roughly equivalent to three voice channels: 9000 ÷ 3000 = 3 channels (although more channels can be derived by applying other technologies). However, if one examines the bandwidth between 10^7 and 10^8, the full bandwidth is 90,000,000 Hz.

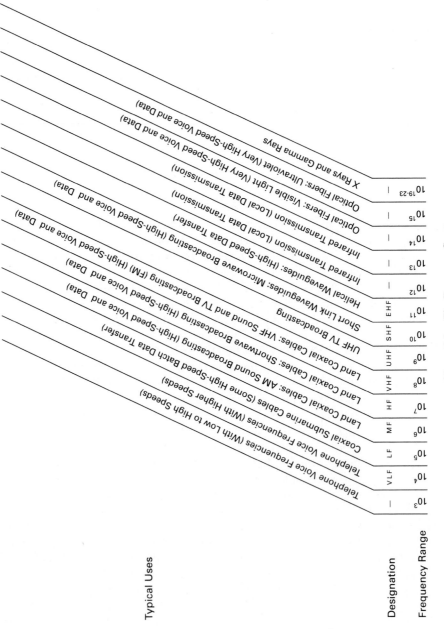

Figure 1-8. The Frequency Spectrum

Typical Uses

Telephone Voice Frequencies (With Low to High Speeds)		
Telephone Voice Frequencies (With Higher Speeds)		
Coaxial Submarine Cables (With Higher Speeds)		
Land Coaxial Cables (Some High-Speed Batch Data Transfer)		
Land Coaxial Cables: AM Sound Broadcasting (High-Speed Voice and Data)		
Land Coaxial Cables: Shortwave Broadcasting (High-Speed Voice and Data)		
UHF TV Broadcasting: VHF Sound and TV Broadcasting (FM) (High-Speed Voice and Data)		
Short Link Waveguides		
Helical Waveguides: Microwave Broadcasting (High-Speed Voice and Data)		
Infrared Transmission (Local Data Transmission)		
Optical Fibers: Infrared Transmission (Local Data Transmission)		
Optical Fibers: Visible Light (Very High-Speed Voice and Data)		
Ultraviolet (Very High-Speed Voice and Data)		
X Rays and Gamma Rays		

Designation		VLF	LF	MF	HF	VHF	UHF	SHF	EHF					
Frequency Range	10^3	10^4	10^5	10^6	10^7	10^8	10^9	10^{10}	10^{11}	10^{12}	10^{13}	10^{14}	10^{15}	$10^{19\text{-}23}$

16

If we divide 3000 Hertz, the voice-grade channel band, into this bandwidth, then theoretically we can derive 30,000 voice-grade channels. (In reality, fewer channels are obtained, due to the need to "separate" the channels from each other.) Simply stated, more things are happening faster as signals occupy channels in the greater frequency spectrum. More channels can be derived at these high-frequency rates.

The transmission of audio signals at their original frequency precludes more than one voice-grade transmission from occupying the channel; the multiple signals at 300–3300 Hz interfere with each other. However, the greater bandwidths of coaxial cable and microwave allow the 3 kHz voice-grade bands to occupy different portions of the frequency spectrum. For example, two voice-grade channels serving two DTEs can be placed onto higher band channels of coaxial cable as follows:

$$
\begin{array}{ccc}
 & 300 & 10{,}030{,}300 \\
\text{voice grade channel 1:} & \updownarrow & \updownarrow \\
 & 3300 & 10{,}033{,}300 \\
\\
 & 300 & 10{,}034{,}300 \\
\text{voice grade channel 2:} & \updownarrow & \updownarrow \\
 & 3300 & 10{,}037{,}300 \\
\end{array}
$$

Since the DTEs' two voice-grade channels now occupy different frequency spectra, the signals can use the same physical media, because they are *linear* in that they behave as if they are independent of each other. The signals are said to occupy or use *subchannels*.

The concept of several transmissions at different frequencies occupying the same physical medium (for example, a wire) at the same time is often quite confusing. An analogy to a more familiar phenomenon—light—should help remove the mystery. The "white" light we see in the sun's beams is actually comprised of many frequencies that fall within the visible light frequency spectrum. Yet, the frequencies of white light yield colors (frequencies) such as red, green, violet, and blue. We can think of the blue frequencies as occupying one "subchannel" of the white light spectrum and the red frequencies as occupying another. The prism provides us the tool to separate or combine the frequencies to travel through the atmosphere (channel) as combined colors (signals). These "prism" capabilities are provided by techniques discussed in the next section.

Bandwidth is a limiting factor on transmission capacity within the network. Other limiting factors are the actual signal power of the transmission and the amount of noise in the channel. The channel noise is a problem that is inherent to the channel itself and can never be completely eliminated. Noise results from several factors. For instance, atmospheric noise emanates from electrical disturbances in the earth's atmosphere. Space noise can come from the sun and other stars which radiate electromagnetic energy over a very broad frequency spectrum. Noise can also be found on a wire conductor or coaxial conductor because the random movement of electrons within the conductor generates thermal energy. (See Appendix A for a discussion of electron movement.)

CONNECTING THE ANALOG AND DIGITAL WORLDS

Digital Signals

When DTEs communicate with each other by use of a telephone path, the signal must accommodate itself to a voice-oriented analog world. However, DTEs "talk" in *digital* forms. As illustrated in Figure 1-9, the digital waveform looks considerably different from the analog waveform. It is similar in that it is continuous, repeats itself, and is periodic, but it is very different from the standpoint that it is *discrete*—it has very abrupt changes in its voltage state. Computers and terminals use digital, binary images because semiconductor transistors are basically two-state, discrete devices. (It should be noted that Figure 1-9 shows an ideal digital signal. Due to the electrical properties of the channel, the signal is actually less discrete and square-shaped.)

Digital transmission is available in many systems today. It has several distinct advantages over the analog channel, and is discussed in more detail in Chapter Nine. However, analog channels still dominate the local connections of DTEs into the telephone companies' channels.

The Modem

A method is needed to allow two digital devices to "talk" to each other through the dissimilar analog environment. The *modem* provides this digital/analog interface. It alters either the amplitude, the frequency, or the phase to represent the binary data as an analog signal.

The modem is our first example of a DCE. It provides the interface between the digital and analog worlds, as well as the capability to transmit from a digital DTE across the analog channel to a receiving digital DTE. The word "modem" is a shortened term for *mo*dulation/*dem*odulation. The process modulates the signal at the transmitting modem and demodulates the transmission at the receiving modem.

To be precise, the exact definition of modulation is: the modification of a frequency to carry data. This frequency is called the *carrier* frequency. The data that modulates the carrier (i.e., the data coming from the terminal or computer) is called the *baseband* signal. The term "baseband" usually refers to an unmodulated signal.

The modem modifies the carrier signal (either its amplitude, frequency, or phase) to carry the baseband signal. As illustrated in Figure 1-10, the AM modem

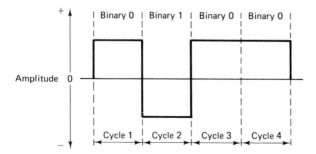

Figure 1-9. The Digital Signal

changes the amplitude of its carrier in accordance with the bit stream to be sent. In this instance, a higher amplitude represents a zero and a lower amplitude represents a one. A more popular modem is called an FM modem (frequency modulation modem) in which the amplitude remains constant and the frequency varies. A binary 1 is represented by one frequency and a binary 0 by another frequency. Another device is the PM modem (phase modulation modem). This modem abruptly alters its phase to represent the change from a 1 to a 0 or a 0 to a 1.

Appendix C provides information on the EIA-232-D and V.24/V.28 interfaces, which are recommended standards used to connect DTEs, DCEs, and DSEs. Review Appendix C if these interfaces are unfamiliar, or if more detailed information is needed.

SYNCHRONIZING NETWORK COMPONENTS

In order for computers and terminals to communicate, they first need to notify each other that they are able and wish to communicate. Second, once they are communicating, they must provide a method which keeps both devices aware of the ongoing transmissions. Let us address the first point. A transmitter, such as a terminal or a computer, must transmit its signal so that the receiving device knows when to search for and recognize the data as they arrive. In essence, the receiver must know

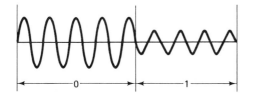

(a) Amplitude Modulation

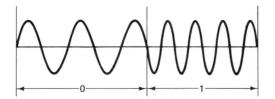

(b) Frequency Modulation

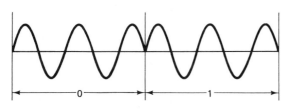

(c) Phase Modulation   **Figure 1-10.**   Modulation Techniques

the exact time that each binary 1 and 0 is coming across the communications channel. This requirement means that a mutual time base or a "common clock" is necessary between the receiving and transmitting devices.

In this sense, machine communications are analogous to the communications between people. For example, during a party where many people are conversing intermittently among and between themselves, two individuals (say, Mr. Dietz and Ms. Jones) must first recognize they are to establish communications with each other. If Ms. Jones' back is turned to Mr. Dietz, he must first send a preliminary signal, such as "Hello," or "Ms. Jones." This, in effect, establishes a common time base between the two individuals who wish to converse. If an individual simply began the conversation without previous notification, it is quite likely the receiving individual would miss the first part of the transmission; i.e., the first part of the first sentence. Since Ms. Jones is busy and occupied with other matters, Mr. Dietz must interrupt her current activity to get her attention.

In the same manner, a transmitting machine must first send to the receiving machine an indication that it wishes to "talk" with it. If the transmitter sends the bits down the channel without prior notice, the receiver will likely not have sufficient time to adjust itself to the incoming bit stream. In such an event, the first few bits of the transmission would be lost. Consequently, like Ms. Jones, the receiving DTE must receive a preliminary signal.

This process is part of a communication protocol and is generally referred to as *synchronization*. Short connections between machines often use a separate channel, or line, to provide the synchronization. This line transmits a signal that is turned on and off or varied in accordance with preestablished conventions. As the clocking signal coming across this line changes, it notifies the receiving device that it is to examine the data line at a specific time. It may also resynchronize the receiver's clock so that the receiver stays very accurately aligned on each incoming data bit. Thus, clocking signals perform two valuable functions: (1) they synchronize the receiver into the transmission before the data actually arrive, and (2) they keep the receiver synchronized with the incoming data bits.

Synchronization Codes

When long distances exist between computers and terminals, it makes more sense economically to incorporate the timing into the signal itself instead of using a separate clocking channel. This is known as a self-clocking code. Non-self-clocking codes present a problem in that the clock and the data can be altered as they propagate through separate channels. The clocking signal speeds up or slows down relative to the data signal, which means the receiver has difficulty "locking" onto the data signal.

A self-clocking code is one in which the receiving device can periodically check itself to see that it is sampling the line at the exact time a data bit is propagating into the receiver. This requires (under ideal conditions) the line to change its state very often. The best clocking codes are those in which the state of the line changes frequently, because these state changes (for example, voltage shifts) allow the receiver to continue to readjust itself to the signal.

The "clock" simply provides a reference for the individual binary 1s and 0s. The idea is to have a code with regular and frequent level transitions on the channel. The transitions delineate the binary data cells (1s and 0s) at the receiver, and sampling logic continuously looks for the state transitions in order to delineate the bit streams. Receiver sampling usually occurs at a higher rate than the data rate in order to more precisely define the bit cells.

Figure 1-11 provides an illustration of several common binary coding schemes used in the industry. We will discuss each of these briefly and describe their advantages and disadvantages. Their introduction here is necessary to an understanding of material in the subsequent chapters. (Be aware that the signals are not as sharp and square as Figure 1-11 suggests. Figure 1-11(e) depicts an actual signal.) All these signals exhibit one or several of the following four characteristics:

- *Unipolar code.* No signal below zero voltage or no signal above (i.e., algebraic sign does not change: 0 volts for 1, 3 volts for 0).
- *Polar code.* Signal is above and below zero voltage (opposite algebraic signs identify logic states: $+3$ volts and -3 volts).
- *Bipolar code.* The signal varies among three levels.
- *Alternate mark inversion (AMI) code.* Uses alternate polarity pulses to encode binary 1s.

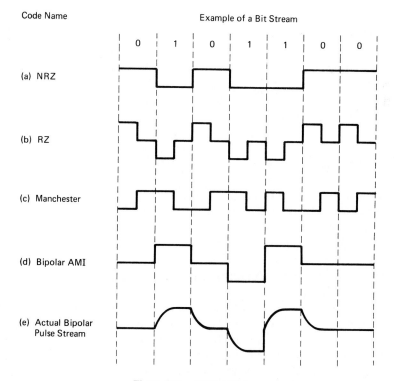

Figure 1-11. Digital Codes

Figure 1-11(a) shows the non-return-to-zero code (NRZ). Notice the signal level remains stable throughout the bit cell. In this case, the signal level remains low for a bit 1 and goes to a high voltage for a bit 0. (Opposite voltages are also used in many devices.) NRZ is a widely used data communications coding scheme because of its relative simplicity and low cost. The NRZ code also makes very efficient use of bandwidth, since it can represent a bit with each baud (signal change). However, it suffers from the lack of self-clocking capabilities, since a long series of continuous 1s or 0s would not create a signal state transition on the channel. As a consequence, the receiver's clock could possibly drift from the incoming signal and not sample the line at the right time; the transmitter and the receiver might actually lose synchronization with each other. The NRZ code can be polar or bipolar, depending on the actual implementation. NRZ is widely used in communications because it requires no encoding or decoding and it uses a channel's bandwidth very effectively.

The return-to-zero code (RZ) usually entails the changing of the signal state at least once in every bit cell. This scheme is illustrated in Figure 1-11(b). Since RZ codes provide a transition in every bit cell, they have very good synchronization characteristics. The RZ code's primary disadvantage is that it requires two signal transitions for each bit. Consequently, an RZ code would require twice the baud of a conventional NRZ code. We find this type of code in some of the more sophisticated systems dealing with local area networks (Chapter Six), lightwave technologies, and optic fibers.

Figure 1-11(c) illustrates another very popular code found in many communications systems today, the Manchester code. This code provides a signal state in every bit cell. Consequently, it is a good clocking code. However, like the RZ code, it requires twice the baud for the bit rate. In addition, the interface devices used to achieve this higher baud are considerably more expensive than the NRZ interfaces. Manchester code is commonly found in magnetic tape recording, optic fiber links, coaxial lines, and local area networks.

Figure 1-11(d) shows one code used by AT&T, the Bell Operating Companies, and other carriers. This was originally called the Bell System PCM Code. This signalling structure is an example of bipolar AMI wherein alternate polarity pulses are used to encode logic 1. This particular code presents some problems when a long series of zeros are located in the transmission. The components in the system have no way to synchronize with zero bit cells because there are no changes in the state of the line. We will see in Chapter Nine that carriers have other methods to ensure that there is a signal state change on the line periodically, even though a long series of zeros may exist in the data stream. Finally, Figure 1-11(e) shows an actual direct current (dc) signal as it exists in the channel.

Asynchronous and Synchronous Transmission

Many computers and terminals communicate with each other and with DCEs through the non-return-to-zero (NRZ) code. Consequently, clocking becomes a major consideration with these devices. Two data formatting conventions are used to help achieve synchronization. These two methods are illustrated in Figure 1-12. The first approach is called *asynchronous* formatting. With this approach, each data byte (each character) has start and stop signals (i.e., synchronizing signals) placed around it. The purposes of these signals are, first, to alert the receiver that data are arriving, and second, to give the receiver sufficient time to perform certain timing functions before the next byte arrives. The start and stop bits are really nothing more than unique and specific signals which are recognized by the receiving device.

Asynchronous transmission is widely used because the interfaces in the DTEs and DCEs are inexpensive. Since the synchronization occurs between the transmitting and receiving devices on a character-by-character basis, some allowance can be made for inaccuracies between the transmitter and receiver because the inaccuracy can be corrected with the next arriving byte. A "looser" timing tolerance translates to lower component costs.

A more sophisticated process is *synchronous* transmission, which uses separate clocking channels or a self-clocking code. Synchronous formats eliminate the intermittent start/stop signals around each character. The preliminary signals are usually called synchronization or sync bytes. The more modern systems call them flags or preambles. Their principal function is to alert the receiver that user data are arriving. This process is called framing. It can be seen that a long synchronous data message without intermittent start/stop bits could present problems because the receiver could drift from the signal. We discussed in the last section two methods to deal with this problem: (1) provide a separate clocking channel, or (2) provide a signal code that is self-clocking, such as return-to-zero or Manchester code. The latter approach allows the receiver to develop its timing from the line transitions.

We now have enough information on codes and formats to move to other components in the network. However, we will come back to this subject several times. It will be more evident in later sections that the knowledge of codes and signalling states is important to gain an understanding of other aspects of networks and protocols.

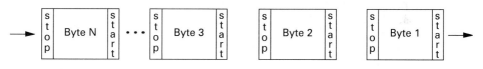

(a) Asynchronous Format

(b) Synchronous Format

(c) A Typical Synchronous Ttansmission

Figure 1-12. Formats

MESSAGE FORMATS

A more realistic depiction of synchronous formats is shown in Figure 1-12(c). Data transported through a computer network usually contain a minimum of five parts:

- sync bytes
- an identification (address) of the data (at a minimum, the receiver or transmitter identification)
- control field(s) which implement(s) the protocol; that is, manages the movement of the data through the network
- user data (the application process data)
- an element to check for a transmission error, typically called an error-check field, or the frame check sequence (FCS) field.

It should prove useful to pause here to define the term *frame*. A frame is the basic unit of information transmitted across the communications channel. In most systems, it contains those fields shown in Figure 1-12(c). The user data field typically contains end-user data or control information used by other control protocols in the communications system. Notwithstanding, even though the contents of the user data field may be other protocol control information, a frame treats these control fields simply as user data. Consequently, the data field in a frame remains transparent to the frame level protocol. Later in this book we will define other terms such as *packet, datagram,* and *segment* and further explain how they differ from a frame.

Network protocols require the exchange of non-user data frames among DTEs, DCEs, DSEs, and control centers to effectively manage traffic flow, diagnose problems, and perform day-to-day operations. In fact, a substantial amount of network traffic is non-user, overhead frames. The purpose of such overhead is to perform the necessary protocol and interface functions to support user data frames.

The identification (ID) field usually provides a name or number for the receiver as well as for the transmitter. Either the ID or control fields contain sequence numbers, which are used to further identify the specific frames from each sender.

The error-check field is appended by the transmitting site. Its value is derived from a calculation on the contents of the other fields. At the receiving site, an identical process computes another error-check field. The two are then compared; if they are consistent, the chances are very good that the packet was transmitted error-free. This process is called the *cyclic redundancy check* (CRC), and the field is called the *frame check sequence* (FCS).

THE COMMUNICATIONS PORT

The illustration in Figure 1-1 showed the connection of a DTE into a DCE. A DTE can also connect or interface directly into another DTE. A very common approach is a computer connecting directly to a graphics device, a printer, a terminal, or another computer. Later, we will also examine systems in which DCEs interconnect directly to each other. Regardless of where the connection is made, the input/output communications channel interfaces into the DTE through a communications *port*.

Vendors and technicians have other names for ports, including communications adapter interface, serial port, serial board, board, USART (universal synchronous/ asynchronous receiver transmitter), and a network interface card (NIC). We describe these terms more fully in other parts of the book. At present, we need only to understand that a port is usually a small microprocessor with its own separate clock, memory, registers, and, often, a central processing unit (a full-fledged microcomputer). The intelligence of the port is highly variable, depending on the type of interface needed. Obviously, the more sophisticated an individual port is, the more expensive it is. The main purpose of the communications port is to interface the communications channel into the DTE and provide for the functions of moving data into and out of the device.

ADDITIONAL NETWORK COMPONENTS

The network configurations discussed thus far have consisted of a few channels and devices. In many organizations, the structure is similar to the configuration in Figure 1-13. We have added several other components to a communications system. First, the DTE (the computer) is connected through various kinds of ports to other computers, terminals, disk files, tape files, and devices such as printers and graphic plotters. One major difference between this picture and previous illustrations is the connection of the computer to a *front-end processor*.

The purpose of the front-end processor (which may or may not be used in your organization) is to offload communications tasks from the mainframe host computer. Many of the communications protocols reside here. The front-end processor is especially designed to do a very limited number of functions but to do them quite efficiently. For instance, it may be responsible for handling the errors of the devices attached to it without interrupting the host computer.

Several of the devices in Figure 1-13 have been discussed previously. Remember, the *modems* act as an interface between the digital systems and the analog facilities. In addition, several other devices we have not yet discussed are explained below.

The *multiplexer* (MUX) is a device found in many installations. Its primary function is to allow multiple DTEs or ports to share one communications line. (The specifics of multiplexing techniques are covered in later chapters.) This practice assumes the channel has sufficient capacity to allow its shared use. In this illustration, the telephone line is a private, leased channel devoted exclusively to the use of the two attached multiplexers. The use of multiplexers can reduce substantially the number of communications channels required. Their cost is usually more than offset by the reduction of line costs. Multiplexers are also very useful in a local (nontelephone line) environment because they can reduce the amount of cable pulled through a building for each terminal's connection to a computer. Notice that a multiplexer is used at each end of the channel.

Another common component found in data communications systems today is the *data service unit* (DSU). This device provides a digital channel from end to end.

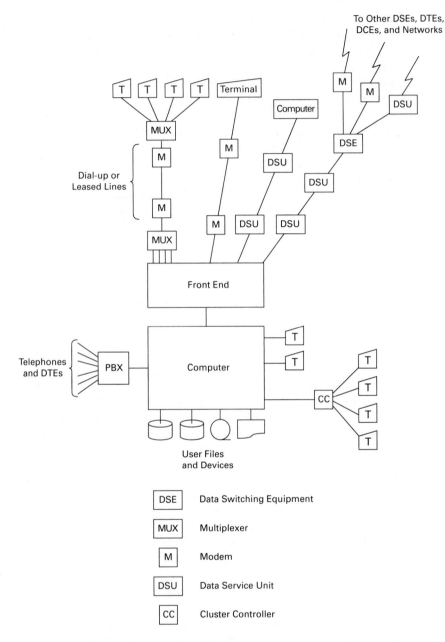

Figure 1-13.   A Typical Computer/Communications Structure

Stated another way, the channel is not an analog channel, but a digital facility transmitting 1s and 0s as discrete digital forms from one DTE to the other. There are several significant advantages in using a DSU instead of a modem, which we will address in Chapter Nine.

A *data switch* (DSE) is also illustrated in Figure 1-13. This switch is really the backbone of a computer communications network. While it is shown here as a very simple arrangement, much of this book is devoted to the discussion of how these switches can be used to build complex communications networks. Consequently, we will not address this topic in detail now, but we have included it in this figure to illustrate how it might fit into a network structure, perhaps similar to one found in your company or organization.

Also illustrated is a *private branch exchange* (PBX), the private telephone switch which is located in many offices and is playing an increasing role in computer networks. PBXs are covered in Chapter Twelve. Finally, the *cluster controller* (CC) is used to manage a group of terminals. The cluster controller receives commands or data from the host computer and directs messages to and from the remote terminals. This arrangement is similar to the multiplexer, but the multiplexer structure uses a like component at each end of the line. Cluster controllers are discussed in Chapters Four and Eleven.

SUMMARY

Computer networks are made up of a wide variety of components organized to create various types of network topologies. These topologies serve to reduce costs and to provide reliability, high throughput, and low delay in the networks. The telephone network performs a basis for many computer-based networks, with value-added services (protocols) added to the basic telephone media. Many systems today use local area networks and PBXs to enhance wide area network capabilities.

2

Communications Between and Among Computers and Terminals

INTRODUCTION

This chapter provides a general description of how DTEs exchange data. The term *protocol* is used to describe the procedures and logic for this process. (See Chapter One and Appendix A for a definition of protocol.)

The more experienced reader may wish only to review the material in this chapter, since it is meant as a tutorial. Whatever your experience level, the protocol classification tree in Figure 2-5 should be examined, since it is used throughout the book.

TRAFFIC CONTROL AND ACCOUNTABILITY

Typically, several different protocols cooperate to manage the communications. For example, one protocol is responsible for controlling the flow of the traffic on each channel; a second protocol usually selects the best channel (among several) for the first protocol to use. The first protocol is classified as a *link* or *line* protocol (also a *data link control*). The second protocol is called a *switching* or *routing* protocol. Additional protocols are also involved and are explained in later chapters.

Figure 2-1 illustrates several important points about network communications. A terminal (DTE) at San Francisco is to transmit data to a remote computer (DTE) located in Atlanta. The transmission goes through an intermediate point, a computer located in Dallas. The Dallas site performs routing and switching functions, since it also has lines to Denver and Houston, and thus fits our definition of data switching equipment (DSE). The most common approach in network communications is to pass the data, like a baton in a relay race, from site to site until they

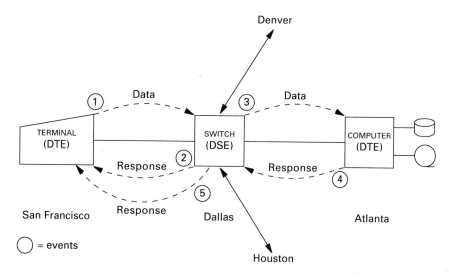

Figure 2-1. Traffic Control and Accountability

finally reach the destination. One important aspect of the process is in event 2, where Dallas sends an acknowledgment of the data received to the San Francisco terminal. This acknowledgment means the Dallas site has checked for possible errors occurring during the transmission of the frame, and as best the Dallas site can determine, the data have been received without any errors. It so indicates by transmitting another frame back on the return path indicating acceptance.

The data communications industry uses two terms to describe the event 2 response. The term ACK denotes a positive acknowledgment; the term NAK represents a negative acknowledgment. A NAK usually occurs because the transmission (i.e., the signal representing the data) is distorted due to faulty conditions on the channel (lightning storm, etc.). The frame in event 2 to San Francisco will either be an ACK or a NAK. In the event of an error in the transmission, the terminal in San Francisco must receive a negative acknowledgment (NAK) so it can retransmit the data. It is also essential that the processes shown in events 1 and 2 are completed before event 3 occurs. If Dallas immediately transmitted the data to Atlanta *before* performing the error check, Atlanta could possibly receive erroneous data. (ACKs and NAKs are represented by the codes discussed in Appendix A.)

If the San Francisco site receives an ACK in event 2, it assumes the data have been received correctly in Dallas, and the communications system in San Francisco can purge this message from its queue. (The application process often saves a copy on disk or tape for accounting, audit, or security reasons.)

Continuing the process in events 3 and 4, assume that an ACK is returned from Atlanta to Dallas. The end user in San Francisco may assume through event 2 that the data arrived in Atlanta. A false sense of security could result, because event 2 indicates only that the data arrived safely in Dallas. If the data are lost between the Dallas and Atlanta sites (it *can* happen), the San Francisco terminal assumes no problem exists. This scenario provides no provision for an end-to-end acknowledgment. If an end user wishes to have absolute assurance that the data arrived at the remote site, event 5 is required. Upon receiving event 4 at the Dallas site, Dallas sends another acceptance (ACK) to San Francisco. In other words, event 5 says that Atlanta also accepts the data.

End-to-end protocols add overhead and costs. Consequently, end users may not choose to have end-to-end acknowledgment with low-priority, unimportant traffic. However, if the data are important—for instance, a transfer of $20 million to an Atlanta bank over a funds-transfer network—a prudent user would want to have absolute assurance that the funds arrived and were posted to an account. In this case, the user would want event 5 to occur.

The preceding statements point out another aspect of a data communications system. Even though it usually provides for all five of the transactions, the actual posting of the funds transfer to a bank account ordinarily is *not* performed by the communications software. The applications process is responsible for the posting and data base update. Therefore, be aware that event 5 means the communications system in Atlanta received the data correctly. In turn, it passes the data to an applications process for the data base update. If a data base problem or an applications software failure prevents the funds transfer from being posted, it is the responsibility of the applications process to send an indicator back to the terminal user in San Francisco. It is rarely the responsibility of the communications system to perform the application-to-application accountability of traffic.

Checking for Errors

The most common method used today for error checking is *cyclic redundancy checking* (CRC) (other methods are explained in Chapter Eleven). The technique uses a constant derived from a CRC polynominal [an algebraic expression consisting of two or more terms: $(x - 1) \times (x^{15} - x - 1)$] to divide the constant into a binary representation of a data field (such as the contents of a frame). The quotient of the division is discarded, but the remainder is retained and used at the receiver to check for transmission errors.

At the receiving end, the transmitted CRC field (usually 16 bits) is compared to the answer of an identical CRC calculation. If they are consistent, the frame is considered to be error-free. CRC is explained in more detail in Chapter Four.

WIDE AREA AND LOCAL NETWORKS

The previous discussion explains in general terms how the DTEs communicate directly. The concern with errors is evident. The use of error-checking techniques and ACKs/NAKs are necessary to ensure the integrity of user data.

Practically speaking, the user data may not warrant such careful attention; each data character may not have to arrive error-free. A one-bit error in the transmission of a business letter (electronic mail) would distort only one character of the entire letter—better than the performance of most typists. Moreover, the scenario depicted in Figure 2-1 assumes the communications channel is unreliable, experiencing frequent errors. Such is the case with a conventional voice-oriented telephone line, but other communications channels are of better quality and are more reliable. For example, optic fiber channels are of significantly higher quality than metallic circuits.

If the user does not require each character to be received correctly and/or the communications channel is reliable, the expense to perform the elaborate functions depicted in Figure 2-1 may not be warranted. The issue is important under the simple arrangement in the figure. It is equally important when the user ties into a more complex network with several layers of protocols such as the *wide area network* (WAN) in Figure 2-2.

This network consists of DSEs (switching computers) connected together by high-speed, leased channels (for example, 56 kbit/s lines). Each DSE uses a protocol responsible for routing data and providing support to the end-user computers and terminals attached to it. The DTE support function is often called a PAD *(packet assembly/disassembly)*. The DSE acts as the PAD into and out of the network for the DTEs. (This definition of a PAD is acceptable now. In Chapter Eight, we expand the definition to include other support functions.) The network control center (NCC) is responsible for the efficient, reliable operations of the network.

A portion of Figure 2-2 is expanded in Figure 2-3. Notice the DTEs' varied connections into the PAD/switch:

A   A user-site computer is connected to the DSE through an asynchronous protocol, with dial-up analog lines into a DSE-dedicated port (a port reserved exclusively for the user).

B   A user-site front-end processor is connected to the DSE through a synchronous protocol, with dedicated 56 kbit/s digital lines using data service units (DSUs).

C   A user-site asynchronous terminal (or personal computer) is connected to the DSE, with dial-up analog lines into a DSE nondedicated port.

D   A user site has a dedicated DSE on premises connected into the network using private network 56 kbit/s digital lines with data service units (DSUs).

Figures 2-2 and 2-3 depict a topology for a wide area network (WAN). This type of network is noted for the following characteristics:

•   Wide area links are usually provided by an interexchange carrier (such as MCI or AT&T), at a monthly cost for leased lines and usage cost for dial-up lines.

•   The links are relatively slow (1200 kbit/s to 1.544 Mbit/s). DTE connections into DSE are usually slower (150 bit/s to 19.2 kbit/s).

•   DTEs and DSEs are located several miles to several hundred miles apart.

•   Links are relatively error-prone (if using conventional telephone circuits).

The *local area network* (LAN) is significantly different from a wide area network. The LAN is one of the fastest growing sectors in the communications industry. The LAN is noted for the following characteristics:

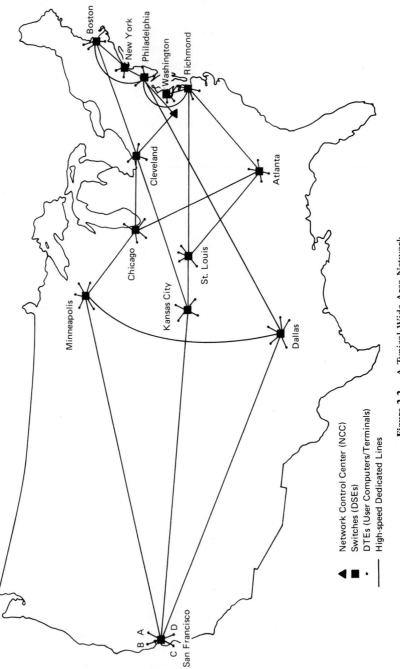

Boston
New York
Philadelphia
Washington
Richmond
Cleveland
Atlanta
Chicago
St. Louis
Kansas City
Minneapolis
Dallas
B A
C D
San Francisco

◄ ■ • Network Control Center (NCC)
Switches (DSEs)
DTEs (User Computers/Terminals)
High-speed Dedicated Lines

Figure 2-2. A Typical Wide Area Network

- Links are usually owned by the user organization.
- Links operate on very high-speed lines (1 Mbit/s to 400 Mbit/s). DTEs are attached to network with lower speed channels (600 bit/s to 56 kbit/s).
- DTEs are located closely together, usually within a building or plant. A DSE is used for switching in some configurations, but not as frequently as in a WAN.
- Links are of better quality than WAN channels.

Because of these major differences between wide area and local area networks, their topologies often take different shapes. A WAN structure tends to be more irregular due to the need to multidrop and/or multiplex terminals, computers, and switches onto the lines. Since the channels are leased on a monthly basis (at considerable expense), a user organization strives to keep the lines fully used. This requirement often creates the need to "snake" the channel through a geographical area, connecting the various DTEs, wherever they may be located, to one channel. Consequently, a WAN topology often has an irregular shape.

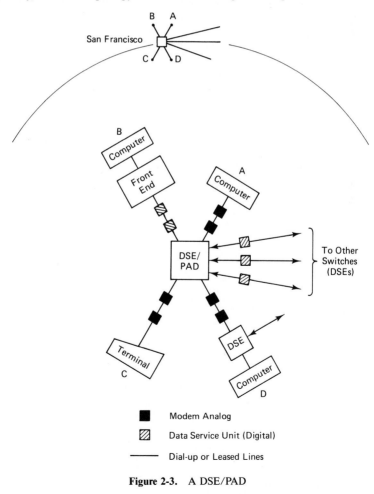

Figure 2-3. A DSE/PAD

The LAN owner is not as concerned with maximum utilization of the channels, which are inexpensive in comparison to their bit-rate capacity (and LAN bottlenecks usually occur in the software, anyway). Consequently, clever multidropping and multiplexing schemes are not as critical in a local environment as they are on a wide area network. Moreover, since local networks usually reside within a building, the topology inherently tends to be more ordered and structured, taking such shapes as the bus, ring, or star configurations. (Chapter Six provides more information on specific LAN systems and standards.)

CONNECTION-ORIENTED AND CONNECTIONLESS NETWORKS

The DTEs in Figures 2-2 and 2-3 communicate through the network DSE/PAD by one of two techniques. One technique is *connection-oriented;* another technique is *connectionless.* As illustrated in Figure 2-4, a connection-oriented network is one in which no logical connection initially exists between the DTEs and the network. The network connection between the two DTEs is in an idle state. In order for computers or terminals to communicate through a connection-oriented network, they must go through connection establishment, which is called a "handshake." Once a connection is established, the data-transfer state is entered; the user data are exchanged through a preestablished protocol. The DTEs subsequently perform a connection release, after which they return to the idle condition.

The connection-oriented network provides a substantial amount of care for the user data. The procedure requires a specific acknowledgment that the connection is established, or the network informs the requesting DTE if the connection is not established. Flow control (i.e., making certain that all the data arrive correctly, in order, and do not saturate the DSEs and DTEs in the various parts of the network) is also required of the network. Error checking is performed, as well as error recovery. Connection-oriented networks maintain a continuous awareness of all DTE-to-DTE sessions and attempt to assure that user data are not lost in the network. The care provided by this type of network requires considerable overhead because of the many support functions.

The connectionless (also called *datagram*) network goes directly from an idle condition (the two DTEs are not logically connected to each other) into a data-transfer mode, followed directly by the idle condition. The major difference is the absence of a connection-establishment phase and a connection-release phase. Moreover, a connectionless network has no network-wide acknowledgments, flow control, or error recovery, although these services may be provided on a link-by-link basis. Obviously, the connectionless network involves less overhead.

Connection-oriented networks are often compared conceptually to the telephone system (either dial-up or leased lines). The caller knows when a connection is made because he is talking to someone at the other end of the line. The connectionless network is comparable to mailing a letter. A letter is placed into the postal system with the assumption it will arrive at its destination. The letter usually arrives safely, but the letter writer never knows it. The post office sends nothing back to tell the letter writer that the letter arrived. The end recipient of the letter must initiate a

CONNECTION-ORIENTED

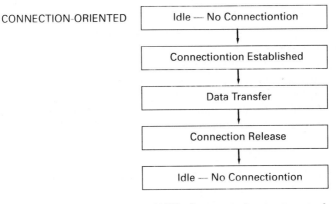

[ACKs, flow control, error recovery]

CONNECTIONLESS

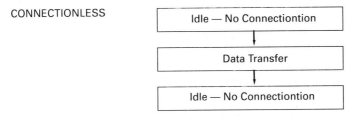

[No ACKs, no flow control, no error control]

Figure 2-4. Connection-oriented and Connectionless Networks

response indicating acceptance, usually in the form of another letter, which in communications parlance is called a *higher-level protocol*.

The tradeoffs between connection-oriented and connectionless networks center around overhead required versus functions provided. A connection-oriented network is rich in functions, yet these functions add to the costs of the system. In contrast, the connectionless network requires less overhead because it is limited in the support it provides the user application process. The issue is really one of deciding where transmission and reception integrity are assured—within or outside of the network.

Connection-oriented networks have dominated computer wide area networks (WAN) because of the inherent error-prone nature of the telephone system. Consequently, systems using the telephone channel perform many functions to ensure data integrity is maintained between the communicating devices. A connectionless network makes more sense with a local area network (LAN). A LAN channel is usually within one building and privately owned. Based on its technology, a LAN is much less error-prone. It is relatively unusual for data to be distorted on a LAN channel. A typical telephone channel connected with a WAN experiences an error rate in the approximate range of $1:10^3$ to $1:10^5$—one bit in error to every 1,000 to 100,000 bits transmitted. A LAN typically experiences an error rate of approximately $1:10^8$. The error performance between a WAN and a LAN differs by several orders of magnitude. Consequently, it may make little sense in a connectionless network (especially if it is a LAN) to perform the expensive overhead options of flow control, error control, and recovery, because the rare occurrence of an error is not worth all the expense of avoiding it.

Of course, a valid response to this rationale could be, "Yes, that may be true, but on the rare occasion that the error does occur, it may be catastrophic to the organization." To allow for this contingency, one practical alternative is to "push" error control up into the application process (or a higher-level protocol), instead of having the lower-level communications protocols deal with it. An error-prone network should not present erroneous data to the application, because the application frequently is forced to devote resources to the error-correction task. However, if errors are rare, placing error-correction capabilities in the application obviates having the functions in the communications system, which translates to a simpler, less expensive network.

Many networks today are designed to use connectionless protocols within the network and in relay systems between networks. End-to-end integrity is provided by logic (an upper layer) outside the network. This layer is called the transport layer. These connectionless-mode networks and the transport layer are described in more detail in Chapters Six and Eight.

CLASSIFICATION OF COMMUNICATIONS PROTOCOLS

DTEs communicate with each other by the techniques depicted in Figure 2-5. The DCE, PAD, and DSE also use these methods to communicate with each other and the DTEs. The "classification tree" in Figure 2-5 will be used throughout the book to assist the reader in understanding communications protocols. The classification tree is not meant to be all-encompassing, but is used to provide the reader a structure from which to gain an understanding of communications techniques.

The majority of the protocols depicted in the figure are called *line (link or channel) protocols* or *data link controls* (DLC). They are so named because they control the traffic flow between stations on one physical communications channel. In later chapters we examine other higher-level protocols that provide additional services to the DTE and application process. Our goal in the remainder of this chapter is to provide a general description of each of the protocols shown on the classification tree.

Data-link protocols manage all communications traffic on a channel. For example, if a communications port had several users accessing it, the DLC would be responsible for ensuring all users had their data transported error-free to the receiving node on the channel. The DLC is generally unaware that the data on the channel are from multiple users.

Data-link controls follow well-ordered steps in managing a communications channel:

- *Link establishment.* Once the DCE has a physical connection to the remote DCE, the DLC "handshakes" with the remote DLC logic to ensure both systems are ready to exchange user data.

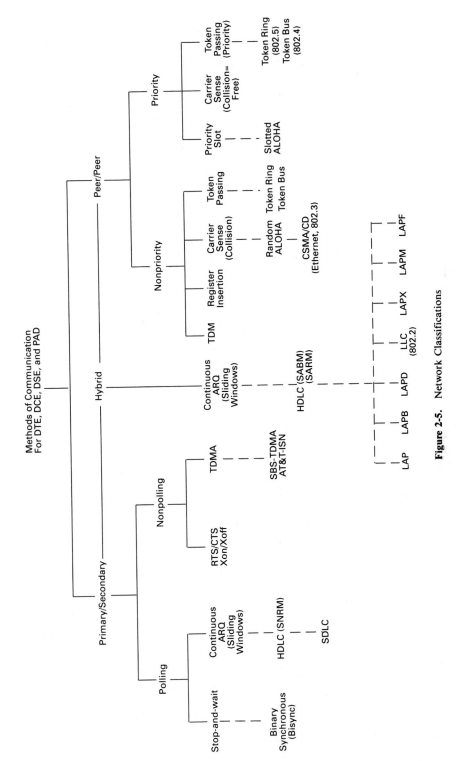

Figure 2-5. Network Classifications

37

- *Information transfer.* User data are exchanged across the link between the two machines. The DLC checks all data for possible transmission errors and sends acknowledgments back to the transmitting machine.
- *Link termination.* The DLC relinquishes control of the link (channel), which means no data can be transferred until the link is reestablished. Typically, a DLC keeps a link active as long as the user community wishes to send data across it.

A widely used approach to managing the communications channel is through a *primary/secondary* (sometimes called master/slave) protocol. This technique designates one DTE, DCE, or DSE as the primary station on the channel. The primary station (usually a computer) controls all the other stations and dictates when and if the devices can communicate. Primary/secondary systems are implemented with several specific technologies depicted in Figure 2-5. We discuss these techniques generally in this chapter and in more detail in later chapters.

The second major approach is through a *peer-to-peer* protocol. This technique has no primary station and typically provides for equal status to all stations on the channel. However, nodes may not have equal access to the network, since they can have preestablished priority over others. Nonetheless, the absence of a primary site usually provides for an equal opportunity to use network resources. Peer/peer systems are often found in local area networks (LANs) with ring, bus, and mesh topologies, and in certain hybrid systems as depicted in the figure.

POLLING/SELECTION SYSTEMS

The first example of a primary/secondary system is *polling/selection,* usually shortened to polling. The configuration in Figure 2-6 shows a host computer at site 1 and a terminal at site 2. There could be many other configurations (for example, a multidrop line or a ring topology). Polling/selection works the same conceptually with computers linked to other computers; it is possible to have primary/secondary computers, as well as terminals.

Polling/selection systems revolve around two commands, *Poll* and *Select.* The purpose of the *Poll* command is to transmit data to the primary site. The purpose of the *Select* command is just the opposite: to transmit data from the primary site to the secondary site. Select commands are no longer needed on the newer protocols, because the master site reserves resources and buffers at the receiver during link establishment, thereby sending data at the discretion of the master node.

A hierarchical network typically exists as an ordered form of a primary/ secondary relationship. *Poll* and *Select* are the principal commands needed to move data to any site on a channel or in the network. Let us examine how this is accomplished, referring to Figure 2-6(a). First, a *Poll* command is sent from the master site to secondary site 2. The poll says, in effect: "Secondary site 2, have you data for me?" The poll is sent to secondary site 2 and if data are waiting to be transmitted, they are sent back to the polling site. The primary site checks for errors and sends an ACK if the data are correct or a NAK if they are incorrect. These two events of data

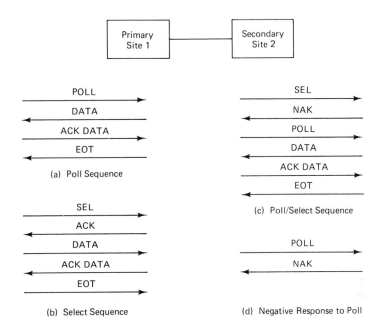

Figure 2-6. Polling/Selection Systems

and ACK/NAK may occur many times until the secondary site has no more data to send. The secondary station must then send an indicator that it has completed its transmission, such as the end-of-transmission code (EOT), or a bit in a control field.

The *Select* command is illustrated in Figure 2-6(b). *Select* means: "Secondary site 2, I am selecting you because I have data for you. Can you receive?" The ACK to the select means: "Yes, I am available and ready to receive your data." The data are transmitted, checked for errors, and acknowledged. (As stated earlier, newer systems reserve resources at link establishment and assume the receiver can indeed receive the data. Therefore, no selects are required with this approach.) The process can repeat itself. Eventually, an EOT control indicator is transmitted, meaning: "I have no more traffic to send."

Figure 2-6(c) shows the complexities of polling/selection. It is called the select/poll sequence. Notice the select is transmitted to secondary site 2, but the site responds with a negative response (NAK) to the select. This dialogue means: "Secondary site 2, I have data for you, can you receive?" The response is: "No, I cannot." There are a number of reasons the site cannot receive. It may be busy doing other things or it may have no memory (buffer space) available to receive data. As another example, it may have data to send to the primary site. The poll/selection system handles the problem by the primary site initiating a poll, which allows the secondary site to send data and clear its buffers.

The last sequence of operations [Figure 2-6(d)] shows what happens in the polling/selection network when a poll is issued to the secondary site and it responds negatively. In this case, the system uses a NAK to indicate a negative response to a poll. Simply stated, it means: "Secondary site 2, have you data for me?" The NAK means: "No, I do not." In newer systems, the indication of a willingness to receive or transmit is called a Receive Ready; unwillingness is called a Receive Not Ready.

A disadvantage of a polling/selection system is the number of negative responses to polls, which can consume precious resources on the channel. This overhead is especially evident in systems *without* multiplexers or terminal cluster controllers. These devices can accept a *general* poll to any device, scan their attached devices for an active request, and transmit to the primary.

Another approach to decreasing the effect of polling overhead is to use dynamic polling/selection tables. If a device continues to be polled and does not respond after a certain number of attempts, its priority is moved down within a polling table. Therefore, it is serviced less and polled fewer times. The nonresponding station is dropped to a lower priority, and those devices which have been responding positively to the poll are moved up in the priority table. It is also conceivable to design the table to provide multiple entries in the table by the same device. Station A might be polled, then station C, then A again, because A has been busy and responded positively to polls. Dynamic polling/selection eliminates some of the overhead found in the conventional static polling/selection systems.

Figure 2-7 shows the polling/selection system used to manage traffic between two DTEs on the same channel. DTE B wishes to communicate with DTE A. In order for this transmission to take place, event 1 requires that the primary site poll DTE B. The data are not sent to A directly, but to the primary site. The data are checked for errors, an acknowledgment is sent in event 3, and an EOT is sent in event 4. When the data arrive at the master site, they can then be relayed (onto the same channel) to DTE A. This is accomplished with (as you can probably guess) the select. (Remember, the poll moves data into the host, the select moves data out of the host.) Event 6 shows the select is ACK'd, the data are sent across the link in event 7, and they are acknowledged in event 8, completing the accountability. The user data in event 2 are a copy of the user data shown in event 7.

These examples illustrate once again the hierarchical aspect of the primary/secondary system. All traffic comes into and goes out of the primary host. The hierarchical topology presents some potential bottleneck problems, since all traffic is managed by one device. The configuration also has some reliability problems—if the primary site goes down, the entire network is lost. Hierarchical systems should provide for some form of backup in the event the primary site is lost.

Chapter Four examines more efficient primary/secondary networks including such widely used technologies as the international standard HDLC (high-level data-link control) and IBM's SDLC (synchronous data-link control).

Selective and Group Polling

Selective polling is the technique we have just examined and is a common mechanism for multidrop communications links. *Group polling* is more common on a ring or loop topology, or on a line with cluster controllers. Both techniques use a primary node to issue the poll command. The multidrop topology has each poll addressing a specific station on the channel. The station responds with data or a negative response to the poll. The ring configuration uses a group or broadcast poll

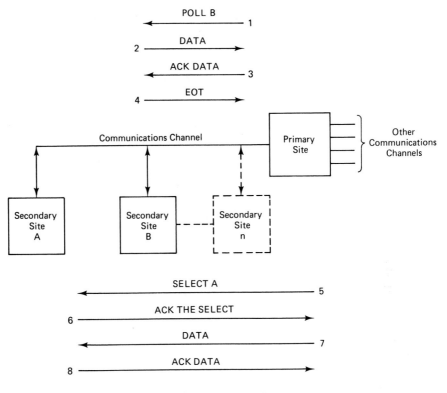

Numbers 1–8 indicate the sequence of events

Figure 2-7. Polling/Selection Combined

to all stations on the channel. Each station can use the poll and respond accordingly, passing the poll (and perhaps data) to the next station on the loop. A station may "piggyback" its transmission onto the data passing around the ring.

Stop-and-Wait Polling/Selection

One of the simplest and oldest forms of polling/selection is the *stop-and-wait* technique. It is so named because a DTE transmits a frame and waits for a reply. It is inherently half-duplex (two-way alternate) because the transmissions are in both directions, but only in one direction at a time. Stop-and-wait is a widely used approach because it is relatively inexpensive; the software is simple, with little logic involved. Most stop-and-wait systems use sequencing, in which stations use sequence numbers to maintain accountability and to control the flow of traffic.

Figure 2-8 shows a situation in which data are transmitted with a sequence number of 0 from station A (in Vancouver) to station B (in Toronto). Sequence numbers are added to each transmission. Recall from the discussion of frame formats that sequencing usually exists inside the data stream, perhaps in a header. As illustrated in the figure, the data are checked in Toronto; the computer responds with an ACK (event 2). The ACK uses a 0 in the header to account for the data sent to it. Upon receipt of the ACK, station A in Vancouver then transmits another data frame, and this time it changes the sequence number to a 1 (event 3). The data are checked for errors at Toronto and an ACK of 1 is sent.

Some protocols do not actually require the sending stations to insert a sequence number. Rather, the sequence number is inferred, alternately changing from a 1 to a 0. The transmitting station simply "flips" a counter from 1 to 0 as it sends a frame, and then looks for the corresponding ACK of 1 or 0.

The reason for the sequence number can be seen in the next data flow. Traffic can be lost in the network because of complexities of the traffic pattern, logic problems ("bugs"), or failed components. The data may also be lost because the frame is damaged en route, for example, by being routed over a microwave communications link through a rainstorm. The frame with ACK 1 can be distorted so severely that the Vancouver site receives "noise" on the line and the traffic is indecipherable.

In such an event, the Vancouver site performs a *timeout*. A timeout means that Vancouver, after not receiving a reply to its transmission within a given period, retransmits the data. The data transmitted in event 5 are exactly the same as in event 3. If a sequence number did not exist to identify the duplicate traffic, Toronto may not detect the duplicate frame. Indeed, the Toronto site might send the duplicate transmission to a data base, in which case a redundant update could be applied to the data. However, Toronto is expecting a different sequence number, a 0. Therefore,

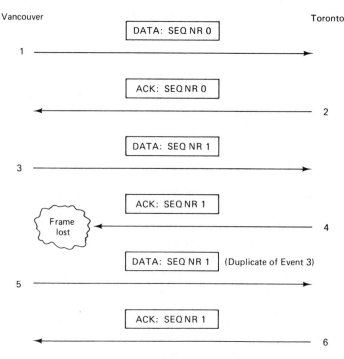

Numbers 1–6 indicate sequence of events

Figure 2-8.   Stop-and-Wait Sequencing

Toronto discards the duplicate data and retransmits the ACK 1 to complete the accountability (event 6).

Continuous ARQ (Sliding Windows)

Another example of polling systems is the *Continuous ARQ* (automatic request for repeat) technique. Continuous ARQ is so named because a station is allowed to request automatically a retransmission from another station. This approach can utilize full-duplex (two-way simultaneous) transmission, which allows transmission in both directions between the communicating devices. Because Continuous ARQ has several advantages over the stop-and-wait, half-duplex system, it has seen increasing use in the industry during the past several years. We introduce the topic of Continuous ARQ here; Chapter Four provides more detail and specific illustrations of the technique.

Continuous ARQ devices use the concept of transmitting and receiving *windows*. A window is established on each link to provide a reservation of resources at both DTEs. These resources may be the allocation of specific computer resources or the reservation of buffer space for the transmitting DTE. In most systems, the window provides both buffer space and sequencing rules. During the initiation of a link session (handshake) between the DTEs, a window is established. If DTE A and DTE B are to communicate with each other, DTE A reserves a window for B, and B reserves a window for A. The windowing concept is necessary to full-duplex protocols because they entail a continuous flow of frames into the receiving site without the intermittent stop-and-wait acknowledgments. Consequently, the receiver must have a sufficient allocation of space to handle the continuous incoming traffic.

The windows at the transmitting and receiving site are controlled by *state variables,* which is another name for a counter. The transmitting site maintains a *send state variable* [V(S)]. It is the sequence number of the next frame to be transmitted. The receiving site maintains a *receive state variable* [V(R)], which contains the number that is expected to be in the sequence number of the next frame. The V(S) is incremented with each frame transmitted and placed in the send sequence field in the frame.

Upon receiving the frame, the receiving site checks for a transmission error and the send sequence number with its V(R). If the frame is acceptable, it increments V(R) by one, places it into a receive sequence number field in an acknowledgment (ACK) frame, and sends it to the original transmitting site to complete the accountability for the transmission.

If the V(R) does not match the send sequence number in the frame, or an error is detected, something has gone awry. After a timeout occurs, a NAK [with the receiving sequence number containing the value of V(R)] is sent to the original transmitting site. Most protocols call this NAK a Reject or a Selective Reject. The V(R) value informs the transmitting DTE of the next frame that it is expected to send. Since the transmitter has already sent a frame with this value, it knows something is wrong and must then reset its V(S) and retransmit the frame whose sequence number matches the value of V(R).

Many systems use the numbers of 0 through 7 for V(S), V(R), and the sequence numbers in the frame. Once the state variables are incremented through 7, the numbers are reused beginning with 0. Because the numbers are reused, the DTEs must not be allowed to send a frame with a sequence number that has not yet been acknowledged. For example, the protocol must wait for frame number 6 to be ACK'd before it uses a V(S) of 6 again. The process is shown in Figure 2-9. Frames 6 through 4 are not yet acknowledged. If another frame was sent with a sequence number of 6, the corresponding ACK of 6 would not indicate *which* frame 6 was acknowledged.

The use of numbers 0–7 permits seven frames to be outstanding before the window is "closed." Even though 0–7 gives eight sequence numbers, the V(R) contains the value of the *next* expected frame, which limits the actual outstanding frames to 7.

Window size is an important design consideration. The larger the window, the more frames that can be transmitted without a response from the receiver. Yet the larger window size also means that the receiver must allocate more resources and larger buffers to handle the incoming transmissions. The line protocols used in the industry today typically allocate a window of seven at session-initiation time, which means that a transmitting DTE is allowed to send seven frames without receiving an acknowledgment back to it. However, in the event the seven frames are sent without an acknowledgment, the transmitting station's window is closed to its session partner, the receiver DTE. Window closing is necessary to prevent the transmitting station from saturating the receiver, which could overflow buffers and result in lost data. Window closing also provides the master a means to service the other sessions on the channel.

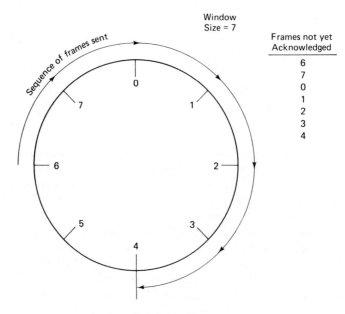

OUTSTANDING: Frames 6 through 4

Figure 2-9. Window Management

When the receiving station transmits a positive acknowledgment (ACK) to the transmitter, the transmitter's window is opened. For example, if the receiver transmits four ACKs back to the transmitter, then the transmitter's window is opened by four frames.

The goal of line protocols is to keep the windows open for all user sessions on the line. In so doing, the transmitting application and receiving application are more likely to experience fast response time. The Continuous ARQ protocols also are designed to keep the expensive communications channel as busy as possible.

The concepts of sliding windows are relatively simple, yet it should be realized that under a primary/secondary system, the primary DTE is tasked with efficient transmission, data flow, and response time between itself and all the secondary sites attached to it. The primary host must maintain a window for every station with which it has a connection. It must ensure that the windows stay open and manage traffic in a manner to keep the stations as busy as possible. This is no small feat, considering that polling and selection systems may have hundreds of terminals or computers attached to a master computer.

Continuous ARQ protocols, if using a window of seven, require at least three bits to provide the windowing and sequencing operations. (For example, the binary number 111 equals 7 in base 10.) Sequencing is required for these systems because more than one frame may be outstanding on the channel at any one time. Therefore, the receiver must indicate to the transmitter the positive acknowledgment (ACK) or the negative acknowledgment (NAK) of each specific frame. As noted earlier, the acknowledgment is accomplished through the use of sequence numbers. For example, if the transmitting site sends frames 1, 2, 3, and 4 to the receiver, the receiver is required to indicate through ACKs and NAKs the specific frames that were received correctly or incorrectly.

In this regard, Continuous ARQs provide several notable advantages over the stop-and-wait systems. One advantage is called *inclusive acknowledgment.* Using the above example, the receiver could send an ACK of 5. ACKs of 1, 2, 3, and 4 are not transmitted. The ACK of 5 means "I have received and acknowledge everything up to and including 4; the next frame expected should have a 5 in its send sequence field." It is evident from this simple example that continuous ARQ protocols with inclusive acknowledgment can reduce considerably the overhead involved in the ACKs. In this example, one ACK acknowledges 4 frames, considerably better than the stop-and-wait systems, in which an ACK is required for every transmission.

Polling Continuous ARQ protocols are used extensively with wide area networks (WANs). Consequently, error control is an important feature in the systems. A considerable amount of the logic found in polling Continuous ARQs is devoted to error detection and resolution. Continuous ARQ uses one of two methods to detect and retransmit erroneous data. The first, *Selective Repeat,* requires that only the erroneous transmission be retransmitted. The second approach, *Reject,* requires that not only the erroneous transmission be repeated, but all frames that were transmitted behind it as well. Selective Repeat and Reject are illustrated in Figure 2-10.

Both techniques have advantages and disadvantages. Selective Repeat provides better line utilization, since the erroneous frame is the only retransmission. However, as shown in Figure 2-10(b), site B must hold frames 3, 4, and 5 to await the retransmission of frame 2. Upon its arrival, frame 2 must be inserted into the proper

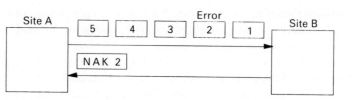

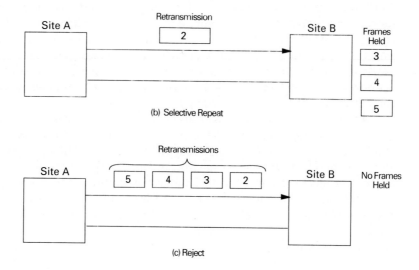

(a) Frames 1 Throught 5 Transmitted with an Error in Frame 2

(b) Selective Repeat

(c) Reject

Figure 2-10.   Retransmission of Errors

sequence before the data are passed to the end-user application. The holding of frames can consume precious buffer space, especially if the DTE has limited memory available and several active links.

Reject is a simpler technique. Once an erroneous frame is detected, the receiving station discards all subsequent frames in the session until it receives the correct retransmission. Reject requires no frame queuing and frame resequencing at the receiver. However, its throughput is not as high as Selective Repeat, since it requires the retransmission of frames that may not be in error.

In subsequent chapters, the following primary/secondary polling systems are covered in more detail: binary synchronous (bisync), HDLC, LAP, LAPB, LAPD, LLC, LAPX, LAPM, and SDLC.

NONPOLLING SYSTEMS

Let us continue our discussion and classification of network communications protocols by branching in our classification tree (in Figure 2-5) to the primary/secondary nonpolling systems. As depicted in the figure, the following are nonpolling systems:

1. request to send/clear to send (RTS/CTS);

2. Xon/Xoff;

3. time division multiple access (TDMA).

The first two approaches, RTS/CTS and Xon/Xoff, are rather simple; the third approach, TDMA, is more sophisticated and is used in several satellite systems.

Request to Send/Clear to Send

Request to send/clear to send (RTS/CTS) is considered a rather low-level approach to protocols and data communications. Nonetheless, it is widely used because of its relationship and dependence upon the frequently used physical interface EIA-232-D. (If you are not familiar with EIA-232-D, review Appendix C.)

The use of EIA-232-D to effect communications between DTEs is most common in a local environment, because EIA-232-D is inherently a short-distance interface, typically constraining the channel to no greater than a few hundred feet. As shown in Figure 2-11(a), devices can control the communications between each other by raising and lowering the RTS/CTS signal on the EIA-232-D channel (pins 4 and 5, respectively). A common implementation of this technique is found in the attachment of a terminal to a simple multiplexer. The terminal requests use of the channel by raising its RTS line (4). The multiplexer responds to the request by raising the CTS line (5). The terminal then sends its data to the multiplexer through the transmitted data line (2).

Xon/Xoff

Another widely used primary/secondary nonpolling technique is Xon/Xoff [see Figure 2-11(b)]. Xon is an ANSI/IA5 transmission character (see Appendix A for ANSI/IA5 code). The Xon character is usually implemented by DC1. The Xoff character, also an ANSI/IA5 character, is represented by DC3. Peripheral devices such as printers, graphics terminals, or plotters can use the Xon/Xoff approach to control traffic coming into them. The master or primary station, typically a computer, sends data to the remote peripheral site, which prints or graphs the data onto an output media. Since the plotter or printer is slow relative to the transmission speed of the channel and the transmission speed of the transmitting computer, its buffers may become full. Consequently, to prevent overflow it transmits back to the computer an Xoff signal, which means stop transmitting or "transmit off."

Upon receiving the Xoff, the computer ceases transmission. It holds any data until it receives an Xon signal. This indicates that the peripheral device is now free (for instance, its buffers now have been cleared) and is ready to receive more data.

As you can see, the Xon/Xoff approach is quite simple; it is of a fairly low level, generally using the EIA-232-D pin connections, a V.24, or some other interface. For example, pins 2 and 3 can be used to support this protocol. The data are transmitted across pin 2 from the computer to the peripheral device and the Xon/Xoff signals are transmitted back to the computer through pin 3.

An inquiring reader might question why RTS/CTS and Xon/Xoff are included in a classification of network protocols. After all, one might say, these

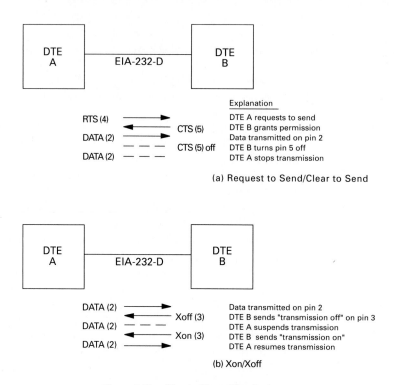

Figure 2-11. Simple Nonpolling Systems

systems are too basic to be considered a protocol. The answer to this question is simply that these systems are used extensively in DTE and DCE communications, especially with multiplexers, modems, printers, and plotters, so you should be aware of them. It is likely that your installation uses these approaches for some of your interfaces. While they may not be as complex as a Continuous ARQ, they are quite useful and inexpensive.

Time Division Multiple Access (TDMA)

A more elaborate approach to primary/secondary nonpolling systems is time division multiple access (TDMA). This technique is a sophisticated form of time division multiplexing (TDM) introduced in the last section of Chapter One and discussed further in the following section. Figure 2-12 provides an illustration of a TDMA satellite network. Site C is designated as a master station (often called the *reference station* [REF]). The responsibility of the reference station is to accept requests from the secondary stations, which are an indication that the secondary station wishes to use the channel. The requests are sent as part of the ongoing transmissions in a special control field. Periodically, the reference station transmits a control frame indicating which stations can use the channel during a given period. Upon receiving the permission frame, the secondary stations adjust their timing to transmit within the predesignated slot.

TDMA does not use a polling selection system. Nonetheless, it does fit into our classification of primary/secondary networks, because the TDMA reference

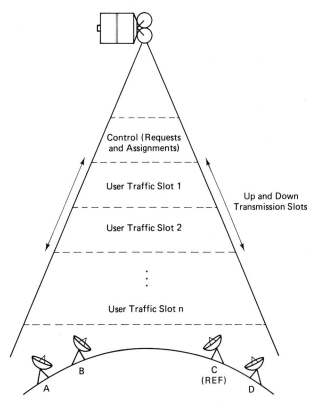

Control (Requests and Assignments)

User Traffic Slot 1

User Traffic Slot 2

Up and Down Transmission Slots

User Traffic Slot n

B

C (REF)

A

D

Figure 2-12. Time Division Multiple Access (TDMA)

station has the option of assigning or not assigning stations to a slot. The assignments, made in response to requests, are based on the relative priority of the station or the type of traffic from the station. TDMA is discussed in more detail in Chapter Five.

PEER-TO-PEER NONPRIORITY SYSTEMS

Time Division Multiplexing (TDM) or Slot

We now turn our attention to the second major classification of network protocols—the peer-to-peer technique. First, let us examine peer-to-peer nonpriority systems. Time division multiplexing (TDM) is probably the simplest example of peer-to-peer nonpriority systems. Under a TDM system, each station is given a slot of time on the communications channel and the slots are divided equally among the users. Each user has the full use of the channel during that slot of time. TDM is actually a simple form of TDMA discussed in the previous section. The TDM approach is found in both local area networks and wide area systems. Some vendors might not classify a TDM as a protocol; nonetheless, the approach is used in the networking of computer and terminals on both bus and ring topologies.

Register Insertion

A number of ring-based networks use the register-insertion technique to control traffic. Any station can transmit whenever an idle state exists on the link. If a frame is received while the station is transmitting, the frame is held in a register and transmitted behind the station's frame. This approach permits the "piggybacking" of multiple frames on the ring. Register insertion is a sophisticated form of a slotted ring.

Carrier Sense (Collision) Systems

Carrier sense (collision) networks are another example of peer-to-peer nonpriority systems. This approach is also widely used in local networks. Several implementations use this technique with the Ethernet specification and IEEE 802.3 standard discussed in Chapter Six. A carrier sense network considers all stations equal, so the stations contend for the use of the channel on an equal basis. Before transmitting, the stations are required to monitor the channel to determine if the channel is active (that is, if another station is sending data on the channel). If the channel is idle, any station with data to transmit can send its frame onto the channel. If the channel is occupied, the stations must defer to the passing signal.

Figure 2-13 is an illustration of a carrier sense collision network. Stations A, B, C, and D are attached to a bus or channel (providing a horizontal topology) by bus interface units (BIUs). Let us assume stations A and B wish to transmit; however, station D is currently using the channel, so the BIUs at stations A and B "listen" and defer to the passing frame being transmitted from station D. Upon the line going idle [Figure 2-13(b)], stations A and B attempt to seize the channel.

Carrier sense networks provide several methods for channel seizing (see Table 2-1). One technique, the *nonpersistent* carrier sense technique, provides the facility for all stations to transmit immediately upon sensing the idle channel, with no arbitration before the transmission. In the event the channel is busy, the stations wait a random period of time before sensing the channel again. Another technique used on slotted systems, the *p-persistent* carrier sense, provides a waiting algorithm at each station (*p* stands for probability). For example, stations A and B do not transmit immediately upon sensing a line going idle; rather, each station invokes a routine to generate a randomized wait, typically a few microseconds. If a station senses a busy channel, it waits a slot (time period) and tries again. It transmits to an idle channel with a probability p and it defers to the next slot with a probability of $1 - p$. Yet another technique, *1-persistent* carrier, has a station transmitting immediately upon sensing an idle channel. When a collision occurs, the stations wait a random period before sensing the channel. The method is called 1-persistent because the station transmits with a probability of 1 when a channel is sensed as idle.

The *p*-persistent technique is designed to meet a 1-persistent goal of reduced idle channel time *and* a nonpersistent goal of reduced collisions. However, *p* must be set to a low value to achieve proper performance. Perhaps surprisingly, 1-persistent is favored by many vendors and standards groups (discussed further in Chapter Six).

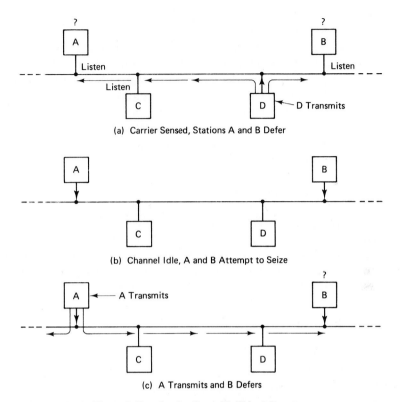

Figure 2-13. Carrier Sense (Collision) Systems

To continue the discussion, we assume that station A in Figure 2-13(c) seizes the channel before station B has an opportunity to finish its randomized wait. A short time later, after B's randomized threshold has expired, it listens and determines that A has transmitted and seized the channel. Consequently, it must continue to adhere to one of the three techniques for busy conditions until the channel goes idle again.

Since A's transmission requires time to propagate to station B, station B may be unaware that a signal is on the channel. In this situation, channel B may transmit its frame even though channel A has supposedly seized the channel. This problem is called the *collision window*. The collision window is a factor of the propagation

TABLE 2-1. CARRIER SENSE NETWORKS

Condition	Nonpersistent	*p*-persistent	1-persistent
Channel idle	transmit immediately	transmit with *p;* defer with $1 - p$	transmit immediately
Channel busy	randomized wait & sense	transmit with *p;* defer with $1 - p$	continually sense
Collision	randomized retransmission	randomized retransmission	randomized retransmission

delay of the signal and the distance between the two competing stations. For instance, if A and B are one kilometer apart (.6 of a mile), it takes approximately 4.2 microseconds for station A's signal to reach station B. During this period, B has an opportunity to transmit, which results in a collision with station A.

Carrier sense networks are usually implemented on local area networks because the collision window lengthens with a longer, wide area channel. The long channel gives rise to more collisions and reduces throughput in the network. Generally, a long propagation delay (a long delay before one station knows the other is transmitting) gives rise to a greater incidence of collisions. Longer frames can mitigate the effect of long delay.

In the event of a collision, the stations have a facility to detect the distorted data. Each station is capable of transmitting and listening to the channel simultaneously. As the two signals collide, they create voltage irregularities on the channel which are sensed by the colliding stations. Both stations turn off the transmission and, after a randomized wait period, attempt to seize the channel again. The randomized wait prevents the collision from recurring, since it is unlikely that the competing stations will generate the same randomized wait time.

Carrier sense systems are explained in detail in Chapter Six.

Token Passing

Token passing is another widely used method for implementing both peer-to-peer nonpriority and priority systems. The priority systems are discussed later. The technique is found in many local area networks. Some token-passing systems are implemented with a horizontal bus topology; others are implemented with a ring topology.

Token Ring.   The ring topology is illustrated in Figure 2-14. The stations are connected to a concentric ring through a ring interface unit (RIU). Each RIU is

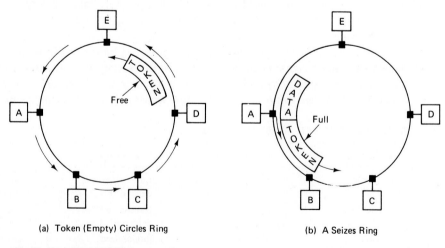

(a) Token (Empty) Circles Ring   (b) A Seizes Ring

■ Ring Interface Unit (RIU)

Figure 2-14. Token Ring

responsible for monitoring the data passing through it, as well as for regenerating the transmission and passing it to the next station. If the address in the header of the transmission indicates that the data are destined for a station, the interface unit copies the data and passes the information to the user DTE or DTEs attached to it.

If the ring is idle (that is, no user data is occupying the ring), a "free" token is passed around the ring from node to node. The token is used to control the use of the ring by a free or busy indication. A busy token is an indication that a station has seized the ring and is transmitting data. A free token indicates that the ring is free, and any station that has data to transmit can use the token to transmit data. The control of the ring is passed sequentially from node to node around the ring. This technique is called an *implicit* token system because any station is allowed to transmit data when it receives a free token.

During the period that the station has seized the token, it has control of the ring. Upon seizing the token (i.e., marking the token busy), the transmitting station (station A in Figure 2-14) inserts data behind the token and passes the data through the ring. As each RIU monitors the data, it regenerates the transmission, checks the address in the header of the data, and passes the data on to the next station. Eventually the data are received at the original transmitting station. This station is required to mark the token free, absorb the data, and pass the token on to the next station on the ring. This requirement prevents one station from monopolizing the entire ring. If the token passes around the ring without being used, then the station can once again seize the token and transmit data.

Some systems provide for the token to be removed from the ring, another user frame placed behind the first data element, and the token placed behind the last data transmission. This allows a "piggybacking" effect (similar to register insertion) on the network with multiple user frames circling the ring. Piggybacking is especially useful for large circumferential rings that experience a long delay in the transmission around the ring.

Token Bus. Token-bus systems provide a horizontal channel (bus), yet provide access to the channel as if it were a ring. The protocol eliminates the collisions found in the carrier sense (collision) systems and allows the use of a nonring (bus) channel. Figure 2-15 gives a simple illustration. Keep in mind that the token bus requires no physical ordering on the bus. The station can be logically configured to pass the token in any order.

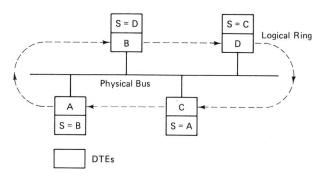

S = Address of Next Station to Send Token (Successor)   **Figure 2-15.** Token Bus

The protocol uses a control frame called an *access token* or *access right*. This token gives a station the exclusive use of the bus. The token-holding station uses the bus for a period of time to send and receive data (or even to poll other stations), then passes the token to a designated station. In the bus topology, all stations listen and receive the access token, but the only station allowed to seize the channel is the station so designated in the access token. All other stations must wait their turn to receive the token.

The stations receive the token through a cyclic sequence, which forms a logical ring on the physical bus. This form of token passing is called an *explicit* token system, because the bus topology causes an ordering of the nodes' use of the channel.

PEER-TO-PEER PRIORITY SYSTEMS

The last major classification of network communications systems is the peer-to-peer priority technique. As indicated in Figure 2-5, the technique is illustrated with three approaches: priority slot, carrier sense (collision-free), and token passing (priority). The systems are introduced here and described in more detail in Chapters Five and Six.

Priority Slot

The priority-slot system is similar to the conventional time division multiplexing approach discussed earlier. However, the use of the channel is determined on a priority basis. For instance, the following criteria can be used to establish the priority for use of the channel:

- prior ownership of the slot
- response time needs for a station
- amount of data to be transmitted
- time-of-day transmission requirements.

Priority slot can be established without a master station. The loading of priority parameters into logic at each site provides the control of the use of the slots. We discuss priority slot systems in more detail in Chapter Five.

Carrier Sense (Collision-free) Systems

Carrier sense (collision-free) systems have many similarities to the carrier sense (collision) networks. The major difference is the use of logic to prevent collisions from occurring. Collision-free systems may be implemented with techniques resembling the priority slot network. Another approach is to provide an additional facility in the network called a *timer* or *arbiter*. This device determines when a station can transmit without danger of collisions. The timing is determined at each station, with no master site to supervise the use of the channel.

Each port has a predetermined timing threshold. When the timing threshold expires, the port uses a timing parameter to determine when to transmit (similar in concept to "seizing" a token). The timing can be established on a priority basis, with the highest priority port having its timer expire first. If this port chooses not to transmit, the channel remains idle. The next highest priority station senses the channel is idle. Its timer indicates it is within a time threshold to transmit, so it may then seize the channel.

The higher priority stations, if they do not transmit, create an idle condition on the channel, which allows the lower priority stations to use the channel. In conventional slot networks, the idle time translates into wasted transmission opportunities. However, the collision-free network uses the arbiter to allow the next highest priority station on the link to seize the idle time if it has data to transmit. This approach reduces considerably the idle time on the channel.

Token-passing (Priority) Systems

The last example of peer-to-peer priority systems is an enhanced token-passing scheme, in which priorities are added to a token-passing system, usually a token ring. Each system attached to a token network has a priority assigned to it. Typically, eight possible priorities are available. The object of the token-passing priority scheme is to give each station an opportunity to reserve the use of the ring for the *next* transmission around the ring. As the token and data circle the ring, each node examines the token, which contains a reservation field. If the individual node's priority is higher than the priority number in the reservation field, it raises the reservation field number to its level, thus reserving the token on the next round. If another node does not make the reservation field higher, then the station is allowed to use the token and channel on the next pass around the ring.

The station seizing the token is required to store the previous reservation value in a temporary storage area at its location. Upon releasing the token when it finishes a complete loop around the ring, the station restores the network to its previous lowest priority request. In this manner, once the token is made free for the next round, the station with the highest reservation is allowed to seize the token. Token-passing priority systems are widely used in local area networks (LANs) and are explained in more detail in Chapter Six, which highlights the IEEE 802.5 token-ring standard.

SUMMARY

Computer networks consist of a wide variety of communications protocols. With few exceptions, these protocols are organized as a primary, secondary, or peer-to-peer relationship. Many older networks exhibit primary/secondary operations, principally in a conventional wide area network environment. Peer-to-peer networks are found predominantly in local area networks utilizing both priority and nonpriority schemes. Some communications protocols are hybrids of the primary, secondary, and peer-to-peer systems. The widely used HDLC protocol provides a hybrid feature.

3

Layered Protocols, Networks, and the OSI Model

INTRODUCTION

The previous chapters provided a general foundation for understanding how network components communicate with each other. In this chapter our goal is to gain an understanding of the conceptual framework of a computer network. This understanding is needed before moving into a more detailed discussion of the classification tree. The Open Systems Interconnection (OSI) model is used as a basis for our discussions. The first part of this chapter explains the rationale for the use of layered protocols in networks. The second part discusses the relationship of layered protocols to the OSI model. We begin with a general discussion of layered protocols.

GOALS OF LAYERED PROTOCOLS

The modern computer network is designed around the concept of layered protocols or functions. These techniques were developed over the past 20 years to meet the following goals:

- provide a logical decomposition of a complex network into smaller, more understandable parts (layers);
- provide for standard interfaces between network functions—for example, standard interfaces between software program modules;
- provide for symmetry in functions performed at each node in the network. Each layer performs the same functions as its counterpart in other nodes of the network;

- provide for a means to predict and control any changes made to network logic (software or microcode);
- provide a standard language to clarify communications between and among network designers, managers, vendors, and users when discussing network functions.

NETWORK DESIGN PROBLEMS

Networks require the writing of hundreds of software programs, entailing thousands of coding statements. Invariably, such complex systems have "bugs" (logic errors) in the code which are difficult, and sometimes impossible, to find. During the past several years, as networks have grown in size and complexity, the supporting communications software, hardware, and microcode have assumed more tasks and have grown in size and function. Network maintenance (through software and microcode changes) has often experienced serious problems when changes were made that resulted in unpredictable consequences.

Moreover, many networks have evolved without any standard by which to design them. The components within the network system sometimes have had poorly defined interfaces. It is not uncommon in some networks for a change in a program at one site to adversely affect a seemingly unrelated component at another site in the network.

The vendors' approach to designing systems has been another major problem in networks. Until recently, each vendor had its own approach to (a) designing networks, (b) developing the hardware and software for the networks, and (c) establishing how end-user interfaces were integrated into the networks. Since each vendor provided a different and unique approach, a user often had to incorporate multiple vendor protocols when integrating the different vendors' products at the user site. Certain major organizations (for example, IBM, General Motors, and AT&T) have established defacto standards because of their dominant position in the industry.

Notwithstanding these informal standards, the lack of a cohesive approach among the different vendors has left the user holding the protocol bag (or more aptly, many bags). The data communications industry has lagged far behind other industries in vendors coming together to support the end user. Paraphrasing an industry leader's statements, it is philosophically inane and economically ludicrous for each vendor to build its own "railroad gauge."

The basic idea of common standards is to develop a core of approaches among all vendors and to provide a reasonable point of departure when the core approach does not meet all needs.

The next two sections comprise a more detailed explanation of layered protocols. The reader who does not wish this detail should skip to the section on standards organizations.

COMMUNICATION BETWEEN LAYERS

In layered protocols, a layer is a service provider and may consist of several service *functions*. For example, one layer could provide service functions for code conversions such as International Alphabet #5 (IA5) to/from EBCDIC, TELEX to/from ASCII, Videotex to/from EBCDIC, and calendar dates to/from numeric form. A function is a subsystem of a layer (an actual software subroutine in a program, for example). Each subsystem may also be made up of *entities*. An entity is a specialized module of a layer or subsystem.

The basic idea is for a layer to add a value to the upper layers it services. Consequently, the top layer, which interfaces directly with the end-user application, is provided with the full range of services offered by all the lower layers. The actual services invoked are dictated by the upper layers to the lower layers.

Figure 3-1(a) shows the standard terminology for interfacing with a layer or service provider. Four transactions, called *primitives,* are invoked to and from the layer through identifiers called service access points (SAPs). (Some sessions do not require all transactions.)

- *Request.* Primitive by service user to invoke a function.

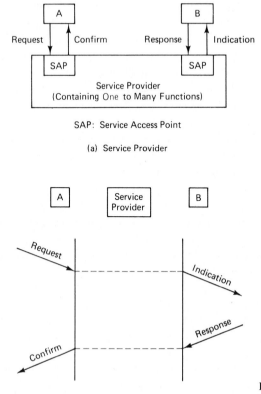

SAP: Service Access Point

(a) Service Provider

(b) Service Provider

Figure 3-1. Communications Through Layered Protocols

- *Indication*. Primitive by service provider to (a) invoke a function or (b) indicate a function has been invoked at a *service access point* (SAP).
- *Response*. Primitive by service user to complete a function previously invoked by an Indication at that SAP.
- *Confirm*. Primitive by service provider to complete a function previously invoked by a Request at that SAP.

Primitives usually are implemented as software procedure calls and the arguments of the call are OSI ICIs (discussed shortly).

As shown in the figure, a user application invokes a service provider function by sending a *request* to the next lower layer. This service request is affirmed by the service provider returning a *confirm*. If the service is going to provide a function for another user (in this case user B), the service provider must send an *indication* to B, after which B is required to provide a *response*. Assuming the service provider is a layer, it connects to users A and B through layer service access points (SAPs). A and B must know the associated SAP to receive the specific service from the service provider. The SAP contains the address or identifier of the specific service function.

Figure 3-1(b) provides another view of the process. The service provider is in the middle of the diagram, with users A and B on each side. The request is sent to the service provider, which sends user B an indication. User B provides a response, which is transmitted through the service provider as a confirm to A.

The process provides a common technique for the layers to "talk" to each other, even if the layers are implemented on different vendor systems. Remember that the service provider could be a layer, a function, or an entity within the layer, and the process is merely establishing a common means of communication among and between the layers.

In much the same way, humans have a common approach to interacting with each other: (a) establishing communications with a greeting, such as "hello"; (b) adhering to an accepted convention of talking (and occasionally, listening); (c) terminating the communications with a farewell, such as "goodbye." The purpose of such a dialogue might be to ask a service provider (for instance, a telephone operator) to connect us to a long-distance party. The service provider (operator) may invoke several service functions or entities to adhere to our request: (a) greeting us, (b) asking what we wish, (c) obtaining our number through information, and (d) dialing the number. The service provider may even invoke more esoteric services, such as language conversions—upon hearing us say "Buenos dias," the operator invokes the English to/from Spanish service entity; e.g., the operator performs a translation for us.

Just as humans must have conventions for asking for services from each other, so must machines. The standard terminology used for layered networks to request services is provided in Figure 3-2. In this illustration, three layers are involved in the communications process: layers $N + 1$, N, and $N - 1$. The lettering and numbering of the layers is relative. In this illustration, layer N is the focus of attention.

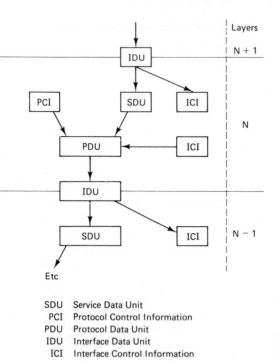

SDU   Service Data Unit
PCI   Protocol Control Information
PDU   Protocol Data Unit
IDU   Interface Data Unit
ICI   Interface Control Information

Figure 3-2. Communications Between Layers

Consequently, the layer above it is designated N + 1 and the layer below it is N − 1. Five components are involved in the layers communicating with each other. Their functions are as follows:

- SDU *(service data unit).* User data transferred transparently by layer N + 1 to layer N, and subsequently to N − 1.
- PCI *(protocol control information).* Information exchanged by peer (the same) entities at different sites on the network to instruct an entity to perform a service function. PCI is a fancy name for header.
- PDU *(protocol data unit).* The combination of the SDU and PCI.
- ICI *(interface control information).* A temporary parameter passed between N and N − 1 to invoke service functions (like a procedure call argument).
- IDU *(interface data unit).* The total unit of information transferred across the layer boundaries; it includes the PCI, SDU, and ICI. The IDU is transmitted across the service access point (SAP).

When the IDU from layer N + 1 passes to layer N, it becomes the SDU to that layer. In turn, the ICI is broken out in layer N, performs its functions, and is discarded. The SDU at layer N has a PCI added to it, as well as another ICI, to become the IDU to layer N − 1. Thus, a full protocol unit is passed through each layer. The SDU has a PCI added at each layer. In effect, this is adding a *header* at each layer. The header is used by the peer layer entity at another node of the network to invoke a function. The process repeats itself through each layer.

A PRAGMATIC ILLUSTRATION

The process may be more easily understood by redrawing Figure 3-2 as in Figure 3-3. In Figure 3-3, we remove the abstract concepts of SDUs and PCIs and simply use the words *user data* and *headers*. As each unit traverses through the layers, it has a header added to it. This becomes the user data unit to the subsequent lower layers. Finally, the full *protocol data unit* is passed onto the communications path, where it arrives at the receiving site, coming up through the layers in the reverse order it went through them from the sending site. The headers added at the peer layers at the transmitting site are used to invoke symmetrical and complementary functions at the receiving site. After the functions are performed, the unit is passed up to the next layer. The header that was added by the peer entity at the transmitting site is stripped off by the peer entity at the receiving site.

On close observation, it can be seen that the header is instrumental in invoking the functions across the network to the peer layer. Again, let us take a more pragmatic approach to these concepts and see what some of these functions may be. Figure 3-3 is expanded in Figure 3-4. Instructions have been placed in the headers to invoke functions in the peer entities at another node in the network. Three layers are involved.

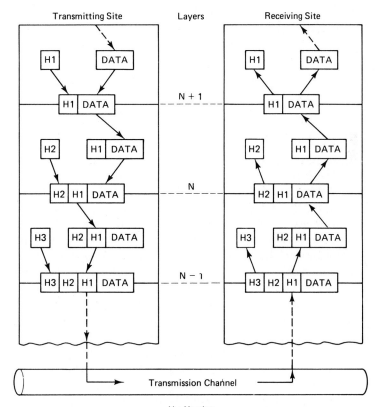

Figure 3-3. Communications Between Two Sites in a Network

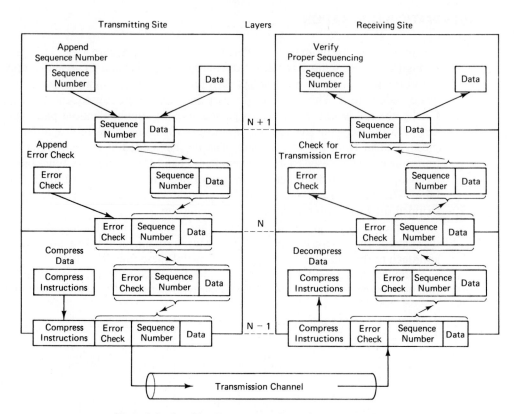

Figure 3-4. Invoking Support Functions with the PCI (Header)

The layers will invoke one service entity from each layer. Layer N + 1 invokes a service entity to provide a sequence-check field at the transmitting site. The receiving site's N + 1 layer checks for any sequence errors in the transmission by using the sequence-check field as a comparison to a receive counter. The service entity in layer N adds an error-check field in the form of a header to be used at the receiving N layer to provide an assurance that data are arriving error free. Last, an entity in N − 1 compresses the code. At the receiving node, the header will be used to instruct the N − 1 layer to convert (decompress) the code back to its original form (although this particular function could be performed without the use of headers).

We can now examine an illustration of the use of the ICI in layered networks. As stated earlier, the ICI is used only between adjacent layers at the *same* node. The ICI provides instructions to be performed by the lower layers going out of the sending node site and the upper layers coming into the receiving node site. For instance, the ICI might issue an instruction to the lower layer that it is to provide expedited routing through its layer. In Figure 3-2, when the N − 1 layer receives the ICI instruction, it knows that it must go through additional functions to increase the throughput of the data it is receiving from this user. Consequently, one approach would be to actually send out multiple data units in parallel, i.e., perform multiplexing operations to expedite the transmission through the lower layers.

INTRODUCTION TO STANDARDS ORGANIZATIONS AND THE OSI MODEL

The Open Systems Interconnection (OSI) model has been in development for several years. It encompasses all the ideas and concepts discussed in the previous section of this chapter. OSI is supported by the major standards organizations, telecommunications administrations, and trade associations. The structure of the major standards groups is depicted in Figure 3-5. A brief description of the organizations is provided in the following paragraphs.

Standards Organizations

The International Telegraph & Telephone Consultative Committee (CCITT) is a member of the International Telecommunications Union (ITU), a treaty organization formed in 1865. The ITU is now a specialized body within the United Nations. CCITT sponsors a number of standards dealing primarily with data communications networks, telephone switching standards, digital systems, and terminals. The State Department is the voting member on CCITT from the United States, although several levels of membership are permitted. For example, the *recognized private operating agencies* (RPOA) are allowed to participate at one level.

The International Organization for Standardization (ISO) is a voluntary body. It consists of national standardization organizations from each member country. The activities of ISO are principally from the user committees and manufacturers,

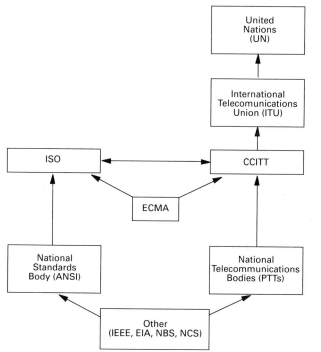

Figure 3-5. Standards Organizations

in contrast to the carriers that are represented in CCITT. The American National Standards Institute (ANSI) is the primary U.S. organization on OSI.

The European Computer Manufacturers Association (ECMA) is dedicated to the development of standards applicable to computer and communications technology. It is not a trade organization, as the name might imply, but a standards and technical review group. Several subcommittees within ECMA work actively with CCITT and ISO.

The American National Standards Institute (ANSI) is a national clearinghouse and coordinating activity for standards implemented in the U.S. on a voluntary basis. In addition to being the U.S. member of the ISO, ANSI is active in developing standards for data communications for the OSI, as well as for encryption activities and office systems.

The Electronic Industries Association (EIA) is a national trade association which has been active for many years in the development of standards. Its best known standard is EIA-232-D (described in Appendix C). The EIA publishes its own standards and also submits proposals to ANSI for publication as U.S. national standards.

The Institute of Electrical and Electronic Engineers (IEEE) has been involved for many years in standards activities. It is a well-known professional society with chapters located throughout the world. Its recent efforts in local area networks have received much attention. The IEEE activity addresses local area networks and many other standards as well.

Several government organizations have important roles in developing international standards. As mentioned earlier, the State Department is the U.S. voting member of CCITT. The National Communications System (NCS) is a consortium of federal agencies that have large telecommunications capabilities. The NCS works very closely with other organizations such as EIA, ISO, and CCITT. One of its jobs is to develop federal input to the international standards organizations. The National Institute of Standards and Technology (NIST) is also very active in international standards committees. Currently, it is working on the upper layers of the OSI standard.

The Layers of OSI

The Open Systems Interconnection (OSI) model is a seven-layer standard. The structure of the layers is shown in Figure 3-6.

OSI and CCITT have developed the OSI basic reference model to define layered networks and layered protocols. The model has received worldwide attention and has been implemented in many vendor products.

The goals of the OSI model are as follows:

- provide standards for communications between systems;
- remove any technical impediment to communication between systems;
- remove concern with description of the internal operation of a single system;
- define the points of interconnection for the exchange of information between systems;

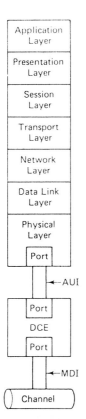

AUI: Attachment Unit Interface   **Figure 3-6.**   Layers of the OSI Network
MDI: Medium Dependent Interface   Model

- narrow the options in order to increase the ability to communicate without expensive conversions and translations between products;
- provide a reasonable point of departure from the standards in the event that they do not meet all needs.

Due to the wide use of these standards, several sections in this book are devoted to explaining their attributes and characteristics.

The lowest layer in the model is called the *physical layer*. The functions within this layer are responsible for activating, maintaining, and deactivating a physical circuit between a DTE and a DCE. There are many standards published for the physical layer. The most notable ones are EIA-232-D and V.24. (Appendix C explains this and other physical layer standards in more detail.)

The *data link layer* is responsible for the transfer of data over the channel. It provides for the synchronization of data to delimit the flow of bits from the physical layer. It also provides for the identity of the bits. It ensures that the data arrive safely at the receiving DTE. It provides for flow control to ensure that the DTE does not become overburdened with too much data at any one time. One of its most important functions is to provide for the detection of transmission errors and provide mechanisms to recover from lost, duplicated, or erroneous data. The majority of the techniques described in Chapter Two are found in the data link layer (see Figure 2-5).

The *network layer* specifies the interface of the user DTE into a packet-switched network, as well as the interface of two DTEs with each other through a packet network. It also specifies network routing and the communications between networks (internetworking). The layer is quite detailed and rich in function. The X.25 specification is included in this layer.

The *transport layer* provides the interface between the data communications network and the upper three layers (generally located at the user premises). It is the layer that gives the user options in obtaining certain levels of quality (and cost) from the network itself (i.e., the network layer). It is designed to keep the user isolated from some of the physical and functional aspects of the packet network. It also provides for end-to-end accountability.

The *session layer* serves as a user interface into the transport service layer. The layer provides for an organized means to exchange data between users, and the users can select the type of synchronization and control needed from the layer, such as:

1. alternate two-way dialogue or a simultaneous two-way dialogue;
2. synchronization points for intermediate checks and recovery for file transfers;
3. aborts and restarts;
4. normal and expedited data flow.

The session layer has specific services, primitives, and protocol data units which are defined in ISO and CCITT documents.

The *presentation layer* provides for the syntax of data in the model, that is, the representation of data. It is not concerned with the meaning or semantics of the data. Its principal role, for example, is to accept data types (character, integer) from the application layer and then negotiate with its peer layer as to the syntax representation (such as ASCII). Thereafter, its functions are limited. The layer consists of many tables of syntax (teletype, ASCII, Videotex, etc.).

The *application layer* supports an end-user application process. Unlike the presentation layer, this layer is concerned with the semantics of data. The layer contains service elements to support application processes such as job management; financial data exchange (ANSI X9); programming language send/receives (ANSI J-Series); and business data exchange (ANSI X12). The layer also supports the virtual terminal and virtual file concept. Standards such as X.400 and FTAM reside in this layer.

The *attachment unit interface* (AUI) is a cable or a circuit card connecting the DTE to the DCE. The most common connections at the AUI interface are EIA-232-D and V.24. The *medium dependent interface* (MDI) connects the DCE into the physical channel. The physical channel may be a pair of wires, coaxial cable, microwave relay, optical fiber, or other kinds of transmission channel technologies.

OSI Status

The layers of the OSI model are now well developed. The fourth layer (transport) was approved in 1984. The top three layers have reached maturation during the past few years. This book addresses the layers in the following chapters:

Physical layer: Chapter One, Appendix C

Data link layer: Chapters Two, Four, Five, Six, Nine

Network layer: Chapters Six, Seven, Eight

Transport layer: Chapter Eight

Session layer: Chapters Three, Thirteen

Presentation layer: Chapters Three, Thirteen

Application layer: Chapters Three, Thirteen

GOSIP

Several countries' federal governments have entered into the computer communications standards activities. In the United States and England the governments sponsor a program designed to foster use of the OSI standards. The program's title is the Government Open Systems Interconnection Profile, or GOSIP. Canada offers a similar program with its Canadian Open Systems Application Criteria, or COSAC.

The National Institute of Standards and Technology (NIST) in the U.S. sponsors the GOSIP workshops. These workshops meet quarterly in Gaithersburg, Maryland, to review ongoing work performed during the prior three months.

Each year a new version of the workshop agreements is published and (with each publication) the standards become more complete and more defined.

GOSIP is published by the U.S. Government as Federal Information Processing Standards Publication #146, or simply FIPS 146. Those wishing to obtain more information should ask NIST for the *Stable Implementation Agreements for Open Systems Interconnection Protocols.*

In addition, anyone is welcome to attend the OSI workshop. Its registration fee is small, and attendance there is a very valuable learning experience. Of course, the workshop members encourage active participation. This makes good sense because it adds intellectual force as more people participate in the standards development.

Why, however, is another body needed to define standards which, in effect, are already written? The answer is that many of the OSI protocols are written in a somewhat generic sense. For example, many fields defined in the PDUs of the OSI standards are fairly general (in the description of the contents). One of the purposes of a program such as GOSIP is to further define and refine the OSI standards and the fields in the OSI PDUs.

In addition, GOSIP provides guidance on testing for conformance and interoperability.

GOSIP establishes that OSI systems are to be used in Request for Proposals (RFPs) for new networking systems. When possible, OSI is to be used when existing networking systems are upgraded and enhanced.

GOSIP is to serve as the one standard reference for government agencies when developing, acquiring, or purchasing information technology systems. GOSIP states that OSI must be used by all federal government agencies.

Conditions may exist in a federal agency or department where it is not feasible to use some of the OSI standards. Under certain circumstances, GOSIP permits the heads of federal agencies and departments to approve waivers to the FIPS. Moreover, the agency head may delegate this authority to an official within the department or agency.

Waivers can be granted only when potential compliance with the OSI standard would negatively affect the agency or department mission. For example, waivers can be granted if compliance would create a severe financial impact on an operator (which could not be offset by the savings from the agency).

Requests for waivers are sent to NIST, to the attention of FIPS Waiver Decisions. They must be sent also to the House of Representatives and the Senate for publication in the *Federal Register*. In addition, the waiver is published in the *Commerce Business Daily*.

The waiver request should contain detailed and adequate backup. Obviously, NIST is going to judge the merit of the request on its validity. Consequently, reasons for granting the waiver should be given. The request should include a detailed description of the systems involved, as well as the total period for which the waiver is requested and a plan for the implementation of GOSIP.

The principle importance of any of these waiver requests is a full description of the negative impact on the agency's mission and, of course, any negative financial impact.

GOSIP, Version 1

GOSIP, Version 1 was published in June, 1988. It still serves as the basis for many of the federal agency and department strategic plans. Figure 3-7 shows the GOSIP, Version 1 profile.

The upper layer protocol implementations are quite simple, as the major aspects deal with FTAM and X.400. In addition, ACSE is required at the applications layer as well as the basic services for the presentation and session layers.

The transport layer is defined only with transport layer class 4. The network layer provides for either an X.25/8208 network interface protocol or the connectionless network protocol (CLNP, published as ISO 8473).

The lower two layers of GOSIP, Version 1 support protocols and interfaces for a wide area network (WAN) or for a local area network (LAN). The left side of the figure shows the lower two-layer protocol stack for a WAN with the use of LAPB, V.35, and RS-232. The right side of the figure shows a protocol stack for LANs with emphasis on the use of CSMA/CD, token bus, and token ring. Resting above all of the LAN protocols, of course, is logical link control (LLC), which must exist on any type of ISO 8802 or IEEE 802 network.

As an aside, you may be somewhat confused by the numbering for the data link and physical layer LAN protocols. The ISO publishes its standards with four digits. The 8802 is functionally equivalent to the IEEE 802. Indeed, the IEEE is the authoritative body for these LAN standards. The ISO publishes them unaltered but with changed numbers.

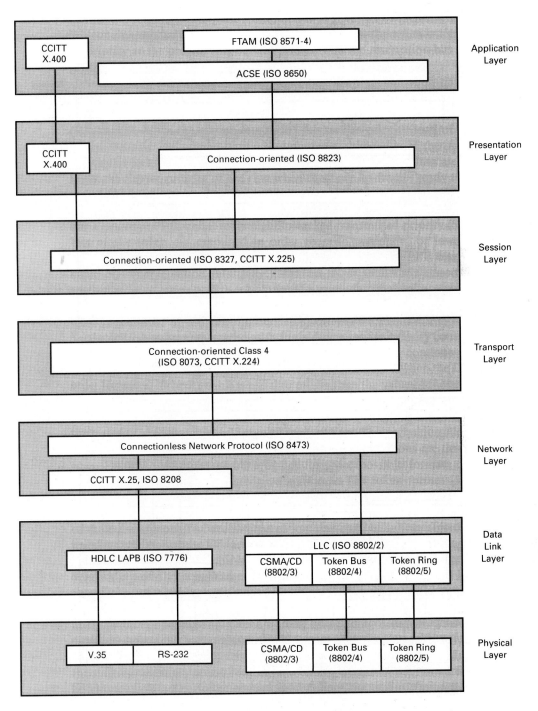

Figure 3-7. GOSIP, Version 1

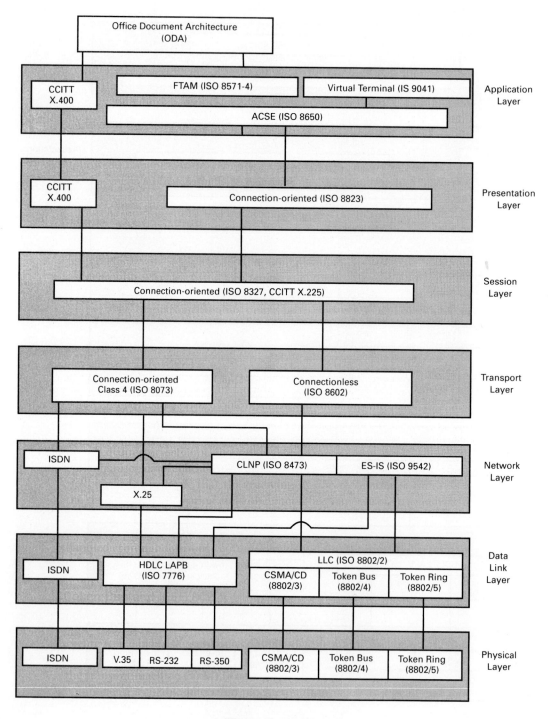

Figure 3-8. GOSIP, Version 2

GOSIP, Version 2

GOSIP, Version 2 (see Figure 3-8) represents a considerable enhancement in functionality over GOSIP, Version 1. The major changes that have occurred in the application layer are the additions of the virtual terminal service published under IS 9041 and the office document architecture (ODA) specifications. Version 2 continues to use the CCITT Red Book X.400 version. Therefore, X.400 still operates at the application and presentation layers. The X.400 Blue Book version moves X.400 into the application layer.

Another major change is the addition of connectionless transport layer protocol services with ISO 8602.

The network layer has also undergone considerable enhancements. For example, the end system-intermediate system (ES-IS) protocol has been added and is published as ISO 9542. The other addition at the network layer is the ISDN network layer service, published as Q.931.

Note the variety of interface and connection options offered through GOSIP, Version 2 with other entities in the network layer, as well as the transport and data link entities.

The changes at the lower layers mainly reflect the addition of ISDN at the data link layer (with the use of LAPD) as well as at the physical layer, principally with the basic and primary access rates. GOSIP, Version 2 also has added RS-350 at the physical layer to provide for higher-speed interfaces than those offered by RS-232.

The GOSIP, Version 2 for LAN protocols remains the same.

In summary, Version 2 adds (at the upper layers) the virtual terminal service (albeit in a somewhat limited form) and office document architecture (ODA).

One of the largest and most significant additions is the provision for the integrated services digital network (ISDN) at the lower three layers. Be aware that the OSI model allows the upper four layers to "ride" the ISDN at the lower three layers, X.25 at the lower three layers, or CLNP at the third layer and LANs at the bottom two layers. These architectures are fairly easy to implement because of the foresight of the OSI architects.

Other major changes include the ES-IS protocol and the connectionless transport service.

SUMMARY

The OSI model is recognized as the foundation for future standards for computer networks. It is based on the concepts of layered protocols. Several federal governments now mandate the use of OSI, and in the U.S. the GOSIP serves as a procurement standard for OSI-based products.

4

Polling/Selection Protocols

INTRODUCTION

This chapter expands the primary/secondary polling systems introduced in Chapter Two. The material covers in more detail the protocols on the left side of the protocol classification tree in Figure 2-5, as well as the hybrid branch. We describe and define the most common standards, as well as some widely used vendor products. Subsequent chapters will complete the description of the protocol classification tree.

Note that many of the functions in these protocols are implemented with communications codes. A description of the prevalent codes can be found in Appendix A.

CHARACTER AND BIT PROTOCOLS

The polling protocols in use today are either character-oriented (also called byte-oriented) or bit-oriented. Most character protocols have control fields that reside in nonfixed locations in the frame. In contrast, the bit protocols' control fields usually reside at fixed locations. Most importantly, the character protocols are code dependent in that the specific code (EBCDIC, IA5/ASCII) dictates the interpretation of the control fields. The bit protocols are code transparent because the protocol control meaning is derived from individual bits; they do not rely on a specific code for the interpretation of the protocol. We will see several examples of these points in this chapter.

BINARY SYNCHRONOUS CONTROL (BSC)

In the mid-1960s, IBM introduced the first general-purpose data-link control to support multipoint and point-to-point configurations. This product, the *binary synchronous control* (BSC) protocol, found widespread use throughout the world. Practically every vendor developed a version of binary synchronous control implemented in a product line. Some people use the term *bisync* to refer to the protocol.

BSC is a half-duplex protocol. Transmissions are provided two ways, alternately. The protocol supports point-to-point and multipoint connections, as well as switched and nonswitched channels. BSC is a code-sensitive protocol, and every character transmitted across a BSC channel must be decoded at the receiver to see if it is either a control character or end-user data. As stated previously, code-dependent protocols are also called byte or character protocols, and they are further distinguished by the fact that the control fields usually reside in variable locations inside the frame.

BSC Formats and Control Codes

The BSC frame formats and control codes are shown in Figure 4-1. The control codes have several functions which depend on the particular line mode at a given moment. (Line modes are explained in the next section.) The figure does not show all the possibilities for the format of a BSC frame, but provides samples of some of the major implementations of the BSC frame format.

Since BSC is a character-oriented protocol, it has a problem in delineating user data fields from control fields. It is possible that a code recognized as BSC control could be created by the user application process. For instance, assume a user program creates a bit sequence which is the same as the ETX (end of text) control code. The receiving station, upon encountering the ETX inside the user data, would assume that the end of the transmission is signified by the user-generated ETX. BSC would accept the ETX as a protocol control character and attempt to perform an error check on an incomplete BSC frame, which would result in an error.

Obviously, control codes must be excluded from the text and header fields. BSC addresses the problem with the DLE control code. This code is placed in front of the control codes STX, ETX, ETB, ITB, and SOH to identify these characters as valid line control characters. The simplest means to achieve code transparency is the use of DLE.STX or DLE.SOH to signify the beginning of noncontrol data (user data) and DLE.ETX, DLE.ETB, or DLE.ITB to signify the end of user data. The DLE is not placed in front of user-generated data. Consequently, if bit patterns resembling any of these control characters are created in the user text and encountered by the receiving station, the receiving station assumes they are valid user data, because the DLE does not precede them.

The DLE places the line into a *transparent text mode,* which allows the transmission of any bit pattern. This capability is important when BSC is used on different types of applications. For example, engineering or statistical departments in a firm often use floating-point notation due to the need for large magnitudes in

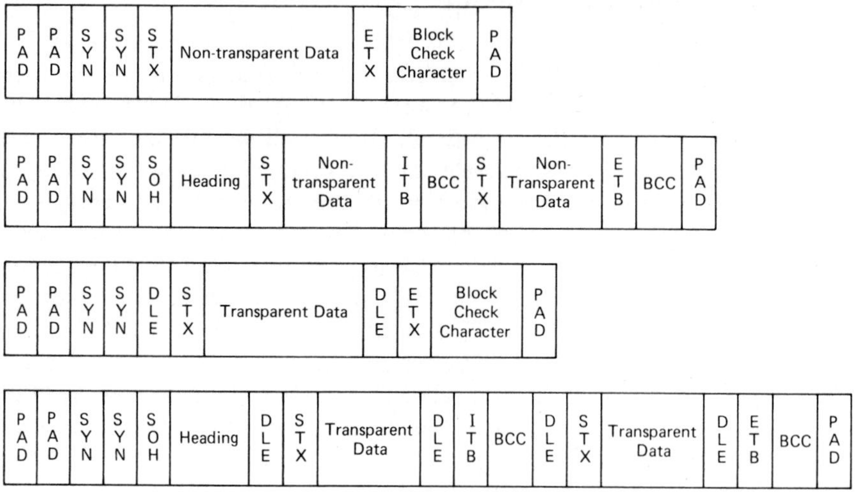

P A D	P A D	S Y N	S Y N	S T X	Non-transparent Data	E T X	Block Check Character	P A D

P A D	P A D	S Y N	S Y N	S O H	Heading	S T X	Non-transparent Data	I T B	BCC	S T X	Non-Transparent Data	E T B	BCC	P A D

P A D	P A D	S Y N	S Y N	D L E	S T X	Transparent Data	D L E	E T X	Block Check Character	P A D

P A D	P A D	S Y N	S Y N	S O H	Heading	D L E	S T X	Transparent Data	D L E	I T B	BCC	D L E	S T X	Transparent Data	D L E	E T B	BCC	P A D

BSC Control Character:

Character	Function
SYN	Synchronous idle (keeps channel active)
PAD	Frame pad (time fill between transmissions)
DLE	Data link escape (used to achieve code transparency)
ENQ	Enquiry (used with polls/selects and bids)
SOH	Start of heading
STX	Start of text (puts line in text mode)
ITB	End of intermediate block
ETB	End of transmission block
ETX	End of text
EOT	End of transmission (puts line in control mode)
BCC	Block check count

Figure 4-1. BSC Formats and Control Codes

numbers or very precise fractions. Accounting departments use fixed-point notation to provide for accurate fractions (two decimal places for cents). BSC accepts these kinds of numeric representations with the use of DLE.

The DLE presents a special problem if it is generated by the end-user application process, since it could be recognized as a control code. BSC handles this situation by inserting a DLE next to a data DLE character. The receiver discards the first DLE of two successive DLEs and accepts the second DLE as valid user data.

The headers illustrated in Figure 4-1 are optional. If they are included, the SOH code is placed in front of the header.

Line Modes

The BSC channel or link operates in one of two modes. The *control* mode is used by a master station to control the operations on the link, such as the transmission of polling and selection frames. The *message* or *text* mode is used for the transmission of an information block or blocks to and from the stations. Upon receiving an invitation to send data (a poll), the slave station transmits user data with either an

STX or SOH in front of the data or heading. These control characters place the channel in the message or text mode. Thereafter, data are exchanged under the text mode until an EOT is received, which changes the mode back to control. During the time the channel is in text mode, it is dedicated to the exchange of data between two stations only. All other stations must remain passive. The two-station text mode is also called the *select-hold* mode.

The polls and selects are initiated by a frame with the contents: *Address.*ENQ (where address is the address of the station). The control (master) station is responsible for sending polls and selects.

A select performs one of two functions: (1) it places the selected station into a slave mode, and (2) it places all other stations (on a multipoint channel) into passive mode. The STX or SOH initiates the passive state. The selected station maintains the slave mode condition until it receives an EOT, ETB, or ETX. The passive stations maintain the passive mode condition until they receive an EOT.

BSC also provides for *contention* operation on a point-to-point circuit. In this configuration, one of the stations can become the master by "bidding" to the other station. The station accepting the bid becomes the slave. A point-to-point line enters the contention mode following the transmission or reception of the EOT.

The ENQ code plays an important role in BSC control modes. To summarize its functions:

- *Poll.* Control station sends with an address prefix.
- *Select.* Control station sends with an address prefix.
- *Bid.* Point-to-point stations send to contend for control station status.

BSC has a rather unusual way of indicating if its control frames are selects or polls. The lower-case code of a station address is used to indicate a select, and the upper-case code is used to indicate a poll.

Line Control

The transmitting station knows the exact order of frames it transmits, and it expects to receive ACKs to its transmissions. The receiving site transmits the ACKs with sequence numbers. Only two numbers are used, a 0 and a 1. This sequencing technique is sufficient, since the channel is inherently half duplex and only one frame can be outstanding at one time. An ACK0 indicates the correct receipt of even-numbered frames; and ACK1 indicates the receipt of odd-numbered frames. (Recall from Chapter Two that the stop-and-wait sequence uses the ACK0/ACK1 technique to account for traffic.)

In addition to the frame-format control codes in Figure 4-1, BSC uses several other line control codes:

ACK0   Positive acknowledgment to even-sequenced blocks of data or a response to a select or bid.

ACK1   Positive acknowledgment to odd-sequenced blocks of data.

WACK   (Wait Before Transmit—Positive Acknowledgment) Receiving station temporarily unable to continue processing or receive transmissions. Signifies a line reversal. Also used as a positive acknowledgment of a transmission. Station will continue to send WACK until it is ready to receive.

RVI   (Reverse Interrupt) Indicates station has data to send at the earliest opportunity. This causes an interrupt of the transmission process.

DISC   For switched lines, forces a disconnection.

TTD   (Temporary Text Delay) Indicates sending DTE cannot send data immediately, but wishes to maintain control of line (examples: its buffer is being filled or its card hopper is empty).

A code-dependent protocol can create dual meanings in line control interpretation. Table 4-1 provides an illustration of how some of these dual meanings can occur in BSC. The meaning of a particular control sequence depends on whether the sequence is sent by a master or slave station, and whether the line is in control or message mode.

TABLE 4-1. BSC MODE INTERPRETATIONS

Message Transmitted	By	Line Mode	
		Control	Message or Text
SYN SYN ENQ	Master	Are you ready to receive?	Repeat your last response
SYN SYN ACK0	Slave	I am ready to receive.	Even block accepted
SYN SYN ACK1	Slave	Not used	Odd block accepted
SYN SYN NAK	Slave	I am not ready to receive.	Retransmit last transmission
SYN SYN EOT	Master	Reset line to control mode	End message mode
SYN SYN EOT	Slave	Negative response to poll (multipoint)	NAK last message and reset to control

Problems with BSC

In our discussions of BSC, several deficiencies of the protocol were discussed. In summary, the half-duplex, code-dependent, multiple-format, and multiple-line modes of BSC present significant problems. Consequently, other line protocols are replacing bisync systems.

HDLC

As discussed in Chapter Three, several organizations have published data communications standards during the past twenty years. One body, the International Organization for Standardization (ISO), is a specialized agency responsible for establishing standards for network protocols and other activities.

HDLC (high-level data link control) is a standard published by ISO that has achieved wide use throughout the world. The standard provides for many functions and covers a wide range of applications. It is considered a superset to several other protocols, as was shown in Figure 2-5. It fits our definition of a Continuous ARQ (sliding-window) protocol. HDLC has several options which make certain parts of the protocol more of a hybrid between the pure primary/secondary and peer/peer schemes, because they diminish the use of polling commands and eliminate select commands. Further explanation of these options follows.

This section addresses the main functions of the superset HDLC. It also covers some of the more important subsets, such as SDLC, LAP, LAPB, LAPD, LAPX, LAPM, and LLC. LAPD and LAPX are discussed more extensively in Chapters Nine and Thirteen. The reader is encouraged to check with specific vendors for their actual implementation of the HDLC structure. Most vendors use HDLC, but they may not implement their products in exact accordance with the HDLC specifications.

This material provides considerable detail on bit-oriented protocols. Those readers wishing an overview can skip to the section entitled "The HDLC Transmission Process."

HDLC Options

HDLC provides for a number of options in its implementation. It supports both half-duplex and full-duplex transmission, point-to-point and multipoint configurations, as well as switched or nonswitched channels. An HDLC station is classified as one of three types:

- The *primary* station is in control of the data link (channel). This station transmits *command* frames to the secondary stations on the channel. In turn, it receives *response* frames from those stations. If the link is multipoint, the primary station is responsible for maintaining a separate session with each station attached to the link.

- The *secondary* station acts as a slave to the primary station. It responds to the commands from the primary station in the form of responses. It maintains only one session, that being with the primary station. It has no responsibility for control of the link.

- The *combined* station transmits both commands and responses and receives both commands and responses from another combined station. It maintains a session with one other combined station.

Stations communicate with each other through one of three logical states:

- The *logically disconnected state* (LDS) prohibits a station from transmitting or receiving information. If the secondary station is under a *normal disconnected mode,* it can transmit a frame only after receiving explicit permission from the primary station to do so. If the station is under an *asynchronous disconnected mode,* the secondary station may initiate a transmission without receiving explicit permission to do so, but the frame must be a single frame, indicating the secondary station status.

- The *initialization state* (IS) is defined by specific vendors and is outside the standards of HDLC.
- The *information transfer state* (ITS) permits the secondary, primary, and combined stations to transmit and receive user information. The information transfer state can be changed by the issuance of disconnect commands (discussed later).

While the stations are in an information transfer state, they are allowed to communicate in one of three modes of operation. These modes can be set and reset at any time during the session, thus allowing a considerable amount of flexibility in how stations communicate with each other.

- *Normal response mode* (NRM) (primary/secondary classification in Figure 2-5) requires the secondary station to receive explicit permission from the primary station before transmitting. After receiving permission, the secondary station initiates a response transmission which may contain data. The transmission may consist of one or more frames while the channel is being used by the secondary station. After the last frame transmission, the secondary station must again await explicit permission before it can transmit again.
- *Asynchronous response mode* (ARM) (hybrid classification in Figure 2-5) allows a secondary station to initiate transmissions without receiving explicit permission from the primary station (usually when the channel is idle). The transmission may contain single or multiple frames of data, or it may contain control information reflecting status changes of the secondary station. ARM can decrease overhead because the secondary station does not need a poll sequence in order to send data.
- *Asynchronous balanced mode* (ABM) (hybrid classification in Figure 2-5) uses combined stations. The combined station may initiate transmissions without receiving prior permission from the other combined station.

Thus far in the discussion we have seen that there are three kinds of *stations* in HDLC operating within three *logical states,* and that within the information transfer state, the stations operate within three *modes.* In addition, HDLC provides for three ways of configuring the channel for primary, secondary, and combined station use.

- An *unbalanced* configuration provides for one primary station and one or more secondary stations to operate as point-to-point or multipoint, half-duplex or full-duplex, or switched or nonswitched. The configuration is called unbalanced because the primary station is responsible for controlling each secondary station and for establishing the mode-setting commands.
- The *symmetrical* configuration was in the original HDLC standard and is used on earlier networks. The configuration provides for two independent, point-to-point unbalanced station configurations. Each station has a primary and

secondary status, and therefore each station is considered logically to be two stations: a primary and a secondary station. The primary station transmits commands to the secondary station at the other end of the channel and vice versa. Even though the stations have both primary and secondary stations as separate entities, the actual commands and responses are multiplexed onto one physical channel. This approach is not used very widely today. We mention it in passing to complete the classification scheme of HDLC.

- A *balanced* configuration consists of two combined stations connected point-to-point only, half-duplex or full-duplex, switched or nonswitched. The combined stations have equal status on the channel and may send unsolicited traffic to each other. Each station has equal responsibility for link control.

To summarize HDLC to this point, the logical stations may consist of primary, secondary, or combined stations. The stations may operate under one of three states: the logically disconnected state, the initialization state, and the information transfer state. Once the stations have entered the information transfer state, they operate in one of three modes: normal response mode, asynchronous response mode, and asynchronous balanced mode.

Finally, the HDLC link is configured in one of three ways: an unbalanced configuration, a symmetrical configuration, and a balanced configuration. These configurations are often labeled unbalanced normal (UN), unbalanced asynchronous (UA), and balanced asynchronous (BA).

HDLC Frame Format

HDLC uses the term *frame* to indicate an independent entity of data transmitted across the link from one station to another [see Figure 4-2(a)]. Three types of frames are allowed.

- The *information format* frame is used to transmit end-user data between the two devices. The information frame may also acknowledge receipt of data from a transmitting station. In addition, it can perform certain limited functions, such as a *Poll* command. We will examine the functions in the information format frame later.
- The *supervisory format* frame performs control functions such as the acknowledgment of frames, the request for the retransmission of frames, and the request for the temporary suspension of the transmission of frames. The actual usage of the supervisory frame is dependent on the operational mode of the link (normal response mode, asynchronous balanced mode, asynchronous response mode).
- The *unnumbered format* frame is also used for control purposes. The frame is used to perform link initialization or link disconnection and other link control functions. The frame contains five bit positions, which allows for a definition up to 32 commands and 32 responses. The particular types of command and response depend on the HDLC class of procedure. (Commands and responses are discussed shortly.)

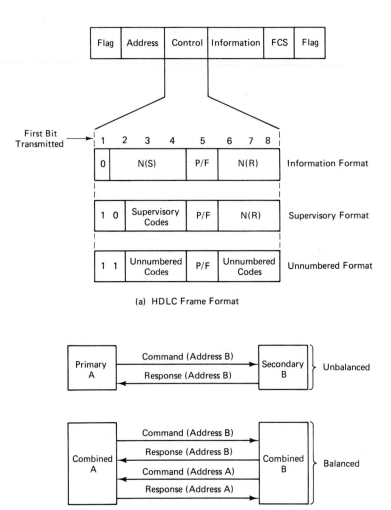

(a) HDLC Frame Format

(b) HDLC Addressing Rules

Figure 4-2. HDLC Formats and Address Rules

The frame consists of five or six fields. All frames must start and end with the *flag fields*. The stations attached to the data link are required to continuously monitor for the flag sequence. The flag sequence consists of 01111110. Flags can be continuously transmitted on the link between HDLC frames. Seven continuous 1s can also be sent to indicate a problem on the link. Fifteen or more 1s keep the channel in an idle state. Once the receiving station detects a non-flag sequence, it knows that it has encountered the beginning of the frame, a problem *(abort)* condition, or an *idle channel* condition. Upon encountering the next flag sequence, the station knows it has found the full frame. The flag performs functions similar to the BSC SYN character.

The *address field* identifies the primary or secondary station involved in the particular frame transmission. A unique address is associated with each station. In an unbalanced configuration, the address fields in both commands and responses contain the address of the secondary station. In balanced configurations, a command frame contains the destination address and the response frame contains the sending station address [see Figure 4-2(b)].

The *control field* contains the command and responses as well as the sequence numbers used to maintain the data-flow accountability of the link between the primary and secondary station. The format and the contents of the control field vary, depending on the use of the HDLC frame. We will examine the actual contents of the control field shortly.

The *information field* contains the actual user data. The information field resides only in the frame under the information format. It is not found in the frame when the frame is a supervisory or unnumbered format.

The *frame check-sequence field* (FCS) is used to check for transmission errors between the two data-link stations. It is similar in function to the BSC BCC character. The transmitting station performs a calculation on the user data stream and appends the answer to this calculation as the FCS field. In turn, the receiving station performs an identical calculation and compares its answer to the appended FCS field. If the answers are consistent, the chances are quite good the transmission occurred without any errors. If the comparisons do not match, it indicates a probable transmission error, in which case the receiving station sends a NAK requiring a retransmission of the frame. The FCS calculation is called a *cyclic redundancy check* and uses the CCITT V.41 generator polynomial of $X^{16} + X^{12} + X^5 + 1$.

The following rules apply to the cyclic redundancy check (CRC) operation:

- The frame contents are appended by a set of zeroes equal in number to the length of the FCS field.
- This value is divided by the generator polynomial which contains one more digit than the FCS and must have high- and low-order bits of 1s. (The data are actually shifted through an exclusive OR register.)
- The *remainder* of the division is placed in the FCS field and sent to the receiver.
- The receiver performs a division with the polynomial on the frame contents *and* the FCS field.
- If the result equals the predetermined number (a zero or, in some other systems, some other number), the transmission is considered error free.

The CRC can detect all possible single-error bursts not exceeding 16 bits and 99.9984% of all possible longer bursts.

Code Transparency and Synchronization

HDLC is a code-transparent protocol. It does not rely on a specific code (ASCII/IA5 or EBCDIC) for line control. In addition, the bit patterns of control fields reside in fixed locations within the frame. The eight-bit flag pattern is generated at the beginning and end of the frame to enable the receiver to identify the beginning and end of a frame. In addition to the unique flag sequence of 01111110, two other signals are used by HDLC. The *abort* signal consists of at least seven but fewer than fifteen 1 bits, and the idle condition consists of fifteen or more 1 bits. The abort signal terminates a frame. The transmission station sends an abort when it encounters a problem that requires it to take recovery action. Flags may be sent after an abort transmission to keep the link *active* so that a transmission can continue. The *idle* signal identifies the channel as being in an idle state.

One use of the idle state is for a half-duplex session to detect the idle pattern and reverse the direction of the transmission in order for it to transmit. The time between the actual transmissions of frames on the channel is called *interframe time fill*. This time fill is accomplished by transmitting continuous flags between the frames. The flags may be eight-bit multiples or they can combine the ending 0 of the preceding flag with the starting 0 of the next flag.

There will be occasions when a flaglike sequence, 01111110, is inserted into the user data stream by the application process or with several codes found in the control field. What happens? This situation can and does occur. To prevent the flag from being inserted into the user data stream, the *transmitting* site inserts a 0 bit after it encounters *five* continuous 1s anywhere between the opening and closing flag of the frame. Consequently, the 0 insertion applies to the address, control, information, and FCS fields. This technique is called *bit stuffing* and is similar in function to the BSC DLE character. After the frame has been stuffed and the flags have been placed around the frame, the frame is transmitted across the link to the receiver.

The *receiver* continuously monitors the bit stream (see Figure 4-3). After it receives a zero bit with five continuous one bits following, the receiver inspects the next bit. If it is a zero bit, it pulls this bit out; in other words, it "unstuffs" the bit. However,

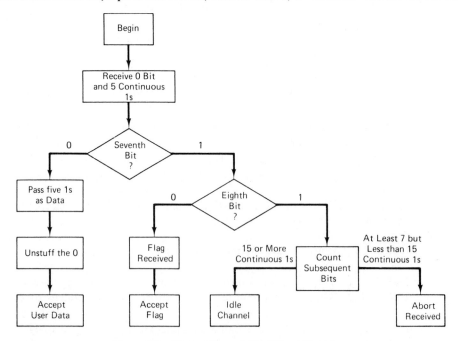

Figure 4-3. Bit Stuffing and Flag/Abort Checking

if the seventh bit is a one, the receiver inspects the eighth bit. If it is a zero, it recognizes that a flag sequence of 01111110 has been received. If it is a one, then it knows an abort or idle signal has been received and takes appropriate action. In this manner, HDLC achieves code and data transparency. The protocol is not concerned about any particular bit code inside the data stream. Its main purpose is to keep the flags unique. Figure 4-3 provides a logical flowchart of the bit-checking technique.

HDLC Control Field

Let us return to a more detailed discussion of the control field, because this field determines how HDLC controls the communications process (see Figure 4-2). The control field defines the function of the frame, and therefore invokes the procedures to control the movement of the traffic between the receiving and sending stations. Recall that the field can be in one of three formats (unnumbered, supervisory, and information). The control field identifies the commands and responses used to control the traffic flow on the link. These commands and responses are depicted in Figure 4-4. The illustration shows the commands and responses used in conjunction with the unbalanced or balanced link configuration. Notice that each of the boxes contains one of three commands: SNRM, SARM, and SABM. These commands are the *mode-setting commands*. HDLC requires a balanced or unbalanced configuration to be established with one of three modes. The illustration also shows some functional extensions of the basic structure. This represents the full HDLC repertoire of commands and responses. Several implementations of HDLC use only a portion of the command/response repertoire. The next section explains the principal functions of the commands and responses depicted in the figure.

The actual format of the control field (information, supervisory, or unnumbered) determines how the field is coded and used. The simplest format is the information format. The actual contents of the control field for this format are shown in Figure 4-2. The information frame control field contains two sequence numbers. The N(S) (send sequence) number indicates the sequence number associated with a transmitted frame. The N(R) (receive sequence) number indicates the next sequence number that is expected at the receiving site. The N(R) serves as an acknowledgment of the previous frames. For example, if the N(R) field was set to 4, the station, upon receiving N(R) = 4, would understand that its transmissions of frames 0, 1, 2, and 3 had been received correctly, and that the station with which it is communicating is expecting the next frame to have a send sequence number of 4 in it. The N(R) field provides for *inclusive acknowledgment;* that is, the N(R) of 4 could inclusively acknowledge more than one message that had preceded it. The concept of send [V(S)] and receive state [V(R)] variables discussed in Chapter Two are used with the HDLC N(S) and N(R) fields. HDLC also uses the Continuous ARQ (sliding-window) protocols discussed in Chapter Two.

The fifth bit position, the P/F or poll/final bit, is recognized only when set to 1 and is used by the primary and secondary stations to provide the following functions:

- The primary station uses the P bit to solicit a status response from a secondary station. The P bit also can signify a poll.

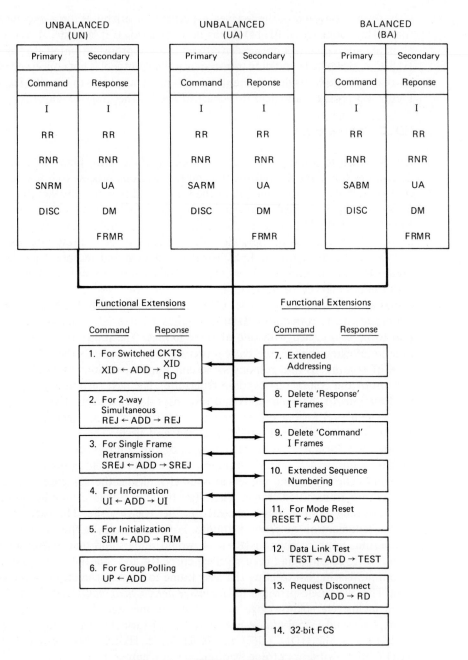

Figure 4-4. HDLC Commands and Responses

- The secondary station responds to a P bit with data or a status frame and an F bit. The F bit also can signify the end of transmission from the secondary station under normal response mode (NRM).

The P/F bit is termed the P bit when used by the primary station and an F bit when used by the secondary. Only one P bit (awaiting an F bit response) should be outstanding at any time on the link. A P bit set to 1 can be used as a *checkpoint*. That is, P = 1 says, "Respond to me, because I want to know your status." Checkpoints are quite important in all forms of automation. It is the machine's technique to clear up ambiguity and discard previous transactions that have accumulated.

The P/F bit is used and interpreted in several ways:

1. In NRM, the secondary cannot transmit until a command with the P bit set to 1 is received. The primary can solicit information (I) frames by sending a frame with the P bit set to 1, or by sending certain supervisory (S) frames (RR, REJ, or SREJ) with the P bit set to 1.

2. In ARM and ABM, information frames can be transmitted without being solicited by a command with the P bit set to 1. The P bit set to 1 is used to solicit a response at the earliest opportunity with the F bit set to 1.

3. In ARM and ABM, following the receipt of a command with the P bit set to 1, a frame with the F bit set to 1 is transmitted.
   - In two-way simultaneous (full-duplex) transfer, where the secondary is transmitting when the command with the P bit set to 1 is received, the F bit is set to 1 in the earliest possible subsequent response.
   - The transmission of a frame with the F bit set to 1 does not require the secondary to stop transmitting. Additional frames may be transmitted following the frame which had the F bit set to 1. In ARM and ABM, the F bit is not to be interpreted as the end of transmission by the secondary; it is to be interpreted only as the indicated response to the previous frame.

Commands and Responses

The *supervisory format* depicted in Figure 4-2 provides for four of the commands and responses shown in Figure 4-4. (Table 4-2 summarizes all the commands and responses.) These are: *Receive Ready* (RR), *Reject* (REJ), *Receive Not Ready* (RNR), *Selective Reject* (SREJ). The purpose of this format and the four commands and responses is to perform numbered supervisory functions, such as acknowledgment, polling, temporary suspension of data transfer, and error recovery. Supervisory format frames do not contain an information field; consequently, as shown in Figure 4-2, they do contain a receive sequence number. The supervisory format can be used to acknowledge the receipt of frames from the transmitting station. The commands and responses used by the supervisory format include the following:

Receive Ready (RR), used by the primary or secondary station to indicate that it is ready to receive an information frame and/or acknowledge previously received frames by using the N(R) field. If the station had indicated it was previously busy by using a *Receive Not Ready* command, it then uses the *Receive Ready* command to indicate it is now free to receive data. The primary station may also use the *Receive Ready* command to poll a secondary station.

TABLE 4-2. HDLC COMMANDS/RESPONSES

Format	Control Field Bit Encoding								Commands	Responses
	1	2	3	4	5	6	7	8		
Information	0	—	N(S)	—	*	—	N(R)	—	I—Information	I—Information
Supervisory	1	0	0	0	*	—	N(R)	—	RR—Receive Ready	RR—Receive Ready
	1	0	0	1	*	—	N(R)	—	REJ—Reject	REJ—Reject
	1	0	1	0	*	—	N(R)	—	RNR—Receive Not Ready	RNR—Receive Not Ready
	1	0	1	1	*	—	N(R)	—	SREJ—Selective Reject	SREJ—Selective Reject
Unnumbered	1	1	0	0	*	0	0	0	UI—Unnumbered Information	UI—Unnumbered Information
	1	1	0	0	*	0	0	1	SNRM—Set Normal Response Mode	
	1	1	0	0	*	0	1	0	DISC—Disconnect	RD—Request Disconnect
	1	1	0	0	*	1	0	0	UP—Unnumbered Poll	
	1	1	0	0	*	1	1	0		UA—Unnumbered Acknowledge
	1	1	0	0	*	1	1	1	Test	Test
	1	1	1	0	*	0	0	0	SIM—Set Initialization Mode	RIM—Request Initialization Mode
	1	1	1	0	*	0	0	1		FRMR—Frame Reject
	1	1	1	1	*	0	0	0	SARM—Set ARM	DM—Disconnect Mode
	1	1	1	1	*	0	0	1	RSET—Reset	
	1	1	1	1	*	0	1	0	SARME—Set ARM Extended	
	1	1	1	1	*	0	1	1	SNRME—Set NRM Extended	
	1	1	1	1	*	1	0	0	SABM—Set SABM	
	1	1	1	1	*	1	0	1	XID—Exchange Identification	XID—Exchange Identification
	1	1	1	1	*	1	1	0	SABME—Set ABM Extended	

* Value is 1 or 0

Receive Not Ready (RNR) is used by the station to indicate a busy condition. This tells the transmitting station that the receiving station is unable to accept additional incoming data. The RNR frame may acknowledge previously transmitted frames by using the N(R) field. The busy condition can be cleared by sending the RR frame, as well as several other frames (discussed later).

Selective Reject (SREJ) is used by a station to request the retransmission of a single frame that is established in the N(R) field. As with inclusive acknowledgment, all information frames numbered up to N(R) − 1 are acknowledged. *Selective Reject* provides the selective repeat capability discussed in Chapter Two. Once the SREJ has been transmitted, subsequent frames are accepted and held for the retransmitted frame.

Reject (REJ) is used to request the retransmission of frames starting with the frame numbered in the N(R) field. Frames numbered N(R) − 1 are all acknowledged. The REJ frame can be used to implement the Reject technique discussed in Chapter Two.

The third and last format of HDLC provides for *unnumbered* commands and responses. This format is used to send the majority of the command and response indicators depicted in Figure 4-4 and Table 4-2. The control field structure of the unnumbered format is depicted in Figure 4-2. Unnumbered commands are further grouped by the function performed:

- *Mode-setting commands:* SNRM, SARM, SABM, SNRME, SARME, SABME, SIM, DISC (SNRME, SARME, SARME for extended addressing)
- *Information transfer commands:* UI, UP
- *Recovery commands:* RESET
- *Miscellaneous commands:* XID, TEST

The commands/responses for the unnumbered format are:

UI *(Unnumbered Information).* This command allows for transmission of user data in an unnumbered (i.e., unsequenced) frame.

RIM *(Request Initialization Mode).* The RIM frame is a request from a secondary station to a primary station for an SIM command.

SIM *(Set Initialization Mode).* This command is used to initialize the primary/secondary session. UA is the expected response.

SNRM *(Set Normal Response Mode).* This places the secondary station in a NRM (normal response mode). The NRM precludes the secondary station from sending any unsolicited frames. This means the primary station controls all message flow on the line.

DM *(Disconnect Mode).* This frame is transmitted from a secondary station to indicate it is in the disconnect mode (inoperational).

DISC *(Disconnect).* This command from the primary station places the secondary station in the disconnected mode, similar to hanging up a telephone. This command is valuable for switched lines. UA is the expected response.

UA *(Unnumbered Acknowledgment)*. This is an ACK to set mode commands (and SIM, DISC, RESET). UA also is used to report the end of a station-busy condition.

FRMR *(Frame Reject)*. The secondary station sends this frame when it encounters an invalid frame. This is not used for a bit error indicated in the frame check-sequence field, but for more unusual conditions. The information field contains the reason.

An FRMR response frame is used under the following four conditions. (This level of detail is necessary to distinguish X.25 from X.75, discussed in Chapter Eight.)

1. receipt of an invalid command or response control field
2. receipt of an information field which is too long
3. receipt of an invalid N(R) field
4. receipt of unpermitted information field or a supervisory/unnumbered frame of an incorrect length.

HDLC provides considerable status information with the FRMR frame. The information field is used to provide the following:

- the rejected control field
- the current value of the receiving station's send [V(S)] and receive [V(R)] state variables
- the rejected frame was a command or response
- the control field is invalid
- the frame was transmitted with an unpermitted information field
- the information field is too long
- the sequence numbers are invalid.

RD *(Request Disconnect)*. This is a request from a secondary station to be disconnected and placed in a logically disconnected state.

XID *(Exchange Station Identification)*. This command asks for the identification of a secondary station. It is useful on switched facilities to identify the calling station.

UP *(Unnumbered Polls)*. (This frame will be explained later during discussion of loop configurations.)

TEST *(Test)*. This frame is used to solicit testing responses from the secondary station.

SARM *(Set Asynchronous Response Mode)*. Sets mode to allow secondary station to transmit without a poll from the primary station. It places the secondary station in the information transfer state (IS) of ARM. Since SARM establishes *two* unbalanced stations, SARM must be issued in both directions on the link:

DTE A sends: B, DISC

DTE B sends: B, UA   A, DISC

DTE A sends: A, UA

DTE B sends: A, SARM

DTE A sends: A, UA   B, SARM

DTE B sends: B, UA

The DISC commands are sent to ensure the link is completely reinitialized.

SABM *(Set Asynchronous Balanced Mode)*. Sets mode to SABM, in which stations are peers with each other. No polls required to transmit, since each station is a combined station.

SNRME *(Set Normal Response Mode Extended)*. Sets SNRM with two more bytes in control field.

SABME *(Set Asynchronous Balanced Mode Extended)*. Sets SABM with two more bytes in control field.

UP *(Unnumbered Poll)*. Polls a station without regard to sequencing or acknowledgment. Response is optional if poll bit is set to 0. Provides for one response opportunity.

RSET *(Reset)*. Transmitting station resets its N(S) and receiving station resets its N(R). The command is used for recovery. Previously unacknowledged frames remain unacknowledged.

HDLC also utilizes the timeout (T1 timer), which is started with the transmission of every frame. T1 is used to initiate a retransmission if it expires. Also, the N2 counter determines the maximum number of retransmissions to be performed upon the expiration of T1. The T1 and N2 variables also are used with the link-establishment commands/responses, such as SABM and UA.

The HDLC Transmission Process

Thus far in this section, we have discussed many terms and concepts. Let us now piece some of this material together with actual examples of the communications process between/among DTEs. Figures 4-5 through 4-9 and Figure 4-11 depict the following types of communications:

- Asynchronous Balanced Mode with half-duplex data flow (Figure 4-5)
- Asynchronous Balanced Mode with full-duplex data flow (Figure 4-6)
- Go-Back-N error recovery (checkpoint) (Figure 4-7)
- Go-Back-N error recovery (reject) (Figure 4-8)
- Selective Reject error recovery (Figure 4-9)
- SDLC with multipoint full duplex (Figure 4-11)

First, let us review the symbols in the figures (using Figure 4-5). The channel has "logical" snapshots taken of it in specific intervals of time (n, $n + 1$, and so on). The symbols within the time slot indicate the contents of the HDLC (or a subset, such as SDLC) frame transmitted by stations A and B at a specific time.

It is quite unlikely that the two stations would transmit at exactly the same instant in time, but the symmetry provides for easier explanation. For example, A's n slot could be depicted as being longer than B's n slot, which would indicate a longer frame being transmitted by A, but the uneven slots unnecessarily complicate an already complex topic. If the reader accepts this small anomaly, the principles illustrated by the graphics are sound. Also, the full-duplex illustrations show some "blank" time slots when the channel is idle. This may or may not happen, depending on how busy the stations are.

The symbols mean the following:

A, B   Station address in the header of the frame

I   An information frame

S = x   Send sequence [N(S)] number x

R = x   Receiving sequence [N(R)] number x

RR, SNRM, SABM, REJ, SREJ   Commands and responses

P/F   Poll/final bit is set to 1

Remember that the receive sequence number indicates inclusive acknowledgment of all traffic transmitted and accepted. The number in the field is actually a value of 1 greater than the last frame acknowledged. For example, R = 4 means frames 0, 1, 2, and 3 are acknowledged and the receiver expects the *next* frame to have a 4 in the transmit station's send sequence field. The P/F bit is discussed (where relevant) in the process depictions.

Each figure is accompanied by a short description of the events in each period of time. Note that the use of station address (A or B) varies in the illustrations. As discussed earlier, HDLC has rules as to which address (the transmitting or receiving station) is placed in the address field: Commands use the receiver's address, while responses use the address of the transmitter. Thus, for a station with address A, if the frame received contains an A, it is a command; if the frame received contains a B, it is a response. [See Figure 4-2(b) for a review of these rules.]

With the exception of Figure 4-11, the addressing conventions for the illustrations conform to Link Access Procedure, Balanced (LAPB). This widely used pro-

			TIME					
n	$n + 1$	$n + 2$	$n + 3$	$n + 4$	$n + 5$	$n + 6$	$n + 7$	$n + 8$
Station A Transmits B, SABM, P		B, I S=0, R=0	B, I, P S=1, R=0				A, RR, F R=2	
Station B Transmits	B, UA, F			B, RR, F R=2	A, I S=0, R=2	A, I, P S=1, R=2		B, RR R=2

Figure 4-5. Asynchronous Balanced Mode with Half-Duplex Data Flow (using P/F for checkpointing)

tocol requires all I frames to be command frames. As a consequence, they contain the address of the receiver. While all these examples are not allowed in LAPB, a consistent address scheme is used to keep the illustrations simple. LAPB is explained in more detail later.

Following are the times and events for the process depicted in Figure 4-5:

n Station A transmits *Set Asynchronous Balanced Mode* (SABM) command with P bit set.

$n + 1$ Station B responds with an *Unnumbered Acknowledgment* (UA) response with F bit set.

$n + 2, 3$ Station A sends information frames 0 and 1, sets P bit.

$n + 4, 5, 6$ Station B acknowledges A's transmission by sending 2 in the receive sequence number field. Station B also transmits information frames 0 and 1 and polls A with the poll bit in $n + 6$.

$n + 7$ Station A acknowledges B's frames of 0 and 1 with a 2 in the receive field of an RR frame.

$n + 8$ B responds with an RR frame. Notice that the receive field is still equal to 2. Why would B respond when it is not acknowledging any new traffic? Typically, the event in $n + 8$ occurs to prevent station A's timer from needlessly timing out and making unnecessary queries to station B. The *Receive Ready* and *Receive Not Ready* commands not only provide negative acknowledgments, but also keep each station informed that the other station is "alive and well."

Following are the times and events for the process depicted in Figure 4-6:

n Stations A and B both transmit an information frame with send sequence number of 0.

$n + 1$ Stations A and B send acknowledgments of the receipt of frames 0 with receive sequence numbers of 1. They also transmit information frames with send sequence numbers of 1. Station A sends a response solicitation with a P bit set to 1.

$n + 2, 3$ Station B issues a *Receive Ready* (RR) to acknowledge A's number 1 frame with a receive sequence number of 2. It also sets its F bit in response to the previous P bit. Under ABM, it can continue to transmit. Station B also transmits information frame 2.

$n + 4$ Station A sends information frame 2 and acknowledges B's 1 and 2 frames with a receive sequence number of 3. Station B sends information frame 3.

$n + 5$ Station A has nothing to send, but acknowledges B's number 3 frame with a receive sequence number of 4. Station B acknowledges A's number 2 frame with a receive sequence number of 3 and transmits frame 4. Station A also solicits a response with P bit set to 1.

$n + 6$ Station B responds to previous P bit with F bit set to 1. The *Receive Ready* frames in $n + 5$ and $n + 6$ emphasize control frames can be issued at

Time

	n	$n+1$	$n+2$	$n+3$	$n+4$	$n+5$	$n+6$	$n+7$	$n+8$
Station A Transmits	B, I S=0, R=0	B, I, P S=1, R=1			B, I S=2, R=3	B, RR, P R=4		B, I S=3, R=5	B, RR, P R=6
Station B Transmits	A, I S=0, R=0	A, I S=1, R=1	B, RR, F R=2	A, I S=2, R=2	A, I S=3, R=2	A, I S=4, R=3	B, RR, F R=3	A, I S=5, R=3	A, RR, P R=4

Figure Assumes Asynchronous Balanced Mode has been Set in Previous Frames

Figure 4-6. Asynchronous Balanced Mode with Full-Duplex Data Flow (P bit does not stop data flow)

Time

	n	$n+1$	$n+2$	$n+3$	$n+4$	$n+5$	$n+6$	$n+7$	$n+8$
Station A Transmits	B, I S=6, R=4	B, I S=7, R=4 (Error)	B, I S=0, R=4	B, I, P S=1, R=4		B, I S=7, R=4	B, I S=0, R=4	B, I, P S=1, R=4	
Station B Transmits					B, RR, F R=7				B, RR, F R=2

Figure Illustrates an Ongoing Session

Figure 4-7. Go-Back-N Error Recovery (Checkpoint) (P and F bits used to perform recovery)

any time when necessary. Typically, a *Receive Ready* would not be issued in a sequence such as is illustrated here because nothing has occurred that warrants a checkpoint at this time.

n + 7   Station A transmits frame 3 and acknowledges B's 4 frame with a receive sequence number of 5. Station B transmits information frame 5.

n + 8   Neither station has data to transmit. Station A sends a *Receive Ready* (RR) to indicate receipt of frame 5. Station B acknowledges A's frame 3 with a receive sequence of 4.

Figures 4-7, 4-8, and 4-9 are examples of how HDLC resolves transmission errors. Figure 4-7 illustrates the use of the receive sequence field to NAK a frame (which we will see can present some problems). Figure 4-8 shows the use of the *Reject* (REJ), and Figure 4-9 shows the use of the *Selective Reject* (SREJ). The illustrations assume an ongoing session, with station A transmitting frame number 6 at time *n*.

Following are the times and events for the process depicted in Figure 4-7 (not supported in LAPB):

n, n + 1, 2, 3   Station A sends information frames 6, 7, 0, and 1. Notice the sequencing wraps back around to 0, since 7 is the largest permissible sequence number. During this period, station B detects an error in frame 7. In *n* + 3, station A sends a poll bit to act as a checkpoint, i.e., to solicit a response from station B.

n + 4   Station B returns a *Receive Ready* (RR) with a send sequence number of 7 and a final bit. This means station B is expecting to receive frame 7 again (and all frames transmitted after 7).

n + 5, 6, 7   Station A retransmits frames 7, 0, and 1 and sets the P bit for a checkpoint.

n + 8   Station B acknowledges frames 7, 0, and 1 with a *Receive Ready* (RR) and a receive sequence number of 2, and sets the F bit.

The use of the N(R) receive sequence field to NAK a frame is not recommended for full-duplex transmissions. Since frames are flowing in both directions across a link, the sending and receiving sequence numbers from the stations often overlap. For example, assume station A's frame 4 [N(S) = 4] is transmitted at about the same time as B's frame which contains N(R) = 4. Station A could assume falsely that its frame 4 is incorrect, when station B was indicating only that it was expecting frame 4 next.

A better approach to error recovery is to indicate *explicitly* the erroneous frame. Figures 4-8 and 4-9 show two techniques to perform explicit NAKs.

Following are the times and events for the process depicted in Figure 4-8:

n, n + 1, 2   Station A sends information frames 6, 7, and 0. Station B detects an error in frame 7, and immediately sends a *Reject* frame with a receive

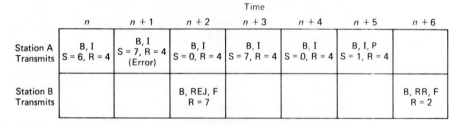

Figure illustrates an ongoing session

Figure 4-8. Go-Back-N Error Recovery (REJ)

sequence number of 7. Station B does not wait for a checkpoint solicitation, but sends the REJ as a response, with the F bit set. If station B had sent the REJ as a command (that is, with the address field containing an A), station A would be required to respond with RR, RNR, or REJ. However, since the REJ is a response, station A immediately retransmits the erroneous frame.

n + 3, 4, 5   Station A retransmits frames 7 and 0, and sets the P bit in time 5.

n + 6   Station B acknowledges frames 7, 0, and 1 with a *Receive Ready* and a receive sequence number of 2. *Note:* For full-duplex systems, the P/F bit is usually not employed to stop data flow, since it inhibits throughput.

Following are the times and events for the process depicted in Figure 4-9 (not supported in LAPB):

n, n + 1, 2   Station A transmits information frames 6, 7, and 0. Station B detects an error in frame 7 and transmits a *Selective Reject* of receive sequence 7. Station B does not require an RR, RNR, or REJ since the frame in n + 2 is not a command.

n + 3, 4   Station A retransmits frame 7 *only* and transmits frame 1 for the first time. Since this is a *Selective Reject,* frame 0 is not retransmitted.

n + 5   Station B acknowledges all remaining frames with a *Receive Ready* and a receive sequence number of 2.

	Time					
	n	n + 1	n + 2	n + 3	n + 4	n + 5
Station A Transmits	B, I S = 6, R = 4	B, I S = 7, R = 4 (Error)	B, I S = 0, R = 4	B, I S = 7, R = 4	B, I, P S = 1, R = 4	
Station B Transmits			B, SREJ, F R = 7			B, RR, F R = 2

Figure Illustrates an Ongoing Session

Figure 4-9. Selective Reject Error Recovery (SREJ)

HDLC Subsets

The acceptance of the HDLC standard has provided a cohesive foundation from which to implement subsets of the HDLC protocol. Several subsets are now available in the industry. These subsets are illustrated in the network classification tree in Figure 2-5.

The terms *subset* and *superset* are used to illustrate that many protocols use the features of HDLC and are called subsets. Conversely, from this description, HDLC is considered a superset. Be aware that some of these so-called subsets may implement options that are not found in the HDLC standard. Thus, the term *subset* should be approached from a general context.

The HDLC superset structure provides for bit-oriented protocols to recognize and use the same procedures among different types of applications. Applications require different modes of operation and different subsets of commands and responses to perform their activities. For example, the needs of multipoint, interactive applications differ from point-to-point, noninteractive systems.

For purposes of clarification, a DTE conforms to an HDLC class if it implements all the commands and responses defined for the class. As stated earlier, the three basic classes of HDLC are as follows:

- Class UN (unbalanced normal response mode)
- Class UA (unbalanced asynchronous response mode)
- Class BA (balanced asynchronous mode)

HDLC provides a set of optional extensions to the basic classes. These extensions are used by vendors and HDLC users to provide more variety to the basic class structure. Again, the options and the HDLC superset are depicted in Figure 4-4. The subset classes are designated by acronyms, such as UN, UA, or BA, plus optional extensions to HDLC, designated by the specific number of the option. For example, a protocol designated as a BA-4 would be a balanced asynchronous protocol providing for the sending of unnumbered information (UI). With this classification scheme in mind, let us examine some of the major subsets of the HDLC standard.

LAP *(link access procedure)* is an earlier subset of HDLC. LAP is based on the HDLC *Set Asynchronous Response Mode* (SARM) command on an unbalanced configuration and rarely is used today. The link setup with LAP is a bit awkward since it requires both stations to send SARM and UA before the link is established. It differs from the widely used LAPB, which is discussed next.

LAPB *(link access procedure, balanced)* is used by many private and public computer networks throughout the world. LAPB is a "subset" of the HDLC commands/responses repertoire. In later chapters we will see LAPB used to support the widely accepted packet network protocol, X.25. LAPB is classified as a BA-2,8 subset of HDLC. This means that, in addition to using the asynchronous balanced mode, it also uses two functional extensions, options 2 and 8. Option 2 provides for simultaneous rejection of frames in a two-way transmission mode (see Figure 4-8). Option 8 does not permit the transmitting of information data in response frames.

This presents no problem, since in an asynchronous balanced mode the information can be transferred in command frames, and since both physical stations are logical primary stations, both can transmit commands.

LAPB also provides for extended sequencing. This means that it may also use the functional extension number 10. Consequently, LAPB may be classified also as BA-2,8,10.

LLC *(logical link control)* is a link layer standard released by the IEEE 802 standards committee (see Figure 4-10). LLC runs on top of a IEEE local area network (LAN). This means that it rests between a LAN data-link control and an undefined network layer.

LLC is modeled on the HDLC standard, but it allows several implementation options. The type 1 option uses the HDLC extension #4 (again, see Figure 4-4). This option is a connectionless protocol in that it has no acknowledgments, no rejects, no sequence numbers, and no flow control operations.

LLC may also be implemented as type 2, which is the conventional balanced asynchronous mode of HDLC with full connection-oriented features such as rejects, acknowledgments, the use of sequence numbers, and flow control measures.

LAPD *(link access procedure, D channel)* is another subset of the HDLC structure, although it has extensions beyond HDLC. LAPD is intended to be used as a data-link control for the emerging integrated services digital network (ISDN). LAPD and ISDN are covered in Chapter Nine, which focuses on digital networks.

LAPX *(LAPB extended)* is another subset of HDLC, used in terminal-based systems and in the emerging Teletex standard. It is a half-duplex rendition of HDLC.

Link access procedure for modems (LAPM) is published by the CCITT in the V.42 Recommendation. This standard establishes SABM procedures operations between modems. In effect, the use of V.42 allows an organization to remove the link protocol from DTEs. The result of this operation is the use of *error-detecting modems.*

V.42 has other attractive features. For example, it provides asynchronous-to-synchronous transmission capabilities (using the V.14 specification). This option allows an asynchronous device, such as a personal computer, to interface into the V.42 modem wherein the asynchronous transmission scheme is transmitted to a synchronous scheme on the communications channel. The synchronous transmission scheme provides for better utilization of the channel and can give the user higher throughput. V.42 provides a simple protocol for a LAPM modem to inquire if the receiving modem supports V.42 and the LAPM operation. If the receiving modem does not respond properly, the V.42 modem falls back to a non-LAPM mode.

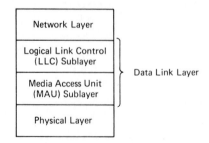

Figure 4-10.   Logical Link Control (LLC)

SDLC

SDLC *(synchronous data-link control)* is IBM's version or rendition of HDLC. SDLC uses the unbalanced normal response mode. In addition, it uses several options of HDLC. Its classification scheme would place it in UN-1,2,4,5,6, and 12. Moreover, SDLC uses several variations of the HDLC scheme, and one classification within the HDLC schema would not fully describe the capabilities and options of SDLC products.

The term "superset" becomes blurred when discussing SDLC, because it uses several commands which are not found in the HDLC standard. These commands and responses provide the ability to establish a loop topology and perform loop or ring polling operations. Consequently, SDLC provides support for point-to-point, multipoint, or loop configurations. The latter topology uses the group-polling features discussed in Chapter Two.

Because of IBM's position in the industry, we will examine the similarities and differences of SDLC and HDLC. (Please note that IBM has several products that are specifically designed to operate with HDLC systems.) Also, an example of the HDLC functions used by IBM is provided to show a different mode of operation. The specific differences between SDLC and HDLC are as follows:

- HDLC provides an option to extend the 8-bit address field by the use of extended bytes. The purpose is to address more terminals or more groups of terminals and devices in computers. SDLC implementations support only a single-byte address field.
- HDLC permits the control field to be extended, as well. Under the extended-format option, HDLC systems may have the control field extended to 16 bits. This provides for extended sequence numbers for the N(R) and N(S) fields. IBM supports only the basic 8-bit format. This becomes an important consideration when using satellite links (see Chapter Five).
- SDLC implementations restrict the information field to an even integral number of bytes. HDLC does not have this restriction.
- As previously discussed, IBM's SDLC provides some additional commands and responses for loop operations.

Figure 4-11 shows an example of an IBM SDLC transmission process. Station A is the primary station in control of stations B and C. Notice the normal response mode under full duplex permits the primary station to transmit frames to one secondary station while receiving frames from another. Figure 4-11 assumes station C's mode has been set and is currently involved in data transmissions. Under normal response mode, the address in the frame always contains that of the secondary station.

Following are the times and events for the process depicted in Figure 4-11:

n, n + 1, 2, 3, 4, 5   Station A first polls B for status. B responds by requesting an initialization mode. Station A sets B to an initialization mode and then normal response mode. B acknowledges both modes.

Time

	n	$n+1$	$n+2$	$n+3$	$n+4$	$n+5$	$n+6$	$n+7$	$n+8$	$n+9$	$n+10$	$n+11$	$n+12$	$n+13$
Station A Transmits	B, RR, P		B, SIM, P		B, SNRM, P		C, RR, P $R=0$	B, I $S=0, R=0$	B, I $S=1, R=0$		B, RR, P $R=0$		C, RR, P $R=3$	B, RR, P $R=2$
Station B Transmits		B, RIM, F		B, UA, F		B, UA, F						B, I $S=0, R=2$	B, I, F $S=1, R=2$	
Station C Transmits								C, I $S=0, R=0$	C, I $S=1, R=0$	C, I, F $S=2, R=0$				

Figure Assumes B in Disconnect Mode
and C in Normal Response Mode

Figure 4-11. SDLC with Multipoint Full Duplex

n + 6   Station A uses *Receive Ready* command to poll station C with poll bit set.

n + 7, 8   Station A sends frames 0 and 1 to B, while station C responds to the previous poll and sends frames 0 and 1 to A on the other channel of the full-duplex circuit.

n + 9   Station C sends information frame 2 and sets final bit.

n + 10   Station A polls B for a checkpoint (confirmation).

n + 11   Station B responds by acknowledging A's 0 and 1 frames with a receive sequence of 2. Station B also sends information frame 0.

n + 12   Station A acknowledges C's frames 0, 1, and 2 with a *Receive Ready* (RR) and a receive sequence of 3. Station B sends frame 1, and sets F to 1 in response to the P bit in *n* + 10.

n + 13   Station A acknowledges B's frames 0 and 1 with a *Receive Ready* (RR) and a receive sequence of 2. Subsequent events would require Stations A and B to respond with F bits set to 1.

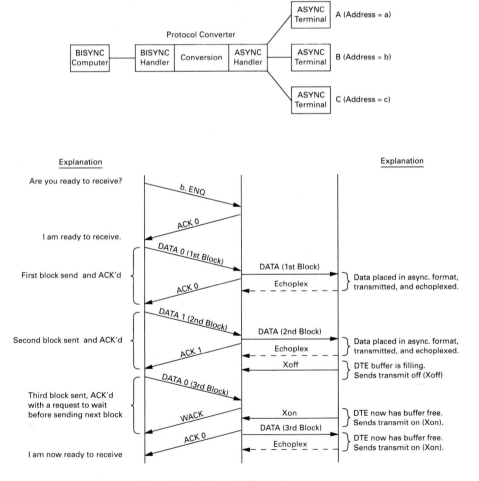

Figure 4-12.   Protocol Conversion

PROTOCOL CONVERSION

It is a rather unusual occurrence when different vendors' products use identical protocols. Certainly, if two machines both use HDLC, for example, the interface problems may not be great. However, even with supposedly similar protocols, vendors often "patch" them to enhance performance for a particular system or need. More obvious is the situation of dissimilar DTEs, perhaps using completely different protocols. For example, synchronous and asynchronous DTEs are quite different in message formats, line control, error handling, and buffer flow control.

One solution to this problem is to use protocol converters (see Figure 4-12). These systems (a software package, a stand-alone microprocessor, or a board) provide the "bridge" between the two protocols. The illustration depicts a binary synchronous (bisync) computer attached through a protocol converter to three asynchronous terminals. (The terminals use an echoplex convention to check for errors.) The converter provides the translation between the two protocols.

SUMMARY

The HDLC family of link protocols continues to evolve and to expand. Their use in X.25, IEEE 802, and digital networks virtually assures that the protocols will be used for many years. However, their emphasis on assuring an error-free transmission will likely diminish as reliable optical fibers and error-correction techniques become more common. In the meantime, their advantages over the BSC (bisync) protocols ensure that, increasingly, they will replace the older, less efficient stop-and-wait systems.

5

Satellite Networks

INTRODUCTION

Man-made satellites have revolutionized communications and, in many instances, the shape of world politics. For example, the graphic, live images of the Vietnam War, conveyed by satellite to the American public, had a dramatic effect on the public's opinion of the war. The startling satellite broadcasts of Ethiopia's famine shocked an otherwise uninformed world. On a lighter side, the live broadcasts of sports events, such as the British Open golf classic and the French Open tennis tournament, have added significantly to the fans' enjoyment of these sports.

In 1945, Arthur C. Clark, with uncanny foresight, described in the magazine *Wireless World* the satellite technology as it exists today. Clark predicted satellite communications would create a communications revolution as profound as that brought about by the telephone. While satellite technology may not have had such a profound effect, it certainly has altered considerably the way in which we communicate and the way in which we perceive the world.

In this chapter we discuss in general terms reasons satellite technology is widely used, its advantages and disadvantages, and how satellite communications facilities provide for computer and terminal networks. We will go into greater detail later in the chapter to describe other protocols of the classification tree in Figure 2-5.

SATELLITE COMPONENTS

Satellite communications use microwave frequency antennas to receive radio signals from transmitting stations on the earth and to relay the signals back down to earth stations. Figure 5-1 illustrates this process. The satellite serves as an electronic relay

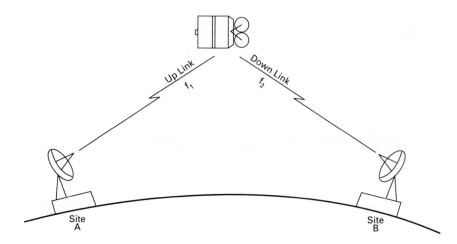

Figure 5-1. Satellite Communications

station. Earth station A transmits signals of a specific frequency (up link) to the satellite. In turn, the satellite receives the signals and retransmits them back down to earth station B on the down-link frequency. The down link can be received by any station that falls within the radiated signal. The signals may be voice images, data transmissions, or television video signals.

The satellite receiving/transmitting capability is supported by a device called a *transponder*. The satellite transponders operate at very high frequencies (see Figure 1-8 for a review of the frequency spectrum), typically in the gigahertz range. The majority of the satellites today use frequencies in the range of 6/4 gigahertz. Other satellites use a higher bandwidth with transponders in the 14/12 gigahertz range. As shown in Figure 5-1, the signal is transmitted from the earth station at a different frequency than this same signal being transmitted from the satellite stations. These signals are noted as f_1 from the up link to the satellite station and f_2 on the down link to the earth stations. This approach prevents the two transmissions (the up and down signals) from interfering with each other because they are operating in different frequency ranges.

Pros and Cons of Satellite Networks

Communications satellites provide several attractive features. First, each satellite has a large transmission capacity. Since the satellites are operating in the broad bandwidth range of the gigahertz level, a satellite can support several thousand voice-grade channels.

Communications satellites have the capability of providing a broad range of coverage. Some satellites can cover the entire United States with one transponder. This feature is quite attractive for organizations that have widely distributed components, for example, branch offices or subsidiaries located around the country or in dispersed regions of the world. However, the wide coverage presents some potential security problems, since a station can pick up another organization's transmission if it is calibrated to the proper channel. Consequently, many satellite carriers implement security measures for the customer, such as encryption devices.

The cost of transmitting the signal is independent of the distance between the two earth sites. It is immaterial if the two sites are five miles or a thousand miles apart. If they are serviced by the same transponder the transmission cost is constant, since the signals transmitted from the transponder can be received by all stations, regardless of their distance from each other.

Communications satellites provide the opportunity to design a switched network without physical switches. In order to establish switches in the LAN-based system, an organization must lease carrier lines and interface these lines into the organization's communications facilities (such as computers, front-end processors, multiplexers, etc.). In contrast, since the earth stations communicating with the satellite transponder are sending and receiving on the same two channels, they need only listen to the down link frequency to determine if the transmission is destined for them. If it is not, they simply ignore the signal. If it is their data, they copy the signal and present it to the end user. This *broadcast* capability can translate into significantly reduced costs when compared to the land-based network that uses numerous physical communications lines and switches.

Satellite communications are not without problems, however. As stated earlier, security can be compromised if the signal is not scrambled or encrypted. Poor weather conditions can interfere with the signal as it traverses up and down the communications channels. It is not unusual for heavy rainstorms to interfere with a signal. Also, since the signal is transmitted over a very great distance (usually 22,300 miles each way to and from the satellite station), a delay occurs in the reception of the signal at the earth station. In some instances, the delay can present problems with line protocols and response time (this subject is discussed shortly).

Periodically, the sun, the earth station, and the satellite are directly aligned with each other. The sun's rays travel directly into the earth station's antenna, creating a *sun transient:* excessive thermal noise in relation to the received signal. Conversely, a *solar eclipse* occurs during the spring and fall when the earth is between the sun and the satellite for a few minutes during a 23-day period. During this time, the solar cells on the satellite may deplete, which creates losses of power to the satellite electronic components.

The communications signal from the satellite may also interfere with other radio signals from land-based systems. Consequently, a careful allocation of frequency spectrum is necessary to prevent such interference.

Finally, a finite amount of frequencies exist for the 6/4 and 14/12 GHz satellites, and a finite number of satellites can be placed in orbit. While spectrum and orbit space has not been a hindrance to the technology in the past, it is becoming a problem and will require increased cooperation of the many nations using communications satellite technology.

Brief History

Before discussing how satellite communications are used in computer and terminal networks, it should prove useful to discuss some of the major landmarks in satellite communications. The interest in satellites happened rather suddenly in 1957, when the Russians launched the famous Sputnik into space. The incident spurred the U.S.

and Canada (and later Europe) to increase their efforts in the satellite communications field as well as in rocket-launching technology. An interesting aside to these early incidents is the somewhat misconceived notion that U.S. technology was inadvertently lagging far behind that of Russia. While the U.S. was lagging, it was because the U.S. had made the first breakthrough in nuclear warfare and did not think it necessary to spend the necessary research money to develop the large launch-capacity vehicles necessary for warfare missiles (and later, the satellite communications field). Nonetheless, the United States soon followed the Russians with the launch of Explorer 1 in January 1958.

Neither Sputnik nor Explorer had communications facilities. The United States Army is credited with the first communications satellite, launched in December 1958. The famous Early Bird, the world's first commercial satellite, was launched from Cape Kennedy in 1965.

These earlier satellites were passive—the signal was merely transmitted up and reflected back down to the earth. As the technology improved, as rockets became more powerful, and as smaller and lighter electronic components emerged, it became possible to install amplifiers in the satellites. Improved technology permitted the signal to be transmitted, received at the satellite, amplified, and transmitted back down to earth.

The earlier satellites had elliptical orbits. They were launched usually no higher than 6,000 miles above the earth. The low orbit resulted in the satellite moving around the earth's horizon faster than the earth's rotation. This presented tracking problems between the earth stations and the satellite because of the satellite's frequent disappearance over the horizon. It is estimated that the North Atlantic region alone would have required 50 elliptically orbiting satellites for continuous coverage.

Today's satellites are in a geosynchronous (or geostationary) orbit. These satellites are launched 22,300 miles above the earth and are positioned on a plane perpendicular to the equator. They are designed to achieve a rotating speed around the earth of 6,879 miles per hour, and the gravitational pull of the earth, counterbalanced by the velocity of the satellite, gives the satellite the appearance of being stationary relative to the earth's rotation. Consequently, the earth station's antenna can remain in a relatively fixed position (which is called an orbital slot), since the satellite's motion is fixed relative to the earth's position. The geosynchronous satellites are often launched in groups of three. These satellites, positioned 120 degrees apart, achieve nearly worldwide coverage.

USING SATELLITES TO COMMUNICATE

Conventional Multiplexing

Communications between the satellite and the earth stations can be controlled in a number of ways. One approach, *frequency division multiplexing* (FDM), is used on some systems. The entire channel spectrum is divided into subchannels, and users are assigned the various subchannels to transmit any traffic they wish within their prescribed spectrum space. Frequency division multiplexing has two significant drawbacks, however. First, much of the available bandwidth has to be utilized as a *guardband* to prevent adjacent channels from interfering with each other. Second, if the users are not all transmitting regularly, then much of the subchannel bandwidth is wasted because of the idle channel conditions.

Another approach is the use of *time division multiplexing* (TDM) in which the time spectrum is divided and users share time slots on the communications channel. The major shortcoming of time division multiplexing is similar to that of FDM. Since the capacity of the channel is preallocated to each potential user, the channel is wasted if the user is not transmitting regularly. (We address this problem shortly when we look at a form of multiplexing called time division multiple access [TDMA].)

Polling/Selection

Satellite communications can also be controlled by a conventional primary/ secondary relationship using polling/selection techniques (see Figure 2-6). The primary traffic is managed by an earth station (designated as a primary site) sending polls and selects up to the satellite to be relayed back down to secondary earth stations. An alternate approach (not used much) is to have the satellite station provide the polls and selects to control the network. Let us examine both approaches to determine the advantages and disadvantages of polling/selection in satellite systems.

First, we assume a satellite computer performs the polling and selection. Since the satellite is located 22,300 miles above the earth and the signal propagates at a rate of 186,000 miles per second, it takes a *minimum* of 120 milliseconds (ms) for the poll or select to reach an earth station (23,000 miles ÷ 186,000 mps = .120 sec). It requires another 120 ms for the response to the poll and select to reach the communications satellite. Consequently, each polling and selection cycle takes 240 ms. Assuming *n* users are to be polled and selected within the network, a full polling and selection cycle would take .240 × *n* seconds. If 100 users were using the satellite system, it would require .240 × 100, or 24 seconds, for a full polling/selection cycle to take place. Obviously, the delay presents some rather serious response-time problems. If a ground station controls the polls and selects, the performance is even worse, since the poll or select is sent up to the satellite *and* down to the earth station. Consequently, with 100 users in the network, a ground station controller would require 48 seconds for the full polling/selection cycle.

The delay is also evident for a session in which only two stations are using the channel. If user A from one station sends a frame on the satellite channel to user B at another site, user A must pause and wait for an acknowledgment (assuming the use of a stop-and-wait, half-duplex protocol). If the two users are sending multiple frames to each other (as in a file-transfer batch transmission), the accumulated delays create an extended time to complete the process, which reduces the effective utilization of the channel. It is easy to see why the once widely used half-duplex binary synchronous control protocol (BSC or bisync, discussed in Chapter 4) has fallen into disfavor. As shown in Table 5-1, it experiences considerable degradation in the utilization of a channel (especially a satellite channel). This table illustrates some of the problems encountered with older protocols and reinforces the idea that full-duplex continuous ARQ protocols are better methods for use on satellite channels.

TABLE 5-1. CHANNEL UTILIZATION

Block (Frame) Size	10 ms delay	38 ms delay	500 ms delay
40 bytes	76.9%	46.7%	6.2%
132 bytes	91.7%	74.3%	18.0%
516 bytes	97.7%	91.9%	46.2%

The larger the block or frame size, the better the channel utilization because the larger blocks mask the delay effect of the long-distance circuit. Half-duplex delay does not create a problem on short-distance channels with short delays (of 10 ms, for example). It is more evident on circuits of several hundred miles (40 ms delay) to several thousand miles (500 ms delay, or more).

The use of a full-duplex Continuous ARQ protocol instead of a stop-and-wait polling system decreases the response time and increases the throughput. As the table shows, satellite delay using polling/selection is especially evident using the half-duplex, stop-and-wait approach. The Continuous ARQ allows the overlapping of transmissions and acknowledgments across a full-duplex channel and reduces the amount of delay incurred in the polling cycle. For example, one station can be polled, and while the poll is being transmitted to that station, yet another station can transmit data on the return channel.

Yet Continuous ARQ also has problems. For example, if the system is transmitting 1,000 bit frames and the channel is operating at 50,000 bits per second, the channel provides the speed for multiple frames to be sent on the up and down links in succession *before* any responses or data are transmitted back. High-speed channels actually increase the effect of propagation delay, because it takes less time to send each frame up and down the channel. Consequently, the window closes faster with high-speed channels and short blocks of data. This problem is illustrated in Figure 5-2.

In order to prevent the channel from becoming idle [as in Figure 5-2(a)], the conventional ARQ window of seven is often expanded. The window expansion prevents the transmitting side from closing its window while awaiting acknowledgments. Some systems use the HDLC extended-sequencing option and expand the window to 127; that is, 127 frames can be transmitted in succession without any acknowledgment from the receiver. The expanded window allows the system to compensate for the propagation delay [see Figure 5-2(b)] and provides for more efficient channel utilization.

Expanded windows present some additional problems, though. In the event of an error, the Go-Back-N technique discussed in Chapters Two and Four necessitates the retransmission of one or more frames. For example, if a transmitting site sends frames 1 through 40, and frame 6 is in error, then frames 6 through 40 must be

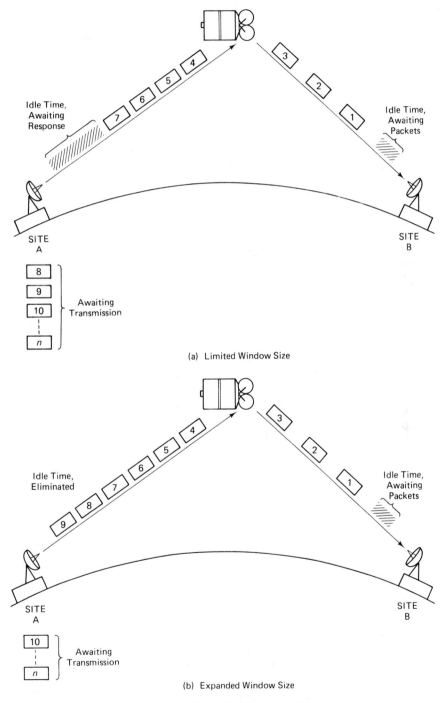

(a) Limited Window Size

(b) Expanded Window Size

Figure 5-2. Effect of Propagation Delay

retransmitted. With the alternative method, Selective Repeat, the receiving station is tasked with queuing and holding several frames to await the retransmission of the single frame. In our example, frames 7 through 40 must be held at the receiver site until frame 6 is retransmitted, because the frames must be passed to the user in sequential order. Consequently, even Continuous ARQ experiences problems with the propagation delay of the satellite channel. Later in the chapter the satellite delay unit (SDU) is introduced as a method to reduce the effect of delay.

Nonpolling Peer/Peer Systems

ALOHA. In the early 1970s, Norman Abramson, at the University of Hawaii, devised a technique for uncoordinated users to effectively compete for a channel. The approach is called the ALOHA system; it is so named because the Hawaiian word is used without regard to whether a person is arriving or departing. The original ALOHA technique used a ground-based radio packet system rather than satellites, but the ideas are applicable to any channel media when users are contending for its use.

As depicted in Figure 5-3, ALOHA is considered to be a peer-to-peer system. Several variations of ALOHA exist. One approach fits the carrier sense collision-detect protocol (*Random* ALOHA). Another variation can be used as a priority slot system (*Slotted* ALOHA). We will use ALOHA to introduce peer-to-peer systems, even though most satellite protocols have implemented more efficient techniques (these will be discussed later in this chapter).

The premise of ALOHA is that users are acting on a peer-to-peer basis—they all have equal access to the channel. A user station transmits whenever it has data to send. Since the channel is not allocated by any primary/secondary structure, it is possible (and probable) that users will occasionally transmit at approximately the same time. Simultaneous transmission results in the signals interfering and distorting each other as the separate signals propagate up to the satellite transponder. (The term to describe several stations transmitting on one frequency to one station is *narrowcasting*. The transmission of one station [the satellite] to many stations is called *broadcasting*.) These "packet collisions" necessitate the retransmission of the damaged packets. (The term "packet" is used in place of "frame" under the ALOHA scheme.) Since the users of the satellite link know exactly what was transmitted onto the up-link channel and when it was transmitted, they need listen only to the down-link channel at the prescribed time to determine if the broadcast packet arrived without damage. If the packet is damaged due to a collision, the stations are required to retransmit the damaged packet. In essence, the idea is to listen to the down-link channel one up-and-down delay time after the packet was sent. If the packet is destroyed, the transmitting site is required to wait a short random period and then retransmit. The randomized wait period diminishes the chances of the competing stations colliding again, since the waiting times will likely differ and result in retransmissions at different times.

Figure 5-3 depicts a typical ALOHA system using satellite communications. Stations A and B are transmitting packets at will on a shared channel. The down-link channel shows that packet 1 from station A is transmitted up and down safely;

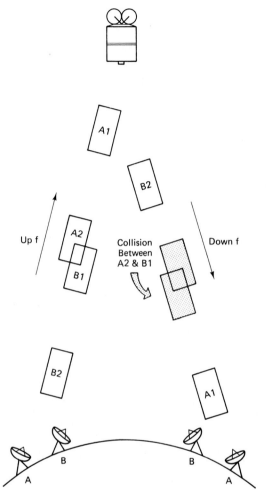

Up f

Collision
Between
A2 & B1

Down f

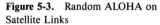

Figure 5-3. Random ALOHA on
Satellite Links

packet 2 from station B is also transmitted without error. However, the second
packet from A and the first packet from B are transmitted at approximately the
same time. As the transmissions of the two stations are narrowcasted up into the
satellite station, the signals interfere with each other, resulting in a collision.

The satellite station is not responsible for error detection or error correction; it
transmits what it receives from the up link. On the down link, stations A and B note
the packets have collided and, upon waiting a random period of time (usually a few
milliseconds), attempt to retransmit. This approach is quite effective when the users
are uncoordinated and are sending traffic in bursts, such as data from keyboard
terminals.

Random ALOHA experiences considerable degradation of throughput when
the channel is heavily utilized. However, keep in mind that what is transmitted
across the channel is *all* end-user data. Unlike the primary/secondary polling systems, ALOHA uses no polls, selects, or negative responses to polls. Only end-user
information is transmitted. Nonetheless, the pure random scheme can be improved

by adapting a more efficient strategy, called Slotted ALOHA, for using the uncoordinated channel.

Slotted ALOHA requires that common clocks be established at the earth stations and the satellite. The clocks are synchronized to send traffic at specific periods. For example, the clocks may require that packets are transmitted only on 20 ms (.020 second) increments. In this example, the 20 ms increment is derived from a 50,000-bit/s channel and 1,000-bit packets (1,000 ÷ 50,000 = .020 second).

The 20 ms increment is referred to as the packet duration, which is the time in which the packet is transmitted on the channel. All stations are required to transmit at the *beginning* of a slot period. A packet cannot be transmitted if it overlaps more than one slot.

The Slotted ALOHA approach increases throughput substantially on the channel, because if packets overlap or collide, they do so completely; at most, only one slot is damaged. However, like pure Random ALOHA, the Slotted ALOHA does offer opportunities for collisions. For example, if two stations transmit in the same clock period, their packets collide. As in the pure Random ALOHA approach, the stations are required to wait a random period of time before attempting to seize a slot for retransmission.

Another refinement to Slotted ALOHA is *Slotted ALOHA with Nonowner*. The channel slots are combined into an ALOHA frame (Figure 5-4). The ALOHA frame must equal or exceed the up-and-down propagation delay. Consequently, a 1,000-bit packet lasting 20 ms would require a minimum of 12 slots to make up the ALOHA frame: 12 slots × 20 ms = 240 ms. The 240 ms period represents the *minimum* up and down propagation delay (120 ms (up) × 120 ms (down) = 240 ms).

Slotted ALOHA with Nonowner requires that a station select an empty slot in the frame. Once the user has seized the slot, it is reserved for the user for successive frames until the user relinquishes the slot. The relinquishment occurs by the station sending a protocol control code, such as EOT (end of transmission). Upon receiving an EOT, the next frame transmitted is empty for that particular slot. A user station then is allowed to contend for the slot with the next subsequent frame. The only collisions occurring on Slotted ALOHA with Nonowner are when stations pick the same slot in the 240 ms frame.

Another variation of Slotted ALOHA is *Slotted ALOHA with Owner*. The slots of each frame are now owned by users. The user has exclusive use of its slot within the frame as long as it has data to transmit. In the event that the user relinquishes the slot, it so indicates with an established code. The slot becomes empty and is available for any other user to seize it. Once another user has seized the slot, it has exclusive rights to the use of the slot until the original owner seizes the slot. The rightful owner can claim the slot at any time by beginning transmissions within its designated slot in the frame. The relinquishment is required when the rightful owner transmits. Obviously, the first time the owner transmits in its slot a collision may occur. On the subsequent frame, the rightful owner retransmits. The relinquishing station then must look for another free slot or go to its own slots if it has them. This refined approach of ALOHA is classified as a peer-to-peer priority structure, since some stations can be given priority ownership over other stations. Thus, it fits into the classification tree as a priority slot system.

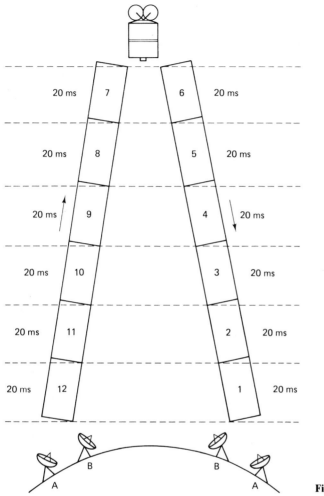

Figure 5-4. Slotted ALOHA

Nonpolling Primary/Secondary Systems

TDMA. In 1981, Satellite Business Systems (SBS) (now defunct) began offering communications services to private and public organizations via geosynchronous satellites and earth stations. Notwithstanding, the system is used in this chapter because it provides an excellent means of discussing another widely used technique for satellite communications. The example in this chapter shows how time division multiple access (TDMA) is used to achieve a primary/secondary nonpolling system. The TDMA technique is used by other satellite carriers, as well. For example, the European Telecommunications Satellite Organization (EUTELSAT) uses TDMA on its Telecom 1 satellite. This explanation covers the specific SBS protocol.

TDMA assigns slots as needed. However, unlike the ALOHA system, the slots are assigned by a primary station called the *reference* (REF). As depicted in Figure 5-5, the reference station accepts requests from the other stations, and, based on the

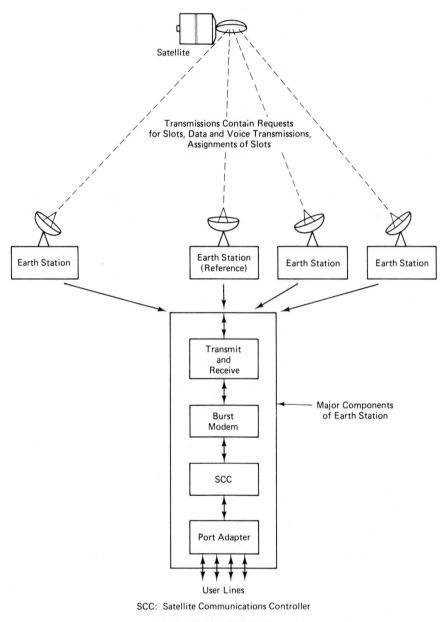

SCC: Satellite Communications Controller

Figure 5-5.   TDMA

nature of the traffic and available channel capacity, the REF assigns these requests to specific frames for subsequent transmission. Every 20 frames, the reference station sends the assignments to the secondary stations. One reference station is assigned to each transponder of the system. TDMA provides for as many as ten active transponders per satellite.

Figure 5-5 also shows the earth station components. The major components consist of the port adapter, the satellite communications controller (SCC), a burst modem, the transmit/receive device, and an antenna.

The port adapter is responsible for interfacing the user lines into the earth station. The adapter accepts voice images at a rate of 32 kbit/s and data at rates varying from 2.4 kbit/s to 1.544 Mbit/s.

All digital images are passed to the satellite communications controller, which is a software-oriented unit that consolidates the functions of timing, station assignment, switching, and processing of voice and data calls. It calculates channel requirements based on the number of voice connections, the number of data ports available, and the number of queued data connection requests. It then assigns these requests to TDMA frames.

The burst modem sends out a 48 Mbit/s signal with 15 ms frames (.015 sec) under the direction of the satellite controller. Thus, each transponder has the capability of operating at 48 megabits per second.

The transmit/receive antennas are responsible for transmitting and receiving the up and down channel links. This protocol operates at 14 gigahertz on the up link and 12 gigahertz on the down link. This transmission band was chosen because it is relatively free from other satellite transmissions and it allows the earth stations to operate relatively free from the terrestrial microwave operations of 4/6 gigahertz.

On a 15 ms frame, illustrated in Figure 5-6, the reference station (REF) transmits an assignment set for all SCCs using the transponder. As mentioned earlier, this transmission is sent every 20 frames. The assignment set specifies the capacity and position of each SCC's traffic burst to the transponder. Recall that assignments are made in response to the requests received in earlier frames. The control field of the frame contains the assignments and the requests from the competing stations. The remainder of the frame consists of the traffic, which contains the traffic bursts from each SCC that was assigned a position by the reference station.

The traffic is packed in 512-bit channels consisting of a 32-bit destination address and 480 bits of data. The 480-bit data frame was chosen to accommodate the requirement for a voice transmission rate of 32 kilobits per second [480 × (1 second ÷ .015 slot) = 32,000].

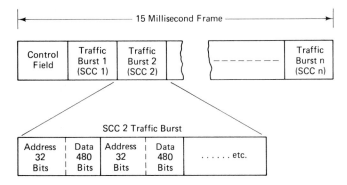

Figure 5-6. The TDMA Frame

The 32 kilobits per second rate uses only a small fraction of the total 48 megabit channel capacity. Consequently, many voice and data transmissions can be time division multiplexed (TDM) efficiently onto the high-speed 48 kbit/s channel. (We return to TDMA in Chapter Nine to examine integrated systems for voice and data.)

SATELLITE DELAY UNITS (SDUs)

In the earlier days of satellite communications (early 1960s), half-duplex protocols were widely employed on user machines. Although half-duplex protocols have fallen into disuse, we discuss an approach that handles this protocol on satellite links because some half-duplex systems still exist today. Satellite vendors have developed methods to compensate for the inherent inefficiency of a half-duplex system on the satellite circuit. The satellite delay compensation unit (SDU) illustrated in Figure 5-7 is one such tool. Stations A and B are to communicate through a satellite channel. However, instead of communicating directly with each other, the two stations trans-

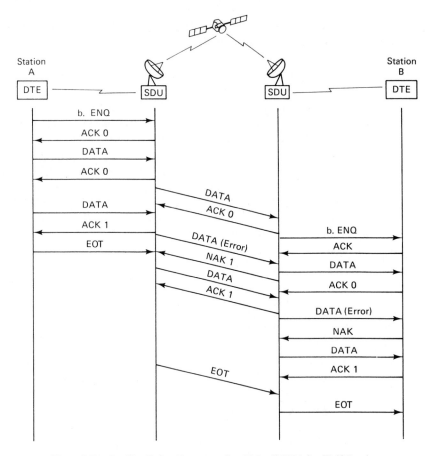

Figure 5-7.   Satellite Delay Compensation Units (SDUs) for Half-Duplex Protocols

mit and receive through a SDU. The SDU is connected to each of the stations through a land-based terrestrial link, such as microwave or optical fibers. Consequently, the delay of signal transmission between the DTE and the SDU is very short.

The SDU is actually a *protocol converter.* It accepts bisync traffic from station A and station B and buffers the traffic locally. Consequently, when station A sends a *Select* command to station B, the SDU servicing station A immediately acknowledges the *Select* with an ACK0. The data are transmitted, checked for errors at the SDU, and then acknowledged. The SDU for A then transmits the data using its own protocol through the satellite circuit for transmission down to the down-link SDU (B). The SDU for B provides an error check and responds with an acknowledgment. The SDU servicing station B then goes through the same sequence of events that DTE A and SDU A performed—it sends a *Select* to station B, which acknowledges the *Select,* receives the data, checks for errors, and responds with an ACK0.

Figure 5-7 shows that the second block of data must be retransmitted between the two SDUs when the data are distorted during the satellite transmission process. Likewise, SDU B and DTE B must pass the data error-free. The SDU servicing station B must retransmit the second data frame, because B sent a NAK to SDU B. Finally, the bisync EOT is sent from station A to tell station B it has no more data to transmit. The EOT is transported across the communications channel, and the remote SDU provides the bisync EOT to terminate the transmission process.

The satellite delay-compensation units provide some immunity from the cumulative effects of delay on half-duplex protocols. However, certain protocols, even though they may be half-duplex, may not benefit from the SDU compensation. For example, if half-duplex messages, such as bisync, are sent *one at a time* for an interactive session, there is no cumulative effect on the delay of these transmissions, even though the long delay could be a problem for extremely high-speed applications. However, half-duplex systems which utilize batch transmission can benefit substantially from the use of the SDU, because the session between the DTEs usually encompasses *many* blocks of transmission. In batch systems, the transmitting SDU can receive and buffer an entire file before it activates the remote SDU session. Likewise, the receiving SDU can buffer the batch file completely and *then* establish the session with the receiving DTE.

THE TELEPORT

The concept of the teleport has received considerable attention in the industry. The teleport is a satellite or several satellites shared by multiple users. Typically, the users are tenants in an office building within an industrial complex. The users of the teleport are linked to the satellite through cable, optical fibers, or microwave links. The basic idea is to share the high-capacity satellite channels in order to reduce users' overall communications costs. The teleport transmits all types of images (voice, data, facsimile, and video) with a wide diversity of data rates. The digital transmission speeds range from 45 kbit/s to 1.544 Mbit/s. Of course, users have the option of lesser data rates through multiplexing techniques.

The primary focus of the teleport is to support private business. However, other users are targeted as well. Some teleport companies are marketing to residential users in the primary form of closed-circuit television broadcasts. Other vendors are supporting hotel and educational organizations.

A teleport provides several options to users. The teleport can be located within an industrial complex or at a user's site. The users can be located far away from the teleport and communicate with the teleport through microwave, optical fiber links, coaxial cable, or a telephone channel. The satellite communications then take the transmission and transport it to other users throughout the country.

The teleport technology emphasizes the controversial bypass issue. *Bypass* describes the use of local media other than the telephone companies' local or subscriber loop. Bypass also includes the use of long-distance media other than AT&T Communications. The Bell operating companies and AT&T state that bypass is a threat to their revenue base and user service. At the same time, Ohio Bell has decided to join the fray. It has purchased 20 percent of the Ohio Teleport Corporation in order to participate in bypassing itself.

SUMMARY

The satellite industry continues to grow. Until 1986, homeowners were able to receive signals from the movie and special-events channels and satellite dishes were springing up all over the country. However, some of these channels are now scrambled, which has somewhat dampened this cottage industry. Some industry watchers believe long-haul optical links will also diminish the use of satellites. Perhaps so, but their broadcast capabilities virtually ensure their place in the industry for many years.

6

Local Area Networks

INTRODUCTION

In the past twenty years, the communications industry has focused on systems which transport data over long distances. The wide area network (WAN) industry has now matured and is a relatively stable field. The local area network (LAN) constitutes a relatively new arena for data communications. LAN technology began to gain attention in the mid-1970s, and today it is one of the fastest growing industries in data communications.

This chapter provides a general background of the most widely used LAN topologies and protocols and discusses some of the major organizations in the market. It also covers, in more detail, some of the emerging LAN standards found in the IEEE 802, the ANSI committees, the ECMA (European Computer Manufacturers Association), the International Organization for Standardization (ISO), and private companies.

A separate discussion of PBXs and LANs can be found in Chapter Twelve. While the PBX/LAN discussion is found in another section, it is not meant to imply that a PBX is not a viable option on the LAN. Any serious considerations of a LAN should include the PBX.

WHY LANs?

Office expenses comprise approximately 25 percent of a company's cost of doing business, and, as the trend toward white-collar employees continues, it is expected that by the end of the decade, office expenses will account for approximately 45 percent of the cost of doing business in a typical company. The driving force for the use of LANs is to increase employee productivity and efficiency. This goal is touted by LAN vendors, office managers, and LAN designers.

The American Telephone and Telegraph Corporation (AT&T) estimates that 70 percent of an office employee's time is spent in communicating with someone else. Naturally, any effort to increase an office worker's productivity can contribute to an organization's profits and mission. Various estimates have been made regarding the ability of a LAN to increase productivity. Some studies suggest that an office worker's productivity may be increased twofold through the use of increased automation and local communications capabilities. While one might question such a large estimate, it is generally recognized by most people working in the industry that the local area network does assist in increasing efficiency and productivity within the office.

The basic idea of a LAN is to provide easy access to DTEs within the office. These DTEs are not only computers (personal, medium-scale, and large-scale), but other devices commonly found in offices, such as printers, plotters, and, increasingly, electronic files and data bases. Like the WAN discussed in previous chapters, the LAN is configured to provide the channel and communications protocols between the work stations and computers.

PRIMARY ATTRIBUTES OF A LAN

Chapter Two introduced the concept of local area networks. Following is a review of some of the major attributes of a local area network:

- The connections between the work stations are usually distances of a few hundred feet, up to several thousand feet.
- The LAN transmits data between user stations and computers (some LANs transport voice and video images, as well).
- The LAN transmission capacity is usually greater than that of a wide area network; typical bit rates range from 1 Mbit/s to 20 Mbit/s.
- The LAN channel is typically privately owned by the organization using the facility. The telephone company is usually not involved in channel ownership or management. However, telephone companies are pursuing the LAN customer with a wide array of options based on their Centrex service.
- The error rate on a LAN is considerably better than a WAN-oriented telephone channel. For instance, error rates in $1:10^8$ are not uncommon. (A WAN error rate ranges from $1:10^3$ to $1:10^5$, with optical fiber systems an exception.)

Broadband and Baseband LANs

LANs are available as either *broadband* or *baseband* systems. A broadband network is characterized by the use of analog technology; it uses a modem to introduce carrier signals onto the transmission medium. The carrier signals are then modified (modulated) by a digital signal. Because of the analog nature of the network, broadband systems are often frequency division multiplexed (FDM), providing the ability to carry multiple carriers and subchannels on one path. Broadband systems are so named because the analog carrier signals operate in the high-frequency radio range (typically 10 to 400 MHz). Not all analog LANs operate at these high frequencies, in which case they are not considered broadband systems.

The baseband network uses digital technology. A line driver introduces voltage shifts onto the channel. The channel then acts as a transport mechanism by which the digital voltage pulses propagate through the channel. Baseband networks do not use analog carriers or FDM techniques. However, multiple access to the medium can be provided by a time division multiplexer (TDM) or protocols discussed in this chapter.

Baseband LANs are quite prevalent. However, some of the small baseband systems (fewer than thirty stations) are being replaced with private branch exchanges (PBX; see Chapter Twelve). Some larger LANs (more than 100 stations) generally use broadband techniques.

IEEE LAN STANDARDS

The Institute of Electrical and Electronics Engineers (IEEE) publish several widely accepted LAN-recommended standards. These standards are very important because they encourage the use of common approaches for LAN protocols and interfaces. As a consequence, chip manufacturers are more willing to spend money to develop relatively inexpensive hardware to sell to (they hope) a large market. The IEEE LAN Committees are organized as follows:

IEEE 802.1	High-Level Interface (and MAC Bridges)
IEEE 802.2	Logical Link Control (LLC)
IEEE 802.3	Carrier Sense Multiple Access/Collision Detect (CSMA/CD)
IEEE 802.4	Token Bus
IEEE 802.5	Token Ring
IEEE 802.6	Metropolitan Area Networks
IEEE 802.7	Broadband LANs
IEEE 802.8	Fiber Optic LANs
IEEE 802.9	Integrated Data and Voice Networks
IEEE 802.10	Security
IEEE 802.11	Wireless Networks

The IEEE standards are gaining wide acceptance. The European Computer Manufacturers Association (ECMA) voted to accept the 802.5 Token Ring as its standard. The NBS, the ISO, and ANSI have accepted these standards, and as we shall see, vendors and user groups are also using them.

In addition to the three basic standards of 802.3, 802.4, and 802.5 the IEEE also publishes the metropolitan area network (MAN) standard under the 802.6 number. An emerging standard, which is not yet complete, deals with integrated voice/data networks. It is identified with 802.9. The IEEE also sponsors standards concerning broadband LANs under 802.7, optical fiber LANs under 802.8, and security aspects for LANs under 802.10.

The IEEE 802.1 includes a number of standards. Network management is published in this standard, as well as the 802.1 bridge.

The IEEE standards are gaining wide acceptance. The European Computer Manufacturers Association (ECMA) voted to accept the 802.5 Token Ring as its standard (ECMA 89). The International Organization for Standardization (ISO) is accepting the 802 standards under ISO 8802. As we shall see, vendors and user groups are also using these standards.

Relationship of the 802 Standards to the ISO/CCITT Model

Chapter Three introduced the concept of layered protocols and the levels of the OSI network model (Open Systems Interconnection, or OSI). The IEEE efforts have emphasized the need to keep the OSI and 802 specifications as compatible as possible. To this end, the 802 committees split the data link layer into two sublayers: medium access control (MAC) and logical link control (LLC). As illustrated in Figure 6-1, MAC encompasses 802.3, 802.4, and 802.5. The LLC includes 802.2.

The MAC/LLC split provides several important features. First, it controls access to the shared channel among the autonomous DTEs. Second, it provides for a decentralized (peer-to-peer) scheme that reduces the LAN's susceptibility to errors. Third, it provides a more compatible interface with wide area networks, since LLC is a subset of the HDLC superset. Fourth, LLC is independent of a specific access method; MAC is protocol-specific. This approach gives the 802 network a flexible interface into and out of the LAN.

The three layers communicate with the exchange of primitives and protocol data units through service access points (SAPs). The convention for naming SAPs is as follows:

PSAP   SAP at top of physical layer
MSAP   SAP at top of MAC layer
LSAP   SAP at top of LLC layer.

Connection Options with LANs

At the onset of the IEEE 802 work, it was recognized that the connection-oriented aspect of the OSI approach would limit the scope and power of a local area network. First, many local applications do not need the data integrity provided by a connection-oriented network. Second, high-speed application processes cannot tolerate the overhead in establishing and disestablishing the connections.

The problem is particularly severe in the local area network, with its high-speed channels and low error rates. Many LAN applications require fast setups with each other. Others require very fast communications between the DTEs. With this in mind, the 802 LAN standards committees have included the concept of connectionless (datagram) systems within the LAN 802 standards. (If the idea of connection-oriented and connectionless networks seems vague, review the material in Chapter Two.)

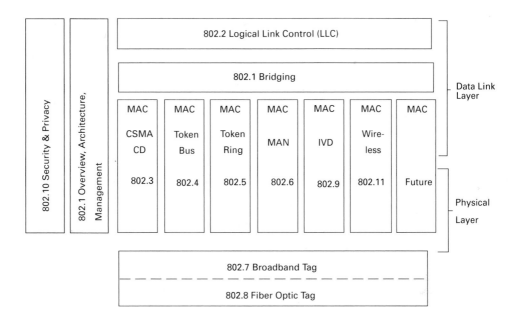

Figure 6-1. The IEEE 802 Standards

The ISO and 802 connection and connectionless modes are compared in Figure 6-2. The connection-oriented model of the ISO's Open Systems Interconnection is depicted in Figure 6-2(a). The two users, A and B, communicate through a service provider (i.e., the LAN) for A and a service provider for B. The connection-oriented model shows a request coming from A, transported across the service providers, and received at B as an indication. In the reverse process, B provides a response, which is transported across the service providers and received at A as a confirm.

The connection-mode transfer requires an agreement between three parties. In Figure 6-2(a), users A and B are two of the parties, and the service provider is the third party. This approach can also be related to the concept of the layers discussed in Chapter Three. Users A and B are the $n + 1$ entities, and the service provider is the n entity.

The other three illustrations of Figure 6-2 depict a service in which there are only two-party agreements—that is, A and B, or A and the service provider. The service provider knows of the connections in Figures 6-2(b) and 6-2(c). In Figure 6-2(d), the service provider has no prior knowledge of the individual agreements between A and B. In the three modes of the IEEE approach, all the information

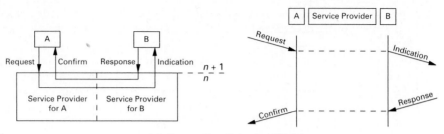

(a) Connection-Oriented Model

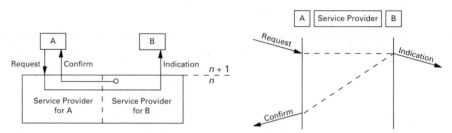

(b) Remote Service Provider Confirms

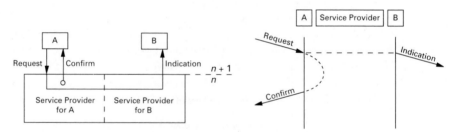

(c) Local Service Provider Confirms

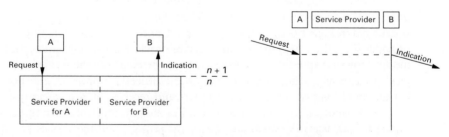

(d) Service Provider Provides No Confirm

Figure 6-2.   ISO and 802 Connection and Connectionless Modes

required to deliver the data unit is presented to the service provider, the *n* layer,
along with the data. Consequently, destination addresses, protocol information,
and error-check fields are all sent as a single entity through the network. Once this
information is exchanged between A and B and the service provider, no further
communication occurs between the service provider and the user layers regarding the

fate or disposition of the data unit. This does not mean that the two parties, A and B, cannot agree beforehand to establish certain acceptable error rates and transfer rates.

The service provider, or *n* layer, is not involved in any prior agreements between the *n* + 1 A and B entities. In a sense, the service provider is a passive conveyor of the data between A and B. Because of this approach, the connectionless orientation provides for a relatively simple environment between A and B, vis-à-vis the service provider.

The service provider considers the data unit transmitted to it as completely unrelated to any other data unit coming from or going to A and B. Consequently, the data units provided to the service provider will not be delivered in any particular order. Sequencing is not part of the connectionless data environment. This provides for considerable flexibility, because the service provider need not become involved in the details of the connection of DTE A and DTE B.

Types of Service.   All 802 networks must provide connectionless service (type 1). Optionally, connection-oriented service can be provided (type 2). Type 1 networks provide no ACKs, flow control, or error recovery; type 2 networks do provide ACKs, flow control, and error recovery. Most type 1 networks actually use a higher-level protocol (i.e., Transport Layer) to provide these functions.

The 802 standard also provides for a third class of service called type 3. Type 3 service is a hybrid service between types 1 and 2. It is connectionless in that no call setup is required between the stations for them to transport traffic. However, traffic is acknowledged between the transmitting entities. The acknowledgment process occurs with a half-duplex protocol in which a station can send one protocol data unit (PDU) and then must wait for the acknowledgment of the PDU from the receiver before it can send the next PDU.

LLC and MAC Protocol Data Units

The LLC and MAC sublayers use *protocol data units (PDUs)* to communicate. The formats for the PDUs are shown in Figure 6-3. The LLC unit contains a destination address (destination service access point [DSAP]), source address (source service access point [SSAP]), and the HDLC control field.

The LLC and MAC sublayers use the *protocol data units* (PDUs) (discussed in Chapter Three) to communicate. The formats for the PDUs are shown in Figure 6-3. The LLC unit contains a destination address (DSAP), source address (SSAP), control field, and information field. The control field is quite similar to the HDLC control field.

The LLC sublayer is a subset of the HDLC standard discussed in Chapter Four. The HDLC-type commands and responses, established in the control field, depend on whether the LAN is type 1, type 2, or type 3. The instruction sets allowed are shown in Table 6-1 (notice the UI frame for connectionless service and SABME for connection-oriented service). The type 3 option for LLC is used for connectionless, yet acknowledged, operations. The sending of an AC0 frame is acknowledged by the station sending back an AC1 frame. In turn, the sending

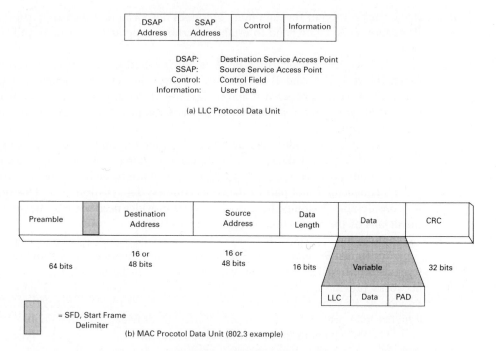

Figure 6-3. The 802.3 Frame

station then sends an AC1 frame which is acknowledged by the responding station with an AC0 frame. In essence, type 3 is a half-duplex protocol in which the stations alternately use AC0 and AC1 to exchange and acknowledge information.

One format for a MAC protocol data unit is shown in Figure 6-3(b). The MAC level CSMA/CD frame for 802.3 is shown in Figure 6-3. The *preamble* is transmitted first to achieve medium stabilization and synchronization. The *start frame delimiter* (SFD) follows the preamble and indicates the start of the frame. The 16- or 48-bit physical address fields contain the MAC addresses of the *destination* and *source addresses*. The destination address can identify an individual workstation on

TABLE 6-1. LLC COMMANDS AND RESPONSES

	Commands	Responses
Type 1	UI	
	XID	XID
	TEST	TEST
Type 2 (I Format)	I	I
(S Format)	RR	RR
	RNR	RNR
	REJ	REJ
(U Format)	SABME	UA, FRMR
	DISC	UA, DM
Type 3	AC0	AC1
	AC1	AC0

the network or a group of stations. The *data length* field indicates the length of the LLC and data fields. If the *data* field is less than a maximum length, the PAD field is added to make up the difference. The *cyclic redundancy check* (CRC) value is contained in the FCS field.

LAN TOPOLOGIES AND PROTOCOLS

This section covers in more detail the prevalent topologies and protocols found in local area networks. It is impossible to discuss in one chapter all the LAN systems found in the industry. We cover the systems that are illustrative of the field. The major systems used and discussed are the following:

- carrier sense multiple access with collision detection (CSMA/CD)
- token ring
- token bus.

In referring to the classification tree in Figure 2-5, it is evident that most LANs use the peer-to-peer approach instead of the primary/secondary relationship. Unlike a wide area network (WAN), the local structure does not normally use a master station to manage the traffic on channel. Since a local area network has short signal propagation times, high channel speeds, and small error rates compared to a WAN, the LAN does not always need the elaborate protocol measures of connection establishment, polling/selection, ACKs, NAKs, and so on established in the connection-oriented Continuous ARQ protocols.

CSMA/CD and IEEE 802.3

The best-known scheme for controlling a local area network on a bus structure is carrier sense multiple access with collision detection (CSMA/CD). CSMA/CD fits into the nonpriority, carrier sense (collision) classification (Figure 2-5). The most widely used implementation of CSMA/CD is found in the Ethernet specification. The Ethernet system was developed partly from the ALOHA concepts discussed in the previous chapter. Xerox Corporation was instrumental in providing the research for CSMA/CD and in developing the first commercial products. In 1980, Xerox, the Intel Corporation, and Digital Equipment Corporation (DEC) jointly published a specification for an Ethernet local network. This specification was later introduced to the IEEE 802 committees and, with some modification, has found its way into the IEEE 802.3 standard.

CSMA/CD Ethernet is organized around the concept of layered protocols. Figure 6-4 illustrates the layers found in CSMA/CD. The user layer is serviced by the two CSMA/CD layers—the data link layer and the physical layer. The bottom two layers each consist of two sublayers. The data link layer provides the logic to control the CSMA/CD network. It is medium independent; consequently, the network may be broadband or baseband—data-link control does not care. The 802 standard includes both broadband and baseband options.

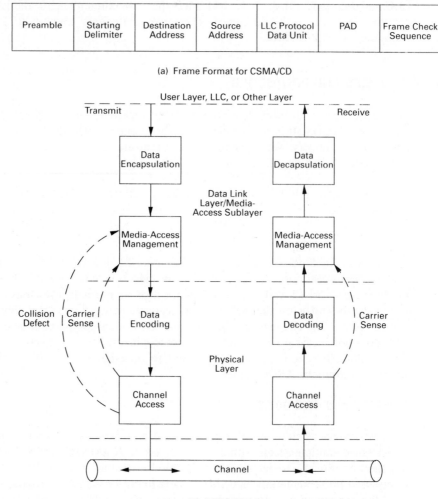

Preamble	Starting Delimiter	Destination Address	Source Address	LLC Protocol Data Unit	PAD	Frame Check Sequence

(a) Frame Format for CSMA/CD

(b) CSMA/CD Layers

Note: IEEE 802.3 combines data encoding/decoding and channel access.
Ethernet specification keeps them seperate.

Figure 6-4.   IEEE 802.3 Format and Layers

The data link layer consists of the data encapsulation/decapsulation entity and the transmit/receive media-access management entity. (The Ethernet specification calls the media-access management entity the link-management entity.) The major functions of these entities are as follows:

Data encapsulation/decapsulation:

- establishes the CSMA/CD frame [the MAC frame—see Figure 6-3(b)]; provides the source and destination address; calculates an error-detection field at the transmitting site and uses the field to calculate an error-detection indicator at the receiving site.

Media-access management:

- transmits the frame into the physical layer and receives the frame from the physical layer,
- buffers the frame,
- provides for collision avoidance (transmit side),
- provides for collision handling (transmit side).

The physical layer is medium dependent. It is responsible for such services as introducing the electrical signals onto the channel, providing the timing on the channel, and data encoding and decoding. Like the data link layer, the physical layer is composed of two major entities: the data encoding/decoding entity and the transmit/receive channel access (although the IEEE 802.3 standard combines these entities in its documents). The major functions of these entities are:

Data encoding/decoding:

- provides the signals to synchronize the stations on the channel (this sync signal is called the *preamble*);
- encodes the binary data stream to a self-clocking code (Manchester code) at the transmitting site and decodes the Manchester code back to binary code at the receiver.

Channel access:

- introduces the physical signal onto the channel on the transmit side and receives the signal on the receive side of the interface;
- senses a carrier on the channel on both the transmit and the receive side (which indicates the channel is occupied);
- detects a collision on the channel on the transmit side (indicating two signals have interfered with each other).

In a CSMA/CD network, each station has *both* a transmit and receive side to provide the incoming/outgoing flow of data. The transmit side is invoked when a user wishes to transmit data to another DTE on the network; conversely, the receive side is invoked when data are transmitted into the cable to the stations on the network.

If you are satisfied with this explanation, skip to the section on token rings. For those seeking more detail, however, the operation of the transmit and receive layers is explained below.

The transmit data encapsulation entity receives the user data and constructs the MAC frame. It also appends the frame check-sequence field to the data and passes the frame to media-access management, which buffers the frame until the channel is free. The channel is sensed as free when it sees a carrier sense signal turned off from the transmit channel-access entity in the physical layer. After a brief delay, media-access management passes the frame to the physical layer.

At the physical layer on the transmit side, data encoding transmits the synchronization signal (preamble). In addition, it encodes the binary data stream to a self-clocking Manchester code. The signal is then passed to transmit channel access, which introduces the signal onto the channel.

The CSMA/CD (MAC) frame is transmitted to all stations connected to the channel. The signal propagates away from the originating node in both directions to the other nodes. A receiving station senses the preamble, synchronizes itself onto the signal, and turns on the carrier sense signal. Then, receive channel access passes the signal up to data decoding. The data decoding entity translates the Manchester code back to the conventional binary data stream and passes the frame up to media-access management.

Like its counterpart on the transmit side, media-access management buffers the frame until the carrier sense signal has been turned off from receive channel access. The carrier sense signal goes off and indicates that all the bits have arrived. Media-access management can now pass the data up to data decapsulation. Data decapsulation performs an error check on the data to determine if the transmission process created errors. If not, it checks the address field to determine if the frame is destined for its node. If it is, it passes it to the user layer with the destination address (DA), source address (SA), and, of course, the LLC data unit.

Collisions. Since the CSMA/CD structure is a peer-to-peer network, all stations are vying for the use of the channel when they have data to transmit. The contention can result in the signals from various stations being introduced on the cable at approximately the same time. When this occurs, the signals collide and distort each other. They cannot be received correctly by the stations.

A central aspect of collisions deals with the *collision window*. This term describes the length of time required for the signal to propagate through the channel and be detected by each station on the network. For example, let us assume that a network has a cable six tenths of a mile long. If stations are situated at the far end of the cable, the furthest station distance is about six-tenths of a mile. It takes approximately 4.2 microseconds for a signal to travel six-tenths of a mile. When station A is ready to transmit, it senses the cable to determine if a signal is on the circuit. If station B had previously transmitted its frame onto the channel, but it had not had time to reach station A, then station A would falsely assume that the channel is idle and transmit its packet. In this situation, the two signals would collide with each other.

Under worst-case conditions for a baseband network, the amount of time to detect the collision (and acquire the channel) is twice the propagation delay, since the collided signal must propagate *back* to the transmitting stations. Propagation delay and collision detection are even longer for a broadband network that uses two cables for send and receive signals. Under worst-case conditions, the time to detect the collision is four times the propagation delay.

A collision is undesirable, since it creates errors in the network. Moreover, if long frames are transmitted, the collision takes more time on the channel than with the use of short frames. CSMA/CD addresses this problem at the transmit media-access management level by stopping the frame transmission *immediately* upon detecting a collision.

Another way to view collisions is through slot time, the time required for a frame to propagate through the entire channel and the delay in acquisition of the channel. An Ethernet 10 Mbit/s channel (baseband) has a propagation delay of 450 bit times ($45\mu s \times 10,000,000 = 450$). Ethernet requires a slot time to be larger than the sum of the propagation time (450 bits) and the maximum jam time (48 bits).

If the signal is propagated to all parts of the channel without collisions, the station that has transmitted the signal is said to have acquired or seized the channel. Once this occurs, collisions are avoided, since all stations have detected the signal and defer to it. However, in the event of the collision, the transmit channel access component notices the interference on the channel (in the form of voltage abnormalities) and turns on a special collision-detect signal to transmit media-access management.

Transmit media-access management performs two functions to manage the collision. First, it enforces the collision by transmitting a special bit sequence called the *jam*. The purpose of the jam is to ensure that the duration of the collision is long enough to be noticed by all the other transmitting stations involved in the collision. The CSMA/CD LAN requires that the jam be at least 32 (but not more than 48) bits. This guarantees that the duration of the collision is sufficient to ensure its detection by all the transmitting stations on the network. Its limited length also ensures that the stations will not falsely interpret it as a valid frame. Any frame containing fewer than 64 bytes (octets) is presumed to be a fragment resulting from a collision and is discarded by any other receiving stations on the link.

Transmit media-access management then performs the second function: After the jam is sent, it terminates the transmission and schedules the transmission for a later time, based on a random wait selection. The termination of frame transmission decreases the effect of a long frame collision manifesting itself on the channel for an extended time.

At the receiving station or stations, the bits resulting from the collision are decoded by the physical layer. The fragmented frames received from the collision are distinguished from valid frames by the receive media-access management layer. It notices that the collision fragment is smaller than the shortest valid frame and discards the fragments. Consequently, the jam is used to ensure all *transmitting* stations notice the collision, and the fragmented frame is transmitted to ensure that any *receiving* station ignores the transmission.

Both Ethernet and 802.3 use a 1-persistent technique to manage collisions and channel contention. However, this 1-persistent algorithm is applied to an integral multiple of a slot time (512 bits), and the scheduling of retransmission is performed by a controlled randomizing process called truncated binary exponential back-off.

At the end of a jam, the media-access layer delays before attempting to retransmit a maximum of 16 times. Each time, the mean value of the random number, r, is doubled:

"The delay is an integral multiple of the slot time. . . . The number of slot times to delay before the nth retransmission attempt is chosen as a uniformly distributed random integer r in the range $0 \le r < s^k$ where $k = min\ (n,\ 10)$." (*min* is a function that selects the lowest value of n or 10.)

CSMA/CD performs best under conditions when aggregate channel utilization is relatively low (less than 30% utilization). An asynchronous terminal-based system should perform well with CSMA/CD. However, alternate LANs are more appropriate for environments that use the LAN network more constantly. For example, the next LAN type, token ring, generally performs better than CSMA/CD under conditions of greater channel utilization.

Token Ring (Priority)

The token ring (priority) uses a token to provide priority access to the network. This approach is used widely in vendor products today and is endorsed in the IEEE 802.5 standard. It has many similarities to a conventional token-passing ring. For example, a token is passed around the ring, and within the token is an indicator sensing the ring as free or busy. The token circles continuously around the ring, passing each station. If a station wishes to transmit data and the token is empty, it seizes or captures the ring by modifying the token to a start-of-user-frame indicator, appending the data and control fields [Figure 6-6(c)] and sending the frame around the ring to the next station.

Each station is required to examine the token. Upon determining that the token is busy, the receiving station then must regenerate it to pass it to the next station. The copying of data is required only if the data are to be passed to the end-user application attached to that particular node. Upon the information arriving back at the original transmitting site, the token is once again "made free" and placed onto the network.

With the token *priority*-passing approach, the stations have priority established for access to the network. This is achieved by placing priority indicators within the token. The priority capability places the token ring in a peer-to-peer priority system within the classification tree (see Figure 2-5).

The next two discussions focus on the operations of a priority token ring. The first illustration presents a general view of a typical token ring. The second discussion offers a more detailed examination of token rings with the IEEE 802.5 protocol.

A General View of the Token Ring.   Assume a token ring has five stations attached to a priority ring (as in Figure 6-5). Station A has a priority access of 1 (lowest priority), stations B and D have priorities of 2, and stations C and E have priorities of 3 (highest priority). We assume station A had already seized the ring and is transmitting data frames. The token has a bit set to indicate that the token is busy. The following sequence of events illustrates one approach to priority token passing:

- Station B receives the frame. It has data to transmit, so it places its priority of 2 in a reservation field within the token. It then passes the token to C.

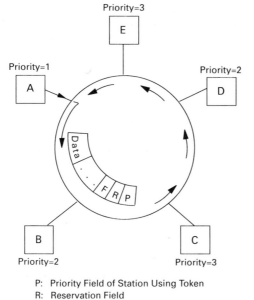

P: Priority Field of Station Using Token
R: Reservation Field
F: Field to Indicate Ring is Busy or Free

Figure 6-5. Token Ring (Priority)

- Station C also determines the ring is busy. It has data to send; it places a 3 in the reservation field, thus displacing the 2 which was inserted by station B. Station C then passes the frame to D. D must defer; it cannot place its priority of 2 into the field because a priority of 3 is already in place. Consequently, it passes the frame to E, which examines the reservation field. Upon seeing the 3 in the field, it does nothing, since its priority is also 3.

- Station A receives the frame back. It makes the ring free by resetting the token and passing the token to B.

- B is not allowed to use the token because the reservation field inside the token is equal to 3—one higher than the priority of B.

- C is allowed to seize the token, since its priority of 3 is equal to or greater than the priority indicator in the token. It places its data on the ring and sends the transmission to D.

- D is now allowed to place its priority of 2 into the reservation field. It does so and passes the frame to E.

- E displaces D's priority of 2 with its priority of 3 and passes the frame to A.

- A must defer any reservation placement, since its priority is 1.

- B must also forgo any priority allocation, since its priority is 2.

- C receives its transmission back; it is required to make the ring free. It does so and transmits the token to D.

- D is not allowed to seize the ring, since its priority of 2 is less than the reserve priority indicator of 3. It passes the token to E.

- E seizes the ring, because its priority of 3 is equal to or greater than the reservation indicator of 3.

As illustrated in Figure 6-5, the token is passed around from node to node. When the node receives the data that are destined for a station at that node, it copies the data for its user station and passes the frame to the next node. As the full (busy) token circles the ring, the stations vie for its use on the *next* pass around the ring. In this particular situation, if all the stations have data to transmit, the token is actually exchanged every other pass between stations C and E, since they have the highest priority on the ring. However, in most situations the higher priority stations are not likely to be transmitting with every pass. Consequently, the priority-ring configuration allows the lower priority stations to seize the ring in the event the higher priority stations are not active.

The IEEE 802.5 Priority Scheme.   The IEEE 802.5 priority scheme is similar to, but considerably more sophisticated than, the previous depiction. The IEEE 802.5 standard provides priority access to the ring through the use of the following fields and registers:

RRR   Reservation bits allow high-priority stations to request the use of the next token.

PPP   Priority bits indicate the priority of the token, and therefore which stations are allowed to use the ring.

Rr   Storage register for the reservation value.

Pr   Storage register for the priority value.

Sr   Stack register to store the value of Pr.

Sx   Stack register to store the value of the token that was transmitted.

Pm   Priority level of a frame queued and ready for transmission.

The priority bits (PPP) and the reservation bits (RRR) contained in the token give access to the highest priority frame that is ready for transmission on the ring. These values are stored in registers Pr and Rr. The current ring service priority is indicated by the priority bits (PPP) and the token, which is circulated around the ring.

The priority mechanism operates in such a way that equal access to the ring is maintained for all stations within a priority level. This is accomplished by having the same station that raised the service priority level of the ring (the *stacking station*) return the ring to the original service priority. The Sx and Sr stacks are used to perform this function.

The priority operation works as follows: When a station has a priority frame to transmit, it requests a priority token by changing the reservation bits (RRR) as the station repeats the token. If the priority level (Pm) of the frame that is ready for transmission is greater than the RRR bits, the station increases the value of the RRR field to the value Pm. If the value of the RRR bits is equal to or greater than Pm, the reservation bits (RRR) are repeated unchanged.

After a station has claimed the token, the station transmits frames until it has completed transmission, or until the transmission of another frame could not be completed before a timer expires, in which case the station generates a new token for transmission on the ring.

If the station does not have additional frames to transmit or if the station does not have a reservation request (contained in register Rr) which is greater than the present ring service priority (contained in register Pr), the token is transmitted with its priority at the present ring service priority and the reservation bits (RRR) at the greater of Rr or Pm, and no further action is taken.

However, if the station has a frame ready for transmission or a reservation request (Rr), either of which is greater than the present ring service priority, the token is generated with its priority at the greater of Pm or Rr and its reservation bits (RRR) as 0. Since the station has raised the service priority level of the ring, the station becomes a stacking station and must store the value of the old ring service priority as Sr and the new ring service priority as Sx. These values are used later to lower the service priority of the ring when there are no frames ready to transmit on the ring whose priority (Pm) is equal to or greater than the stacked Sx.

Upon becoming a stacker, the station claims every token that it receives that has a priority (PPP) equal to its highest stacked transmitted priority (Sx). The RRR bits of the token are examined in order to raise, maintain, or lower the service priority of the ring. The new token is transmitted with its PPP bits equal to the value of the reservation bits (RRR), but no lower than the value of the highest stacked received priority (Sr), which was the original ring priority service level. This approach ensures that the highest priority gets access to the ring.

If the value of the new ring service priority (PPP equal to Rr) is greater than Sr, the RRR bits are transmitted as 0, the old ring service priority contained in Sx is replaced with a new value Sx equal to Rr, and the station continues its role as a stacking station.

However, if the Rr value is equal to or less than the value of the highest stacked received priority (Sr), the new token is transmitted at a priority value of the Sr, both Sx and Sr are removed from the stack, and, if no other values of Sx and Sr are stacked, the station discontinues its role as a stacking station. This technique allows the lower priority stations to use the ring once the high-priority stations are through.

The IEEE 802.5 standard provides for three possible formats for the token ring. These formats are depicted in Figure 6-6. The token format [Figure 6-6(a)] consists of three bytes, the starting delimiter, the access control, and the ending delimiter. The purpose of the two delimiters is to indicate the beginning and ending of the transmission. The access control contains eight bits. Three bits are used for a priority indicator, three bits are used for a reservation indicator, and one bit is the token bit. When the token bit is set to 0, it indicates that the transmission is a token. When it is set to 1, it indicates that a token is being transmitted. The last bit in the access control byte is the monitor bit. This provides for a designated station to monitor the ring for error control and backup purposes. Figure 6-6(b) shows an abort token consisting only of the starting and ending delimiter. This transmission can be sent at any time to abort a previous transmission.

The information-transfer format is illustrated in Figure 6-6(c). In addition to the starting delimiter, access control, and ending delimiter, the standard provides for additional fields. The frame control field defines the type of frame (MAC or LLC data unit) and can be used to establish priorities between two LLC peer entities. The address fields identify the sending and receiving stations. The information field

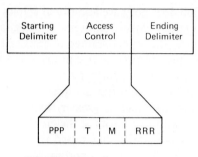

PPP: Priority Bits
  T: Token Bit (0: Token, 1: Data)
  M: Monitor Bit
RRR: Reservation Bits

(a) Token

(b) Abort Token

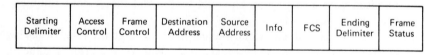

(c) Token and Data

Figure 6-6. IEEE 802.5 Ring Formats

contains user data. The FCS field is used for error checking and the frame status field is used to indicate that the receiving station recognized its address and copied the data in the information field.

The 802.5 recommendation provides for many other features, as well. For example, several timers are used to control the use of the ring, and failures are handled through various control fields, station reporting requirements, and neighbor-node notification of problems.

Token Bus and IEEE 802.4

The token-bus approach recommended by the IEEE 802.4 committee is illustrated in Figure 6-7. This MAC sublayer consists of four major functions: the interface machine (IFM), the access control machine (ACM), the receive machine (RxM), and the transmit machine (TxM). The regenerative repeater machine is another optional component, available in certain repeater stations such as a head-end modulator.

The ACM is the heart of the token-bus system. It determines when to place a frame on the bus and cooperates with the other stations' ACMs to control access to

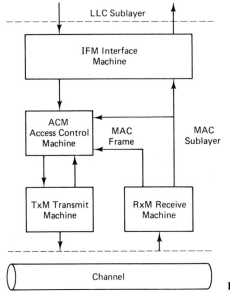

Figure 6-7. Token Bus (IEEE 802.4)

the shared bus. It is responsible also for initialization and maintenance of the logical ring, including error detection and fault recovery. In addition, it controls the admission of new stations and attempts recovery from faults and failures.

The LLC frames are passed to the ACM by the interface machine (IFM). This component buffers the LLC sublayer requests. The IFM maps "quality of service" parameters from the LLC view to the MAC view and performs address checking on received LLC frames.

The TxM and RxM components have somewhat limited functions. The responsibility of the TxM is to transmit the frame to the physical layer. It accepts a frame from the ACM and builds a MAC protocol data unit (PDU) by prefacing the frame with the preamble and starting delimiter (SD). It also appends the FCS and the ending delimiter (ED). The RxM accepts data from the physical layer and identifies a full frame by detecting the SD and ED. It also checks the FCS field to validate an error-free transmission. If a received frame is an LLC type, it is passed from the RxM component to the IFM. The IFM indicates its arrival and then delivers it to the LLC sublayer. Once in the LLC sublayer, it goes through the necessary functions of the HDLC subset to service the end-user application, or another layer provided by ISO or HILI (IEEE 802.1).

The format of an 802.4 frame is identical to the token ring 802.5 frame [Figure 6-6(c)], except that it has no access control and frame status (AC) fields. Obviously the AC is not needed, since this protocol does not use priority (PPP) and reservation (RRR) indicators.

IEEE 802.4 determines the *logical* ring of the *physical* bus by the numeric value of addresses. An MAC or LLC data unit provides the facility for the lowest address to hand the token to the highest address. Then, the token is passed from a predecessor station to its successor station.

The token (right to transmit) is passed from station to station in descending numerical order of station address. When a station hears a token frame addressed to itself, it may transmit data frames. When a station has completed transmitting data frames, it passes the token to the next station in the logical ring. When a station has the token, it may temporarily delegate its right to transmit to another station by sending a request-with-response data frame.

After each station has completed transmitting any data frames it may have, the station passes the token to its successor by sending a token control frame.

After sending the token frame, the station listens for evidence that its successor has heard the token frame and is active. If the sender hears a valid frame following the token, it assumes that its successor has the token and is transmitting. If the token sender does not hear a valid frame following its token pass, it attempts to assess the status of the network and may implement measures to pass around the problem station by establishing a new successor. For more serious faults, attempts are made to reestablish the ring.

If the successor does not transmit, the sending station normally assumes the successor is not operable. The sender then transmits a "who follows" frame with its successor's address in the frame. The failed station is bypassed by all stations comparing this address with the address of their predecessor. The station whose predecessor's address matches the "who follows" address then sends a "set successor" frame with its address. In this manner, the failed station is bridged out of the network.

Stations are added to an 802.4 bus by an approach called *response windows:*

- While holding the token, a node issues a *solicit-successor* frame. The address in the frame is between it and the next successor station.
- Token holder waits one window time (slot time, equal to twice the end-to-end propagation delay).
- If no response, the token is transferred to the successor node.
- If response, a requesting node sends a *set-successor* frame and token holder changes its successor node address. Requester receives token, sets its addresses, and proceeds.

A node can drop out of the transmission sequence. Upon receiving a token, it sends a set-successor frame to the predecessor, which orders the next node to give the token hereafter to its successor.

While Figure 2-5 classifies a token bus system as a peer-to-peer, nonpriority network, options do exist in the 802.4 standard to include *class of service,* which would make the system priority-oriented. The class-of-service option permits stations access to the bus based on one of four types of data to transmit:

- Synchronous—class 6
- Asynchronous Urgent—class 4
- Asynchronous Normal—class 2
- Asynchronous Time Available—class 0

A token-holding station is allowed to maintain bus control passed on priority timers. The timers give more time to the higher classes of traffic.

Metropolitan Area Networks (MANs)

The Metropolitan Area Network (MAN) standards are sponsored by the IEEE, ANSI, and the Regional Bell Operating Companies (RBOCs). Although 802.6 was designed initially for a LAN-to-MAN support service, the telephone companies see it as a technology to provide for the interconnection of LANs to its central office, and even for the interconnection of telephone switching facilities.

802.6 also forms the basis for the Switched Multi-megabit Data Service (SMDS), now being touted as the "WAN bottleneck" solution. Therefore, LAN/ WAN internetworking problems are solved with the use of 802.6 technology for connecting the WAN to LANs.

The MAN standard is organized around a topology and technique called *dual queue dual bus* (DQDB). This term means that the topology uses two buses. Each of these buses transmits traffic in one direction only. The implementation for MAN provides for transfer rates from 34 to 150 Mbit/s.

The DQDB provides for two types of access. One access, *pre-arbitrated* services, guarantees a certain amount of "bandwidth." This access is useful for isochronous services such as voice and video. The second service, *queued arbitrated service,* provides access based on demand. It is designed to accommodate bursty services such as data transmission.

A MAN is designed with two unidirectional busses. Each bus is independent of the other in the transfer of traffic. The topology can be designed as an open bus or a closed bus configuration. Figure 6-8 shows the two alternatives.

DQDB Operations.   The MAN protocol is elegantly simple and is quite attractive because it is distance-independent. Its basic operations may be summarized as follows:

- Node gains access by putting itself in a queue (one for each bus).
- When node is idling, count is made of the requests that pass on bus B (request counter).
- The request counter is decremented by 1 with each empty slot on bus A.
- The node keeps a count of the number of downstream requests and balances that with the number of the empty slot.
- To send, node puts a request on a slot on bus B and remembers the slot count.
- By sending the request counter to a countdown counter, node can determine an empty slot.
- When counter = 0, node uses the slot.

Summary of the 802 Specifications

This part of Chapter 6 emphasizes the work of the IEEE 802 committees. This is not to say that other LANs should be ignored, since other systems exist that are very

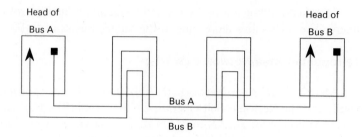

(a) Open Bus Architecture

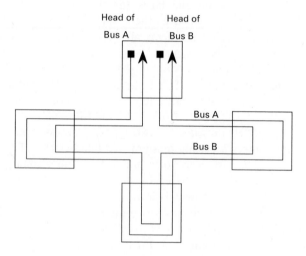

(b) Closed Bus Architecture

Figure 6-8. The MAN Bus Architecture

effective. However, our goal is to gain an understanding of the major LAN protocols and standards. The IEEE 802 specifications have been widely accepted in the
industry and are illustrative of how most LANs operate.

OTHER SYSTEMS

AT&T Information System Network (ISN)

American Telephone and Telegraph (AT&T) has also entered the LAN market with
several offerings. One is the Information System Network (ISN). ISN is similar to
the time division multiple access (TDMA) protocol (discussed in Chapter Five on
satellite networks), thus fitting into the classification tree as a primary/secondary
nonpolling system. It is based on a star topology utilizing twisted-pair cable from a
central controller to the attached DTEs.

Figure 6-9 illustrates the major components of ISN. The system employs three
networks inside a central controller. One network, the contention bus, is dedicated

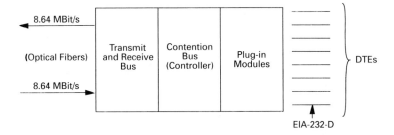

Figure 6-9. AT&T's Local Area Network

to handling access to the network. The other two subnetworks consist of a transmit bus and a receive bus. All three systems operate at 8.64 megabits per second. The purpose of the transmit and receive buses is to provide a high-speed interface to remote components, such as multiplexers or computers. The two input/output modules utilize optical fibers for the transmission media. The central controller directs the traffic into and out of the system through the use of a TDMA arrangement. The DTEs are attached to ISN through conventional interfaces, such as EIA-232-D. The contention bus and its associated logic provide the assignment of transmission time slots to the attached DTEs. The actual allocation of the traffic depends on the nature of the request from the DTE and the amount of traffic to be handled.

The TDMA-like controller allocates 50 millisecond (0.050 sec) time slots. These short data bursts interleave many packets in a short period of time, thereby diminishing the chances of contention. AT&T states that an ISN can switch up to 48,000 of these small 180-bit packets per second. This equates to the 8.64 Mbit/s rate of all three internal systems.

End-user devices are attached through plug-in modules into the system. Up to 42 plug-in modules representing 336 local devices are supported by a central controller. However, multiple controllers can be attached to each other. AT&T claims that a fully loaded ISN will support up to 1,680 end-user devices. The configuration with this capability would require one central controller with four remote concentrators attached to it.

AT&T has taken a major step into IBM's arena with the enhancements that provide BSC or SDLC device attachment to its ISN. Another enhanced package supports the direct attachment of 3270-family devices. AT&T provides these features, not only for the ISN, but for its System 75 and System 85 PBXs. The support packages also allow the networking of an ISN with a System 75 or 85, interfaces into T1 and Dataphone Digital Service (DDS) offerings, and gateways to Ethernet or Starlan local networks. Moreover, the 3270 adapters allow users to replace 3270 coaxial cable with twisted-pair cable. The products are being examined carefully by the industry, especially in view of IBM's delayed entry into the LAN field.

IBM Token Ring

IBM provided considerable input to the 802.5 token-ring standard, and the IBM token ring closely resembles the IEEE LAN standard. This section covers some of the features of the IBM token ring, as well as its format structure.

The ring is a baseband, single token-passing priority configuration which works like the IEEE 802.5 standard discussed previously. We will not repeat how it operates, but will describe additional functions IBM has added to its ring. The format for the ring is depicted in Figure 6-10. In order to assess the similarities and differences between the IEEE standard and IBM's token-ring approach, the reader should review Figure 6-6 and compare it with Figure 6-10.

The physical ring consists of 4 Mbit/s shielded twisted-pair cable or unshielded telephone-type cable. A ring can be connected to another ring through a backbone of 4 Mbit/s twisted-pair cable or 16 Mbit/s optical fiber.

The data link level contains the MAC sublayer 802.5 protocol. However, IBM has implemented more functions in its MAC. Consequently, a native 802.5 MAC device cannot operate with IBM's chip set for this level. The upper level of the data link layer also contains the 802.2 logical link control (LLC) protocol. IBM supports all three of the options in the IEEE 802 model [illustrated in Figures 6-2(b), (c), and (d)].

The IBM token ring also contains support for the SNA/APPC (advanced program-to-program communications). This feature provides a personal computer with a bridge into an SNA network through one of SNA's logical units, LU 6.2 (Chapter Seven describes SNA and LUs). In addition, IBM's Netbios (Network Basic Input/Output System) is provided to allow PCs using MS-DOS 3.1 and above to internetwork with each other. The LU 6.2 and Netbios features provide powerful functions for the IBM token-ring network.

Recognizing that network integrity is an important component of the ring, the IBM ring (and the 802.5 protocol) implemented a token-monitor function on the system. One ring-interface unit on each ring acts as an active token monitor to perform recovery of lost data or lost tokens. The only purpose of the token-monitor function is to provide for token recovery. It performs no functions for managing the data flow between the devices on the ring.

Figure 6-10 shows a monitor count bit flag in the physical control field of the frame. The token-monitor station uses the monitor count flag to detect a continuous circulation of a busy token. When a station seizes the ring, it places the token header around the data. In doing so, the token-monitor field is set to zero. When the busy token circles around the ring and passes by the monitor station, the monitor station notices the busy token and sets the monitor count flag. As the busy token passes around the ring to the original transmitting site, it is removed by the site. However, if the original transmitting site has malfunctioned, the busy token will

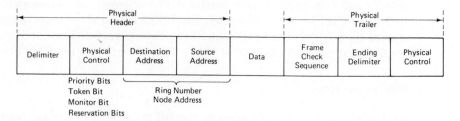

Figure 6-10.   IBM Token Ring Format

pass the token monitor a second time. The token monitor will observe that the count flag is still set; it will assume that the original transmitting station has malfunctioned and will remove the busy token from the ring. It then inserts and issues a free token, and the ring continues its normal operations.

Another possibility is for a token to be lost. In this sense, "lost" means that a ring interface unit (RIU) receives the token, but malfunctions before it has a chance to relay the token out into the ring. Another possibility is for the token to be damaged due to an electrical problem on the circuit and, consequently, is not decipherable as it circles around the ring. Whatever the cause for the lost token, the active monitor handles the situation by maintaining a timer that is reset upon a free or busy token passing it. If the timer expires before the token circles back to the active monitor station, then the token monitor is required to reinitialize the ring by issuing a free token onto the network.

IBM's Cabling System.   The cabling system of IBM is designed to reduce or eliminate the expense of rewiring a building or pulling cable when DTEs such as computers and terminals are installed or moved. It is meant to be an alternative to dedicated coaxial cable, which is used conventionally to attach remote terminals to mainframe computers.

IBM's approach in a LAN configuration is to: (1) minimize the length of the cable pulled through a building, and (2) provide for concentration points in the cabling system or link. The first objective reduces costs and the transmission distance between the DTEs. The second objective facilitates installation, configuration, and reconfiguration of the topology. Most importantly, it facilitates network maintenance and simplifies troubleshooting.

Given these two goals, IBM states one approach is to provide a serial bus connection, as indicated in Figure 6-11(a). While this is quite good for meeting the first goal (very little cable is pulled through a building for a serial bus), the serial interconnection is very poor in meeting the second goal. It is difficult to troubleshoot a serial interconnection, and it is very difficult to reconfigure a serial bus. Option Two provides for concentration points [Figure 6-11(b)]. In contrast to Option One, it is quite poor in meeting the first goal, but quite good in meeting the second.

IBM's approach is to combine Options One and Two as depicted in Figure 6-11(c). The combination provides for concentration points which bridge linear buses (which are actually rings).

The cabling system consists of wiring closets (concentrators) placed in various locations in the building. Each closet has a distribution panel. This panel is used to connect the wiring which runs through the various walls of the offices. Each panel can accept up to 64 cable pairs or, stated another way, 64 individual devices. The wiring closets and their attached cables fan out to special outlets in walls. The wiring permanently connected to the wiring closet permits connections to be made into the outlets in the office walls with a special plug. This concept is quite similar to the electrical outlets we have in our homes and offices, where if we wish to move something (for example, a clock), we simply unplug it and move it to another outlet in the wall.

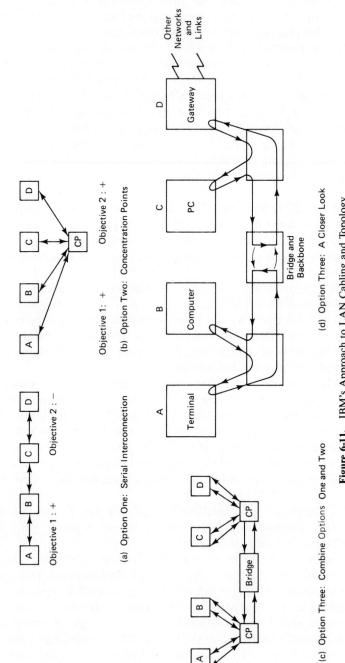

(a) Option One: Serial Interconnection

Objective 1 : +   Objective 2 : −

(b) Option Two: Concentration Points

Objective 1: +   Objective 2 : +

(c) Option Three: Combine Options One and Two

(d) Option Three: A Closer Look

Figure 6-11. IBM's Approach to LAN Cabling and Topology

Figure 6-11(c) depicts the token-ring bridge. This component serves as an off-ring communications link to other ring networks. Ring-to-ring communications are provided by a backbone of 4 Mbit/s twisted-pair coaxial cable or 16 Mbit/s optical fiber. The individual nodes can be outfitted with PC adapter boards, allowing an IBM PC network interface into the token ring.

As stated earlier, IBM supports the conventional telephone-type unshielded twisted-pair cable. The token ring permits each node to utilize this technology. This can be quite attractive for small business or users who wish to use the wiring already installed in a building. However, unshielded telephone twisted-pair cable is subject to more problems than other kinds of media. Consequently IBM also offers higher-quality cable connections, called data-grade cable. If the user chooses the conventional telephone wiring, the maximum number of stations that can be attached to the ring is 72. In addition, the mixing of wires is not permitted on the individual ring.

All stations must use the same type of media. However, this does not preclude two rings using twisted-pair cable connecting to each other through the wiring closet from which the wiring concentrators could use the higher grade cable. The use of twisted-pair cable limits the distance of the devices to no more than 45 meters to the wiring closet. Twisted-pair cable is more subject to noise, jitter, decay, and clocking problems, but the reduced cost may justify its use.

Traffic Management on the IBM Ring.   Each station attached to a ring is provided with a ring-interface adaptor. This adaptor handles the line protocol and physical interface functions associated with the network. The adaptor recognizes and buffers frames, generates and recognizes tokens, provides error detection, and performs address decoding and link error detection.

The work stations can be located in any location throughout a building. The stations are connected to the network through wiring lobes. These lobes are two pairs of conductors for the send and receive channels. They are connected to wall outlets for each of the work stations. In turn, the connectors are attached to wiring concentrators which can be located throughout the building. The lobe is kept on the path only when the work station is active. If the work station is idle and disconnected, the wiring concentrator bypasses the lobe for that particular work station. This approach allows the work station to be moved from one area to another within an office building without the installation of new wiring.

The IBM topology permits several rings to be attached through bridges. The bridges are then connected by a backbone ring. The bridge will provide a cross-ring network function by copying frames that are forwarded from one ring to another.

Previous discussions have focused on how the IEEE 802.5 protocol manages the transmission of traffic around a token ring. The IBM token ring closely adheres to the 802.5 convention. However, since IBM permits a multiple token-ring network, data are transmitted and received between rings through a concept called *source routing*. This technique permits the internetworking of multiple rings and the transmission of data between the rings.

The routing logic for source routing is provided by the insertion of routing information in the data before the data are transmitted between the rings and bridges. This relieves the bridges and intermediate nodes of having to store and update complex routing tables, which in turn gives the bridges more latitude to perform other necessary functions, such as network management. Source routing is performed in the IBM token ring below logical link control (LLC) 802.2.

Data are transmitted across the rings through the bridges in one of two methods. First, the transmitting table can maintain a routing table at its site. Typically, the routing table maintains the routing addresses of those stations that the transmitting station accesses frequently. These routing tables are loaded into the transmission frame as part of the Information (I) field and are then used by the bridges to decide how to relay the traffic across the various multiple token rings. With the second method, if a transmitting station wishes to reach a new station, it sends out a query through its local ring to determine if the station is on the ring. If it is not on the local ring, then a general query is sent through the entire network. The response to this query contains the needed routing information which the transmitting station uses and inserts into the frame. As stated previously, this information is used by the intermediate bridges to determine how to route the traffic through the network. The routing information contains the list of bridges that will be used in relaying the traffic across the multiple token rings and through the backbone stations.

The transmitting station has four options in developing routing directives in the frames it transmits.

- *Ring segment broadcast*. These frames are transmitted only within the network and are not relayed by any of the interconnecting bridges.
- *Limited broadcast*. Frames also can be sent where they are transmitted only once onto each ring in the network.
- *General broadcast*. These frames can be transmitted so that multiple copies may flow over the network. They must appear on each ring segment at least once. However, the list of bridges can be expanded such that multiple copies can be created. This concept is quite similar to packet flooding found in some packet-switch networks.
- *Point-to-point routing*. This frame type can be transmitted such that frames travel specifically from one station to another over a designated route. There is no broadcast aspect to point-to-point routing. Only certain ring and bridge segments are involved.

In order to manage traffic across the bridges and through the multiple token-ring network, logical link control (LLC) detects when traffic is becoming heavy. This automatic congestion detection will then change the size of the transmit window dynamically. For example, as traffic conditions become heavier (or congested), LLC will decrease the size of the transmit window. The effect of this decision means that fewer frames will be outstanding at any one time. For example, if an error occurs or frames are out of sequence, only a limited number of frames have to be transmitted. Conversely, when traffic conditions are light and the network is not congested, the window is expanded to permit a large number of frames to be transmitted and outstanding at any one time.

A transmit window is changed if a lost frame is confirmed at the transmitter. When the transmitter detects that the N(R) of the received frame is out of sequence with its expected transmit state variable, it reduces its window to one. As a consequence, it can send only one frame at a time. It must receive the acknowledgment back before it sends another frame. In effect, LLC becomes a stop-and-wait protocol for a brief period. However, each successful transmission [wherein the transmitter receives back the N(R) number correctly] causes the transmitter to increase its window by one. Each increase eventually brings the window size back up to the original maximum value, which continues to be in effect until problems occur or a lost frame is detected.

ANSI Fiber Distributed Data Interface (FDDI)

ANSI (the American National Standards Institute) has developed a specification for local area networks and optical fibers. The standard is called FDDI (Fiber Distributed Data Interface) and was written by ANSI Committee X3T9.5. The use of optical fibers in local area networks can provide useful functions, and several reasons exist for placing DTEs on optical channels.

First, computers operate at very high speeds. When computers are linked together, the slow path between them can be a bottleneck. Consequently, the high-speed optical fiber can be a complementary path to the high-speed computer. Second, the improving technology of disk units will provide read/write speeds approaching 40 to 50 megabits per second. This extraordinary capability can be hampered by the slow channel between the disk unit and the computer, and optical fibers can relieve this bottleneck. Third, digitized voice conversations require a greater bandwidth than the typical telephone channel provides, especially if the conversations are in an interactive, real-time mode. Optical fibers provide the bandwidth capability to accommodate real-time voice transmissions.

The specifications for the FDDI are as follows. The optical-fiber channel operates at 100 Mbit/s. Up to 1,000 nodes can be placed on one optical-fiber ring. The nodes can be spaced as far as 2 kilometers apart, and the ring circumference can be up to 200 kilometers. These limits, unto themselves, may not make sense to the uninitiated, yet they are important in order to minimize latency; that is, the time it takes the data (or signal) to travel around the ring.

FDDI specifies a topology in which two independent, counterrotating optical-fiber rings are in place (see Figure 6-12), which provides for an overall bit rate of 200 megabits per second, with each channel operating at 100 Mbit/s. The figure shows that the components (DTEs, such as terminals, computers, work stations, or graphics stations) are tied together through a wiring concentrator. The concentrator acts as a reconfiguration and concentration point for all optical wiring and data traffic. The inner channel connects only certain devices. These devices, which have inner and outer rings attached to them, are classified as A devices. The B devices are connected by only one ring. The attractive aspect of this specification is that it allows a user facility to designate those critical stations which need additional backup and higher channel speeds as Class A stations. The other, less important DTEs, such as isolated work stations or low-priority terminals, can then be hooked up as Class B stations, at a lesser cost.

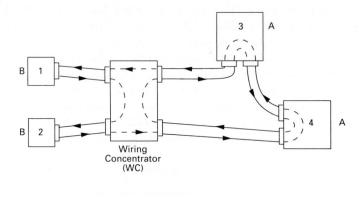

Class A: Inner and Outer RIngs
Class B: Only Outer Ring
     WC: Hub to Connect Stations } Reconfiguration and Backup: <u>Mixed Media</u>

Figure 6-12.   Fiber Distributed Data Interface (FDDI)

The wiring concentrator allows a facility to connect stations and provide for reconfiguration. It also serves to isolate troubleshooting through the concentration point, which is one of the key tenets of IBM's token network (and cabling system). FDDI does not specifically require that all the channels be optical fibers. The wiring concentrator could provide an interface in which a user installs optics in one portion of the LAN and uses coaxial cable or twisted-pair wiring in another portion of the network.

The connectors into the terminals and wiring concentrator are laser diodes which drive the fiber at a rate of over 100 MHz. Several years ago, these devices cost well over a hundred dollars. Light-emitting diodes now can do the same task for under ten dollars each. FDDI stipulates a standard optical lightwave of 850 nanometers.

In a building or plant, severed channels are not uncommon. Figure 6-13 depicts a possible reconfiguration in the event of a lost channel or channels. In the figure, the channel between devices 3 and 4 is lost. FDDI provides a reconfiguration by changing the loops through devices 3 and 4. As can be seen from the figure, the network remains intact. All devices have access to the net through the reconfiguration of the inner and outer loops from the wiring concentrator to devices 3 and 4.

If a station malfunctions and goes down, FDDI also stipulates that the node can be bypassed. In essence, a mirror directs the lightwaves through an alternative

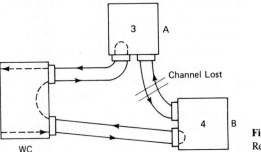

Figure 6-13.   FDDI System
Reconfiguration

path. In Figure 6-13, if device 4 malfunctions and becomes inoperable, the signals can be diverted away from the device by using the same channels and the mirrors.

FDDI stipulates a very unique approach to timing and clocking on the network. The reader may recall from previous discussions that the best code to be used in a network is one which provides frequent signal state changes. The changes provide the receiver with the ability to continue to adjust to the incoming signal, thereby assuring that the transmitting device and the receiving device are synchronized with each other. The Manchester code used in the IEEE 802.3 standard is only 50 percent efficient, because every bit requires a two-state transition on the line (i.e., two baud). Using Manchester code, a 100-megabit transmission rate requires 200 megabits of bandwidth (a 200 MHz rate). In other words, Manchester code requires twice the band for its transmission.

ANSI, recognizing that the 200 MHz rate would create more expense in manufacturing the interfaces and clocking devices, devised a code called 4B/5B, in which a four-bit code is used to create a five-bit code. For every four bits transmitted from a DTE, FDDI creates five bits. The five bits provide clocking for the signal itself. Consequently, the 100 Mbit/s rate on FDDI requires only 125 MHz of band. The 4B/5B code structure is shown in Table 6-2.

FDDI uses a multiple token-passing protocol. The token circles the ring behind the last transmitted packet from a device. Any station wishing to transmit data seizes the token, removes the token, places the packet or packets on the ring, and then issues the new token directly behind the data stream. This is in contrast to IEEE 802.5, in which only one station uses the token.

TABLE 6-2.   4B/5B CODE STRUCTURE

USER DATA		4B/5B CODE	
Binary	Hex	Code	Symbol
0000	0	11110	0
0001	1	01001	1
0010	2	10100	2
0011	3	10101	3
0100	4	01010	4
0101	5	01011	5
0110	6	01110	6
0111	7	01111	7
1000	8	10010	8
1001	9	10011	9
1010	A	10110	A
1011	B	10111	B
1100	C	11010	C
1101	D	11011	D
1110	E	11100	E
1111	F	11101	F

The token-passing scheme is predicated on the need for real-time applications on the network, so the timing is structured such that a node has assurance of getting a token within a certain time. As the packet circles the ring with the token behind, each station retimes and regenerates the packets.

Like many LANs, the network uses a *timed token* approach. Each node measures the time it takes for the token to return to it, called token rotation time (TRT). It then compares the time to a prenegotiated target time (PTT) for its arrival. If the token comes back sooner than the threshold in PTT, this indicates, in all likelihood, a light load on the network. The node is allowed to transmit as long as its full transmission stream does not exceed PTT. However, if the token comes back later than PTT, indicating the probability of heavy network load, then a node is allowed to transmit only high-priority traffic. Low-priority traffic must be deferred until the load on the network becomes lighter.

Two points should be emphasized with this protocol. First, as stated before, upon seizure of the ring the token is stripped off, data are placed on the ring, and the token is placed behind the data. However, when the station seizes the token, the ring is made idle for a brief period of time while the packet is being set up. This allows for more time between the DTE and the ring interface unit to structure and move the packet across the interface. This relative simplicity translates into a less expensive interface. Second, since the token is transmitted immediately after the packet, another station down the line could also use the token if the token rotation time and prenegotiated target time fall within the established parameters. This approach provides for much more efficient utilization for large rings which might have much latency in transfer around them. Third, the FDDI optic ring provides for priorities by establishing the parameters in the TRT and PTT variants.

SUMMARY

The LAN industry is quite diverse, and this brief chapter precludes examining all of the systems and products. The IEEE standards and the IBM token ring were highlighted due to their position in the industry. In Chapter Eleven, we will consider LANs for personal computers.

7

Switching and Routing in Networks

INTRODUCTION

Imagine the effect the telephone switch has on our ability to communicate with practically anyone we wish. Without such a switching system, a point-to-point telephone line would have to be established to every single number we wanted to dial, including banks, business associates, relatives, and friends. Switching is a vital element for computer and terminal communications, as well. If we wish to use a computer in a remote part of the country, we first connect to some form of switching apparatus, thus obviating a separate point-to-point channel. This chapter provides a general discussion of switching systems, with a more detailed view of packet-switching protocols.

TELEPHONE SWITCHING SYSTEMS

The telephone line is a commonly used channel to connect computers and terminals. The telephone network uses a technology called *circuit switching* to connect communicating DTEs. The major characteristics of circuit switching are:

- Once a call is established, the users have a direct path through the switches in the network. The direct path is equivalent to two wires connecting the users.
- The switches provide no intermediate storage capability (such as disk units).
- Because of the absence of storage capability at the switches, blockage is possible on a circuit switch (a busy or engaged condition).
- The circuit switch provides limited value-added functions. For example, line protocols such as those discussed in Chapter Two are generally not available

on the circuit switch. Additional software or microcode must be added to a circuit switch to provide for these value-added functions.

The telephone switching systems today are classified as either *electromechanical* or *stored program control* (SPC). Electromechanical systems are described here briefly for historical interest. In most industrialized countries, they have been replaced with stored program control systems. However, electromechanical systems still do exist in certain parts of the world. Additionally, their description provides information on how telephone switching systems have evolved.

Electromechanical systems are controlled by wired circuits. The electromechanical switches are motor driven, electromechanically operated, or driven by electrical impulses. In wired logic systems, routing logic is designed into the hardware. Stored program control (SPC) systems use software for the switching logic. The program controls the sequencing of operations to establish the telephone call. In this section, we discuss these two technologies and consider their development.

Figure 7-1 illustrates a typical telephone call between people or between DTEs through a dial-up facility. (Many computers and terminals have automatic dial-up facilities.) The flowchart is self-explanatory with the inclusion of the following definitions:

On-hook. Telephone or DCE is not requesting a call.

Off-hook. A call request is being made to the central office (CO). A person lifts the phone off its cradle, or a DCE electronically performs a similar function.

Register. Storage area for the dialed number. (Number is also called the address.)

Intraoffice (Intraexchange). Call within same central office (exchanges).

Interoffice (Interexchange). Call between central offices (exchanges).

Hierarchy. Telephone network structure.

Trunk group. Set of trunks (channels) with common routing and connection characteristics; can be used interchangeably.

Private, nonswitched lines do not require the procedure shown in Figure 7-1. The simplest class of private line has no signalling services performed by the telephone network. The DCE (such as a modem) provides the alerting function with a signal to the receiving site. For human "receivers," the originating site usually sends a signal to the terminating end. This *automatic ring-down* (a loop closure and a 20 Hz signal) alerts the receiving DCE or human of a call on a private circuit.

The major circuit-switching systems developed during the past few decades are as follows:

Electromechanical
Switchboard
Step-by-Step
No. 1 and No. 1A Crossbar
Crossbar Tandem

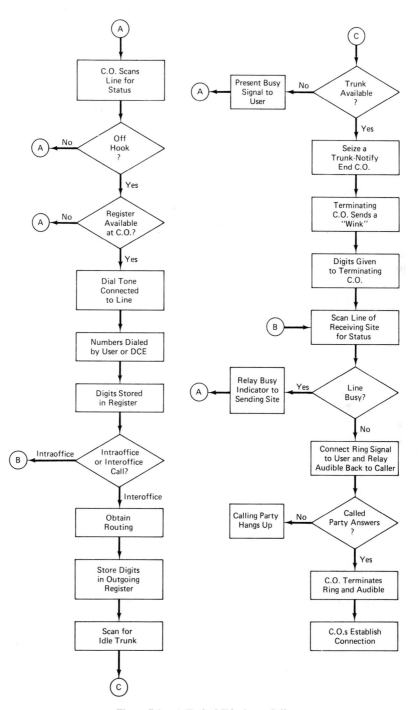

Figure 7-1. A Typical Telephone Call

4A Crossbar
No. 5 Crossbar

Stored Program Control (SPC)
No. 1ESS and 1AESS
No. 2ESS and 2AESS
No. 3ESS
No. 4ESS
No. 5ESS
DMS-10
DMS-100/200

Electromechanical Systems

The earliest switches were adapted from telegraph technology. Consisting of brass strips that looked like door hinges, the "hinge" contacts provided the switch between two channels. The first telephone *switchboard* was developed in 1878 by Charles Scribner of Western Electric. He devised the sockets and jacks used in early private branch exchange (PBX) switchboards. The switching system was a person, who serviced eight lines and 21 subscribers. The familiar terms *tip* and *ring* referring to two parts of the switchboard plug are still used to describe a two-wire pair (tip is the ground).

The *step-by-step* (or Strowger) system was first installed in Kansas City in 1892 by a mortician named Strowger, who, as legend has it, invented the device to prevent the town operator from manually routing potential business to his competitor. The first commercial switch was installed in La Porte, Indiana, in 1893. The modern step-by-step system is a *progressive control* system and gets its name from the way its electromechanical switches are actuated progressively as each digit of the called number is dialed by the customer. For example, the number 3 lifts a Strowger switch up a rack by three positions. The system is called a *direct* progressive control system because the dial pulses directly control the stepping switches. Depending on the type of office, the step-by-step system can accommodate from 100 to 10,000 customer lines.

During the 1940s, the increased traffic volume made it very difficult for human operators to handle telephone demand. Moreover, the method of a subscriber dialing and controlling connections and network setups was very slow. The concept of *register-progressive control* was developed to remove the subscriber as a bottleneck. This system requires the subscriber to dial the number to a control mechanism, which stores it for use. Initially, the Bell designers feared that subscribers would be reluctant to give up the use of verbal communications with an operator, but studies revealed that metropolitan subscribers actually preferred the direct-dialing mode.

AT&T/Bell did not begin using the step-by-step systems until 1919 because they were not economically attractive. The Automatic Electric Company initially installed the systems. In 1926, AT&T/Bell developed its own design for the step-by-step switch.

The *No. 1 crossbar* was first used in 1938 in Brooklyn, New York. It was developed for use in large metropolitan areas to handle calls within the telephone network. Although still electromechanical, it was the first switching system to use *common control devices*, in which many functions are performed by shared elements. Also, the entire number is received before switching logic is invoked. It sets up calls faster than its predecessors and requires less maintenance. As of January 1, 1983, 180 systems still remained in operation (serving four million lines).

Crossbar switches differ considerably from step-by-step systems. The crossbar is a matrix of crosspoints established by vertical and horizontal bars that close by "hold magnets" being activated to select a crosspoint. The crosspoints (or contacts) are the switch paths. The earlier crossbar switches allowed ten calls to pass through a switch simultaneously, in contrast to only one call in a step-by-step switch.

The *crossbar tandem* was first used in 1941. The tandem system is used primarily in areas where central offices (COs) have step-by-step or No. 1 crossbar switching equipment. In effect, a tandem performs functions that other switching equipment cannot do. Among the functions it performs are the recording of calling information for billing, serving as an "interpreter" between different types of COs, and centralizing the equipment needed for public announcement services, such as weather and time information.

The *No. 4 crossbar* was first used in 1943 in Philadelphia and is designed to establish connections on a nationwide basis. It is capable of routing a call automatically over a "first-choice" route or other predetermined alternate routes (discussed in Chapter One). The No. 4A crossbar, an enhancement of No. 4, was the first switching system to separate the transmit path from the receive path (to reduce the effect of echo). It is sometimes called "four-wire." The introduction of the 4A crossbar system made direct distance dialing (DDD) possible. The 4A crossbar system has been replaced for the most part by the new No. 4ESS, or a similar digital switching system.

The *No. 5 crossbar* was first used in 1948. A further advance in the crossbar system, the No. 5 crossbar switching system can serve as a combination CO and tandem office, and some systems employ centrex and common control (discussed later). The No. 5 crossbar was designed to handle traffic in areas ranging from suburban residential areas to small cities where many calls are completed within the same CO. The last new No. 5 crossbar was installed in November 1977. In the 1970s, it served more than 40 percent of the AT&T/Bell telephones.

Stored Program Control Systems

During the 1950s and early 1960s, Bell Labs developed electronic switching systems to meet growing demands for faster, more reliable, and more flexible switches. These systems use the stored program control (SPC) concept introduced at the beginning of this chapter. The first trial of electronic switching took place in 1960 in Morris, Illinois, with the first ESS switch cutover in May 1965 in Succasunna, New Jersey.

The *No. 1ESS* was designed for use in metropolitan areas with heavy traffic. Like all ESS systems, the No. 1ESS completes connections between customers faster than the electromechanical switching systems and does it with a relatively small amount of equipment. The initial No. 1ESS could handle 100,000 calls in the busy hour. Like all electronic switching, it is directed by computers and programs.

Among the features provided by the No. 1ESS are local switching, with connections to all types of switching facilities and special services such as WATS, centrex (centralized PBX), and the custom calling services: call waiting, call forwarding, three-way calling, speed calling, and conference calling. It also records billing information.

The *No. 2ESS* was first used in 1970. It was designed for use in suburban residential COs and provides features similar to the No. 1ESS, but handles fewer lines (2,000–10,000). The system is designed for simplicity, with diagnostics and testing handled remotely.

The *No. 3ESS* was first used in 1976. It was designed for use in rural areas serving fewer than 4500 lines. It is similar to the No. 1ESS in that it is a stored program control (SPC) device, but with newer equipment. The No. 3ESS uses better technology (less expensive computer, faster processor).

The *No. 4ESS* was first used in 1976. It is a four-wire *digital* switching system. It performs the same basic functions as the electromechanical 4A crossbar switching system connecting trunks to trunks, but it handles more than four times as many calls per hour as the No. 4A crossbar.

In addition, the 4ESS uses the 1A computer processor to carry over 550,000 busy-hour calls. In the electromechanical No. 4A crossbar system, each call had a dedicated, continuous physical connection through the switching equipment; but with the No. 4ESS, the same conversations are connected only intermittently. Each connection is connected and disconnected thousands of times per second. The gaps are too small to affect voice transmission, yet the No. 4ESS can use these time gaps to sample other calls. This process is called time division (digital) switching, and is discussed in more detail in Chapter Nine. The 1A processor also has been used to enhance the 1ESS system. The enhanced version is called 1A ESS and serves 130,000 lines. The 1A also is used with 2ESS, which doubles its traffic capacity.

The *No. 5ESS* system, a local digital switching system, was introduced in 1981. It is designed for use in local offices to handle 1,000 to 100,000 lines. Figure 7-2 is a simplified view of this SPC system. The interface modules terminate the lines and trunks into the system. A module accepts digital or analog signals and adds eight bits of control information for switching, routing, and control functions.

The administrative module provides routing control and administrative functions. It consists of two Western Electric 3B20 computers. The administrative module also contains the input/output processors, which provide access to terminals and other peripheral devices for technicians operating the switch. The communications module houses the switching facilities. A message switch interfaces the administrative module with the communications module. The TMS (time multiplexed switch) connects user channels (voice or data) from one interface module to another.

The *DMS-10* was first introduced in 1981. This local digital switching facility is produced by Northern Telecom, Ltd., and is designed for local COs. It has a capacity of up to 6,000 lines and can provide service to a 13,000 calls-per-hour peak. In 1983, the *DMS 100/200* was standardized for AT&T/Bell use and is also in operation.

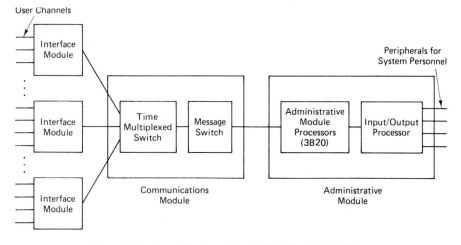

Figure 7-2. Stored Program Control Switching (No. 5ESS)

Electronic switching and stored program control were used in other parts of the telephone system, as well, notably the toll services performed by operators. In 1969, 1ESS was used to implement the *traffic service position system* (TSPS). The following are services we take for granted today that were made possible by the computer and stored program control (software):

- operator-assisted calls (without manual cords)
- guest-originated calls from hotels
- immediate billing, if necessary
- obtaining billing information for credit calls.

The power of the computer is also evident in the telephone network's *automatic intercept system* (AIS). This system uses 2ESS and became available in 1970. When you make a call to a changed, unassigned, or disconnected number, 2ESS routes the call to an operator or automatic answering device. Both use large data bases to track down an answer for you. A large metropolitan area has over 500,000 records on line and experiences as many as 18,000 changes per day—a gargantuan task that would not be possible without the computer and electronic switching.

Of course, user computers and terminals (DTEs) often use the telephone network directly to communicate with each other (through switched or nonswitched lines). In addition, many organizations add other types of switches to the telephone network to provide for specific services to the user DTEs. These "value-added" switches are classified as message or packet switches and are designed to support data traffic instead of voice traffic. The remainder of this chapter addresses these systems from the standpoint of how they support end-user systems and, in some instances, the telephone network as well.

MESSAGE SWITCHING

In the 1960s and 1970s, the pervasive method for switching data communications traffic was message switching. The technology is still widely used in certain applications, such as electronic mail. Figure 7-3 illustrates a message switch. The switch is typically a specialized computer. It is responsible for accepting traffic from terminals and computers attached to it through dial-up or leased telephone lines. It examines the address in the header of the message and switches (routes) the traffic to the receiving DTE. Unlike circuit switching in telephones, message switching is a *store-and-forward* technology because of the storage capability at the switch, usually in the form of disk units. Since the data are usually stored, the traffic is not considered to be interactive or real-time. However, traffic can be sent through a message switch at very high speeds by establishing levels of priority for different types of traffic. High-priority traffic is queued for a shorter period than low-priority traffic. This approach can support interactive applications.

The queuing onto disk provides a method to smooth traffic by queuing the lower priority traffic during peak periods. The queuing also decreases the chance of blocking traffic in the event certain portions of the network are busy. The traffic can be stored temporarily and later routed to sites when they are free to accept it. In addition, message switches can use tape files to perform backups of disk files for billing records and audit trails of transactions processed by the switch.

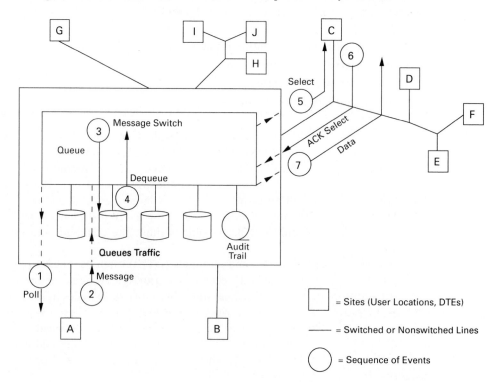

Figure 7-3.   Message Switch

The message-switching technology usually operates with a master/slave relationship. Typically, the switch performs polling and selection to manage the traffic coming into and going out of it. For example, in Figure 7-3 we assume user DTE A has data for user DTE C. The switch performs a polling cycle of the attached sites. Upon polling A, the message is transmitted to the switch. Based on priority, the data are stored in one of several disk queues. Depending on overall traffic conditions and the message priority, the switch de-queues the message and sends a select command to C. At site C, an ACK is sent to the switch and the message is transmitted to C.

While message switching has served the industry well, it suffers from three deficiencies. First, since it is inherently a master/slave structure, the entire network can be lost if the switch fails, since all traffic must go in and out of the message switch. Consequently, many organizations provide for a duplicate (duplexed) message switch in which the second switch assumes the functions of the first switch in the event of failure. The second major deficiency stems from the hub arrangement of many message switches. Since all traffic must go through the switch, the switch itself is a potential bottleneck. Degraded response time and decreased throughput can result from such an arrangement. Third, message switching does not utilize the communications lines as efficiently as other techniques discussed in the next section.

PACKET SWITCHING

Because of problems with message switching, in the 1970s the industry began to move toward a different data communications switching structure known as packet switching. Packet switching distributes the risk to more than one switch, reduces vulnerability to network failure, and provides better utilization of the lines than does message switching.

Packet switching is so named because user data (for example, messages) are broken down into smaller pieces. These pieces, or packets, have protocol information placed around them and are routed through the network as independent entities.

A packet-switching network is illustrated in Figure 7-4. The topology is obviously different from message switching. First, more switches allow the network load to be distributed to multiple switching sites. Second, additional communications lines are attached to the switches. The arrangement provides the opportunity to perform alternate routing arrangements around failed or busy nodes and channels. As a consequence, a packet-switching network has high availability to end users.

Packet switching gained interest initially as a means to provide for secure voice transmissions. During the 1960s research was conducted by the United States Department of Defense with the intent to develop a network to switch packets containing voice conversations. It was believed an individual voice conversation, broken into small pieces, could be routed on different channels throughout the system. In the event an adversary tapped a particular communications line and was able to discern the actual intelligence of the voice image, the espionage would reveal only a piece of the entire conversation. Since the full conversation was "packetized" onto different paths, an individual line would not divulge the full intelligence of the

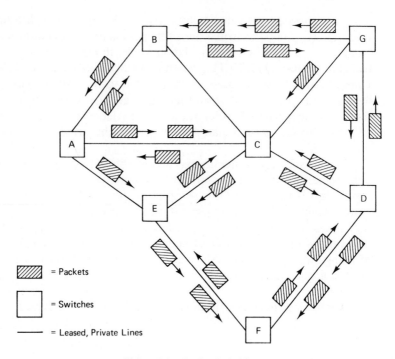

Figure 7-4.   Packet Switching

communication. The project was abandoned in these early years, however, because technology was not sufficiently advanced to deal with the need for "constant bandwidth" for voice communications. These pioneering efforts were designed around bursty transmission protocols which did not fit voice communications well.

It was soon recognized that packet switching would work well with data communications traffic, because many devices, such as keyboard terminals, transmit traffic in bursts. The data are sent on the channel, which is then idle while a terminal user inputs more data into the terminal or pauses to think about a problem. The idle channel time translates into wasted line capacity. One of the concepts of packet switching is to interleave multiple transmissions from *several terminals* onto one channel, in effect achieving time division multiplexing across a communications line. This approach provides better use of the expensive communications channel.

Packet switching goes one step further than simple multiplexing of the communications lines. Packet logic can also multiplex multiple user sessions onto a single communications port of the computer. Instead of dedicating a port to one user, the system interleaves the bursts of traffic from multiple users across one port. The user perceives a dedicated port is being used when the user DTE or program is actually sharing a port with other users.

Port and channel multiplexing are referred to as a *virtual channel* or *virtual circuit*. "Virtual" means that a user thinks it has a dedicated resource when, in fact, the resource is shared.

The Department of Defense (DOD) conducted a study several years ago on the nature of data (nonvoice) traffic. The study revealed that over 99 percent of data transmissions are shorter than voice transmissions. The DOD study showed that 25 percent of data transmissions last less than one second, 50 percent last less than five seconds, and 90 percent last less than fifty seconds. Packet-switching technology is designed to address these characteristics by interleaving several users' bursts of traffic (packets) onto one channel. (Of course, these techniques are available through time division multiplexing techniques. However, we will see that packet switching does more than simple multiplexing.)

Studies also have revealed that communications traffic is often asymmetrical; that is, communications occur more in one direction between two DTEs than in the other. A good example of asymmetrical communications is in computer-to-terminal traffic: the terminal often transmits less data than it receives from the computer. Packet switching provides a facility to smooth the asymmetrical flow across the channel by interleaving multiple users onto the channel. In Figure 7-4, for instance, what might be a computer at B and a terminal at G from one user session could be reversed by having another user share the same line with the opposite structure: a terminal at B and a computer at G. Packet switching balances the traffic across many channels by switching traffic among the many users to decrease the asymmetrical aspect of the traffic flow.

Packet switching also provides an attractive feature for connecting the DTEs together for a session. In a circuit-switched telephone structure, connect time is often slow. Recall from earlier discussions in this chapter that a switched telephone call requires that a number be dialed and that all circuits be set up for the call to be routed to the destination. However, with a packet-switching system, dedicated leased lines are available for multiple users to interleave their data traffic. The lines do not require any circuit setups, since they are permanently connected through the system. The technique can improve the slow connect time associated with multiple telephone circuit switches.

When and When Not to Use Packet Switching

How does an organization determine when to use, or not to use, packet-switching systems? With the preceding discussion in mind, one way to address this question is to compare four alternatives for connecting DTEs (see Figure 7-5):

- public telephone dial-up system
- private, nonswitched telephone channels
- public packet networks, or private circuit-switched networks
- private packet networks.

Organizations with relatively low data-transfer rates benefit from using public dial-up lines. If sessions between DTEs are short and the connections between the DTEs are local, the dial-up approach makes good sense, *if* the user does not mind the dial-up delay and an occasional busy signal. Since dial-up charges are based on time and distance, infrequent and short-distance transmissions favor the use of the public telephone system.

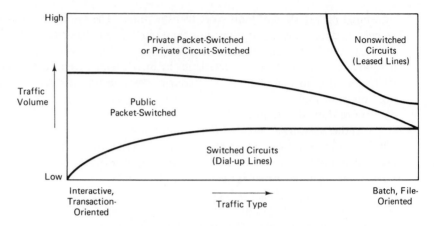

Figure 7-5. Options for DTE Communications

Private leased lines are a viable option for organizations that experience heavy, constant traffic throughout a 24-hour period and/or cannot tolerate the delays of dial-up. The organization can use the permanently connected leased lines continuously. Moreover, companies that establish multidrop connections on their private channels usually benefit from using the leased channel option, because the multi-drops permit a more effective sharing of the channel.

Public packet networks are sometimes called value-added carriers (VAC) because they provide value-added services to their customers. For example, VACs lease lines from the telephone carrier, add packet switches and PADs to the lines, and sell the service to any customer willing to pay the fees. Organizations with low to medium traffic volumes can usually benefit from subscribing to a public packet network. The public network can accommodate organizations with occasional traffic for transmission. Also, for organizations that are spread out over a large geographical area, the public packet network may be better economically, since most of the public packet carriers charge on *volume* of traffic, not distance between DTEs.

Many organizations have established private packet networks or private circuit-switched systems. There are several reasons for private systems. For medium to high traffic volumes, private networks are more cost-effective than dedicated private lines. Moreover, if an organization has "bursty" traffic conditions, a private packet network usually provides better and more economical service than the dedicated facilities.

Figure 7-5 provides a graphic depiction of the tradeoffs between dial-up lines, private lines, public packet networks, and private packet networks. Be aware that changing carrier offerings and tariffs require a careful analysis of the options vis-à-vis a company's needs. Moreover, the value-added aspects of packet networks (such as X.3 PADs and the X.25 connection orientation discussed in Chapter Eight) could alter a user organization's decisions to favor a packet network alternative.

In summary, the major goals of packet switching are to accomplish the following:

- provide for multiplexing capabilities of the channel and the port

- smooth the asymmetrical traffic among multiple users
- provide for fast response time to all users of the facility
- provide for high availability of the network to all users
- provide for distribution of risks and sharing of resources.

Packet Routing

Network routing entails the use of logic (software, hardware, or microcode) at the switches to move the data packets through the network to the end destination. As a general statement, network routing has three primary goals to fulfill:

- provide for the shortest possible delay and highest throughput
- route the packet through the network at the least cost
- provide each packet with the maximum possible security and reliability.

Keep in mind that these three goals pertain to the general idea of routing. Each enterprise develops its own notion of what routing goals should be. Indeed, most networks today have a rather simplistic view of routing based on the fewest number of nodes. Interestingly, this often translates to routing the traffic through the shortest possible delay path and routing the traffic at the least possible cost. In the last few years, however, network administrators have begun to use more sophisticated routing logic (other than the minimal hop). Increasingly, networks are using criteria based on delay and throughput.

Network routing is categorized in a number of ways. One approach is *centralized* or *distributed* routing. A centralized routing network (almost defunct) provides for one network control center (NCC) to determine the routing of the packets through the network. The packet switches are not as intelligent as the central site, which can translate into decreased costs at the switching nodes. However, centralized control suffers from the vulnerability of possible failure of one central site. Consequently, NCCs are usually duplicated (duplexed).

The centralized approach also entails considerable overhead, with the requirement for the network control center to distribute routing information to its subordinate packet switches. As the industry has migrated toward powerful route discovery protocol, the centralized approach has fallen into disfavor.

Distributed routing requires more intelligent nodes in the network. However, it provides more network resiliency, because each node makes its own routing decisions without regard to a centralized network control center. Distributed routing is also more complex, as we will see shortly.

Before discussing the actual routing technologies, it is necessary to define some terms.

- *Traffic multiplication effect* (TME). A given packet generates additional, identical packets.
- *Node "route-around."* Bypassing a failed or busy node or channel.
- *Packet die-out (packet kill).* Diminishing the effect of TME.

Most packet networks perform routing by the use of a routing directory or table. The directory contains the entries that inform the switches to transmit a packet to one of several possible output channels at the switch. Packet network directories are organized around three approaches.

- *Fixed (or static) directory.* Changes at system generation time only. Remains static for *every* user session.
- *Session-oriented directory.* Changes with *each* user session. Static for an individual session.
- *Adaptive or dynamic directory.* Changes *within* each user session.

The directory systems are further classified as partial-path directory or full-path directory. A *partial-path* directory contains only the adjacent nodes to a particular switch, i.e., those nodes connected directly to the switch. A *full-path* directory contains the entire set of intermediate nodes for the packet to traverse to its final destination.

The routing techniques described in this section illustrate the wide diversity of methods used by network designers. Some of these techniques are used extensively and others are used only occasionally or are research projects. We will consider how they work and the extent of their use, as well.

Packet Flooding.   One approach to network routing is packet flooding. Every possible path is used between a transmitting and a receiving DTE; duplicate packets are placed onto all output channels and routed through the network. An advantage to flooding is that since every path through the network is used, the first copy of the packet to arrive at the end site will have gone through the shortest delay (which meets one of the major goals of network routing). However, the traffic multiplication effect (TME) is quite severe with packet flooding, and the load on the network is proportional to the connectivity of the network. In other words, more channels and alternate paths create more traffic. However, packet flooding provides for a highly resilient network since a packet copy will always get through to the end destination as long as one path exists between the sending and receiving stations. Some military networks use this technique because it is very robust.

The traffic multiplication effect can be diminished by adding some additional bookkeeping logic at each switch. For example, the design can be set up as follows: If each receiving node recognizes a duplicate packet, it discards the packet and does not send out any additional copies of the packet. In other words, it forwards only one copy of the packet. This die-out (or packet kill) process substantially reduces TME. Packet copies gradually disappear as the packets make their way toward the end destination.

Many LANs control routing operations through packet flooding. A more common term for LANs is *broadcasting.* The use of broadcasting on a LAN is relatively straightforward since most LANs have one channel with devices attached. Broadcasting in networking where multipoint links, various LANs, and packet switch topologies exist is more complex. Notwithstanding, packet flooding/broadcasting is a common approach for the exchange of routing information. For networks with complex topologies, such as wide area networks (WANs), packet flooding/broadcasting is less common for the exchange of data packets.

Random Routing.   Random routing is another technique used for network packet switching. This approach requires the software at each switch to randomly select an output channel. Under a pure random-routing pattern, the output channel may include the path over which the packet was received. If, for example, a packet switch had three output ports, it "randomizes" to each of the ports. Consequently, 33 percent of the time it selects port A; 33 percent, port B; and 33 percent, port C. Less logic is required at the switches to perform random routing, and traffic is, on average, distributed to all switches. Random routing provides for load leveling across the entire network.

However, random routing has serious disadvantages. First, the total path through the network is (on average) considerably longer than with other techniques. Also, the delay through the network is longer, which greatly compromises a major goal of packet switching—to reduce delay. Third, while the packet "wanders around" the network, eventually finding its destination, a finite chance exists that the packet may never reach its destination. Fourth, because of the "wandering," random routing experiences the traffic multiplication effect (TME). Consequently, this technique is not used frequently.

Directory Routing.   As stated earlier, the more widely used routing techniques employ a directory or table. The three directory approaches introduced earlier will be explained by an examination of existing networks. The *fixed, static directory* is illustrated by IBM's System Network Architecture (SNA). The *session-oriented directory* technique is explained by the public packet network Tymnet. (Although the example that follows is, in fact, an older version of Tymnet, it serves to explain a session-oriented directory.) Finally, the *adaptive* or *dynamic directory* approach is illustrated by the Department of Defense's ARPANET.

SNA can best be introduced by an examination of the *System Services Control Point* (SSCP) and two other fundamental parts of the architecture: *physical units* (PU) and *logical units* (LU). These three elements are called *network addressable units* (NAUs). In SNA, an NAU can be an originator or a receiver of traffic, and every NAU in the network is assigned a unique address. For example, an NAU is assigned to elements such as the host-access method (VTAM or TCAM), the front-end network central program (NCP), cluster controllers, terminals, and certain applications. Communications lines are also assigned addresses, but they are not NAUs since they do not originate or receive traffic.

SSCP is responsible for the SNA network. It resides in the host telecommunications access method (either ACF/TCAM or ACF/VTAM). Each part (domain) of an SNA network is assigned to an SSCP. The major functions of an SSCP are as follows:

- establishing user sessions in the network
- controlling all resources in the domain
- bringing up the network.

End users in an SNA network are individuals or applications programs. An end user is not considered part of SNA, so a logical unit (LU) acts as an access point into the network. The logical unit is software or microcode. An end-user-to-end-user session requires an LU-to-LU session to acquire the resources for the end users. The LUs provide for any buffers, data conversion, editing, flow control, and software required to satisfy the end-user requirements. Each LU has a network name associated with it used by SNA to determine a network address and the actual location of the needed resources. The end user is not concerned with the physical aspects of the network.

SSCP sends commands to a PU, which then manages the resources attached directly to it. A PU actually contains a subset of the SSCP capabilities and performs functions such as recovery procedures, activating a data communications link, and terminal control.

SNA communicates through a *session,* which is a temporary logical connection between network-addressable units (NAU). The goal of session management is to create an LU-to-LU session in order for end users to communicate with each other. In doing so, the SSCP first establishes a session with the logical unit's physical unit (SSCP-PU), then with the logical unit (SSCP-LU). Finally, the two logical units establish a session for applications processing (LU-to-LU).

The SNA directory is responsible for routing traffic through the SNA network. Figure 7-6 depicts a typical SNA topology. SNA is organized around the concept of domains and nodes. Nodes constitute domains. Two kinds of nodes exist. The subarea node contains a mainframe computer and/or a front end and has the intelligence to make routing decisions. Peripheral nodes contain cluster controllers and/or terminals and do not make routing decisions.

When a user wishes to use the SNA network, a class of service (COS) must first be defined. The user defines a preferential route and a preferential level of service [i.e., a class of service (COS)]. For example, the preferential route could contain (a) a request for land lines instead of satellite links because of response time considerations, (b) the explicit routing over certain links that are more secure than others, and (c) the bypassing of certain nodes.

The class of service (COS) defines a list of preferential routes called *virtual routes* (VR). A virtual route is a logical route between two end points. A user session is assigned the first operational VR in the COS table. Each virtual route is then mapped into a table to create *explicit routes* (ERs). An explicit route is a sequence of subarea nodes and links from the originating to terminating subareas. Up to eight explicit routes can be defined between each pair of subarea nodes. Each explicit route is also defined in a *transit routing table* (see Figure 7-7). The routing table contains the destination of the subarea addresses as well as explicit route numbers.

SNA provides an option in which routing through SNA is session oriented and fixed at the time the user's profile is generated into the routing table. As with all packet-switching networks, alternate routing entries in the table are provided in the event of problems with nodes or channels.

SNA provides an additional feature called *transmission groups* (TGs). This term describes the grouping of parallel links between adjacent subarea nodes. The

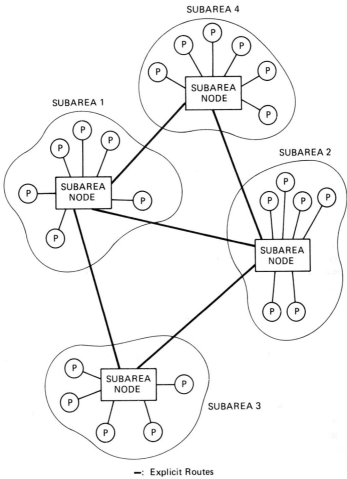

—: Explicit Routes
P: Peripheral Routes

Figure 7-6. SNA Domain

transmission groups consist of links using the same technology (for example, land lines or satellite links).

As stated earlier, the SNA directory is partial—no single subarea has an understanding of the complete end-to-end path. As the routing table in Figure 7-7 shows, the subarea knows only the adjacent nodes to which it is to route traffic. The explicit routes are broken down into route segments. A change in network configuration and topology (for example, adding new nodes or removing nodes from the network) necessitates changing only the transaction routing tables of the adjacent nodes. No other nodes are affected.

The transit routing table consists of three fields: the destination subarea (DSA); explicit route (ER) numbers; and the next node/transmission group (NN/TG) field. When an SNA message, called a path information unit (PIU), is processed by a subarea node, the node checks the PIU header for a DSA and an ER

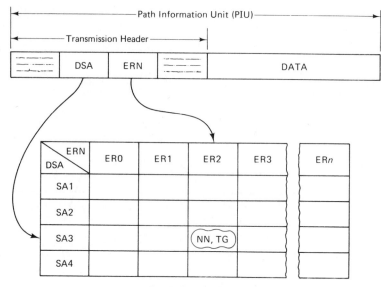

DSA: Destination Subarea
ERN: Explicit Route Number
ER: Explicit Route
NN: Next Node
TG: Transmission Group

Figure 7-7. SNA Transit Routing Table

number. It finds the corresponding entries in the table and places the message in the appropriate outgoing queue.

The next example illustrates an older version of Tymnet's use of session-oriented directory. Tymnet has altered this approach in upgrades, but we use this particular technique because it provides a good illustration of how session-oriented directories are utilized.

TYMNET provides a control center (the "supervisor"), which determines the route through the network for each user session when each user logs on to the network. The network supervisor sets up a session by sending a "needle" packet to the requesting node. The needle packet identifies all the intermediate nodes used to complete the packet transfer to the end site. Upon the needle packet arriving at the source node, the packet is then sent along the path to the intermediate nodes, where buffers are set up and reserved for a two-way session between the two users.

TYMNET establishes the needle packet based on a "link cost": link capacity load conditions of each line, type of link, and type of application session (interactive, batch, etc). Thereafter, a session traverses the same path while the users are logged on to the network. The network supervisor maintains an awareness of the entire network by requiring that each node send status packets to it every few seconds. These packets contain the operational status of each node and provide information on packet delay through the nodes. To terminate the session, a "path zapper" packet is used to release the channels and buffers through the path.

Each TYMNET node is allocated *logical channels,* and the channels are reserved for transmissions when the session is set up with the needle packet. The logical channel number identifies the session and the packets belonging to the session. Figure 7-8 illustrates the logical channel concept (which are called *ports* at the end sites). As the session is set up at node A, the packet is assigned to outbound logical channel 5. The logical channel number 5 is placed in the packet header and sent to node B. Due to the previous session establishment, node B knows inbound logical channel 5 is to be given to outbound logical channel 9. Node B performs the queuing functions and changes the packet header channel number to 9. This number is associated with port 7 at the final destination, node C. An *outbound* logical channel number is associated with an *inbound* logical channel number.

ARPANET is an example of adaptive or dynamic directory routing. It also illustrates the concept of distributed packet systems. Each node maintains an awareness of the entire network topology and independently computes the optimum (shortest) path to each destination node and the final node. Adaptive networks function on the concept of node-adjacency knowledge; that is, a particular node is aware of the status of those nodes adjacent to it. The process is depicted in Figure 7-9, which shows the routing table for node D. The routing table consists of several entries. Three illustrated are final destination, next node, and a calculated overall delay. If node D wishes to transmit packets to node A, it performs a table look-up to final destination A and determines that the next node to route the packets is C. The overall delay from D to C to B to A is seven units of time—shorter than any other path to A.

As the packets are sent out from node D to its adjacent nodes (C, E, and G), the software at D keeps records of the time required to receive an ACK from the adjacent nodes. In addition, each node knows how many packets it has outstanding for other nodes. Every ten seconds the node calculates the delay on each of its outgoing links. Any significant deviation in delay changes are sent by packet flooding to all other nodes. The nodes then use the information to recompute the routing table. Thus, the name *dynamic* or *adaptive* routing is used, because the routing logic changes based on network conditions.

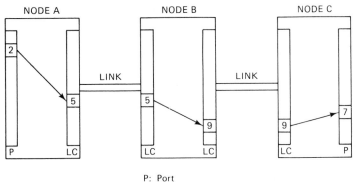

P: Port
LC: Logical Channel

Figure 7-8. TYMNET Logical Channels

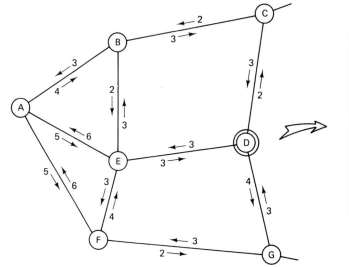

ROUTING TABLE

FD	NN	OD
A	C	7
B	C	4
C	C	2
E	E	3
F	E	6
G	G	4
⋮	⋮	⋮

FD: Final Destination
NN: Next Node
OD: Overall Delay

Figure 7-9.   Adaptive Routing

Adaptive routing is not without its problems, however. First, the software to handle this powerful routing scheme is complex. Second, it is possible that a packet can "oscillate" and become lost in the network when it moves from one node to another during the time that the routing tables are changed. However, if the routing tables are not changed frequently, the lost-packet problem is not serious. Initially, ARPANET exchanged path-update packets with neighbors every 128 milliseconds, which created a variety of problems in the network. Recent approaches have the nodes update their table every ten seconds.

Adaptive routing also presents some unique problems in reassembling packets at the final destination. With the fixed-directory approaches, since the packets follow each other sequentially through a set path in the network, the packets arrive in sequential order. However, adaptive routing allows the packets to take different paths through the network, so that in many instances they arrive out of sequence. (Some people call this method *datagram routing*. We will see, though, that the term *datagram* has a different meaning in the X.25 context.) Out-of-sequence transmissions require the receiving node to queue and hold packets until *all* packets have arrived. They are then given to the user.

Routing Problems.   This section discusses several problems that exist in many packet networks: lost packets, duplicate packets, flow-control problems, network purges, and packet choking.

To describe the lost-packet problem, let us assume a packet is routed to switch B, which acknowledges with an ACK to transmitting node A [Figure 7-10(a)]. However, the switch that sends the ACK (node B) does not send the packet forward, because the switch fails before B has an opportunity to transmit the acknowledged packet out onto the channel. In this case, the packet is lost. If other packets from this session finally arrive at the receiving node, the lost packet cannot be found in the network.

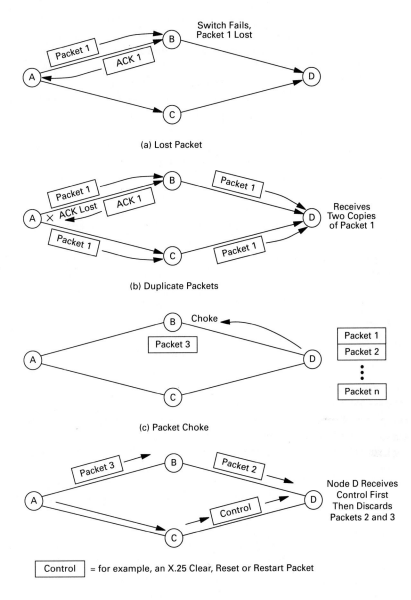

Figure 7-10. Packet Routing Problems

Several methods exist for handling lost packets. One approach is to restrict node B from sending an ACK back to node A until it has actually sent the packet on to node D. Other systems require that end node D transmit status packets back to node A to indicate which packets are missing. The latter approach stipulates packet accountability as an end-to-end function.

Figure 7-10(b) illustrates the problem of *duplicate packets*. In this situation, node B's ACK does not arrive back to node A, even though node B sends the packet successfully to node D. Consequently, node A may assume node B is down and retransmit the packet to node C. Node C will relay this packet to node D, which eventually receives the packet twice.

Duplicate packets can be handled by a number of methods. One is to require a more elaborate sequencing scheme in a header to uniquely identify each packet, and to provide software at the receiving site to discard duplicate data.

Flow-control logic is available at every node to prevent an excessive number of packets from arriving at a node faster than the node can transmit the packets. One approach to handling flow control is through packet choking [see Figure 7-10(c)]. Each node monitors the utilization of its output lines. When the output lines exceed a threshold, the node's logic checks incoming packets to determine if the packets destined for that line are above a threshold. If so, a choke packet is sent back to the node or DTE originating the "problem" traffic. The sending site is required to reduce traffic or hold traffic by a certain amount or period. Once the overload has decreased, the transmitting site can resume sending traffic.

A problem with packet choking occurs when two or more nodes depend on each other to complete an action. For example, if a packet choke is issued to a node because the receiving node has an excessive number of packets, yet the node it "choked" is sending some of the very packets needed for the receiving node to relieve its buffers, then the result is a *deadly embrace*. One solution to the deadly embrace is to require the sending node to request from the receiving node the necessary buffer space for a multipacket session. The receiving site reserves the buffer space ahead of time or denies the call request. TYMNET's "needle" packet is an illustration of reserving buffers before the session begins.

Figure 7-10(d) shows another situation, *network purge,* in which packets can be lost in the network. Due to a number of potential problems (sequencing errors, timing problems, etc.), the network issues a *control packet* to terminate a user session. Typically, when this packet arrives at end node D, subsequent packets for this session are not accepted by D. In this case, packets 2 and 3 would be ignored, and a higher-level protocol would have to initiate recovery of these packets.

The X.25 clear, reset, and restart control packets discussed in Chapter Eight illustrate how the problem shown in Figure 7-10(d) can occur. The value of a higher-level recovery mechanism (the transport layer) is also discussed.

Finally, some networks (such as packet flooding) discard a packet if it has existed within the network beyond a time limit. The packets are given a "time to live" and then discarded if the time expires. After a certain amount of time, the packet loses its value. Adaptive routing networks and connectionless networks sometimes use this approach.

PACKET-SWITCHING SUPPORT TO CIRCUIT-SWITCHING NETWORKS

Several years ago, AT&T recognized the inefficiency of integrating its control signals on the same channel with voice traffic. Consequently, it devised the Common Channel Interoffice Signalling (CCIS) system, which transmitted the signalling information for a group of trunks over a separate channel from the user communications channel. CCIS reduced the call setup time for switched circuits. It also provided for more flexibility and lower costs in high-volume telephone networks. Moreover, since the signalling function was disassociated from the voice channel, control signals could be handled in a highly concentrated manner.

One of the initial problems encountered in implementing CCIS was an occasional connection that had a voice-defective channel. To solve this problem, AT&T tested the connected channel for quality before releasing it for user allocation.

CCIS was the first major packet-switching system implemented by AT&T. The packets were used for call setup and breakdown. Call sets of information were called *signal units,* which consisted of 28 bits (8 bits are used for error detection). CCIS placed 12 signal units into a packet for transmission. The signal units within the packet had the same destination, as depicted in Figure 7-11. Toll office A sent the packets to a signal transfer point (STP). The STP transferred the signal units to an associated outgoing trunk to the distant office (toll office B) to establish the call setup.

CCIS and its CCI 77 counterpart, Signaling System Number 6 (SS6), have performed well enough, but the data link speeds of 2.4 and 4.8 Kbit/s and the limited size of the service unit (SU) limit their capabilities. Also, the band-based routing is awkward to manage. Many telephone companies and administrations have now moved to SS7.

SS7 uses digital 56 Kbit/s trunks. The topology of the network remains about the same as CCIS, but the STPs are configured around only seven regions. The STPs handle both CCIS and SS7 protocols.

SS7 can also be applied to call control for a telephone service (Q.7 and Q.110) and to circuit switched data transmission systems (X.60). Its use in international systems is specified in X.87.

SS7 defines the procedures for the setup and clearing of a call between telephone users. It performs these functions by exchanging telephone control messages and signals between the SS7 telephone exchange and SS7 signalling transfer points (STPs). At the broadest level, the SS7 telephone signalling messages are made up of (a) telephone signalling messages types and, within the types, (b) the identification

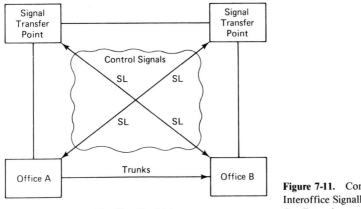

Figure 7-11.   Common-Channel Interoffice Signalling (CCIS) Configuration

of specific components relevant to the telephone call. Q.722 describes these components, and they are summarized in Table 7-1.

TABLE 7-1. EXAMPLES OF FUNCTIONS OF SS7 MESSAGES & SIGNALS

Message Components

- Identifiers of: circuits signalling points, called and calling parities, incoming trunks, and transit exchanges
- Control codes to set up and clear down a call
- Called party's number
- Indicator that called party's line is out of service
- Indication of national, international, or other subscriber
- Indication that called party has cleared
- Nature of circuit (satellite/terrestrial)
- Indication that called party cleared, then went off-hook again
- Use of echo-suppression
- Notification to reset a faulty circuit
- Language of assistance operators
- Status identifiers (calling line identity incomplete; all addresses complete; use of coin station; network congestion; no digital path available; number not in use; blocking signals for certain conditions)
- Circuit continuity check
- Call forwarding (and previous routes of the call)
- Provision for an all-digital path
- Security access calls (called closed user group [CUG])
- Malicious call identification
- Request to hold the connection
- Charging information
- Indication that a called party's line is free
- Call setup failure
- Subscriber busy signal

SUMMARY

Switching systems and routing protocols have evolved from the primitive electromechanical devices used in earlier telephone systems to the sophisticated packet-
switching systems in use today, and most recently to the digital switching that is
virtually taking over the switching industry. This chapter introduced the major
switching and routing systems used in computer networks. In Chapter Nine, after
discussing digital systems, we will continue with a close examination of digital
switching.

8

The X.25 Network and Supporting Protocols

INTRODUCTION

This chapter describes the CCITT recommendation for packet network interfaces, X.25, along with its major protocols and supporting standards. We describe the protocols and explain their uses in the context of an end-user application. The first part of the chapter introduces the major features of X.25. Then, for those seeking it, the section on packet formats offers more detail. Otherwise, skip to the section on X.25 facilities. Familiarity with material in the first seven chapters of this book, as well as Appendices B and C, is assumed.

FEATURES OF X.25

In 1974 CCITT issued the first draft of X.25 (the "Gray Book"). It was revised in 1976, 1978, 1980, and again in 1984 with the 1985 publication of the "Red Book" recommendations. The original document was primarily the proposals from Datapac (Canada), Tymnet, and Telenet (U.S.)—three new packet-switching networks. Since 1974, X.25 has been expanded to include many options, services, and facilities. It is now the predominant user-oriented interface standard into wide area packet networks.

A packet network and the user stations must have control mechanisms when they interface with each other. Perhaps the most important from the standpoint of the network is *flow control:* limiting the amount of traffic from the user stations in order to prevent congestion in the network. The user DTE also needs flow control to regulate the traffic coming from the network. Both the DTE and the network also must have error control procedures to assure all traffic is received without errors. X.25 provides these flow and error control functions.

X.25 defines the procedures for the exchange of data between user devices (DTEs) and a packet network node (DCE). Its formal title is "Interface Between Data Terminal Equipment and Data Circuit Terminating Equipment for Terminals Operating in the Packet Mode on Public Data Networks."

Networks use X.25 to establish the procedures for two packet-mode DTEs to communicate with each other through a network, since X.25 defines the two DTEs' sessions with their respective DCEs. The idea of the recommended standard is to provide common procedures between a user DTE and a packet network (DCE) for establishing a session and exchanging data. The procedures include functions such as identifying packets of specific user terminals and computers (with *logical channel numbers* [LCNs]), acknowledging packets, rejecting packets, and providing for error recovery and flow control. X.25 also provides for some very useful *facilities,* such as the charging of packets to DTE stations other than transmitting DTEs.

Interestingly, the X.25 standard contains *no routing algorithms.* Features such as the fixed or dynamic packet-routing schemes within a network are left to specific vendor implementations, since they are internal to a vendor's product. Also, it should be emphasized that, although the two DTE/DCE interfaces at each end of the network are independent of each other in relation to how X.25 defines their dialogue with the intervening network nodes, X.25 *does* have end-to-end significance because selected traffic is routed end to end. Nonetheless, the recommended standard is *asymmetric:* only one side of the network interface (DTE/DCE) is defined. This important point will be emphasized in several sections of this chapter.

The absence of routing algorithms in X.25 is often a source of confusion. Figure 8-1 shows the relationship of X.25 in the network layer (3) to relay or routing capabilities. The traffic is transmitted from DTE A to an intermediate node, which could be the user's entrance node into the network (in X.25, the DCE). At this node, the physical layer (1), data link layer (2, LAPB), and the network layer (3) are

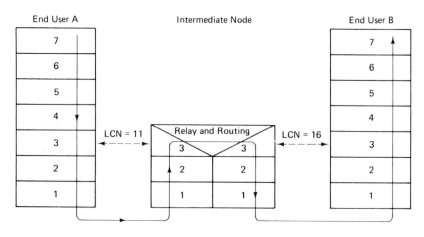

→ : User Data Flow and Routing

Figure 8-1.   X.25 and Relay/Routing

invoked to service user A. In this illustration, user A identifies itself to the network with logical channel number (LCN) 11.

Next, the data are given to relay and routing software, which performs the switching functions discussed in Chapter Seven. These functions are not part of X.25. At the final destination the data are given back to X.25 (and the lower layers) and are transmitted out of the node (which could be the network node [DCE] for user B) to DTE B. The network node assigns LCN 16 to its session with DTE B.

WHY X.25?

The reader might wonder why X.25 is of any real value. "What's in it for me?" There are a number of reasons to use a standard such as X.25. First, the adoption of a common standard among vendors provides an easier way to interface different vendor products. Second, the X.25 standard has gone through numerous revisions and is relatively mature (it is now revised every four years). X.25 has seen considerable use since 1980, and several systems were implemented as early as 1976. Consequently, the changes and adaptations made to the 1984 document reflect a substantial amount of experience relating to the interface with a packet network. Third, a widely used standard such as X.25 can decrease network costs, since off-the-shelf software and hardware are readily available. Fourth, it is much easier to write a request for proposal to a vendor stating the network must conform to X.25 than to write a 180-page specification document. Fifth, the data link layer with HDLC/LAPB provides only for error recovery and data accountability on an individual link between the DTE/DCE (and on the links between the packet-switching nodes within the network). However, X.25 provides a higher level of support by establishing accountability between each sending DTE and its DCE (entrance packet node to the network) and each receiving DTE and its DCE (exit packet node from the network). In other words, it gives more end-to-end support than does HDLC/LAPB. In addition, X.25 provides for enriched functionality well beyond that provided by a data link protocol.

However, the four-year revision cycle concerns some vendors who believe it difficult to achieve stability in communications product lines. Some vendors also have expressed concern that the increasing number of functions being written into X.25 are making the standard too large and complex for efficient use.

LAYERS OF X.25

X.25 and the Physical Layer

As Figure 8-1 illustrates, the X.25 packet-level recommendation is one of the recommended standards for the third layer of OSI's model. It actually encompasses the third layer as well as the lower two layers. The recommended physical layer interface between the DTE and DCE is X.21. (You may wish to refer to Appendix C for a review of X.21.) X.25 assumes the physical layer X.21 keeps circuits T (transmit) and R (receive) active for the exchange of packets. It assumes that X.21 is in state

13S (send data), 13R (receive data), or 13 (data transfer). X.25 further assumes that the X.21 channels C (control) and I (indication) are active. Given that C and I are active, X.25 uses the X.21 physical interface between the DTE and DCE as a "packet pipeline" by transmitting and receiving the packets across the transmit (T) and receive (R) pins.

Since many countries have not implemented X.21 extensively, X.25 also provides a provision to use the X.21 bis/EIA-232-D physical interface (see Appendix C). The term *bis* refers to a second version of a recommended standard, although X.21 *bis* is not close to X.21 in similarity. Both X.21 *bis* and EIA-232-D use the CCITT V.24 circuit assignments discussed in Appendix C. EIA-232-D identifies its circuits with two letters (such as BA); V.24 identifies its circuits with three numbers (such as 103).

In order to use these interfaces, X.25 requires that circuits 105 (CA), 106 (CB), 107 (CC), 108.2 (CD), and 109 (CF) be in the ON condition. Data are exchanged on circuits 103 (BA) and 104 (BB). If these circuits are off, X.25 assumes the physical level is in an inactive state and any upper levels (such as data link [LAPB] and network [X.25]) will not function. Although not stated explicitly, X.25 networks can operate with other physical layer standards (for example, EIA-449 and V.35).

The principal EIA-232-D and V.24 circuits required for X.25 are shown in Table 8-1 (the ground, signaling, and timing circuits are not shown).

TABLE 8-1.   CIRCUITS FOR X.25 STANDARD

	EIA-232-D	V.24
Send Data	BA	103
Receive Data	BB	104
Request to Send	CA	105
Clear to Send	CB	106
Data Set Ready	CC	107
Data Terminal Ready	CD	108.2
Carrier Detect	CF	109

The physical level of X.25 does not perform significant control functions. It is more of a passive conduit, with control provided by the data link and network layers.

X.25 and the Data Link Layer

X.25 assumes the data link layer to be LAPB. This line protocol is a subset of the superset HDLC. It allows, but does not encourage, the use of LAP. Vendors also use other link controls such as bisync (binary synchronous control) for this layer. LAPB and X.25 interact in the following manner:

The X.25 *packet* is carried within the LAPB *frame* as the I (information) field. LAPB's job is to ensure that the X.25 packets are transmitted error-free across an error-prone channel from/to the DTE/DCE. (To differentiate between a packet and a frame, a *packet* is created at the network level and inserted into a *frame,* which is created at the data link level.)

LAPB uses a specific subset of HDLC to support X.25. The thirteen commands and responses are:

Commands	Responses
Information (I)	*Receive Ready* (RR)
Receive Ready (RR)	*Reject* (REJ)
Reject (REJ)	*Receive Not Ready* (RNR)
Receive Not Ready (RNR)	*Unnumbered Acknowledgment* (UA)
Disconnect (DSC)	
Set Asynchronous Response Mode (SARM)	*Frame Reject* (FRMR)
Set Asynchronous Balanced Mode (SABM)	*Disconnect Mode* (DM)

As these entries show, user data in the I field cannot be sent as a response. In accordance with HDLC rules on addressing, this means I frames will always contain the destination address, which prevents any ambiguity in determining the proper interpretation of the frame. If, for example, station A receives a REJ frame with the address of A, it knows it has received a command. If the REJ contains an address of B, the station knows it has received a response.

X.25 requires LAPB to use specific addresses at the data link level. The subscriber DTE must be A (binary 11000000) and the DCE (network node) must be B (binary 10000000).

X.25 allows both SARM and SABM to support LAP and LAPB, respectively. However, SABM is encouraged, while LAP with SARM is rarely used now.

Both X.25 and LAPB use send (S) and receive (R) numbers to account for traffic in their respective layers. LAPB describes its numbers as N(S) and N(R). X.25 uses P(S) and P(R) to describe its sequence numbers.

Companion Standards to X.25

X.25 also assumes other standards are used in addition to the standards discussed in the physical and data link layers. The following companion standards are used as part of the X.25 standard. Appendices D and E summarize these and other recommended standards, and the more prevalent standards are covered in this chapter. The X.25 recommendation makes reference to all these standards:

X.1   User classes of service
X.2   User facilities
X.10   Categories of access
X.92   Reference connections for packets with data transmissions
X.96   Call-progress signals
X.121   International numbering plan
X.213   Network services

X.25 uses a considerable amount of telephone terminology (channels, circuits, calls, etc.). These terms will be defined in the context of packet switching for this chapter.

FEATURES OF X.25

X.25 operates on the premise of virtual circuit services. A virtual circuit is one in which one user perceives the existence of a dedicated physical circuit at a computer he or she is using, yet in reality the "dedicated" physical circuit is allocated to multiple users. Through the use of statistical multiplexing techniques, different users' packets are interleaved onto one physical channel. Ideally, the channel performance is good enough to ensure that each user does not notice degraded service from other traffic on the channel. X.25 uses logical channel numbers (LCNs) to identify the DTE connections to the network. As many as 4,095 *logical* channels and user sessions can be assigned to one *physical* channel.

X.25 Channel Options

We introduce X.25 in more detail by discussing the options for establishing sessions between DTEs that have X.25 logic capabilities. The standard provides four mechanisms to establish and maintain communications:

- permanent virtual circuit (PVC)
- virtual call (VC)
- fast-select call
- fast-select call with immediate clear.

Permanent Virtual Circuit (PVC).   A permanent virtual circuit is analogous to a leased line in a telephone network—the transmitting DTE is assured of obtaining a connection to the receiving DTE through the packet network. [See Figure 8-2(a).] X.25 requires that a permanent virtual circuit be established before the session begins. Consequently, an agreement must be reached by the two users and the packet network carrier before a permanent virtual connection will be allocated. Thereafter, when a transmitting DTE sends a packet into the packet network, the identifying information in the packet (a logical channel number) indicates that the requesting DTE has a permanent virtual circuit connection to the receiving DTE. Consequently, a connection will be made by the network and the receiving DTE without further arbitration and session negotiation. PVC requires no call setup or clearing procedures, and the logical channel is continually in a data-transfer state.

Virtual Call.   A virtual call (also called a switched virtual call) resembles some of the procedures associated with telephone dial-up lines. The process is illustrated in Figure 8-2(b). The originating DTE issues a call-request packet to the network with a logical channel number of 11 (LCN). The network routes the call request packet to the destination DTE. The destination DTE receives the call request packet as an incoming call packet from its network node with an LCN of 16.

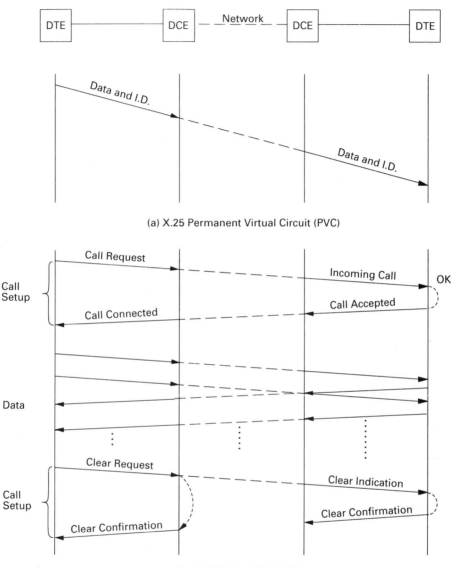

(a) X.25 Permanent Virtual Circuit (PVC)

(b.) X.25 Virtual Call (VC)

Figure 8-2. Packet Network Options

Logical channel numbering is done at each end of the network; the main requirement is to keep the specific DTE-to-DTE session identified at all times with LCN 11 and LCN 16. Logical channel numbers specifically identify the various user sessions for each physical circuit at each end of the network. Inside the network, the intermediate packet-switching nodes also may perform their own LCN numbering.

If the receiving DTE chooses to acknowledge and accept the call request, it transmits to the network a call-accepted packet. The network then transports this packet to the requesting DTE in the form of a call-connected packet. The channel enters a data-transfer state after call establishment. To terminate the session, a clear

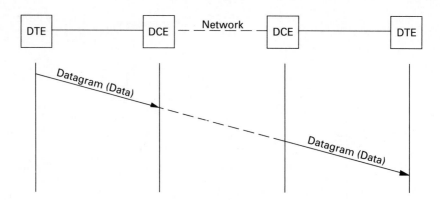

(c) Datagram (Not Supported in X.25)

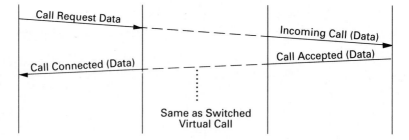

(d) X.25 Fast Select Call

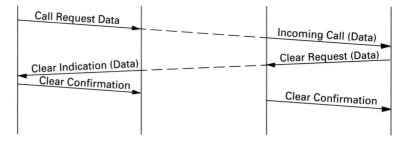

(e) X.25 Fast Select Call with Immediate Clear

Figure 8-2   *(Continued)*

request is sent by either DTE. It is received as a clear indication and confirmed with the clear-confirm packet. To summarize the connection-establishment procedure:

Packet	LCN Selected By
Call Request	Originating DTE
Incoming Call	Destination packet network node (DCE)

| Call Accepted | Same LCN as in Incoming Call |
| Call Connected | Same LCN as in Call Request |

By reviewing carefully the preceding paragraphs, you may recall earlier discussions in this book relating to connection-oriented networks. The connection-oriented network requires that a connection establishment be made before data are exchanged. Once the receiving or called DTE accepts the call request, data are exchanged in accordance with the X.25 standard.

Demise of X.25 Datagram.   The datagram facility is a form of connectionless service. Datagram service was supported in earlier releases of the standard [see Figure 8-2(c)]. However, it received little support from the commercial industry. Consequently, the 1984 and 1988 releases of the X.25 standard do not contain the datagram option. However, the datagram-connectionless service remains an important feature of other networks, as evidenced by the IEEE 802 standards and the Internet Protocol (IP).

Fast Select.   The basic premise of the datagram (eliminating the overhead of the session establishment and disestablishment packets) makes good sense for certain applications, such as those with very few transactions or short sessions on the network. Consequently, the fast select facility was incorporated into the standard. The 1984 release of X.25 provides the fast select as an essential facility, which means that vendors or manufacturers implementing X.25 are encouraged to implement fast select in order to be a certified X.25 network supplier.

Fast select provides for two options. The first option, *fast select call,* is depicted in Figure 8-2(d). A DTE can request this facility on a per-call basis to the network node (DCE) by means of an appropriate request in the header of a packet. The fast select facility allows the call request packet to contain user data of up to 128 bytes (octets). The called DTE is allowed to respond with a call-accepted packet, which also can contain user data. The call request/incoming call packet indicates if the remote DTE is to respond with clear request or call accepted. If a call accept is transmitted, the X.25 session continues with the normal data transferring and clearing procedures of a switched virtual call.

Fast select also provides for a fourth call-connection feature of the X.25 interface, the *fast select with immediate clear.* This option is depicted in Figure 8-2(e). As with the other fast select option, a call request contains user data. This packet is transmitted through the network to the receiving DTE, which, upon acceptance, transmits a clear request (which also contains user data). The clear request is received at the origination site as a clear indication packet. This site returns clear confirmation. The clear confirm packet cannot contain user data. Thus, the forward packet sets up the network connection and the reverse packet brings the connection down.

The idea of the fast selects (and the defunct datagram) is to provide support for user applications that have only one or two transactions, such as inquiry/

response applications (point-of-sale transactions, credit checks, funds transfers). These applications cannot effectively use a switched virtual call because of the overhead and delay required in session establishment and disestablishment. Moreover, they cannot benefit from the use of a permanent virtual circuit, because their occasional use would not warrant the permanent assignment of resources at the sites. Consequently, the fast selects have been incorporated into X.25 to meet the requirement for specialized uses of a network, as well as to provide for more connection-oriented support than the datagram offered. Both DTEs must subscribe to fast select, or the network will block the call.

Fast select was designed for transaction-based applications, but its use in remote job entry (RJE) and bulk file transfer (large amounts of data, such as a tape file) can provide another valuable user service. For example, a fast select call request may contain 128 octets of user data that could be examined by the receiving DTE to determine if it can accept a long-running, data-intensive session. The call-accept response could then grant permission—perhaps including rules to govern the data transfer between the end-user applications.

FLOW-CONTROL PRINCIPLES

X.25 allows the user device (DTE) or packet exchange (DCE) to limit the rate at which it accepts packets. This feature is very useful in preventing excessive traffic from arriving at either station.

Flow control can be established separately for each direction and is based on authorizations from the stations. As we shall see, flow control is implemented with certain X.25 control packets as well as packet-level sequence numbers.

OTHER PACKET TYPES

In addition to the packets described in the previous discussion, the X.25 recommendation uses several other packet types. (See Table 8-2.) The remaining packets are explained in this section.

The *interrupt* procedure allows a DTE to transmit one nonsequenced packet to another DTE without following the normal flow-control procedures established in X.25. (Flow control is discussed in more detail shortly.) The interrupt procedure is useful for situations in which an application requires the transmittal of data under unusual conditions. For example, a high-priority message could be transmitted as an interrupt packet to ensure the receiving DTE accepts the data. User data (32 octets) is permitted in an interrupt packet. The use of interrupts has no effect on regular data packets within the virtual call or permanent virtual circuit. As Table 8-2 shows, the interrupt packet requires an interrupt confirmation before another interrupt packet can be sent on the logical channel.

The *Receive Ready* (RR) and *Receive Not Ready* (RNR) packets are used in a fashion quite similar to the same commands in the HDLC and LAPB subset (Chapter Four). They serve the important function of user-device initiated flow control.

TABLE 8-2.   PACKET TYPES

Packet Type		Service	
From DCE to DTE	From DTE to DCE	VC	PVC
Call Setup and Clearing			
Incoming call	Call request	X	
Call connected	Call accepted	X	
Clear indication	Clear request	X	
DCE clear confirmation	DTE clear confirmation	X	
Data and Interrupt			
DCE data	DTE data	X	X
DCE interrupt	DTE interrupt	X	X
DCE interrupt confirmation	DTE interrupt confirmation	X	X
Flow Control and Reset			
DCE RR	DTE RR	X	X
DCE RNR	DTE RNR	X	X
	DTE REJ	X	X
Reset indication	Reset request	X	X
DCE reset confirmation	DTE reset confirmation	X	X
Restart			
Restart indication	Restart request	X	X
DCE restart confirmation	DTE restart confirmation	X	X
Diagnostic			
Diagnostic		X	X
Registration			
Registration confirmation	Registration request	X	X

VC = Virtual Call   PVC = Permanent Virtual Circuit

Both these packets provide a receive sequence number in the packet field to indicate the next packet sequence number expected from the transmitting DTE. The RR packet is used to tell the transmitting DTE/DCE to begin sending data packets and also uses the receive sequence number to acknowledge any packets that have been previously transmitted. Like the RR response in HDLC, the RR packet can be used to acknowledge packets received when there are no data packets to convey back to the transmitting site.

The RNR packet is used to request the transmitting site to stop sending packets and it also uses the receive sequence field to acknowledge any packets that have been previously received. The RNR is often used when a station is temporarily unable to receive traffic. Thus, both packet types provide flow control. It should be noted that an RNR issued for a specific DTE will likely cause the network to issue RNR to the other associated DTE to prevent excess traffic from entering into the network. The network packet-switching nodes have a finite amount of buffering and queuing capability. Consequently, an RNR often requires "choking" both sides of the DTE/DCE session.

These two packet types provide X.25 with an additional form of data flow control beyond the data link support level of LAPB, so flow control and windows are provided at the data link layer with LAPB *and* at the network layer with X.25. However, remember from previous chapters that the data link level provides effective flow control for individual user devices (DTEs); but, at the network level, X.25 uses RR and RNR with specific logical channel numbers to accomplish individual flow control. This flow control can be provided by anything that has a logical channel number assigned to it (terminals, personal computers, application programs). In some networks, blocks of logical channel numbers are assigned to a host computer and the host manages the LCNs for its attached terminals and programs.

The *reject* (REJ) packet specifically rejects the received packet. If it is used, the station requests retransmission of packets, beginning with the count in the packet receive sequence field.

The *reset* packets are used to reinitialize a switched virtual call or a permanent virtual circuit. The reset procedure removes in each direction between the two stations (for one logical channel session) all data and interrupt packets which may be in the network. Reset procedures may be necessary when problem conditions arise, such as lost packets, duplicate packets, or packets that cannot be resequenced properly. Reset is used only during a data-transfer state. A reset can be set by the DTE (reset request) or the network (reset indication).

The *restart* procedure is used to initialize or reinitialize the packet-level DTE/DCE interface. Up to 4,095 logical channels on a physical port can be affected. The procedure clears *all* the virtual calls and resets *all* the permanent virtual circuits at the interface level. The restart might occur as a result of a severe problem, such as a crash in the network (for example, the network control center computer fails). All outstanding packets are lost and must be recovered by a higher-level protocol.

Sometimes the network will use a restart when reinitializing or starting up the system to ensure all sessions are reestablished. Upon a DTE sending a restart, the network must send a restart to each DTE that has a virtual circuit session with the DTE that issued the restart. Restart packets also can contain codes indicating the reason for the restart.

From discussions on packet networks in earlier chapters, you may recall that user data packets can be lost in a network. Packet loss is also possible in an X.25 network. The clear, reset, and restart packets can cause undelivered packets to be discarded by the network. A situation such as this is not all that unusual, since these control packets often arrive at the destination node before all user data packets. Control packets are not subject to the delay inherent in the flow-control procedures used with user data packets. Consequently, higher-level protocols are required to account for these lost packets. Later in this chapter we examine the transport layer; one purpose (among others) of this layer is to provide end-to-end integrity of the users' traffic.

The *clear* packet is used for a number of functions in the X.25 network, although primarily to clear a DTE-DTE session. One of its other uses is to indicate that a call request cannot be completed. If the remote DTE refuses the call (because of the lack of resources, for example), it issues a clear request to its network node. The packet is sent through the network to the originating network node and a clear indication is sent to the originating DTE. [See Figure 8-3(a).] If the network cannot complete the call (for example, the remote network DCE node has no logical channel free, or

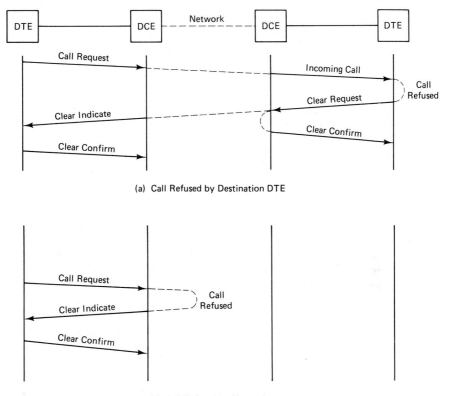

(a) Call Refused by Destination DTE

(b) Call Refused by Network

Figure 8-3. X.25 Call Clear Packets

the network is congested), it must send a clear indication to the originating DTE [see Figure 8-3(b)]. The fourth octet of the packet contains bit codes to indicate the reason for the clear. One of these codes is rather unique; it is used in maritime communications to indicate a ship is absent (sunk?!) and cannot accept a call on a radio or satellite circuit. X.25 provides several codes to indicate the reason for the clear packet.

The *diagnostic* packet is used by X.25 networks to reveal certain error conditions that are not covered by other methods of indications, such as reset and restart. The diagnostic packet with LCN = 0 is issued only once (and only by the network DCE) for a particular problem; no confirmation is required on the packet. X.25 defines 66 diagnostic codes to aid in determining network or DTE problems. These codes also can be used with the clear, reset, and restart packets.

Here are some examples of X.25 diagnostic codes:

- unidentifiable packet
- packet too long or too short
- unauthorized interrupt confirmation
- time limit expired
- invalid address
- no logical channel available

- facility not provided
- unknown international address
- remote network problem
- temporary network routing problem.

Finally, the *registration* packets are used to invoke or confirm the X.25 facilities (discussed later in this section). This 1984 addition allows the end user to request changes to facilities in an on-line mode, without the manual intervention and negotiation of the network vendor. A registration confirmation is returned to provide a status of the request.

X.25 LOGICAL CHANNEL STATES

Logical channel states provide the foundation for managing the DTE/DCE connection. Through the use of the various packet types, the logical channel may assume the following states:

State Number	State Description
p1 or d1 or r1	packet level ready
p2	DTE waiting
p3	DCE waiting
p5	call collision
p4	data transfer
p6	DTE clear request
p7	DCE clear indication
d2	DTE reset request
d3	DCE reset indication
r2	DTE restart request
r3	DCE restart indication

An example of a call establishment is provided in Table 8-3 to illustrate how channel states are used.

TABLE 8-3.   CALL ESTABLISHMENT PROCEDURE (EXAMPLE)

Sequence of Events	Packet	From	To	Channel State From	To Current Channels
1	Call Request	local DTE	local DCE	p1	p2
2	Incoming Call	remote DCE	remote DTE	p1	p3
3	Call Accepted	remote DTE	remote DCE	p3	p4
4	Call Connected	local DCE	local DTE	p2	p4

TIMEOUTS AND TIME LIMITS

The majority of communications protocols have timers, and X.25 is no exception. Timers are used to establish limits on the length of time it takes to get connections, clear channels, reset a session, etc. Without such timers, a user might wait indefinitely for an event if that event did not go to completion. Timers simply force X.25 to make decisions in the event of problems; hence, they facilitate error recovery.

X.25 provides DTE time limits and DCE timeouts. These timers are described in Table 8-4, as well as the results when the timers expire. In all cases, if problems persist and the timers are reset and retried, eventually the channel must be considered out of order and network diagnostics/trouble-shooting measures should then be performed.

TABLE 8-4(a). DTE TIME LIMITS

Time-Limit Number	Time-Limit Value	Started When	State of the Logical Channel	Normally Terminated When
T20	180 s	DTE issues a Restart Request	r2	DTE leaves the r2 state
T21	200 s	DTE issues a Call Request	p2	DTE leaves the p2 state
T22	180 s	DTE issues a Reset Request	d2	DTE leaves the d2 state
T23	180 s	DTE issues a Clear Request	p6	DTE leaves the p6 state
T28	300 s	DTE issues a Registration Request	Any	DTE receives the Registration Confirmation or a Diagnostic packet

TABLE 8-4(b). DCE TIMEOUTS

Time-Limit Number	Time-Limit Value	Started When	State of the Logical Channel	Normally Terminated When
T10	60 s	DCE issues a Restart Indication	r3	DCE leaves the r3 state
T11	180 s	DCE issues an Incoming Call	p3	DCE leaves the p3 state
T12	60 s	DCE issues a Reset Indication	d3	DCE leaves the d3 state
T13	60 s	DCE issues a Clear Indication	p7	DCE leaves the p7 state

PACKET FORMATS

The length of a default user data field in a data packet is 128 bytes or octets, but X.25 provides options for other lengths. The following options are also available: 16, 32, 64, 256, 512, 1024, 2048 and 4096 octets. The latter two sizes were added in the 1984 revision. If the user data field in the packet exceeds the network-permitted maximum field, the receiving DTE will reset the virtual call by issuing a reset packet.

Every packet transferred across the DTE/DCE interface to the network must contain at least *three octets* (or bytes). The three octets comprise the packet header. Other octets may also be used to make up the header. The header for data and nondata packets is illustrated in Figure 8-4. The first four bits of the first octet of the header contain the logical channel group number (introduced earlier and discussed in more detail shortly). The last four bits of the first octet contain the general format identifier. Bits 5 and 6 of the general format identifier (SS) are used to indicate the sequencing for the packet sessions. Two sequencing options are allowed in X.25. The first option is *Modulo 8,* which permits sequence numbers from 0 through 7. *Modulo 128,* which permits sequence numbers ranging from 0 through 127, is also available. The seventh bit, or D bit, of the general format identifier is used only with certain packets. (We discuss the D bit shortly.) The eighth bit is the Q bit, used only for end-user data-type packets. It qualifies two levels of user data to the network (explained later with X.29).

The second octet of the packet header contains the logical channel number (LCN). This 8-bit field, combined with the logical channel group number, provides the complete logical channel identification of 12 bits, which provide a possibility of a total of 4,095 logical channels (2^{12} less the 0 channel). The 0 LCN is reserved for control use (restart and diagnostic packets). Networks use these two fields in various ways. Some networks use the two together; others treat them as separate fields.

Logical channel numbers are used to identify the DTE to the packet node (DCE), and vice versa. The numbers may be assigned to: (a) permanent virtual circuits; (b) one-way incoming calls; (c) two-way calls; (d) one-way outgoing calls. The term "one-way" refers to the direction in which the call establishment occurs (see Figure 8-5). It is possible that the DTE and DCE may use the same LCN when beginning a communication process. For example, a DTE call request could use the same LCN as a DCE call connection. To minimize this possibility, the network (DCE) looks for a number starting at the low-order end and the DTE starts at the high-order end. If the outgoing call (call request) from a DTE has the same LCN as an incoming call (call connected) from the network DCE, X.25 stipulates that the incoming call be cleared and the call request processed.

The third octet of the X.25 packet header is the packet type identifier octet for nondata packets and sequencing octet for data packets. This field identifies the specific nondata packet types illustrated in Table 8-2.

Figure 8-4(c) illustrates additional fields inside the X.25 packet. For call establishment packets, the DTE addresses and address lengths are included. The addressing convention could use a standard such as X.121 (see Appendix E). The address fields can be in the fourth through nineteenth octet (maximum length) of the call

*: Modulo 128 Uses a Fourth Octet for Extended Sequencing
SS = 01 for Modulo 8
SS = 10 for Modulo 128

(a) Data Packet Header

(b) Nondata Packet Header

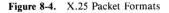

(c) Nondata Packet

P(R):	Receiving Sequence Number	SS: Modulo Bits
M:	Packet Category Indicator	LCGN: Logical Channel Group
P(S):	Sending Sequence Number	FFL: Facilities Field Length
LCN:	Logical Channel Number	TDA: Transmitting DTE Address
Q:	Qualifier Bit	RDA: Receiving DTE Address
D:	Delivery Confirm Bit	TDAL: Transmitting DTE Address Length
A:	Address Bit	RDAL: Receiving DTE Address Length

Figure 8-4. X.25 Packet Formats

request packet. These address fields are used in the call establishment packets to identify the calling and called stations. Thereafter, the network uses the associated logical channel numbers to identify the DTE-to-DTE session. In addition, the facility fields may also be used in the event the DTEs wish to use options contained in the X.25 standard. Finally, user call data may exist in the packet. The maximum limit in the call request packet for user data is 16 octets. This field is useful for entries, such as passwords and accounting information, for the receiving DTE. It is used also for the X.29 protocol (discussed shortly). For certain options, such as fast select, 128 octets of user data are allowed.

The packet header is modified to facilitate the movement of user data through the network. As can be seen from Figure 8-4(a), the third octet of the header, normally reserved for the packet type identifier, is broken into four separate fields:

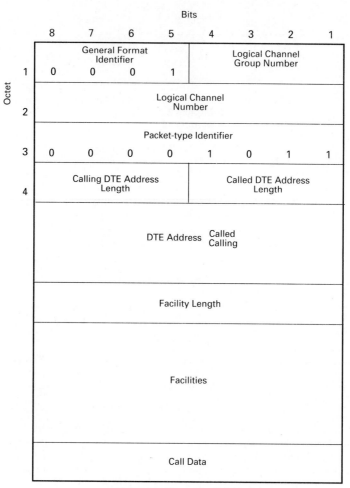

(d) Another View of an X.25 Packet

Figure 8-4. *(Continued)*

Bits   *Description or Value*

1   0

2-4   Packet send sequence [P(S)]

5   More data bit [the M bit]

6-8   Packet receive sequence [P(R)]

     The functions of these fields are as follows: The first bit of 0 identifies the packet as a data packet. Three bits are assigned to a send sequence number [P(S)]. One bit is assigned to an M bit function (more about this later). The three remaining bits are assigned to a receiving sequence number [P(R)]. We will see how all these fields are used shortly.

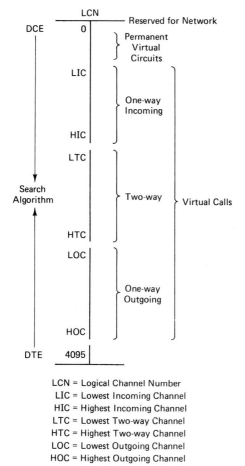

LCN = Logical Channel Number
LIC = Lowest Incoming Channel
HIC = Highest Incoming Channel
LTC = Lowest Two-way Channel
HTC = Highest Two-way Channel
LOC = Lowest Outgoing Channel
HOC = Highest Outgoing Channel

Figure 8-5.   X.25 Logical Channels

Some vendors and the majority of X.25 documents depict the packet format as shown in Figure 8-4(d). The packet contents are the same; the octets are drawn in a staking arrangement, instead of serial sequences as in Figures 8-4(a), (b), and (c).

The sending and receiving numbers are used to coordinate and acknowledge transmissions on each virtual circuit between the DTE and DCE. As the packet travels through the network from node to node, an internal network header is often added to the packet. This header contains sufficient routing information to allow the network nodes to route the traffic to the receiving exit point of the network.

Figure 8-4 shows that the receiving DTE or DCE must know which packet-receiving sequence number to send back to the transmitting device to properly acknowledge the specific packet. These features of X.25 are similar to those found in the second OSI level, data link control (Chapter Four). The use of P(R) and P(S) at the network level requires the P(R) to be one greater than the P(S) in the data packet.

The D Bit

The D-bit facility was added to the 1980 version of X.25. It is used to provide for one of two capabilities. First, when the bit is set to 0, the P(R) value indicates that acknowledgment of receipt of the data packets is by the network. Second, when D is set to 1, the P(R) field is used to provide for an end-to-end acknowledgment of the packet, i.e., from one DTE to the other DTE. The function of the D bit for network acknowledgment or DTE-to-DTE acknowledgment is illustrated in Figure 8-6. With the use of D bit = 1 option, X.25 assumes one of the functions of the transport layer: end-to-end accountability.

The M Bit

The M (more data) bit identifies a related sequence of packets traversing through the network. This capability aids the network and DTEs in preserving the identification of blocks of data when the network divides these blocks into smaller packets. For example, a block of data relating to a data base needs to be presented to the receiving DTE in the proper sequence. This capability is quite important when networks are internetworking each other, a topic discussed later.

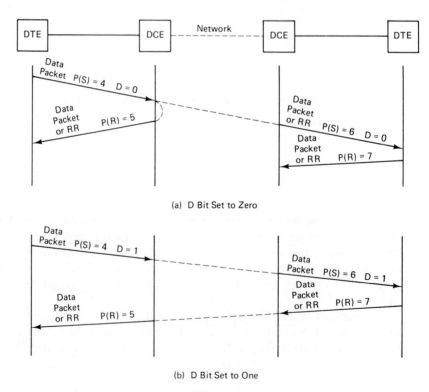

Figure 8-6.   X.25 D Bit

A and B Packets

The combination of the M and D bits provides for two categories in the X.25 standard. These categories are designated as *A packets* and *B packets*. This feature allows a DTE or DCE to indicate a sequence of more than one packet (see Figure 8-7) and allows the network to combine packets. X.25 defines a complete packet sequence as a single category B packet and all preceding, contiguous category A packets (if any).

The category B packet also ends a related sequence of packets. In contrast, category A packets represent the ongoing packets and must be full, with M = 1 and D = 0. Only category B packets can have a D bit set to 1 for an end-to-end acknowledgment. Category A packets and the immediately following B packet can be combined into one packet by the network. B packets themselves must maintain separate entities as separate packets. Combining packets may be useful when different packet sizes are used along the route through a network, or in internetworking when the subnetworks use different packet sizes. It allows the packets to be tracked as a logical whole. If this is the case, the M bit can be used to indicate to the receiving DTE that there is a related sequence in the packet flow.

Table 8-5 shows how X.25 treats M and D bits sent by the source DTE.

As previously stated, one goal of M and D bit specifications is to combine packets. For example, if the receiving DTE's data field is longer than the transmitting DTE's, then the packets within a complete sequence can be combined by the network. To illustrate the concept, consider the flow of packets in Figure 8-7. Packets 1, 2, 3, and 4 are related; the setting of the D bit in packets 1, 2, and 3 indicate they are A packets. Packet 4 is a category B packet, which ends one packet sequence and allows the four packets to be combined. Packets 5, 6, and 7 belong to another sequence, and packet 7 (a category B packet) uses the M bit set to 0 to identify the complete packet sequence.

The Q Bit

This bit is optional and may be used to distinguish between user data and control information. Since one of the PAD standards, X.29, uses the Q bit, we will defer discussion of this bit until we discuss the PAD standards (put in the same format as the Q bit above).

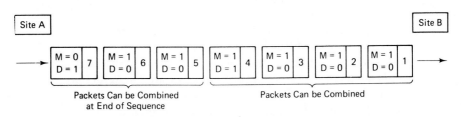

Figure 8-7.   X.25 Category A and B Packets

TABLE 8-5. X.25 PROCESSING OF M AND D BITS FROM SOURCE DTE

Category	M Bit	D Bit	Full?	Combine with Subsequent Packets?
B	0 or 1	0	no	no
B	0	1	no	no
B	1	1	no	no
B	0	0	yes	no
B	0	1	yes	no
B	1	1	yes	no
A	1	0	yes	yes

The A Bit

The A bit facility was added to the 1988 Blue Book release of X.25. It is in the same bit position as the Q bit and is used only for connection management packets, call setups, call releases, and so on. In turn, the Q bit is used only for data packets. The purpose of the A bit is to allow an "escape" from the conventional addresses in X.25 (which are usually X.121). If the A bit is set to 1 in the call set-up packet, it is an indication that other forms of addresses can reside in the address fields. The standards for these address spaces are stipulated in CCITT X.213 and XA and allow other address forms such as E.164 (an ISDN address), telex addresses, and so on to be used during the session.

FLOW CONTROL AND WINDOWS

X.25 uses flow-control techniques and window concepts that are quite similar to those of HDLC, LAPB, SDLC, and other line protocols. As seen in Figure 8-4, a data packet combines two sequence numbers (send and receive) to coordinate the flow of packets between the DTE and DCE. The extended numbering scheme allows for a sequence field to contain a maximum number of 127, using Modulo 128. At the DTE/DCE interface, the data packets are controlled separately for each direction, based on the authorizations coming from the user in the form of the receive sequence numbers or the *Receive Ready* (RR) and *Receive Not Ready* (RNR) control packets.

Why have flow control at the data link and packet levels? Since X.25 multiplexes multiple users onto one physical link, the issuance of a link-level RNR would throttle traffic for *all* logical channel connections on the link. X.25 flow control allows the throttle to be applied more selectively. Moreover, sequencing at the network interface adds an additional level of accountability and security of user data.

The numbering of the packets at this third level proceeds in the same fashion as it does with the second-level HDLC/LAPB standard. The packet sequence number cycles through the entire range of 0 through 7 and returns back to 0 again. If Modulo 128 is used, the sequence number cycles through the entire range of 0 through 127.

The data flow of the D-bit arrangement in Figure 8-6 shows how the sending and receiving sequence numbers are coordinated. X.25 uses the windows established by the Modulo scheme to prevent an overflow of the packets. However, with X.25, a standard window size of 2 is recommended for each direction of flow, although other window sizes can be made available by networks. The value of 2 limits the flow of packets that are outstanding at any one time. This limitation necessitates faster acknowledgment of the packets from the receiver. The limited window size also limits the number of packets that are outstanding in the network at any one time.

X.25 FACILITIES

X.25 contains several facilities. The major facilities are described briefly here. Some of these features are not required for a vendor to be "X.25 certified," yet they provide some very useful functions to end users, and some are considered "essential" to a network. The facilities are requested by specific entries in the call request packet. The facilities are classified as:

1. international facilities [in recommendation X.2 (Appendix E)]
2. CCITT-specified DTE facilities
3. facilities offered by originating public data network (PDN)
4. facilities offered by destination PDN.

On-Line Facility Registration.   This facility permits the DTE to request facilities or to obtain the parameters (values) of the facilities, as understood by the DCE. The DTE/DCE dialogue takes place with the registration packets (see Table 8-2), and the packets indicate whether the facility value can be negotiated.

Extended Packet Numbering.   This facility provides sequence numbering using Modulo 128. In its absence, sequencing is done with Modulo 8 (sequence numbers 1–7). This 1984 addition was deemed important in order to contend with the long propagation problems of satellite channels and radio transmission of ships at sea.

D-Bit Modification.   This facility is intended for use by DTEs developed prior to the introduction of the 1980 D-bit procedure. It allows the DTEs to operate with end-to-end acknowledgment.

Packet Retransmission.   A DTE may request retransmission of one to several data packets from the DCE. The DTE specifies the logical channel number and a value for P(R) in a reject packet. The DCE must then retransmit all packets from P(R) to the next packet it is to transmit for the first time. This facility is similar to the Go-Back-N technique used by the line protocols at the second level of the OSI model.

Incoming Calls Barred. Outgoing Calls Barred.　These two facilities prevent incoming calls from being presented to the DTE or prevent the DCE from accepting outgoing calls from the DTE.

One-Way Logical Channel Outgoing. One-Way Logical Channel Incoming.　These two facilities restrict a logical channel to originating calls only or receiving calls only. These two facilities are similar to Incoming/Outgoing Calls Barred, except they are applicable to *individual* channels.

Nonstandard Default Packet Sizes.　This provides for the selection of default packet sizes that are supported by the network. Registration packets can be used to negotiate the packet sizes.

Nonstandard Default Window Sizes.　This facility allows the window sizes [P(R), P(S)] to be expanded beyond the default size of 2 for *all* calls.

Default Throughput Classes Assignment.　This facility provides for the selection of one of the following throughput rates (in bit/s): 75, 150, 300, 600, 1200, 2400, 4800, 9600, 19200, 48000. Other values can be negotiated.

Flow-Control Parameter Negotiation.　This facility allows the window sizes [P(R), P(S)] to be negotiated on a per-call basis. A DTE often suggests window and packet sizes during call establishment. Some networks require these parameters to be the same for both DTEs.

Throughput Class Negotiation.　This allows the throughput rates to be negotiated on a per-call basis.

Closed User Groups (CUG).　A set of features allow users to form *groups* of DTEs from which access is restricted. The CUG facility provides a measure of security/privacy in a public network. The facility has several options, such as outgoing or incoming access only. Typically, the calling station specifies the required closed user group by the facility fields in the call request packet. If the called station is not a member, the call is rejected by the network.

Bilateral Closed User Groups.　This facility is similar to CUG, but allows access restrictions between *pairs* of DTEs.

Fast Select. Fast Select Acceptance.　These two facilities were discussed earlier in this chapter.

Reverse Charging. Reverse Charging Acceptance.　These facilities allow the packet network charges to accrue to a receiving DTE. It can be used with virtual calls *and* fast selects. The facility is like calling "collect" on a telephone.

Local Charging Prevention.   This facility authorizes the DCE to prevent the establishment of calls for which the subscribing DTE must pay. For example, a DTE may not be allowed to accept reverse charging to its account from *all* calling DTEs.

Network User Identification.   This facility enables the transmitting DTE to provide billing, security, or management information on a per-call basis to the DCE. If invalid, the call is barred.

Charging Information.   This facility requires the DCE to provide the DTE information about the packet session relating to the charges.

RPOA Selection.   This allows a calling DTE to specify one or more recognized private operating agencies (RPOA) to handle the packet session. The RPOA is a carrier. AT&T in the U.S. is an example.

Hunt Group.   This facility distributes incoming calls across a designated grouping of DTE/DCE interfaces. This 1984 addition gives users the ability to select multiple ports on a front-end processor or computer or to select different front-ends or computers at a user site. The facility is quite valuable for organizations with large computing facilities that need flexibility in directing jobs to various, different resources. It is similar in concept to the familiar port selector found in most installations.

Call Redirection.   This facility redirects packet calls when the DTE is out of order, busy, or has requested a call redirection. It allows a call to be rerouted to a backup DTE, which provides the very valuable function of keeping problems and failures isolated from the end user. The call redirection could also permit calls to be redirected to different parts of a country due to time-zone considerations.

Called Line Address Modified Notification.   In the event a call is redirected, this facility informs the calling DTE why the called address in a call connected or clear indication packet is different from the DTE's call request packet.

Call Redirection Notification.   In the event a call is redirected, this facility so informs the alternate DTE and also gives the reason why and the address of the DTE that was originally called.

Transit Delay Selection and Indication.   This last facility permits a DTE to select a transit delay time through the packet network. This feature can be quite valuable to an end user by giving the user some control over response time in the network.

The facilities are invoked by the use of specific fields in an X.25 control packet. Figure 8-4(c) provides a general view of the relationship of the facilities fields to the X.25 packet.

OTHER STANDARDS AND LAYERS

The Pad

As the X.25 recommendation developed in the 1970s, the standards groups recognized that the majority of terminals in operation were unintelligent, asynchronous devices. Obviously, an interface was needed to connect these terminals into packet networks. Consequently, standards were developed to provide for *protocol conversion* and *packet assembly/disassembly* (PAD) functions for the asynchronous terminal. After the initial 1976 draft of the X.25 standard, the standards committees followed up in 1977 with recommendations for three specifications to support X.25 with asynchronous terminal interfaces: X.3, X.28, and X.29. These recommendations have been enhanced with the 1984 release.

The purpose of a PAD is to provide protocol conversion for a user device (DTE) to a public or private network and a complementary protocol conversion at the receiving end of the network. The goal is to furnish a transparent service to the user DTEs. While X.3 and its companion standards, X.28 and X.29, address only asynchronous devices (which constitute many of the devices in operation today), many vendors offer other PAD services to support protocols such as BSC and SDLC. These nonasynchronous PAD capabilities do not fall within the framework of X.3, X.28, and X.29.

The PAD standards provide for several configurations. Figure 8-8(a) shows a connection between user non-packet DTE and a packet-mode DTE. Notice that the PAD (X.3) and X.28 are needed only for the asynchronous DTE. Figure 8-8(b) illustrates another common example in which two asynchronous DTEs wish to communicate with each other. Both DTEs use X.3 and X.28. The last example, Figure 8-8(c), illustrates a PAD located outside the network, perhaps at a user premises. In this situation, the PAD appears as an actual X.25 device to the network. The reader should also note that X.29 is used to support communications between a PAD and an X.25-mode DTE or between two PADs.

X.3. X.3 provides a set of 22 parameters the PAD uses to identify and service each terminal communicating with it. When a connection to a PAD from the DTE is established, the PAD parameters are used to determine how the PAD communicates with the user DTE. The user also has the option of altering the parameters after its log-on to the PAD. Each of the 22 parameters consists of a reference number and parameter values. These parameters and references are explained in Table 8-6. The parameters do not lend themselves to interpretation easily. A few examples are provided here to explain how the PAD parameters could be used.

Parameter 3 = 0   Instructs the PAD to forward only a full packet.

Parameter 3 = 2   Instructs the PAD to forward a packet upon the terminal sending a carriage-return character.

Parameter 6 = 1   A terminal user wishes to receive the PAD service signals (useful during troubleshooting).

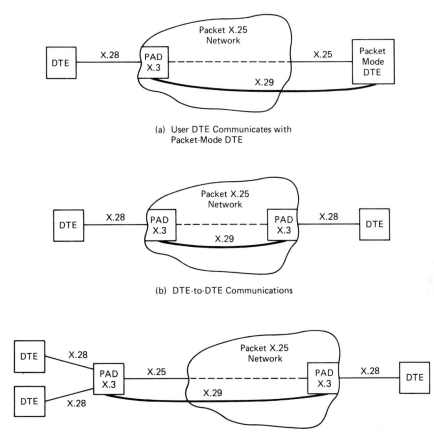

(a) User DTE Communicates with
Packet-Mode DTE

(b) DTE-to-DTE Communications

(c) A PAD Outside the Network

Figure 8-8. PADs and X.25

Parameter 7 = 1   Upon receiving a break character from the terminal, the
PAD sends an interrupt packet to the receiving DTE.

X.28.   This standard defines the procedures to control the data flow between
the nonpacket mode user terminal and the PAD. Upon receipt of an initial connection from the user DTE, the PAD establishes a connection and provides services
according to X.28. As illustrated in Table 8-7(a), the user DTE evokes X.28 commands to the PAD, which requests an X.25 virtual call to a remote DTE. The PAD
is then responsible for transmitting the appropriate X.25 call-request packet. The
table summarizes the procedures for the following:

- the establishment of the path
- the initialization of service
- the exchange of data
- the exchange of control information.

TABLE 8-6.   PAD PARAMETERS

X.3 Parameter Reference Number	Description	Values
1 PAD recall	Escape from data-transfer mode to command mode	0 not possible 1 DLE character 32–125 user-defined characters
2 Echo	Controls the echo of characters sent by the terminal	0 no echo 1 echo (default)
3 Data forwarding	Defines the characters to be interpreted by the PAD as a signal to forward data	0 full packet only 1 alphanumerics 2 carriage return (default) 4 ESC, BEL, ENQ, ACK 6 carriage return, ESC, BEL, ENQ, ACK 8 DEL, CAN, DC2 16 ETX, EOT 18 carriage return, EOT, ETX 32 HT, LT, VT, FF 126 all other characters in col. 1 & 2 of IA5
4 Idle timer delay	Selects a time interval of terminal activity as a signal to forward data	0 no timer 1–255 delay value in twentieths of a second
5 Ancillary device control	Allows the PAD to control the flow of terminal data using X-ON/X-OFF characters	0 not operational 1 X-ON (DC1)/X-OFF (DC3)—data transfer 2 X-ON/X-OFF—data transfer and command
6 Control of PAD service signals	Allows the terminal to receive PAD messages	0 no service signals 1 transmit service signals 5 transmit service and prompt signals 8–15 network-dependent format service signals
7 Operation of the PAD on receipt of break signal from DTE	Defines PAD action when a break signal is received from the terminal	0 no action 1 interrupt packet 2 reset packet 4 indication of break 5 interrupt & indication of break 8 escape from data-transfer state 16 discard output to start/stop DTE 21 1 + 4 + 16 combined
8 Discard output	Controls the discarding of data pending output to a terminal	0 normal data delivery 1 discard output to start/stop DTE
9 Padding after carriage return	Controls PAD insertion of padding characters after a carriage return is sent to the terminal	0 no padding 1–7 number of padding character inserted

TABLE 8-6. *(Continued)*

X.3 Parameter Reference Number	Description	Values	
10 Line folding	Specifies whether the PAD should fold the output line to the terminal	0 no line folding 1–255 number of characters per line	
11 Binary speed of DTE	Indicates the speed of the terminal	0 110 bit/s 1 134.5 bit/s 2 300 bit/s 3 1200 bit/s 4 600 bit/s 5 75 bit/s 6 150 bit/s 7 1800 bit/s 8 200 bit/s 9 100 bit/s	10 50 bit/s 11 75/1200 bit/s 12 2400 bit/s 13 4800 bit/s 14 9600 bit/s 15 19200 bit/s 16 4800 bit/s 17 56000 bit/s 18 64000 bit/s
12 Flow control of the PAD	Allows the terminal to flow-control data being transmitted by the PAD	0 not operational 1 use X-ON (DC1) and X-OFF (DC3)	
13 Linefeed insertion	Controls PAD insertion of linefeed after a carriage return is sent to the terminal	0 None 1 after carriage return to DTE 2 after carriage return from DTE 4 after echoed carriage return 5 values 1 + 4 6 values 2 + 4 7 values 1 + 2 + 4 (data transfer only)	
14 Linefeed padding	Controls PAD insertion of padding characters after a linefeed is sent to the terminal	0 none 1–7 number of pads inserted (data transfer only) 8–255 optional extension	
15 Editing	Controls whether editing by PAD is available during data-transfer mode	0 off 1 on	
16 Character delete	Selects character used to signal character delete	127 DEL character other characters from IA5 (optional)	
17 Line delete	Selects character used to signal line delete	24 CAN character other characters from IA5 (optional)	
18 Line display	Selects character used to signal line display	18 DC2 character other characters from IA5 (optional)	
19 Editing PAD service signals	Controls the format of the editing PAD service signals	0 no editing 1 editing for printing terminals 2 editing for display terminals 8 editing using characters from range 32–126	

TABLE 8-6. *(Continued)*

X.3 Parameter Reference Number	Description	Values
20 Echo mask	Selects the characters which are not echoed to the terminal when echo (Parameter 2) is enabled	0 all characters echoed 1 no echo of carriage return 2 no echo of LF 4 no echo of VT, HT, FF 8 no echo of BEL, BS 16 no echo of ESC, ENQ 32 no echo of ACK, NAK, STX, SOH, EOT, ETB, ETX 64 no echo of editing characters 128 no echo of all characters in col. 1 & 2 of IA5 plus DEL
21 Parity treatment	Controls the checking and generation of parity on characters from/to the terminal	0 no parity detection or generation 1 parity checking 2 parity generation 3 value 1 + 2
22 Page wait	Specifies the number of lines to be displayed at one time	0 no page wait 23 number of linefeed characters before waiting (mandatory value); other optional values

X.28 requires the PAD to return a response when a terminal issues a command to it. [These signals are summarized in Table 8-7(b).] It also specifies that two profiles can be defined for providing service to the user DTE. The *transparent* profile means the servicing PAD is transparent to both DTEs—the DTEs "think" they have a direct virtual connection to each other. In this situation, the remote DTE is responsible for some PAD functions, such as error checking. The *simple* profile makes use of the fully defined X.3 standard and the parameter functions to satisfy the user DTE requests.

X.3 offers a user the flexibility to tailor additional characteristics for a particular terminal. This is provided by the PROF PAD command signal (explained in Table 8-7). The PROF command could give packet network vendors additional flexibility in tailoring a PAD to support interfaces for more protocols, such as the BSC and SDLC data link controls.

A typical X.28 command and service signal is as follows:

SET 3:0, 6:1

This means: set PAD parameter 3 to 0 and PAD parameter 6 to 1.

X.29.   This standard provides directions for the PAD and a remote station to exchange control information on an X.25 call. In the context of X.29, a remote station refers to either a PAD or an X.25 DTE—X.29 allows the exchange of information to occur at any time, either at a data-transfer phase or any other phase of the virtual call.

TABLE 8-7(a).   PAD COMMAND SIGNALS

PAD Command Format	Description
STAT	Request status information regarding a virtual call connected to the DTE
CLR	Clear a virtual call
PAR? (Parameters)	Request the current values of specified parameters
SET? (Parameters)	Request changing or setting of values of specified parameters; Request current values of specified parameters
PROF (Identifier)	Give to PAD a standard set of parameter values
RESET	Reset the virtual call
INT	Transmit an Interrupt packet
SET (Parameters)	Set or change parameter values
Selection PAD	Set up a virtual call

TABLE 8-7(b).   PAD SERVICE SIGNALS

PAD Service Format	Description
Linefeed	Acknowledgment of a command signal
COM	Indication of Call Connected
RESET DTE	Remote DTE has reset the call
RESET ERR	Call has been reset due to a local procedure error
RESET NC	Call has been reset due to network congestion
ERROR	PAD command is in error
PAR $<n:n>$	Response to set or read PAD command; n indicates the parameter number and parameter value in decimal
PAR $<n:INV>$	Response to an invalid parameter setting request in a set or set and read PAD command.
ENGAGED	Response to "STATUS" PAD command when a call is established
FREE	Response to "STATUS" PAD command when a call is not established

As introduced earlier in the chapter, the X.25 Q-bit sequence controls certain functions of X.29. The Q bit (or data-qualified bit) is contained in the header of the data packet. It is used by the remote DTE to distinguish a packet containing user data (Q = 0) from one containing PAD control information (Q = 1). X.29 is quite useful when a host computer needs to change the X.3 operating parameters at the terminals communicating with it. By sending an X.29 control packet to a PAD (Q = 1), the host can "reconfigure" its attached workstations.

X.29 defines seven control messages, called PAD messages. These messages are as follows:

Set: Changes an X.3 value.

Read: Reads an X.3 value.

Set and Read: Changes an X.3 value and requires PAD to confirm the change.

Parameters Indication: Returned in response to above commands.

Invitation to Clear: Allows X.25 call clear by remote DTE; PAD clears to local terminal.

Indication of Break: PAD indicates terminal has transmitted a break.

Error: Response to an invalid PAD message.

PAD: Packet Formats and Packet Flow

The PAD packet is similar in format to the conventional X.25 packet format (see Figure 8-9). The three-octet header is required, after which follows a one-octet control field and the PAD parameter numbers and values.

To summarize the PAD, Figure 8-10 depicts states and state transitions between a user DTE and a PAD. This illustration shows a call-establishment and data-transfer possibility with parameter 6 set to 1. (Table 8-6 explains parameter 6.) The states perform the following functions:

1—Active: DTE and DCE exchange 1 across interface.

2—Service Request: Enables PAD to detect data rate and code used by DTE and to select the initial profile.

3A—DTE Waiting: Interface is in a waiting state.

4—Service Ready: State entered after PAD transmits PAD identification signal.

5—PAD Waiting: PAD waits for data or control signals.

6—PAD Command: State entered from various wait states. Allows commands to be transmitted to PAD.

7—Connection in Progress: State entered as PAD initiates a network connection.

8—Service Signals: Allows all service signals with this state.

9—Data Transfer: Allows transfer of data across interface.

10—Waiting for Command: State entered to allow DTE to receive PAD command or data.

The Transport Layer

The fourth layer of the OSI communications network model is the transport layer. It sits just above the network layer. The International Organization for Standardization (ISO) approved the transport layer on June 25, 1984, and it is now implemented in many vendor products. The layer has been under development for several years

Figure 8-9.   X.25/PAD Packet

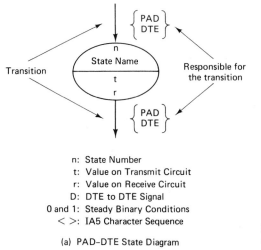

n: State Number
t: Value on Transmit Circuit
r: Value on Receive Circuit
D: DTE to DTE Signal
0 and 1: Steady Binary Conditions
< >: IA5 Character Sequence

Figure 8-10. PAD/DTE
Communications (parameter 6 set to 1)

(a) PAD-DTE State Diagram

and was eagerly (even anxiously) awaited by some members of the data communications community. Its importance lies in the fact that it gives the end user several options as to how the network (below it) serves the user.

The transport layer requires the end user to specify a *quality of service* (QOS) from the network. (The transport layer must know the types of services offered by the network below it.) Upon receiving the user's request for a quality of service, the transport layer selects a class of protocol to match the user's quality of service request. Even though a variety of networks may exist (connection-oriented, connectionless, etc.), the transport layer ensures a consistent level of service is provided to the end user.

The quality of network services rests on the types of networks available to the end user and the transport layer. CCITT, ISO, and ECMA have defined three types of networks.

Type A   Network provides acceptable error rates and acceptable rates of signalled failures (acceptable quality).

Type B   Network provides for acceptable error rates, but an unacceptable rate for signalled failures (unacceptable signalled errors).

Type C   Network connection provides an error rate not acceptable to user (unreliable).

The idea of defining network types is simply to recognize that different qualities of networks exist, yet give the user a consistent level of service, regardless of the network type. For example, a Type C network could be one in which the transmissions might take place in connectionless mode. On the other hand, a Type B network would likely be one using the full X.25 functions and capabilities. Remember that X.25 conditions, such as restarts and clears, do not provide for recovery of the lost data packets in the network. The layer also gives the user options to obtain network services on a per-connection basis at a minimum cost.

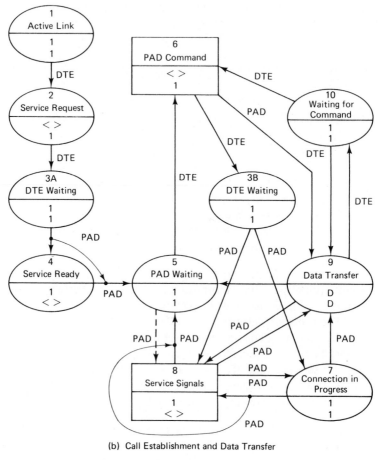

(b) Call Establishment and Data Transfer

Note: Check X.3 specifications for more detail

Figure 8-10. *(Continued)*

Given that different kinds of networks exist, the transport layer allows the user to establish the following quality of service parameters (QOS):

- throughput
- accuracy
- reliability
- transit delay
- priorities
- protection
- multiplexing
- flow control
- error detection
- segmenting.

The transport-layer service definition uses *primitives* to specify the services to be provided through the transport and network layers. The parameters associated with each primitive action (see Table 8-8) provide the specific actions and events to be provided by the layers. During the connection-establishment phase in the network, the characteristics of the connection are negotiated between the end users and the transport layer. The primitives and the parameters of the primitives provide the negotiation. It is possible that no connection will be made if the network or an end user cannot provide or agree upon the requested quality of service.

After the parameters are accepted between the two negotiating parties, data transfer is provided at one site from the transport layer through the bottom three layers and the channel. At the remote site, the data pass through the three layers into the transport layer. Figure 8-11 illustrates the use of the transport-layer primitives to establish and disestablish transport-layer sessions.

As stated earlier, the transport layer is responsible for selecting an appropriate protocol to support the quality of service (QOS) parameters established by the user. Since the transport layer knows the characteristics of a network (Types A, B, or C), the layer can choose five classes of protocol procedures to support the QOS request from the user:

Class 0 Simple class

Class 1 Basic error recovery class

Class 2 Multiplexing class

Class 3 Error-recovery class

Class 4 Error-detection and recovery class

Class 0 protocol provides for a very simple transport connection establishment to support a Type A network. Class 0 provides for a connection-oriented support during both the network connection and release phases. It does *not* provide for any support of user transfer data during connection establishment. This protocol is able to detect and signal protocol errors. If the network layer signals an error to the transport layer, the transport layer releases the connection to its network layer. The end user is informed about the disconnection.

TABLE 8-8. TRANSPORT LAYER PRIMITIVES

Primitive Name	Type of Primitive	Parameters to Primitive
T-Connect	Request indication	To transport address; from transport address; expedited data option; quality of service; TS-user data
T-Connect	Response confirmation	Responding address; quality of service; expedited data option; TS-user data
T-Data	Request indication	TS-user data
T-Expedited Data	Request indication	TS-user data
T-Disconnect	Request	TS-user data
T-Disconnect	Indication	Disconnect reason, TS-user data

T = Transport Layer   TS = Transport Layer Service

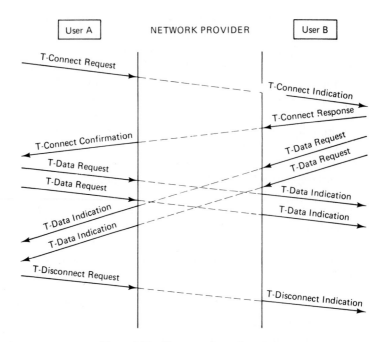

Figure 8-11. Transport Layer Sequences

The Class 1 protocol is associated with networks, such as an X.25 packet network. The Class 1 protocol provides for a segmenting of data, if necessary; retention of all data and acknowledgment; and resynchronization of the session in the event of an X.25 network reset indication packet. The protocol is also required to support expedited data transfer. It responds to disconnect requests and responds to protocol errors. It also is responsible for resynchronization and performing reassignments in the event of a network failure.

It is sequenced to aid in ACKs/NAKs and error recovery. The ACKs release the copies of the data units at the transmitting sites. Class 1 also provides for either user acknowledgment or network acknowledgment. It should be emphasized that Class 1 can recover only from errors that are signalled from the network. It does *not* use timers to detect delays or nondeliverables.

Class 2 protocol allows a multiplexing of several transport connections into a single X.25 network session. It also provides for flow control to prevent congestion from occuring at the end DTE sites. Class 2 provides neither error detection nor recovery. If an X.25 reset or clear packet is detected, this protocol disconnects the session, and the user is informed. The Class 2 protocol is designed to be used over very reliable Type A networks. The flow control provided in this protocol uses the familiar concept of windows (described in previous chapters). User data can be transmitted in the connection-request data unit.

The Class 3 protocol provides for the services included in the Class 2 structure. It also provides recovery from a network failure *without* requiring the notification of the user. The user data are retained until the receiving transport layer sends back a positive acknowledgment of the data. This class has a very useful mechanism to retransmit data. The packets in transit through a network are given a maximum "lifetime" through timers. All data requiring a response are timed. If the timer expires before an acknowledgment is received, retransmission or other recovery procedures can be invoked. The Class 3 protocol assumes a Type B network service.

The Class 4 protocol includes the flow control functions of Classes 2 and 3. Like Class 3, expedited data are allowed *and* the ACKs are sequenced. This protocol allows for "frozen" references—upon a connection release, the corresponding references cannot be reused, since the network layer could still be using the references.

Class 4 is used when a network could lose or corrupt data. It uses several sophisticated mechanisms to check for errors, sequence number problems, and lost packets. It is the only transport class that retransmits data when a timer expires and resequences data at the receiving end. Because it retains a copy of the data until they are acknowledged by the receiver, transport layer Class 4 can recover from network failure.

Due to the many functions provided by Class 4, it might be assumed that the protocol is inefficient. Such is not the case. Its functionality is not inefficient if the end-to-end timers are implemented properly.

Table 8-9 summarizes the five classes of protocols and their respective functions. Consult CCITT X.224 for more detail and for some variations of this table.

INTERNETWORKING

As networks proliferate and grow in functionality, end users often need to access more than one network to obtain a service. For example, a terminal that normally uses network A may need to access a data base at a computer that subscribes to network B. Thus, the end-to-end service requires that networks A and B be interconnected. This feature is called *internetworking*.

The ECMA and ISO divide the network layer into three functional groups. At the top is the *subnetwork independence convergence function* (SNICF), which provides the relay and routing services for internetworking. This sublayer contains the internetwork protocols to support data and transfer between networks. The middle group is the *subnetwork dependent convergence function* (SNDCF), which may be used to bring the interconnecting networks up to a level needed for the interconnection. The lowest sublayer is the *subnetwork access function* (SNAF), which contains the services relevant to each of the interconnecting networks, for example, an X.25 network.

At the broadest level, internetworking by SNICF is achieved by a *gateway* or a *relay*. With the gateway concept, the internetworking control and routing/address data are provided and used only by the end users and the gateways. The connecting networks do not provide this data; they carry the data transparently through their networks from the end users through the gateways. The subnetworks treat this information as end-user data. The gateway does not care about the internal routing or the organization within the lower-level networks, which remain transparent to the

TABLE 8-9.   TRANSPORT LAYER PROTOCOL FUNCTIONS

Protocol Function	Variant	Protocol Class				
		0	1	2	3	4
Assignment to network connection		X	X	X	X	X
TPDU transfer		X	X	X	X	X
DT TPDU length and segmenting		X	X	X	X	X
Concatenation and separation			X	X	X	X
Connection establishment		X	X	X	X	X
Connection refusal		X	X	X	X	X
Release	Implicit	X				
	Explicit		X	X	X	X
Implicit termination		X		X		
DT TPDU numbering	Normal		X	X	X	X
	Extended			O	O	O
Expedited data transfer	Normal		X	X	X	X
	Expedite		O			
Reassignment			X		X	
Reassignment after failure			X		X	
Retention until acknowledgment of TPDUs	Confirmation		O			
	Receipt AK		X		X	X
Resynchronization			X		X	
Multiplexing and demultiplexing				X	X	X
Explicit flow control						
With				X	X	X
Without		X	X	O		
Checksum (use of)						X
(non-use of)		X	X	X	X	O
Frozen references			X		X	X
Retransmission on timeout						X
Resequencing						X
Inactivity control						X
Treatment of protocol errors		X	X	X	X	X
Splitting and recombining						X

TPDU = Transport Protocol Data Unit   O = optional

gateway. It should be noted that the gateway performs routing decisions, and as such has the necessary logic to choose appropriate output channels and possibly alternate networks.

The relay SNICF is more limited than a gateway SNICF. In this protocol, the interconnecting networks are aware of the control and routing addresses and usually generate them. They are responsible for maintaining an awareness of the global addresses and the networks that are interconnected to each other. As a consequence, the relay SNICF accepts routing requests that have been determined by a subnetwork to be at a destination address in other networks. The relay SNICF then routes the data unit according to the furnished address.

CONNECTIONLESS-MODE NETWORKS

During the past few years many vendors and standards organizations have published specifications for connectionless-mode network service (see Chapter Two for a discussion of connectionless service). These protocols reside in the network layer of the OSI model. Usually, the Class 4 transport layer protocol resides above the connectionless network layer to provide end-to-end service.

Connectionless-mode systems are frequently used for connecting networks through the use of the *Internetwork Protocol* (IP). The network layer provides the necessary routing functions between networks and the transport layer provides end-to-end reliability. Since the transport layer provides this support, internetwork accountability is not a prime concern. In fact, connection-oriented internetworking often results in degraded performance due to the additional overhead of network-to-network (called hop-to-hop) accountability and services.

The IP rests over the data link layer and provides network-to-network communications independent of the specific networks' functions. IP requires very little from each of the networks. It even can be operated over a telephone line that uses a data-link protocol like HDLC (LLC, LAPB, etc.).

The network layer protocols are not affected by IP. It simply accepts the network *protocol data unit* (PDU) and transports it to the next network within its own *protocol data unit* (IPDU). The IPDU contains the necessary routing information and addresses to move the data through all hops to the final destination.

X.75

X.25 is designed for users to communicate through one network. However, users operating on two separate networks often need to establish communications to share resources and exchange data. X.75 is designed to meet this need. It also is used within a network to connect the packet exchanges to each other.

The object of X.75 is to allow internetworking of X.25-based networks. To accomplish this, X.75 provides a relay for a user to communicate through multiple networks with another user. The standard assumes the networks use X.25 procedures.

Figure 8-12 shows how X.25 and X.75 operate. A user in network C logs on to a PAD and establishes an X.25 session with the network. Network C recognizes that user X wishes to communicate with DTE Z in another network. By previous arrangement, network C establishes a logical session with user Z's parent X.25 network, B. Network B completes the connection between DTE X and DTE Z by establishing an X.25 session with user Z. X.75 remains transparent to each user; the PAD or DTE-to-DCE interface is still X.28 or X.25, respectively.

X.75 is quite similar to X.25. It has the features described earlier with X.25, such as switched virtual circuits, logical channel groups, logical channels, and several of the control packets depicted in Table 8-2. The architecture is divided into physical, link, and packet levels, with X.75 placed above X.25 in the network layer. In addition, X.75 assumes the following standards are used by the participating networks:

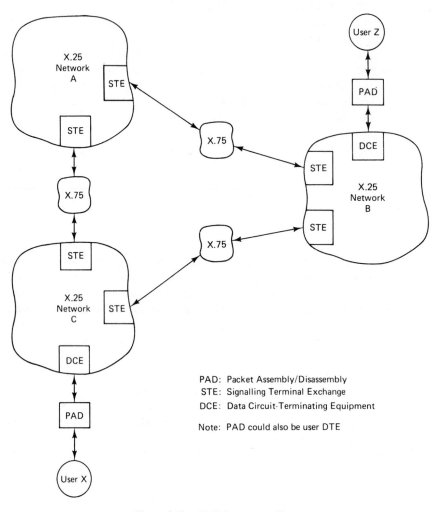

Figure 8-12.   X.75 Internetworking

X.1   User classes of service

X.92   Logical links A1, G1

X.180   Administrative arrangements for international closed user groups

An overview of these recommended standards can be found in Appendix E.

X.75 defines the operation of international packet-switched services. It describes how two terminals are connected logically by an international link while each terminal is operating within its own packet-mode data network. X.75 uses a specific term for the network interface—*signaling terminal exchange* (STE).

Figure 8-13 shows some key features of X.75. The STE contains two major functions—packet-signaling procedures and packet-transfer procedures. The signaling procedures cover the physical level of the ISO model. Like X.25, the physical

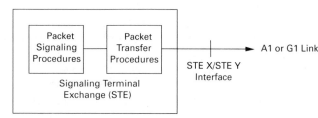

A1:   Link between Two Adjacent Gateway Data-Switching Exchanges
      (DSEs) in an International Connection
G1:   Link Between a Source Gateway DSE and a Destination Gateway
      DSE in an International Connection
STE X: STE of International Exchange
STE Y: STE of Other International Exchange

Figure 8-13.   X.75 Signaling Terminal, Interfaces, and Links

level can be implemented with X.21 or appropriate V-series recommendations (such as V.24). X.75 requires the signaling to be performed at 64 kbit/s. (An optional rate is 48 kbit/s.) The physical link is assumed to be an A1 or G1 data link in conformance with recommendation X.92 (see Appendix E).

The STE uses the same packet format that is created by the X.25 subnetwork. It simply modifies the logical channel number to obtain an STE-to-STE dialogue. The STEs then relay the traffic between the interconnecting networks. The X.75 STEs perform no encapsulation of the X.25 header; it is reused. Also, the STE-to-STE interface is like the X.25 DTE-to-DCE or X.28 DTE-to-PAD interfaces: it has local significance only.

X.75 adds a network-level utilities field for the STE/STE session and does not use the X.25 packet call indication, clear indication, and call accepted indication, since they are relevant only to the DTE-to-DCE interfaces.

The second level of X.75 uses the HDLC subset LAPB. (X.75 does not support LAP.) The X.75 STE also uses the LAPB frame-reject response (FRMR) to note three additional situations beyond conventional LAPB (see Chapter Four for LAPB FRMR discussions):

1. Receipt of a LAPB supervisory frame with an F bit set to 1.
2. The receipt of an unexpected, unnumbered acknowledgment (UA) or disconnected mode (DM) response.
3. The receipt of an invalid N(S) field.

The X.25 and X.75 link levels also support the *multilink procedure* (MLP). This procedure provides for the use of multiple links between STEs. MLP establishes the rules for link transmission and link resequencing for delivery to/from the multiple links. Multilink operations allow the use of parallel communications channels between STEs in such a manner that they appear as one channel with a greater capacity.

The multilink operation also provides for more reliability than can be achieved on a single channel. MLP sends the data across a single link through LAPB. If the link is faulty or producing excessive retransmissions, MLP can place the traffic onto another single link in its MLP group. It also can transmit multiple copies of a data unit across more than one link. The receiving MLP entity discards duplicate copies.

Multilink procedures exist at the upper part of the data link level (see Figure 8-14). The X.25 network layer perceives it is connected to a single link, and the LAPB single links operate as if they are connected directly to the network layer. MLP is responsible for flow control between layers 2 and 3, as well as resequencing the data units for delivery to the network layer. The network layer then operates with a higher bandwidth in the data link layer.

The X.75 HDLC-oriented command and responses are depicted in Table 8-10. The commands and responses are identical to LAPB, the data link level supporting X.25.

COMMUNICATIONS BETWEEN THE LAYERS

This section provides an example of the relationships and communications between the physical, data link, network, and transport layers. Figure 8-15 is used to provide this integrated view of the data communications network. The figure is divided into six parts to facilitate understanding the process.

The transport layer sends a connection request to the network layer, as shown in Figure 8-15(a). The network layer responds by sending a connection request to the data link layer, which, in turn, sends an activate request to the physical layer. These primitives are requesting a link be established to provide a path for a user dialogue. As this request passes through the network and data link layers, the layer states change from disconnect to pending. At the physical layer, X.21 logic turns the C channel on. (Recall from earlier discussions that the X.21 C channel is similar to EIA-232-D pin 4 and the CCITT standard V.24 circuit 105.)

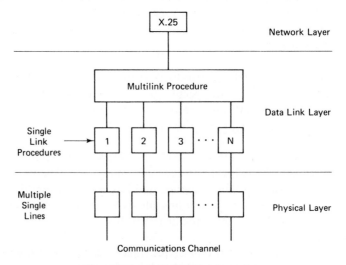

Figure 8-14.   X.75 Multilink Procedures

TABLE 8-10. X.75 COMMANDS AND RESPONSES

Format	Command	Response	Control Field 1	2	3	4	5	6	7	8
Information transfer	(Information)		0	N(S)			P	N(R)		
Supervisory	RR (receive ready)	RR (receive ready)	1	0	0	0	P/F	N(R)		
	RNR (receive not ready)	RNR (receive not ready)	1	0	1	0	P/F	N(R)		
	REJ (reject)	REJ (reject)	1	0	0	1	P/F	N(R)		
Unnumbered	SABM (set asynchronous balanced mode)		1	1	1	1	P	1	0	0
	DISC (disconnect)		1	1	0	0	P	0	1	0
		FRMR (frame reject)	1	1	1	0	F	0	0	1
		UA (unnumbered acknowledgment)	1	1	0	0	F	1	1	0
		DM (disconnected mode)	1	1	1	1	F	0	0	0

The signal is transmitted through the network (the actions within the network are not described in this scenario). The signal arrives at receiving site B, and the physical layer activates the X.21 I circuit. (The X.21 I circuit is similar to EIA-232-D pin 5 and the V.24 circuit 106.) The physical layer creates a physical activate indication; the data link layer immediately turns this to a physical activate response. Site B X.21 then activates its C pin and transmits the signal to the network. The signal is received at site A, and the physical level I pin is turned on with a physical activate confirmation indication.

It is possible that the physical link can be established without the signals from the upper layers. For example, a link start-up procedure at the beginning of the business day might initiate the physical level without regard to higher level requests.

The effect of the signals in Figure 8-12(a) can be seen in Figure 8-15(b). The network layer is still not involved in any transport of packets at this time. The reader will see when going through these figures that first the physical level is activated, then the data link level, next the network level, and finally the transport level. Figure 8-15(b) shows the data link layer moving from a pending state to a data state. The logic at the data link level starts the process by sending a *Set Asynchronous Balanced Mode* (SABM) command to the network. This is accepted by the physical layer and transported across the physical layer T channel. (The X.21 T channel is similar to the EIA-232-D pin 2 and the V.24 circuit 103). The data are transported across the network to receiving site B; they are passed through the physical layer across the R circuit. (The R circuit for X.21 is similar to EIA-232-D pin 3 or V.24 circuit 104.) The SABM command is passed to site B's data-link layer, which in turn acknowledges the command with an unnumbered acknowledgment (UA). This is

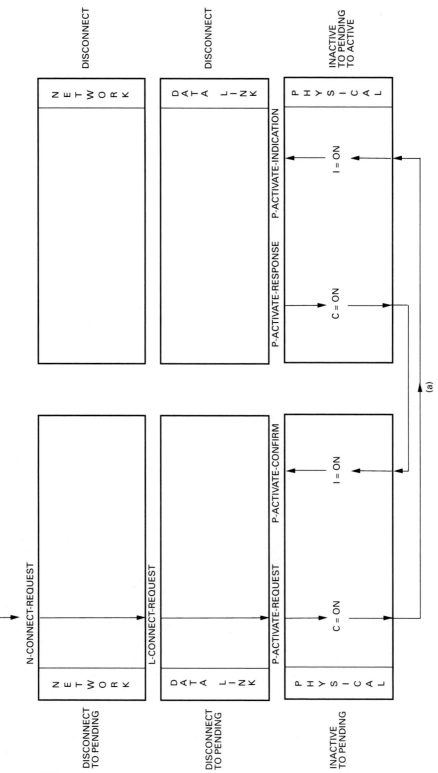

Figure 8-15. Communications Between Layers

216

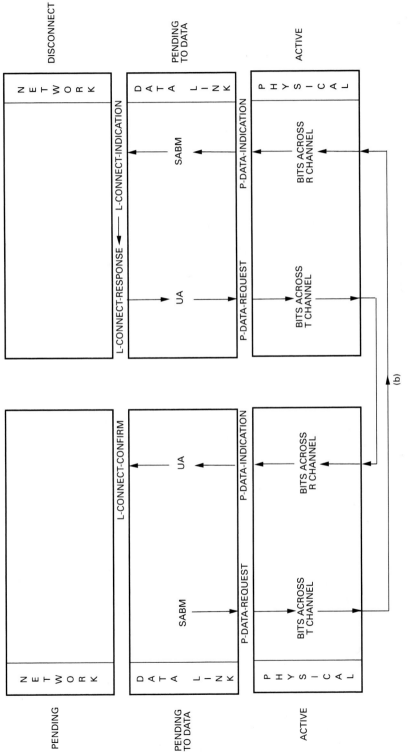

Figure 8-15. *(Continued)*

217

passed back down through the layers across the network, where it is received by site A's data link layer, which then initiates a link-connection confirmation signal.

The data-link start-up may be part of an operational procedure between the user site and the network node. The link is established after the physical level is operational. Thereafter, a path is available for the transmission of packets and user data. The SABM is not required for each packet transmission; the link normally stays active to accept the packets as they are sent to the data link layer.

Now that the data link layers have been activated between the two sites, the link-connection confirmation sent to the packet layer in the previous illustration enables the packet layer to initiate a call request packet from the X.25 logic [Figure 8-15(c)]. The call request is sent with a logical channel number (LCN) of 75 in the packet header. The packet is transmitted to the LAPB data link layer where the packet is placed into the I field of the LAPB frame. The LAPB sending and receiving sequence numbers are established in this illustration; the sending sequence number is set to 0 to indicate the first frame sent across the link. The frame is transported through site A's layers, and through the network to receiving site B. It is then passed to the data link layer, which performs an error check. The error check indicates the transmission is correct.

The packet is then passed up to the network layer, where it is received as an incoming call packet, with a logical channel number of 106. The network layer sends a network connection indication signal to the transport layer and responds with a call accepted packet (issued from X.25). This packet is passed to the data link layer, which places it inside an information frame. The data link layer sets the receive sequence field to 1 to acknowledge the frame sent to it from site A. The frame is transported across the physical layers in the network. It is received at site A's data link layer, which performs an error check. The error check indicates the transmission occurred without problems. The packet is then passed to the network layer, which receives it as a call connect packet in the X.25 logic.

Let us pause at this point and review some aspects of our scenario. The sequence of events occurring in Figure 8-15 conforms precisely to the principles of connection-oriented networks discussed in several sections of this book. For example, Figure 2-4 and Figures 3-1, 3-3, and 3-4 depict the sequence of events we are explaining in this section. Also, Chapters Four and Eight describe the sequences that occur at the LAPB and X.25 levels. You may wish to review these sections of the book if concepts illustrated in this summary seem unfamiliar.

All layers are now in a data, or active, state. Figure 8-15(d) shows that (at last) a packet with user data is transmitted. Actually, this might not be user data; it could be control data from the transport layer. However, for purposes of brevity, we assume the packet contains user data.

Notice the packet transmitted from the network layer at site A contains sequence numbers. These are labeled $P(S)$ and $P(R)$ to distinguish them from the data link sequence numbers, which are labeled $N(S)$ and $N(R)$. As stated several times in this chapter, both layers have the ability to perform sequencing, which is necessary to provide for accountability among peer layers. For instance, if a problem occurs at the data link layer, it normally does not necessitate retransmitting any units at the levels above. Rather, the data link layer provides the NAK and a retransmittal occurs

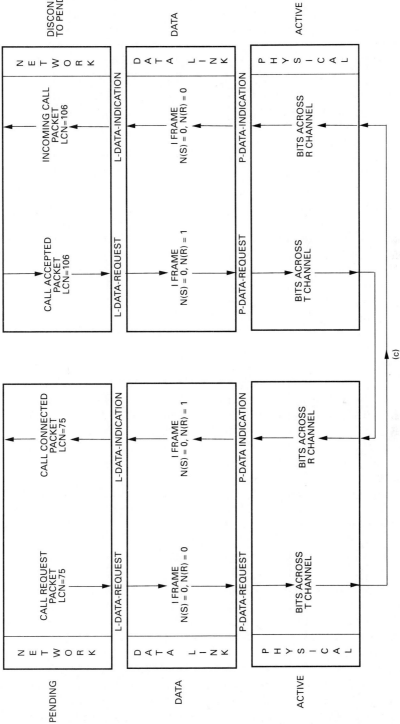

Figure 8-15. *(Continued)*

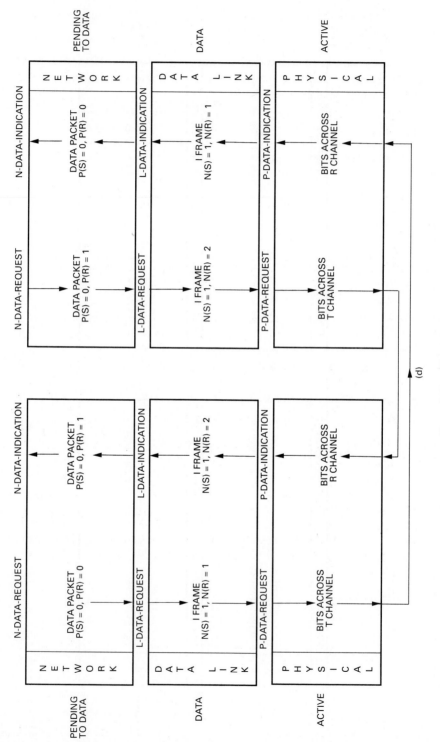

Figure 8-15. *(Continued)*

at this layer without disturbing the packet sequencing at the network layer. This process will become evident in Figure 8-15(e).

Continuing our discussion in Figure 8-15(d), the packet is passed (at site A) to the data link layer's LAPB. Notice that site A's LAPB sequence numbers are coordinated with site B's LAPB. [Examine Figure 8-15(c) to see the relationships of the sending and receiving sequence numbers as they occur in Figure 8-15(d).] The frame is transmitted to site B; LAPB examines it for errors and transmits the data packet to the network layer. Likewise, the network layer appends the proper sequence numbers and transports the data out of the network layer at B.

The sequence numbers at the network level are relevant to the network level only, and the sequence numbers at the data link level pertain only to the data link level. This concept is fundamental to understanding the relationship of the network layer to the data link layer. Since multiple X.25 sessions can be multiplexed onto one physical link, it is quite possible that a data link can carry the logical channels (different users) in the order shown in Table 8-11.

The LAPB data link is simply "dropping" each packet from the logical session assigned to it into the I field and asking the receiving node for an error check and an acknowledgment. Once more we iterate the theme that the task of the level 2 data link layer is to provide an error-free transmission of the level 3 packets through the network.

Recall that the receiving sequence number for both the packet and data level is set with a number greater than the actual transmission previously received. This technique, in effect, says "I received and accept everything up to and including 0. The next packet or frame that I receive from you must have the number 1 in the sending sequence number."

Figure 8-15(e) shows the effect of an error occurring at the data link level. The data packet is from site A to the data link layer at site B. Site B determines an error has occurred. In this case, it issues a *Reject* (REJ) command with sequence number 2. The reject frame is passed back to site A. Site A's data link still has the packet outstanding.

In Figure 8-15(f), site A's data link layer initiates a retransmission of the erroneous frame. The frame is transmitted to site B, checked for errors, and the packet is passed up to the next level. Site B's X.25 network layer appends the proper sequence numbers in the packet header, passes this to site B's data link layer, which appends its own sequence numbers into the frame, and passes it back to the net-

TABLE 8-11. EXAMPLE OF ORDER OF LOGICAL CHANNELS

Logical Channel	X.25 Packet Send Sequence	LAPB Frame Send Sequence
LC 16	$P(S) = 3$	$N(S) = 3$
LC 40	$P(S) = 6$	$N(S) = 4$
LC 28	$P(S) = 4$	$N(S) = 5$
LC 40	$P(S) = 7$	$N(S) = 6$
LC 40	$P(S) = 0$	$N(S) = 7$

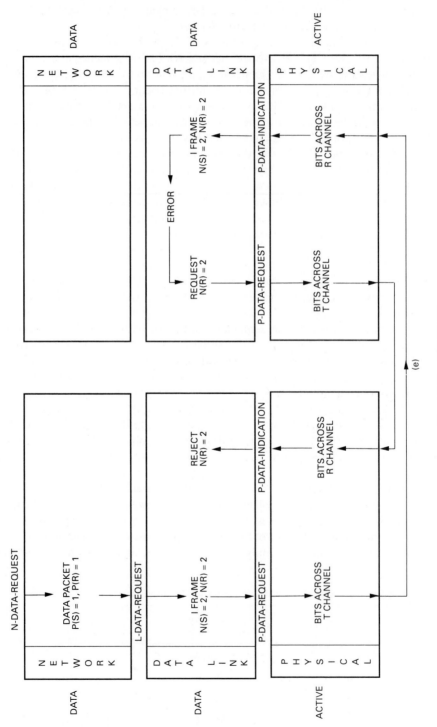

Figure 8-15. *(Continued)*

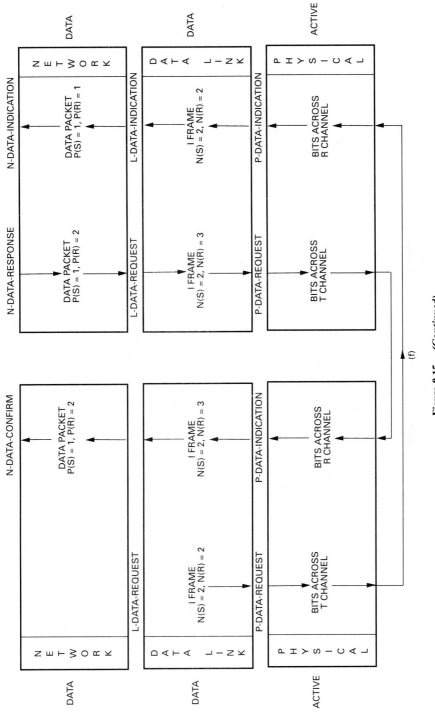

Figure 8-15. *(Continued)*

work. Site A uses the sequence numbers to acknowledge the frame at the data link layer and the packet at the network layer.

The reader should notice that the data link error remained transparent to the X.25 network level. *Only* when the events in Figure 8-15(e) were resolved did the X.25 network layer receive the data.

Although not depicted in this illustration, problems may occur at the packet level, which should remain transparent to the data link level. For instance, let us assume that a packet sequence number is in error. This packet is passed through the bottom two layers at the transmitting site and up through the layers at the receiving site. The packet level at site B detects a sequencing error and transmits a reset control packet. This would be placed in the information field of a frame at the data link layer. LAPB would treat the reset packet as an ordinary information packet at site B. Likewise, LAPB at site A would pass this packet back up to the site A packet level. It would then be used as a reset command, in which the two packet layers between sites A and B would initiate recovery operations. The data link and physical layers would not be concerned with this problem.

FRAME RELAY AND X.25

A technology that has gained increased attention recently is *frame relay*. Its popularity stems from the fact that transmission systems today are experiencing far fewer errors and problems than they did in the 1970s and 1980s. During that period X.25 was developed and implemented to cope with error-prone transmission circuits. However, with the increased use of optical fibers and highly conditioned lines, protocols that expend resources dealing with errors become less important.

The second factor which has contributed to the increased use of frame relay is the need for higher-capacity network interfaces (in bits/second). The technology of the 1980s focused on kilobit rates which are inadequate for applications that need large transmissions of data, such as bit-mapped graphics, telemetry systems, and large data-base transfers. In addition, X.25 was designed to support relatively "unintelligent" devices, such as nonprogrammable terminals. Today, these devices operate with powerful microprocessors and have many capabilities. They are able to handle many tasks that were heretofore delegated to network components.

In the past few years LANs and WANs have been interconnected with bridges, routers, gateways, and packet-switched networks. These internetworking units are interfaced into the LANs and WANs through individual leased communications channels. The use of these lines to connect internetworking units and LANs and WANs, however, is a very expensive process. Moreover, reliability problems occur because individual point-to-point leased lines have no backup capability. In addition, the extensive processing of the traffic (edits, error checks) have created unacceptable time delays for certain applications.

A better approach is to develop a LAN/WAN-carrier network which provides efficient switching technologies for backup purposes as well as high-speed circuits. Frame relay is designed to eliminate and/or combine certain operations residing in layers 3 and 2 of a data communications 7-layer model. It implements the operational aspects of statistical multiplexing found in X.25 protocol and the efficiency of circuit switching found in TDM protocols. The end effect of this approach is increased throughput and decreased delay and the saving of "CPU cycles" within the network, because some services are eliminated.

It should be emphasized that frame relay provides for a better delay performance than X.25, but it cannot match TDM performance because TDM does little processing of the traffic. In addition, frame relay (and X.25) support variable lengths of data units, which makes for a flexible arrangement when internetworking different types of networks (LANs and WANs). However, variable data units translate into variable delay. Consequently, frame relay does not work well in systems that are delay sensitive (digitized voice, compressed video).

The Frame Relay and X.25 Stacks

Figure 8-16 shows the relationship of the X.25 and frame relay layers. On the left is a depiction of the X.25 protocol stack which encompasses the physical, data link, and network layers. In contrast, the frame relay stack virtually eliminates the network layer and several aspects of the data link layer. Small wonder that frame relay is fast, as it does very little.

In summary, X.25 is attractive for its port sharing, line sharing, and STDM capabilities. Because of its variable slots, it is well suited to "bursty" environments. It is also well suited to systems such as LANs, which usually use large data units, and WANs, which usually use small data units. However, X.25 suffers from relatively low throughput and relatively high delay due to its very strict virtual circuit design and the resulting processing overhead.

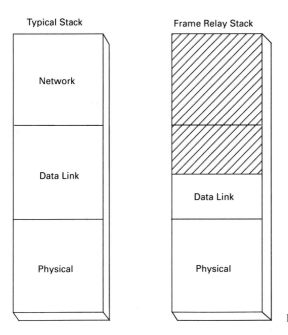

Figure 8-16. Frame Relay Layers

TDM and its use of circuit switching is attractive because of high throughput and very low delay. These performance factors stem from the fact that TDM uses fixed slots. Such an approach does not work well in bursty environments such as data transfer, but it is appropriate to environments that require fixed bandwidths, such as voice processing.

Frame relay exhibits low delay and high throughput because many of the features typically found in the virtual connection network are not performed. It is attractive to bursty environments because it allows the sharing of the line in a dynamic fashion and uses STDM techniques to support variable data units.

Only the future will tell if frame relay will supplant the widely used X.25 standard.

INTERNATIONAL X.25 NETWORKS

Almost every industrialized country in Europe and the Far East has a national public packet network. International networking using X.75 has increased dramatically in the last several years. For example, Figure 8-17 shows the United Kingdom international packet-switched service. The London International Data Centre uses X.75 to link to several of the X.25 networks.

Does a Standard Assure Compatibility?

Even though vendors, telephone companies, and Postal and Telegraph Ministries (PTTs) may be using the same recommended standard (such as X.25 or LAPB) to

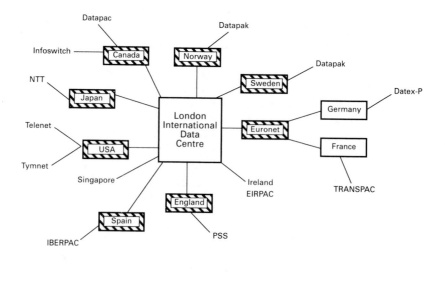

 = International Gateway

Figure 8-17.   International Networking Example (not all inclusive)

design their systems, the systems are not necessarily compatible with one another. To illustrate, various countries and vendors provide different responses to the LAPB *Frame Reject* command (FRMR). Certain networks initiate a disconnect response (DISC) upon receiving a *Frame Reject* (FRMR) command. These networks issue the disconnect *before* resetting the link with a link-setting command such as *Set Asynchronous Balanced Mode* (SABM). The problem lies in the fact that the disconnect causes a restart at the packet X.25 level. The reader may recall that the restart procedure as established by the X.25 specification reinitializes and clears all virtual calls.

Some vendors use the above technique; others do not issue the DISC command. Consequently, a vendor utilizing the disconnect before setting the SABM will necessarily have trouble interfacing with a vendor that does not use the same approach.

There is no easy answer to the problem of different interpretations of recommended standards. One solution is to provide an extremely detailed standards document. However, such a detailed standard would be agonizing to develop through a standards committee. What is more, it would certainly hinder flexibility at the design level. Another choice is to provide more opportunities for the design teams from PTTs, telephone companies, and vendors to work with certification bodies to ensure that interpretation of the standards is in adherence with the intent of the specification itself.

The third option is to certify the vendors' products or the PTT networks as meeting the standard. This option is being exercised in several countries today. In the U.S., the National Bureau of Standards publishes FIPS PUB 100/FS 1041, which provides guidelines to determine conformance to X.25. This document provides the details to perform tests to simulate an X.25 DCE or an X.25 DTE at the physical, data link, and packet levels. Many vendors now have their own certification programs.

SUMMARY

X.25 is the most widely used network interface standard in existence. Although based on technology such as error-prone links and unintelligent devices, X.25 continues to grow and is now found in practically every vendor's communications product. Notwithstanding, newer technologies that provide higher throughput and less delay will probably supplant some of the X.25 interfaces in the future. Presently, frame relay is designed to do so.

9

Digital Networks

INTRODUCTION

Since the early 1960s, telephone companies, specialized carriers, and network vendors have increasingly implemented systems with digital technology. Today, many transmission components use digital technology, including such diverse devices as PBXs, multiplexers, and switches.

Why has digital technology become so pervasive in the industry? First, many digital devices are less expensive than their analog counterparts. For example, digital multiplexers are less expensive than analog multiplexers. Moreover, digital systems are built around large-scale integration circuitry (LSI), which is quite rugged and reliable. Second, it is possible to use digital technology for transmission of all images—digital networks transmit not only voice, but data, television video images, and facsimile on the same channel. Third, digital techniques overcome many of the transmission and storage limitations of analog technology. We address this point in more detail in the next section.

This chapter provides a tutorial on digital networks and also gives the reader a more detailed view of the new digital technology, such as integrated digital systems, digital switching, and packet voice transmission.

ADVANTAGES OF DIGITAL SYSTEMS

The process of digitization was developed at Bell Laboratories in the 1960s with the aim of overcoming some of the limitations of analog transmission and image recording. An analog signal experiences a continuous variance of amplitude over time. When an individual speaks into a telephone, for example, the physical, mechanical oscillations of the air (high and low air pressure) are transformed into an electrical signal with similar waveform characteristics. The telephone acts as a transducer to change a signal from one form of energy (sound) to another (electrical). As the signal is transmitted down the communications channel, it must be amplified periodically to prevent excessive signal decay.

Several problems arise regarding the analog signal and how it is transmitted across the channel. First, the signal is relayed through amplifiers and other transducers. The relaying function is designed to be as linear as possible. Linear means the waveform representing the signal maintains its characteristics from one end of the channel to the other. A deviation from this linearity creates a distortion of the waveform. All analog signals exhibit some form of nonlinearity. Unfortunately, the intervening components, such as amplifiers, increase the nonlinearity of the signal.

The second problem relates to noise on the channel. As explained in Appendix A, an electrical signal is composed of the nonrandom movement of electrons. Thermal noise is created on a wire or cable channel by the random variations of the electrons in the channel or transducer. You have heard noise on a telephone line—it sounds like hiss. Noise is also introduced in radio transmissions by electrical disturbances in the earth's atmosphere and by radiation from the sun and stars.

Third, if a signal is stored on a recording medium, such as a tape or disk, the medium itself is a source of noise. For example, the roughness of the surface of a recording disk or tape and its granularity (due to the size of the magnetic domains on the medium) can also create noise.

Fourth, all signals are weakened (or attenuated) during transmission across the medium. This signal decay can make the transmission so weak that it is unintelligible at the receiver. A high-quality wire cable with a large diameter certainly mitigates decay, but it cannot be eliminated.

Digital systems overcome these problems by representing the analog waveform with digital and binary images. In essence, the analog waveform signal is converted to a series of digital numbers and transmitted on the communications channel as binary data. The digital numbers represent samples of the waveform.

The digital signals are subject to the same kinds of imperfections and problems as the analog signal—decay and noise. However, the digital signal is *discrete:* the binary samples of the analog waveform are represented by discrete levels of voltages, in contrast to the nondiscrete levels of an analog signal. As the signal traverses the channel, it is necessary only to sample the *absence or presence* of a digital binary pulse, not its *degree,* as in the analog signal. The mere absence or presence of a signal pulse can be more easily recognized than the magnitude or degree of an analog signal. The digital signals can then be completely reconstituted before they deteriorate below a specified threshold. Consequently, noise or attenuation can be completely eliminated from the reconstructed signal.

The periodic sampling and reconstitution process is performed by regenerative *repeaters.* The repeaters are placed on a channel at defined intervals. The spacing depends on the quality and size of the conductor, the amount of noise on the conductor, its bandwidth, and the bit rate of the transmission. Early digital systems used a 6000-foot spacing. Today, optical fiber channels can transmit reliably with regeneration occurring every 50 to 70 miles.

SIGNAL CONVERSION

Many methods are used to change an analog signal into a digital string of binary images. The first widely used approach, *pulse code modulation* (PCM), was developed in 1939 by A. H. Reeves of Bell Labs. Even though PCM entails many processes, it is generally described in three steps: sampling, quantizing, and encoding (see Figure 9-1). The devices performing the digitizing process, called channel banks or primary PCM multiplexers, have two basic functions: (1) to convert analog signals to digital form (and vice versa at the other end); and (2) to combine the digital signals into a single time division multiplexed (TDM) data stream.

Pulse code modulation is based on Nyquist sampling theory. If an analog signal is sampled at regular intervals at a rate at least twice the highest frequency in the channel, the samples will contain sufficient information about the signal to allow its reconstruction. The accepted sampling rate in the industry is 8000 samples per second. Based on Nyquist sampling theory, this rate allows the accurate reproduction of a 4 kHz channel. The 8000 samples are sufficient to capture the signals in a 3 kHz telephone line.

The samples are stored and collected at a predetermined rate and translated into a binary image. Each sample is called a *pulse amplitude modulation* (PAM) signal. Once the sampling has taken place, the PAM signal is subjected to the second major component of the translation, *quantizing*. The purpose of quantizing is to assign a value to each PAM signal. Quantizers assign a range of values of either 1 to 128 or 1 to 256 to each PAM signal. If the quantizer assigns one of 128 values to the signal, 7 bits are required for each sample ($2^7 = 128$). If the quantizer uses 256 possible values, 8 bits are required for each sample ($2^8 = 256$). The 128-quantum-step quantizer requires a 56,000 bit/s rate ($8000 \times 7 = 56,000$). The 256-quantum-step quantizer requires a rate of 64,000 bit/s ($8000 \times 8 = 64,000$).

Experiments have shown that 2048 quantizing steps provide for adequate voice signal quality. However, eleven bits per sample (2^{11}) would require an 88 kbit/s data rate ($2^{11} = 2048$), so a reduction in the number of quantum steps is highly desirable. One solution is the use of *companding* (discussed shortly).

Once the PAM values have been assigned a binary value by the quantizing process, the third step encodes the samples into a binary bit string. As stated earlier, the binary values for the 8000 samples carry enough information to reconstruct the analog signal at the other end of the channel.

In order to reconstruct the signal properly, the data must be presented to a digital-to-analog (D/A) converter at the same rate the signal was sampled originally. The converter develops a voltage to represent each of the 8000 data values and presents these voltages to the D/A function. The digital-to-analog conversion process results in a signal that is a near replica of the original analog waveform.

Digital transmission is not without its problems. A digital signal can be distorted in a number of ways. First, inadequate sampling can create a distortion in the signal. The problem can be solved by more frequent sampling, but this would require more expensive components and larger bandwidths (higher bit rates) on the channel to carry the increased data rates. No technique exists to completely eliminate sampling distortions because of the analog nature of the waveform. The fun-

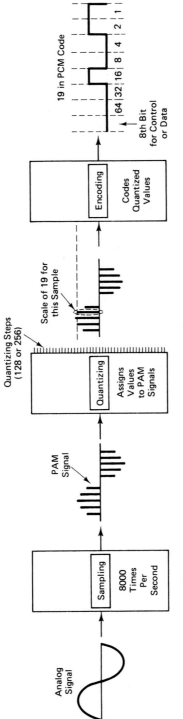

Figure 9-1. Signal Conversion

damental anomaly results from applying discrete (digital) samples to a nondiscrete (analog) signal.

The second problem arises through quantizing errors. The quantizing process does not represent exactly the amplitude of the PAM signal. Since the signal distortion in the process is proportional to the step size, one approach to solve the problem is to increase the number of quantizing steps available to represent the signal. However, increased levels of quantizing increases the costs of the components and the number of bits required to represent the signal. Nonetheless, the 128-step quantizer has been replaced by the 256-step quantizer.

Earlier systems exhibited a linear relationship between PAM signals and PCM code (called *linear coding*). As a consequence, equal changes in the signal amplitude would produce equal changes in the PCM codes. This effect created significant quantization distortion in lower amplitude signals.

Newer techniques compress the higher amplitude signals to a smaller amplitude range for a given number of quantization levels. The smaller amplitude signals are expanded. This technique increases the number of available quantization levels and decreases the overall quantization distortion. After the signal is decoded, it is restored to its original amplitude level. This combination of compressing and expanding is called *companding*.

Modern systems also use another concept called *nonlinear coding*. This process represents small-amplitude PAM signals by larger coding variations than similar changes in large-amplitude PAM signals. The quantization error is reduced as the PAM signal level is reduced. As a consequence, a constant *signal to distortion (S/D) ratio* is maintained over a wide range of PAM signals.

The nonlinear coding process is defined by a logarithmic relationship in the form of the *mu law* (used in North America and Japan) and the *A law* (used in Europe). The laws are quite similar except the A law uses a linear relationship in the small-amplitude range. The minimum step size is 2/4096 for the A law and 2/8159 for the mu law. The nonlinear companded analog voice signals in a time division multiplexed (TDM) system are implemented in a segmented process. The mu law is represented by 15 segments; the A law is approximated by 13 segments. Both laws exceed the minimum requirements in reducing lower signal level distortions.

DIGITAL CARRIER SYSTEMS

In 1962 AT&T/Bell began the commercial use of digital telephone systems. The system, implemented in the Chicago area, was labeled the T1 carrier system. Since then, a family of T carriers have evolved, and today T1-based inter-city facilities are pervasive throughout North America and other parts of the world. Table 9-1 shows the digital carrier system. The systems range from the T1 carrier supporting 1.544 Mbit/s to the sophisticated optical fiber system (FT-4E-432) operating at 432 Mbit/s. The channels of the lower T carriers are combined into larger bundles to make efficient use of transmission facilities and routes on the network.

The T1 signals are applied directly to the channel (for example, wire pairs) in a bipolar format. (Figure 1-11 shows the T1 alternate mark inversion bipolar code.)

TABLE 9-1. DIGITAL FACILITIES

System Name	Voice Grade Channels	Bit Rate (Mbit/s)
T1	24	1.544
T1C	48	3.152
T2	96	6.312
T3	672	44.736
T4M	4032	274.176
FT3C	1344	90.524
FT-4E-144	2016	140.000
FT-4E-432	6048	432.000

This code has the significant advantage of providing detection of any single-bit transmission error: If a 1 is converted erroneously to a 0, adjacent 1s will be of identical polarity, violating the alternate mark inversion (AMI) coding rule. If a 0 is converted erroneously to a 1, then two successive 1s of identical polarity will violate the rule.

Why is the 1.544-megabit rate used for the T1 carrier? The answer to this frequently asked question comes from the use of time division multiplexing (TDM) techniques on the T1 channel. The T1 carrier is designed to support 24 simultaneous voice-grade transmissions. We know from previous discussions that each channel is operating with 8000 samples per second. We will assume 8 bits per sample are required for the transmission. If 24 individual transmissions are carried across the channel, and 8000 samples constitute each transmission, the total bit rate required is: 8000 samples × 24 channels + 1 framing bit = 1,544,000 bit/s.

Yet another question focuses on the rationale for 24 TDM channels: Why not 22 or 28? Initially, AT&T/Bell judged that an effective and economical bandwidth of 750 kHz could accommodate a 1.544 Mbit/s throughput. Based on the initial bandwidth considerations, the 24 channels were derived as follows:

- 1 second ÷ 1,544,000 × 8 bits per sample = 5.18 μsec (.000005176).
- In other words, 5.18 μsec are required for each sample.
- 5.18 μsec × 8000 = .0414 second utilized by *each* of the 24 channels.
- 1 second − .0414 = .9586.
- Therefore, about 95 percent of the channel's TDM slots are available for other transmissions.
- Therefore, .0414 second × 24 = .9936.
- Hence, over 99 percent of T1 channel's slots are effectively used.

A user DTE may not be able to use the full 64 kbit/s channel rate. On some systems, the carrier uses one bit out of every eight for network signaling. Consequently, user throughput is actually 56 kbit/s through the channel. Other systems "borrow" the eighth bit in every sixth sample, which gives 7⅚ bits per sample.

The T carrier frame is shown in Figure 9-2. Each frame contains one sample from each of the 24 voice-grade channels. Some versions of the T family use the eighth bit of each sample for control signaling. Others use every sixth sample. Figure 9-2(b) illustrates the use of time division multiplexing to interleave the PAM samples into the 193-bit frame.

The 1.544 Mbit/s rate is the commonly accepted standard in North America. Europe uses a slightly different approach. Its digital scheme encompasses a 32-channel system, where 30 channels transmit signals derived from incoming telephone trunks and the remaining two channels are used to provide for signaling and synchronization signals. The European scheme uses an overall bit rate of 2.048 Mbit/s.

CHANNEL AND DATA SERVICE UNITS

Digital transmission between computer and terminals occurs through devices known generically as customer premises equipment (CPE). Prior to deregulation, the CPEs were in the telephone company's domain. As a result of Federal Communications Commission rulings, neither AT&T nor the Bell operating companies are permitted to install equipment a customer can provide. This equipment includes the digital CPEs. In the 1970s and early 1980s, a user DTE interfaced into a digital channel with a Western Electric 500A, a combined channel service unit (CSU) and data service unit (DSU). In 1981, at the requests of customers, AT&T provided a separate device for bipolar signal conversion, called the 500-B DSU. Today, a customer interfaces into a digital network through a channel service unit (CSU), a data service unit (DSU), or a combination of the two (CSU/DSU). (See Figure 9-3.) The DSU converts the DTE-oriented data signals into bipolar digital signals. The DSU also performs clocking, signal regeneration, and equalization of the channel. The CSU has more limited functions than the DSU. The CSU performs functions such as line conditioning (or equalization), which keeps the signal's performance consistent across the channel bandwidth; signal reshaping, which reconstitutes the binary pulse stream; and loop-back testing, which entails the transmission of test signals between the CSU and the network carrier's office channel unit (OCU).

ANALOG-TO-DIGITAL TECHNIQUES

In addition to pulse code modulation (PCM), several analog-to-digital techniques are used by telephone companies and other vendors. The techniques fall into two broad classifications, *waveform analysis* and *parameter coding*.

Waveform Analysis

The pulse code modulation technique discussed earlier is categorized as waveform analysis or waveform synthesis. It is so named because the analog waveform is analyzed and sampled to provide digital codes for a later reproduction of the waveform. Today's systems have more sophisticated approaches than the conventional PCM technique. One widely used system is called *differential pulse code modula-*

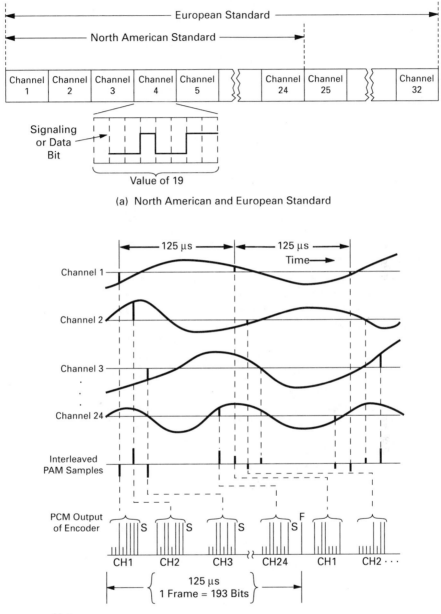

(a) North American and European Standard

(b) Time Division Multiplexing

Notes:
1. Framing Bit is 193rd Bit (F)
2. Signaling Bit is 8th Bit in Each Channel in One Frame Out of Six (S)
3. The Output Pulse Rate Shown is 1.544 Mbit/s, the DS1 Level in the TDM Hierarchy

Figure 9-2. Digital TDM Frame

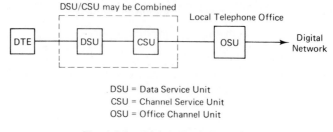

DSU = Data Service Unit
CSU = Channel Service Unit
OSU = Office Channel Unit

Figure 9-3. Digital Circuit Structure

tion (DPCM). This technique transmits the differences between samples of the signal instead of the actual samples. Since an analog waveform's samples are closely correlated with each other (almost sample-to-sample redundant), the range of sample differences requires fewer bits to represent. DPCM uses a differential quantizer to store the previous sample in a sample-and-hold circuit. The circuit measures the change between the two samples and encodes the change. Differential PCM achieves a smaller *voice digitization rate* (VDR) than do the conventional PCM techniques (32 kbit/s, for example).

A special case of DPCM is *delta modulation* (DM), which uses only one bit for each sample. Delta modulation measures the polarity of difference of successive samples and uses a 1 bit to indicate if the polarity is rising in amplitude and a 0 to represent a signal that is decreasing in amplitude [see Figure 9-4(a)]. The signal is encoded as a "staircase" of up-and-down sequences. The digital code can later be used to reconstruct the analog signal (analog-to-digital [A/D] process) by "smoothing" the staircase back to the original signal.

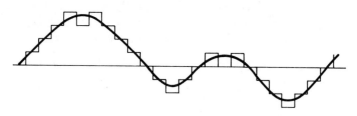

(a) Delta Modulation (Nondistortion)

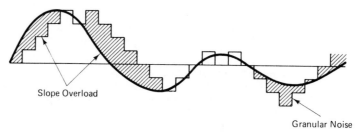

Slope Overload

Granular Noise

(b) Distortion

Figure 9-4. Delta Modulation

Delta modulation is simple to implement. However, it requires a higher sampling rate than PCM or DPCM because each sample does not carry much information. Delta modulation assumes the encoded waveform is no more than one step away from the sampled signal. However, a signal may change more rapidly than the staircase modulator can reflect, producing a problem called *slope overload.* In contrast, a slow-changing signal also creates distortions, called *granular noise.* [See Figure 9.4(b).] This effect of inaccurate representation of the waveform is called *quantization noise;* it also occurs with PCM and DPCM systems.

One widely used variation of delta modulation is *continuously variable slope delta modulation* (CVSD). (Another term for this technique is *delta modulation with companding.*) CVSD transmits the difference between two successive samples and employs a quantizer to change the actual quantum steps based on a sudden increase or decrease of the signal. CVSD increases the staircase step size when it detects the waveform's slope increasing and reduces the step size upon detecting a decrease in the slope. As stated earlier, PCM and DPCM can also employ companding techniques to reduce errors. By changing the quantum steps, the quantization errors are reduced.

CCITT has standardized a companding PCM technique called *adaptive differential PCM* (ADPCM). This approach uses a bit rate of 32 kbit/s, carrying 4 bits per sample. Many systems have now adapted CCITT's ADPCM techniques.

Parameter Coding (Vocoders)

In addition to the waveform analysis techniques just discussed, the industry has devoted considerable research to a technique called *parameter coding* (other terms to define this approach are *modeling, analysis synthesis,* and *vocoding*). Parameter coding systems are not used on the telephone network because they are designated to encode *speech* signals only and cannot accommodate other analog signals, such as modem transmissions. In contrast, PCM can convey data or voice.

Parameter coding does not preserve the character of the input waveform; rather, the input waveform is processed into parameters which measure vocal characteristics. The speech is analyzed to produce a *time varying model* of the waveform. Parameter coding then computes a digital signal that most closely resembles the original speech. These modeling parameters are transmitted through the channel (or stored on disk) to allow for later reproduction of the speech signal. Vocoders are commonly used for recorded announcements (e.g., weather information), personal computer voice output, and electronic video games.

Linear predictive coding (LPC) (see Figure 9-5) is a widely used form of parameter coding. LPC is based on the fact that speech produced by a vocal tract is either voiced or voiceless. The vowel "e" in *keep* is a voice sound; the "s" in *sir* is a voiceless sound. Both of these mechanisms are sampled to produce a stream of impulses. The impulses can then be stored as digital images for later use.

The pattern of a speech signal is then defined in 20–50 millisecond durations called *speech segments* or *parcels.* The speech segment is sampled and processed by the LPC function, which determines a predicted value of the sample. Several calculations are performed on the sample. When the values have been calculated, all the

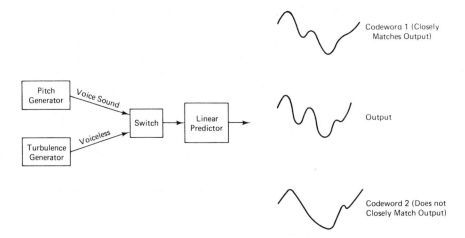

Figure 9-5. Parameter Coding

values are used to produce a predicted value for the speech segment in question. The idea of the iterative calculations is to reduce the error between the input speech segment and the predicted output. The LPC continuously adapts by periodically developing a new set of predicted values.

Before the signal is transmitted onto the channel, the signal to be transmitted is compared against a table of values. The entry in the table that is closest to the actual value is used as the actual transmitted value. In the LPC system, the signal is matched against a library of values. This library is called a *code book*. The library member whose values give the best match to the signal is selected as the code word. The advantage of this approach is that each code word can be represented by a very few number of bits. For example, if a library has 4000 members, only 10–12 bits are required to represent and/or transmit the information about the full LPC speech segment.

This technique is attractive because the LPC code book allows transmission at only 2.4 kilobits per second. A high-quality 9.6 kbit/s telephone line supports four time division multiplexed (TDM) 2.4 kbit/s LPC transmissions. This data rate is substantially lower than the waveform techniques of 64 kbit/s, 32 kbit/s, and 16 kbit/s. The main disadvantage of LPC is that speech reproduction is not as high quality as PCM.

FUTURE DIGITAL SYSTEMS

During the last twenty years, the industry has made extraordinary progress in developing integrated digital systems for representing and transmitting voice, data, and other images. The ability to digitize, store, and "play back" the human voice is leading to new applications in many fields. However, the real power of voice digitization will be seen in the future as techniques are improved to decrease the bandwidth and data rate requirement and to increase the ability to capture the intelligence of voice. Much work remains to be done, because true speech recognition is very difficult. The intelligence of speech lies not in the ability to recognize one word, but to recognize a complex thought or idea that is spread out over several words or perhaps several sentences. Research continues in developing machines and software to extract and make intelligible the semantics, stress, and syntax of the immensely complex human language.

INTEGRATED DIGITAL NETWORKS

A tremendous amount of attention has focused on the *integrated services digital network* (ISDN) during the past few years. The purpose of this section is to describe the goals and characteristics of ISDNs, as well as their capabilities and shortcomings.

The strict definition of the term *ISDN* encompasses concepts that are still in development. However, integrated digital systems are in operation today, and some people use the term *ISDN* to describe these ongoing operations. These ISDNs do not conform to the emerging standards of CCITT, yet they provide integrated services for digital transmission of all images. We first examine an existing ISDN with Satellite Business Systems' (SBS) integrated satellite network. Next we examine the conceptual aspects of the ISDN, with a review of the ISDN standards from CCITT.

SBS Integrated Network

We will continue the discussion of SBS begun in Chapter Five. (Figures 5-5 and 5-6 illustrate major features of the SBS network.) SBS provides integrated voice, data, and image communications services. The TDMA frame (Figure 5-6) can contain voice or data intelligence.

SBS allocates one voice channel per frame to accommodate the 32 kbit/s digitized voice. Each traffic burst is 15 milliseconds (.015 sec) and contains 480 data bits (1 second ÷ .015 × 480 = 32,000 bits). Multiple channels can be allotted for data-only transmissions of greater than 32 kbit/s.

The port adapter in Figure 5-5 is shown in greater detail in Figure 9-6. The voice port uses a 32 kbit/s companded delta modulation scheme (also called logarithmic companded delta modulation [LCDM]). LCDM provides good tolerance to noise, a low data rate, and acceptable performance over a wide range of input signals. The way the voice port handles a call is similar to the telephone company procedure.

- Calling party goes off-hook (telephone or PBX).
- SBS sets up software to record connection and sends dial tone to caller.
- Port accepts dialed digits from caller.
- Calling satellite communications controller sends "attempt connect" signal to called SCC based on the TDMA protocol discussed in Chapter Five.
- If resources are available at called SCC, an "attempt response" is returned and the called party is dialed.
- Upon the called party going off-hook, the called SCC transmits "connect," and the calling SCC responds with "connect response."

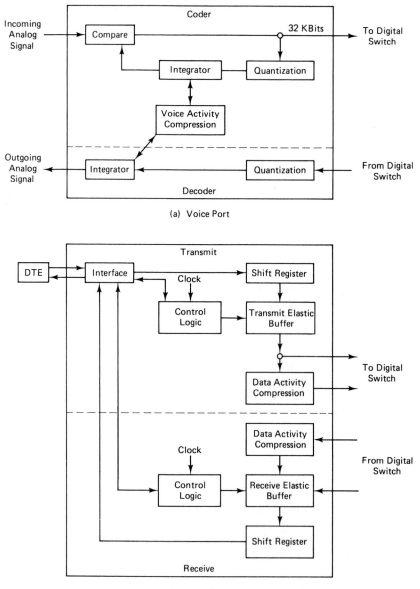

Figure 9-6. SBS Voice and Data Ports

- The parties converse, with the voice ports digitizing the analog signals for insertion into the TDMA frames.
- Either party hangs up and the SCC transmits "disconnect." Other SCC responds with "disconnect response."

The voice port also performs *voice activity compression* (VAC). A voice conversation includes periods of silence (listening and pausing). VAC takes advantage of the quiet periods by transmitting data from the coder corresponding to signals above a certain level. Only speaking persons require channel slots, so VAC makes it possible to share satellite channels among multiple voice conversations. Forty conversations may require only 25 channels.

The digital data port (Figure 9-6b) accepts data rates from 2.4 kbit/s to the T1 rate of 1.544 Mbit/s. A user can interface into the port as if it were a DCE (modem) or DTE (terminal). The "elastic buffer" compensates for user clocks and the SCC clocks (see Chapter One and earlier discussions in this chapter on clocks and synchronization). The shift registers convert user bytes into serial-bit data streams.

The digital port also uses a compression technique, *data activity compression* (DAC). When a 480-bit channel slot contains a string of characters that are the same as the previous channel, that channel slot is not transmitted on the link. The receiving DAC reconstructs the original data stream by using the last channel slot received from the specific port to repeat the last characters for channel reconstruction.

Thus, through the use of voice ports, data ports, and time division multiplexing, SBS integrates voice-data transmissions. After the signals are digitized, they are all treated the same, and the demands and problems for the channel require only one technology.

The Integrated Services Digital Network (ISDN)

An integrated services digital network (ISDN) provides end-to-end digital connectivity to support a wide range of services. In essence, all images (voice, data, television, facsimile, etc.) are transmitted with digital technology. ISDN has five major goals:

1. to provide a worldwide uniform digital network which supports a wide range of services and uses the same standards across different countries;
2. to provide a uniform set of standards for digital transmission across and between networks;
3. to provide a standard ISDN user interface, such that internal changes to a network are transparent to the end user;
4. in conjunction with the third objective, to provide for end-user application independence—no consideration is made as to their characteristics in relation to the ISDN itself;
5. as an adjunct to goals three and four, to provide portability for user DTEs and applications.

ISDN is centered on three main areas: (1) the standardization of services offered to subscribers in order to foster international compatibility; (2) the standardization of user-to-network interfaces in order to foster independent terminal equipment and network equipment development; and (3) the standardization of network capabilities in order to foster user-to-network and network-to-network communications.

Much literature on the subject claims ISDN is a revolutionary technology, which is not true—the ISDN is an *evolutionary* technology. The committees, common carriers, and trade associations working on the standards recognize that the ISDN is based on the ongoing telephone integrated digital network (IDN). Consequently, many of the digital techniques discussed previously in this chapter will be utilized for future ISDN systems. This includes signaling rates (e.g., 32 kbit/s), transmission codes (e.g., bipolar), and even physical plugs (e.g., the jacks to the telephone). The foundations for ISDNs have been in development for the past twenty years.

The ISDN recommendations have received criticism. Some people believe them to be overly complex; others state they are not supportive of a true integrated system; still others claim they do not use the right technology to achieve their goal. We will discuss these criticisms as we describe the ISDN.

ISDN Interfaces.   Figure 9-7 illustrates the standard end-user ISDN network interfaces. The ISDN-recommended standard provides a small set of compatible interfaces which are intended to economically support a wide range of user applications. The standard recognizes that different interfaces are required for applications that have different information rates and requirements. Consequently, more than one interface type is available. Before explaining Figure 9-7, two terms must be defined:

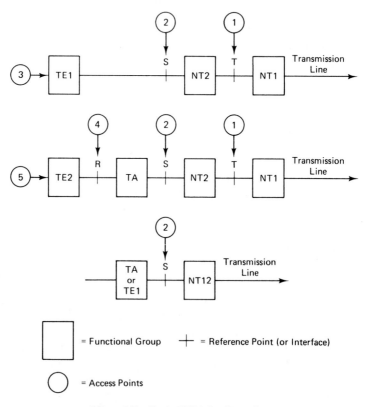

Figure 9-7.   Basic ISDN Configurations

- *Functional groupings* are a set of capabilities needed in an ISDN user-access interface. Specific functions within a functional grouping may be performed by multiple pieces of equipment and software.
- *Reference points* are the points dividing the functional groupings. Usually, a reference point corresponds to a physical interface between pieces of equipment.

Figure 9-7 illustrates a reference configuration for the ISDN user-network interface. The six functional groupings depicted use three different types of reference points. Reference points S and T use the recommended channel interface structures of the specific ISDN standard I.412 (more about this standard later). The physical interface for reference point R is in accordance with other CCITT recommendations or EIA recommendations (for example, X.21, V.24, and EIA-232-D).

The ISDN also provides access points. The definitions of the access points are as follows: Access point 1 (reference point T) and access point 2 (reference point S) are the access points for *bearer services* supported by the ISDN. Bearer services involve the lower three levels of the ISO ISDN model (the ISDN layers are illustrated in Figure 9-9).

Access points 3 and 5 use *teleservices,* which encompass the upper layers of the ISO ISDN model (and may use bearer services as well). Access point 4 encompasses other CCITT-standardized services, which depend on the specific X and V recommendations being utilized by terminal adaptors (TA).

Functional grouping NT1 (network termination 1) includes functions equivalent to the physical layer of the OSI reference model. These functions are associated with the physical and electrical connections in the network. The major NT1 functions are:

- termination of the line
- layer 1 line maintenance and performance monitoring
- transmission signaling and timing
- provision for power for the channel
- possible multiplexing at the layer 1 level
- interface termination, including multidrop terminations if necessary.

The NT1 can define the boundary of the carrier's ISDN; it may be controlled by the network carrier. It provides the user a fixed, standard interface into the ISDN. NT1 gives the user *transparency* into the network and isolates the user from the physical aspects of the ISDN.

The NT2 (network termination 2) functions are equivalent to the physical layer and higher layers of the OSI model. Examples of an NT2 function are private telephone branch exchanges (PBXs), local area networks (LANs), and terminal or cluster controllers. In other words, the NT2 functions as an end-user equipment interface. As illustrated by the figure, end-user equipment terminates into the NT2 through an S-connection reference point. Since the NT2 can be a PBX, local area network, or terminal controller, it can perform functions such as switching, multiplexing, and protocol handling. Its principal responsibilities encompass layers 2 and 3 protocol handling.

The actual functions performed are not stipulated in the ISDN recommendations. However, latitude is given to allow a PBX to perform functions at layers 1, 2, and 3, whereas a simple time division multiplexer (TDM) would probably perform only layer 1 functions.

The NT12 (network termination 1, 2) is a multiple-function device containing the combined capabilities of the NT1 and NT2 equipment. Devices interface into this function with an S reference-point connector. The evolving fourth-generation PBXs fit into this function.

The NT2 and the NT12 functions are as follows:

- protocol handling for layers 2 and 3
- multiplexing for layers 2 and 3
- switching functions
- concentration functions
- ongoing network maintenance functions
- termination of the layer 1 functions.

The TE (terminal equipment) functions represent the end-user equipment (DTEs). They include not only DTEs, but other devices such as end-user digital telephones and integrated workstations found in offices. The TE functions are as follows:

- higher-level protocol handling
- maintenance functions
- interface functions
- connection functions to other equipment.

ISDN defines two kinds of TEs. TE1 (terminal equipment, Type 1) works with an ISDN network using an ISDN interface. The TE2 function (terminal equipment, Type 2) requires the more conventional interface, such as EIA-232-D or one of the V or X series standards.

The TA (terminal adaptor) is actually a protocol converter which changes existing interfaces such as EIA-232-D, V.24, or X.21 into the standard ISDN interface. The ISDN standards allow the TA function to be combined with an end-user DTE device, as well. Its principal function is supporting an ISDN connection for a TE2 device.

The ISDN specifications provide for considerably more flexibility than what might be inferred from Figure 9-7. Figure 9-8 shows eight other possible ISDN configurations. The configurations in Figures 9-8(a) and 9-8(b) provide the ISDN interfaces at reference interfaces S and T. Figures 9-8(c) and 9-8(d) illustrate configurations where the ISDN interfaces occur at the interface S only. Figures 9-8(e) and 9-8(f) illustrate the ISDN interface occurring at reference T only. Finally, Figures 9-8(g) and 9-8(h) depict a single ISDN interface, where S and T are located at the same place.

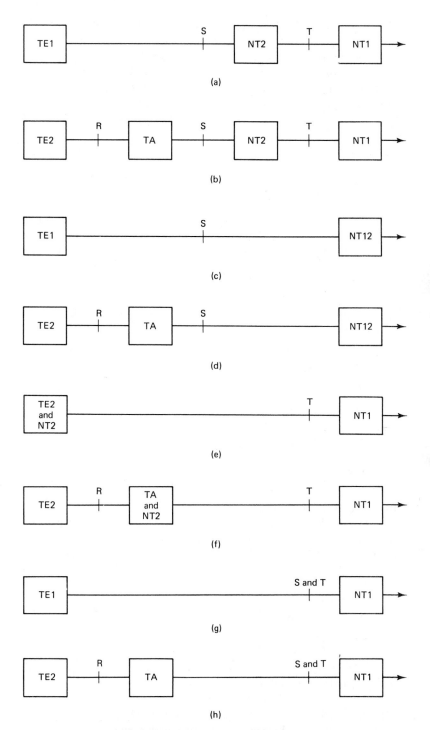

Figure 9-8.   Other Possible ISDN Interfaces

The physical characteristics of the S and T interface have now been established by an ISDN working group (W-G3). Three candidates were studied—the United States, the United Kingdom, and the Federal Republic of Germany. The U.S. proposal was adopted because it has been widely used and tested throughout the country for several years. The standard connector for ISDN is an eight-channel version of the four-channel connector commonly used in the telephone plugs in homes and offices. The eight-wire connector for the ISDN plug and jack is self-latching and compatible with existing plugs. Experience in the U.S. indicates it is inexpensive to implement and use. Again, the ISDN plug applies to the S and T interfaces in conformance with the ISDN standards.

ISDN Channels. The most common ISDN interface supports a bit rate of 144 kbit/s. The rate includes two 64 kbit/s channels, called the B channels, and one 16 kbit/s channel, called the D channel. In addition to these channels, ISDN provides for framing control and other overhead bits, which totals to a 192 kbit/s bit rate. The 144 kbit/s interfaces operate synchronously in the full-duplex mode over the same physical connector. The 144 kbit/s signal provides time division multiplexed provisions for the two 64 kbit/s channels and the one 16 kbit/s channel. The standard allows the B channels to be further multiplexed in the subchannels. For example, 8, 16, or 32 kbit/s subchannels can be derived from the B channels. The two B channels can be combined or broken down as the user desires.

The B channels are intended to carry user information streams. They provide for several different kinds of applications support. For example, B can provide for voice at 64 kbit/s; data transmission for packet-switch utilities at bit rates less than or equal to 64 kbit/s; and broadband voice at 64 kbit/s or less.

The D channel is intended to carry control and signaling information, although in certain cases ISDN allows for the D channel to support user data transmission as well. However, be aware that the B channel does not carry signaling information. ISDN describes signaling information as s-type, packet data as p-type, and telemetry as t-type. The D channel may carry all these types of information through statistical multiplexing.

The ISDN committees also are working on provisions for other kinds of channels (the E channel and H channels). These are intended for channels at faster speeds. The E channel is a 64 kbit/s channel used to carry signaling information for circuit switching. The H channels are categorized as follows:

H0:   384 kbit/s
H11: 1536 kbit/s
H12: 1920 kbit/s

ISDN requires the B-channel interfaces for points S and T to comply with one of three interface structures:

Option One: B channel interface structures. The basic interface structure is composed of two B channels and one D channel. The basic interface structure requires that two B channels and one D channel always be present at the user network interface; the D channel bit rate is 16 kbit/s. This option is known as 2 B + D.

Option Two: Primary rate B channel interface structures. This alternative provides for structures corresponding to the common bit rates of 1.544 Mbit/s and 2.048 Mbit/s. The primary channels are composed of B channels and one D channel. The bit rate for the D channel with this option is 64 kbit/s. The North American 1.544 Mbit/s standard requires the interface structure to consist of 23 B channels and one D channel (23 B + D). The European approach of 2.048 Mbit/s requires an interface structure to consist of 30 B channels and one D channel (30 B + D).

Option Three: Alternative primary rate B channel interface structures. This option can be used when an NT2 device connects to the network by more than one B channel. For the 1.544 Mbit/s rate, the interface structure would consist of 23 B channels and one E channel (23 B + E). For the 2.048 Mbit/s rate, the interface structure would consist of 30 B channels and one E channel (30 B + E).

Other interfaces are also supported in the ISDN, and additional interfaces are under study.

ISDN Layers.   The ISDN approach is to provide an end user with full support through the seven layers of the OSI model. In so doing, ISDN is divided into two kinds of services—the *bearer* service, responsible for providing support for the lower three levels of the seven-layer standard; and *teleservices* (for example, telephone, Teletex, Videotex, message handling; see Chapter Thirteen), responsible for providing support through all seven layers of the model and generally making use of the underlying lower-level capabilities of bearer services. The services are referred to as low-layer and high-layer functions, respectively. The ISDN functions are allocated according to the layering principles of the OSI and CCITT standards. The functions are depicted in Figure 9-9. Various entities of the layers are used to provide a full end-to-end capability. These layered capabilities may be supplied by PTTs, telephone companies, or other suppliers.

Let us piece some of the ISDN components together and describe how two end users can be supported going through an ISDN D channel and an X.25 packet-switching network. Figure 9-10 provides an illustration of packet-switched communications through an ISDN. DTE A, which under the ISDN terminology is configured as a TE1, uses the seven layers provided at its site. The DTE interfaces into the physical layer of ISDN, with the S/T interface into an NT1 device. In turn, the NT1 machine passes user information to a packet handler. (A packet handler would not be required if the DTE were an X.25 packet-mode device.) The packet handler interfaces with the packet-switched network through the X.75 protocol (discussed in Chapter Eight). The data traverse through the packet-switched network. They are transmitted to the remote packet handler, to the NT1, and finally to the end-user DTE B at the S/T interface.

LAPD.   The ISDN provides a data link protocol to allow DTEs to communicate with each other across the D channel. This protocol is LAPD, a subset of HDLC. LAPD operates at the data link layer of the OSI architecture. The protocol is independent of transmission bit rate and requires a full-duplex, bit-transparent channel.

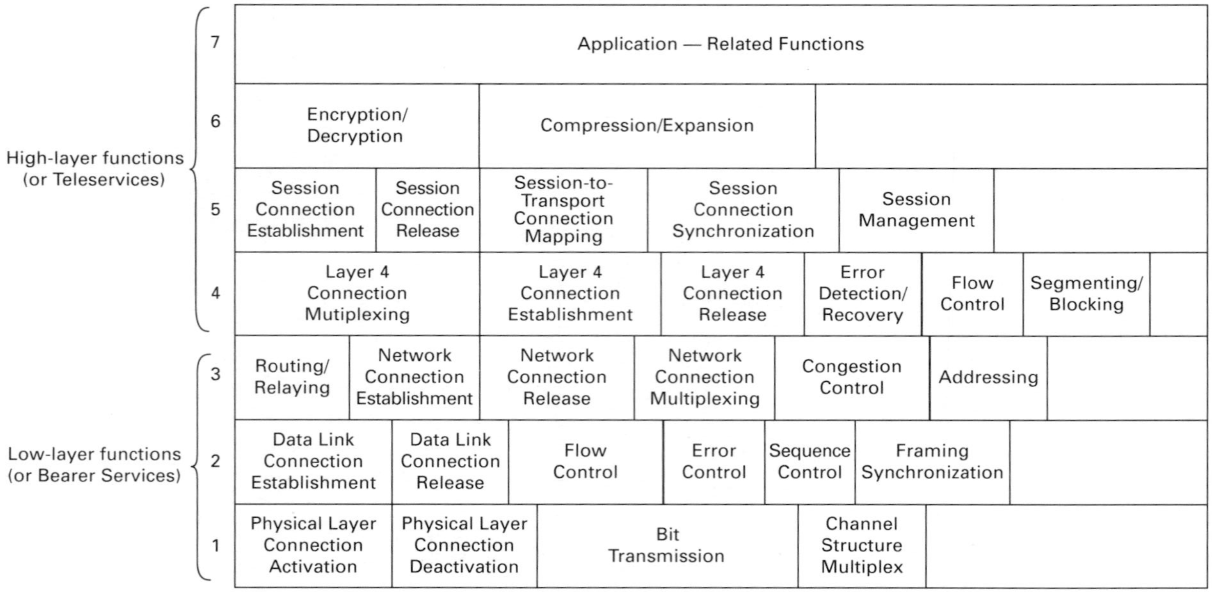

ISDN Layers

High-layer functions (or Teleservices): Layers 7, 6, 5, 4

Layer	Functions
7	Application — Related Functions
6	Encryption/Decryption; Compression/Expansion
5	Session Connection Establishment; Session Connection Release; Session-to-Transport Connection Mapping; Session Connection Synchronization; Session Management
4	Layer 4 Connection Multiplexing; Layer 4 Connection Establishment; Layer 4 Connection Release; Flow Control; Error Detection/Recovery; Segmenting/Blocking
3	Routing/Relaying; Network Connection Establishment; Network Connection Release; Network Connection Multiplexing; Congestion Control; Addressing
2	Data Link Connection Establishment; Data Link Connection Release; Flow Control; Error Control; Sequence Control; Framing Synchronization
1	Physical Layer Connection Activation; Physical Layer Connection Deactivation; Bit Transmission; Channel Structure Multiplex

Low-layer functions (or Bearer Services): Layers 3, 2, 1

Figure 9-9. ISDN Layers

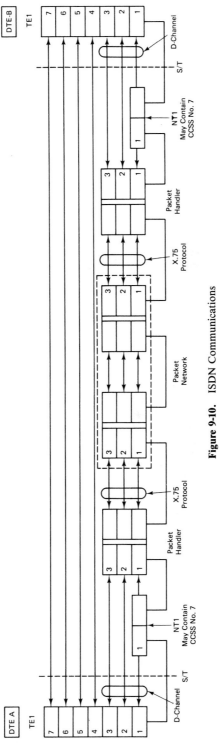

Figure 9-10. ISDN Communications

LAPD has a very similar frame format to HDLC. Moreover, like HDLC, it provides for unnumbered, supervisory, and information transfer frames. Table 9-2 shows the LAPD commands and responses, as well as differences from or similarities with the HDLC superset. LAPD also allows a Modulo 128 operation. The control octet to distinguish between the information format, supervisory format, or unnumbered format is identical to HDLC (Figure 4-2 shows the HDLC and LAPD control-field format). LAPD provides for two octets for the address field (see Figure 9-11). This is valuable for multiplexing multiple functions onto the D channel. The address field contains the address field extension bits, a command/response indication bit, a service access point identifier (SAPI), and a terminal end-point identifier (TEI). These entities are discussed in the following paragraphs.

The purpose of the address field extension is to provide more bits for an address. The presence of a 1 in the first bit of an address field octet signals that it is the final octet of the address field. Consequently, a two-octet address would have a field address extension value of 0 in the first octet and a 1 in the second octet. The address field extension bit allows the use of both the SAPI in the first octet and the TEI in the second octet, if desired.

The command/response (C/R) field bit identifies the frame as either a command or a response. The user side sends commands with the C/R bit set to 0. It responds with the C/R bit set to 1. The network does the opposite—It sends commands with C/R set to 1 and responses with C/R set to 0. The command/response field bit is summarized in Table 9-3.

The *service access point identifier* (SAPI) identifies the point where the data link layer services are provided to the layer above (that is, layer 3). (If the concept of the SAPI is vague, review Chapter Three.)

The *terminal end-point identifier* (TEI) identifies either a single terminal (TE) or multiple terminals. The TEI is assigned automatically by a separate assignment procedure. As stated earlier, the control field identifies the type of frame, as well as the sequence numbers used to maintain windows and acknowledgments between the sending and receiving devices.

Table 9-3 shows two commands and responses which do not exist in the HDLC superset. These are sequenced information 0 (SI0) and sequenced information 1 (SI1). The purpose of the SI0/SI1 commands is to transfer information using se-

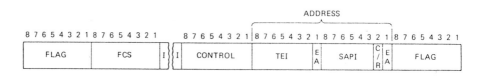

FLAG = 01111110
EA = Address Field Extension Bit
C/R = Command/Response Bit
SAPI = Service Access Point Identifier ⎱ Data Link Connection
TEI = Terminal Endpoint Identifier   ⎰ Identification (DLCI)
I = Information Field
FCS = Frame Check Sequence

Figure 9-11. LAPD Frame Format

TABLE 9-2. LAPD COMMANDS AND RESPONSES

Format	Commands	Responses	Control Field								Same as HDLC?
			8	7	6	5	4	3	2	1	
			— N(R) —			P	— N(S) —			0	
Information Transfer	I (information)		— N(R) —			P	— N(S) —			0	yes
Supervisory	RR (receive ready)	RR (receive ready)	— N(R) —			P/F	0	0	0	1	yes
	RNR (receive not ready)	RNR (receive not ready)	— N(R) —			P/F	0	1	0	1	yes
	REJ (reject)	REJ (reject)	— N(R) —			P/F	1	0	0	1	yes
Unnumbered	SABM (set asynchronous balance mode)		0	0	1	P	1	1	1	1	no
		DM (disconnect mode)	0	0	0	F	1	1	1	1	no
	SI0 (sequenced information 0)	SI0 (sequenced information 0)	0	1	1	P/F	0	1	1	1	no
	SI1 (sequenced information 1)	SI1 (sequenced information 1)	1	1	1	P/F	0	1	1	1	no
	UI (unnumbered information)		0	0	0	P	0	0	1	1	yes
	DISC (disconnect)		0	1	0	P	0	0	1	1	yes
		UA (unnumbered acknowledge)	0	1	1	F	0	0	1	1	yes
		FRMR (frame reject)	1	0	0	F	0	1	1	1	yes

TABLE 9-3. COMMAND/RESPONSE FIELD BITS

	Network C/R	User C/R
Commands From	1	0
Responses To	1	0
Commands To	0	1
Responses From	0	1

quentially acknowledged frames. These frames contain information fields provided by layer 3. The information commands are verified by the means of the end (SI) field. The P bit is set to 1 for all SI0/SI1 commands. The SI0 and SI1 responses are used during single-frame operation to acknowledge the receipt of SI1 and SI0 command frames and to report the loss of frames or any synchronization problems. LAPD does not allow information fields to be placed in the SI0 and SI1 response frames. Obviously, information fields are in the SI0 and SI1 command frames.

The work on layer 2 for ISDN using LAPD is continuing. Although the 1980–84 work has resulted in the resolution of substantive issues by the standards groups, much work remains to define more specific primitives and functions of LAPD. However, as can be seen from this brief discussion, since it uses many of the HDLC concepts, LAPD is moving to full definition and complete specifications.

ISDN addresses layer 3 as well. The layer 3 specification (recommendations I.450 and I.451) encompasses *circuit-switch* connections, *packet-switch* connections, and *user-to-user* connections. The actual alignment of the ISDN layer 3 functions with those of the OSI network are being studied at present. Note that even though the ISDN layer 3 standard contains commands and responses different from that of the OSI X.25 layer 3 standard, it is envisioned that the two standards will complement each other in completing the transmission of user information across the level 3 network.

Circuit-switched calls using layer 3 have some resemblance to the X.21 state diagrams discussed in Appendix C. Tables 9-4 and 9-5 are provided to give a better understanding of the ISDN states and the ISDN session-establishment procedures, as well as information-transfer and disestablishment procedures.

The hybrid of circuit- and packet-switched technologies in ISDN has received strong criticism from certain segments in the industry. The critics believe one technique, packet switching, is sufficient to accommodate all applications in an integrated digital network. For example, Satellite Business Systems (SBS) successfully uses one uniform approach. However, due to the broadcast nature of satellite signals, SBS is not concerned with the actual switching and routing of its signals.

Nonetheless, the standards were approved by the CCITT representatives of 157 countries in October 1984, and several prototypes have been built. For example, British Telecommunications (BT) has completed a 64 kbit/s and two 8 kbit/s systems in London, and ISDN chips are available in England and North America.

The proponents of ISDN believe it to be able to accommodate a wide variety of end-user applications, such as the ability to choose essential and nonessential services, channel options, and variable data rates.

TABLE 9-4. ISDN STATES FOR CIRCUIT-SWITCHED CALLS

U0	*Null state*—No call exists.
U1	*Call unit*—State exists for an outgoing call as a result of user action requesting call establishment.
U2	*Overlap sending*—State exists for an outgoing call while the user is sending call setup information to the network in the overlap mode.
U3	*Outgoing call proceeding*—State exists for an outgoing call when the network has acknowledged receipt of the information required for the call to proceed and the user is awaiting further network response.
U4	*Call delivered*—State exists for an outgoing call when the network has completed processing the call to the point of receiving alert from the user-network interface indicated by the called address, or an alternate interface specified either by the called user or the network.
U5	*Negotiate*—State exists for an incoming call while negotiation for a suitable B-channel is in progress.
U7	*Call received*—State exists for an incoming call when a response/answer from the called user is awaited while alerting.
U8	*Connect request*—State exists for an incoming call while awaiting receipt from the network of a connect acknowledgment.
U9	*Incoming call proceeding*—State exists for an incoming call when the user has acknowledged receipt of the information required for the call to proceed and the network is awaiting further user response.
U10	*Active*—State exists when a call is in the end-to-end communication.
U11	*Disconnect request*—State exists in response to a request by the user to disconnect a call, prior to acknowledgment by the network.
U12	*Disconnect indication*—State exists when the network has indicated disconnect and the user has not yet indicated release or detach.
U13	*Detach request*—State exists when the user has requested a call be detached, prior to acknowledgment by the network.
U14	*Detach*—State exists when the B-channel has been released but the call has not been cleared.
U15	*Suspend request*—State exists in response to user action to initiate terminal move procedures locally, prior to acknowledgment by the network.
U16	*Local suspend*—State exists in response to a suspend request, following receipt of the acknowledgment of the suspend request by the network.
U17	*Resume request*—State exists in response to a request to resume a previously suspended call, prior to acknowledgment by the network.
U19	*Release request*—State exists in response to a release request, prior to acknowledgment by the network.
U20	*Remote facility request*—State exists in response to a request from the network for the activation of a facility, prior to user response.
U21	*Local facility request*—State exists after a request by the user to the network for the activation of a facility, prior to network response.
N0	*Null state*—No call exists.

TABLE 9-4. *(Continued)*

N1	*Dial tone sending*—State exists for an outgoing call when the network sends dial tone prior to the receipt of the first message.
N2	*Overlap sending*—State exists for an outgoing call when the network is awaiting further information from the user before attempting call establishment.
N3	*Outgoing call proceeding*—State exists for an outgoing call when the network has acknowledged receipt of the information required for the call to proceed, and the user is awaiting further network response.
N4	*Call delivered*—State exists for an outgoing call when the network is aware that compatible user equipment exists at the called user interface which can accept the call.
N5	*Negotiate*—State exists for an incoming call when the user and the network are attempting to select a B-channel on which to complete the call.
N6	*Call present*—State exists for an incoming call when the call has been indicated by the network but no user has indicated whether the call can be accepted.
N7	*Call received*—State exists for an incoming call after user equipment has indicated the start of user alerting.
N8	*Connect request*—State exists when an incoming call is awaiting a response to a connect message to the user.
N9	*Incoming call proceeding*—State exists for an incoming call when the user has acknowledged receipt of the information required for the call to proceed and the network is awaiting further user response.
N10	*Active*—State exists when a call is in the end-to-end communication mode.
N11	*Disconnect request*—State exists after a user has indicated disconnect and the network has not yet cleared the connection.
N12	*Disconnect indication*—State exists when the network has indicated disconnect and the user has not yet indicated disconnect.
N13	*Detach request*—State exists when the network has requested a call be detached, prior to acknowledgment by the user.
N14	*Detach*—State exists when the B-channel has been released but the call has not been cleared by either the network or the user.
N15	*Suspend request*—State exists when the network has received a suspend request but has not yet sent a response to the user.
N16	*Local suspend*—State exists when the network has positively acknowledged a request for call suspension.
N17	*Resume request*—State exists when the network has received a resume request but has not yet sent a response to the user.
N18	*Tone active*—State exists after a network disconnect request when the option of sending in-band tone is used.
N19	*Release request*—State exists when the network has initiated the release of a call (that is, disconnection of the B-channel and release of the call reference value) and is awaiting user acknowledgment.
N20	*Remote facility request*—State exists after a request from the network for the activation of a facility, prior to user response.
N21	*Local facility request*—State exists after a request from the user for the activation of a facility, prior to the network response.

TABLE 9-5. ISDN LAYER 3 MESSAGES

Call Establishment Messages	Call Disestablishment Messages
ALERTing	DETach
CALL PROCeeding	DETach ACKnowledge
CONNect	DISConnect
CONNect ACKnowledge	RELease
SETUP	RELease COMplete
SETUP ACKnowledge	

Call Information Phase Messages	Miscellaneous Messages
RESume	CANCel
RESume ACKnowledge	CANCel ACKnowledge
RESume REJect	CANCel REJect
SUSPend	CONgestion CONtrol
SUSPend ACKnowledge	FACility
SUSPend REJect	FACility ACKnowledge
USER INFOrmation	FACility REJect
	INFOrmation
	REGister
	REGister ACKnowledge
	REGister REJect
	STATUS

DIGITAL SWITCHING

A fully integrated digital network must have the ability to switch signals among and between the various components in the network. Increasingly, digital-switching technology is being used to perform the routing and switching functions of the digital pulse-code images. Figure 9-12 shows a simple time division digital switch. The switch controls the gates to a common bus, which are opened and closed at various time periods to allow the digital bits to be transmitted between the devices attached to the switch. In the illustration, assuming that DTE A is communicating with DTE F, the switch closes a gate to DTE A and to DTE F during the same slot period, which permits a segment of speech or data to be transferred across the bus to the receiving device.

From previous discussions in this chapter, we learned that a PCM sampling speed is 8000 samples per second. A digital switch must be able to provide 8000 slots for *each* connection. Therefore, for n sessions, the switch must be switching at a speed of $n \times 8000$. A very small system is capable of switching more than 2 million bits per second, which supports over 30 PCM channels.

Two forms of digital switching are available: *space switching* and *time division switching*. A space switch connects any input time slot (say, 4) to any output time slot 4. The connection through the switch lasts only for the duration of the time slot.

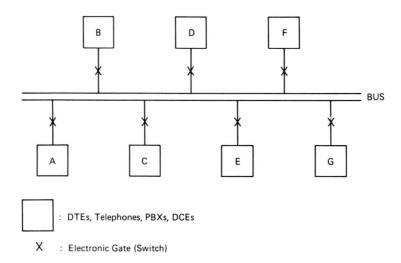

           □   : DTEs, Telephones, PBXs, DCEs

           X   : Electronic Gate (Switch)

Figure 9-12.   Simple Time Division Digital Switch

Earlier discussions also explained the use of a T1 24 and the CCITT 30 voice-channel multiplexed frame. The T1 or CCITT channel bank associates a specific customer's loop with a specified time slot. These specified time slots then can be sent to the digital switch for routing through the digital network.

The more elaborate digital time division switch separates the individual PCM signals and switches them through a *time slot interchange facility* (TSI) (Figure 9-13). The TSI can be a nonblocking switch, in that there are the same number of input slots available as there are output slots. A channel can be switched from time position X in an input frame to time position Y in an output frame. With more complex systems, one TSI is usually connected to another to form a digital switch called the *time multiplexed switch* (TMS). A TMS is essentially an n-by-n switch (n = number of connections); however, the TMS provides for another dimension—time. Unlike other switching systems and many PBXs, which leave the path open for the duration of a call, a TMS is changed for each of the n time slots in the digital frames coming from the time division multiplexer (such as a channel bank).

The concept is similar to the virtual-connection concept of packet switching and X.25. A physical path (or bandwidth) is shared by multiple users. This relationship is evident in Figure 9-13. TSI A accepts a multiplexed stream into its input store register and stores a slot in buffer position 6. Shortly thereafter, it transfers these data to its output store buffer, position 20. The TMS, at a specific time, will connect TSI A output buffer to TSI Z's input buffer. In this case, during slot 20, the samples from TSI A are transferred to TSI Z's number 20 time slot, as well. After this occurs, TSI Z transfers its input store buffer, the 20th slot, to its output store buffer 15, and the data are transmitted. In this manner digital images are switched through a time division digital switch. Although not shown in this figure, a TMS/TSI facility provides for bidirectional transmission—the TMS uses the same

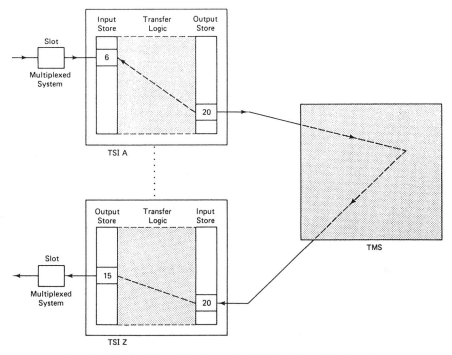

Note: Other Direction of Transmission Between Users (Not Shown) Occurs Simultaneously on
TS I s, Using Same Time Slot on TMS.

Figure 9-13.   Time-Multiplexed Digital Switch

time slot to interleave data going the other direction, thus providing for full-duplex transmission.

Digital switching has found its way into the PBX industry and has overcome one of the major limiting factors of using a PBX for data communications. We discuss this issue in Chapter Twelve.

VOICE TRANSMISSION BY PACKET

Chapter Seven discusses the attributes and pros and cons of packet-switching systems. Emphasis was placed on packet-switching networks for routing computer- and terminal-generated data. This chapter has addressed the translation of analog voice and video images into digital bit streams. We can now take these two subjects, data-packet transmission and digital voice transmission, and join the two technologies. This section discusses a field that is rapidly gaining the attention of the communications industry: packet voice transmission using digital coding techniques.

Chapter Seven briefly discussed the early research done on packet systems: "packetizing" voice. It was recognized that, like data transmission, voice transmission has a "bursty" quality—sound interspersed with periods of silence. Consequently, voice packets can share a common channel, just as data packets do today.

The rationale for voice by packets is much the same as data by packets: to share the transmission and switching facilities. Certainly, the concepts implemented with an integrated digital system such as SBS and the ISDN standards point to a movement to integrated voice-data systems.

The concept of voice by packet is illustrated in Figure 9-14. A packet voice terminal (PVT) is used to provide the interface of the telephone analog handset and a data terminal. The work at this time (primarily by the Defense Advanced Research Projects Agency [DARPA], AT&T Bell Labs, GTE Corp., MIT, and Tymnet) has focused on the analog-to-digital techniques of CVSD (continuously variable slope delta modulation) or LPC (linear predictive coding). The voice processor provides for analog and digital speech conversion. The protocol processor is responsible for controlling the attached PVT modules. It generates and interprets the packets necessary for establishing a call or session. It also contains buffers for the incoming and outgoing packets. The network interface processor is conceived to provide the network-dependent packet interface.

Experiments and research thus far encourage optimistic predictions for using packet-switching networks for both voice and data. However, voice by packet does present some significant problems. First, it is desirable to use existing packet networks for voice transmission to preclude building a redundant network. Data transmission is relatively intolerant of errors, so the packet-switching protocols today, such as X.25, assume the posture of correcting as many errors as possible. However, voice transmission is quite tolerant of occasional errors. For example, a 40-millisecond speech segment, if lost, would not affect the intelligibility of a conversation between two users.

However, error tolerance can place a network designer in a "catch 22" situation. For example, if a connectionless network supports voice by packet, an occasional lost packet may do no harm. On the other hand, a series of lost packets could possibly change the meaning of a conversation. For instance, consider a packet voice conversation such as this, "Yes, our meeting is in the SJO Airport—I will meet you there." The packet relating to the "J" is damaged and interpreted as SFO—San Francisco Airport. The two individuals are going to experience a frustrating "nonmeeting."

Another problem pertains to the delay of the transmission of the packets through intermediate nodes of the network, and the consequent delay of their arrival at the receiver. In data packet networks, packets encounter different delays,

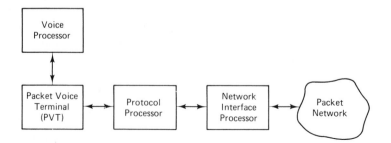

Figure 9-14. Packet-Voice System

especially if they are travelling through a non-session-oriented network. Voice reproduction requires a fixed rate of packet reconstruction and a fixed rate of *playout* at the receiving end to the user. Since packets arrive at variable times, a packet must be delayed and buffered at the receiving site in order to allow the reassembling of any late-arriving packets. A point is reached, however, at which late-arriving, nonarriving, or wandering packets simply must be ignored and the resultant incomplete output packets be given to the end user. This can create gaps in a voice conversation if the delays become severe.

One approach to solve the delay problem is based on choosing a target *playout* by an analysis of the network to determine when the majority of packets arrive. Upon passing the threshold, the packets are presented as output. Several approaches are under study to enhance this technique by dynamically adjusting the delay time based on network conditions at a particular period.

The third problem pertains to the choice of a packet size. To minimize the delay of the packet and to decrease the effect of a lost, damaged, or late-arriving packet, it is desirable to keep the packets as short as possible. Short packets provide for faster response time than long packets. However, long packets provide for better channel utilization, because short packets have more non-user data in the form of packet headers and control fields. Optimum packet size must consider response time, throughput, and the effect of late or lost packets.

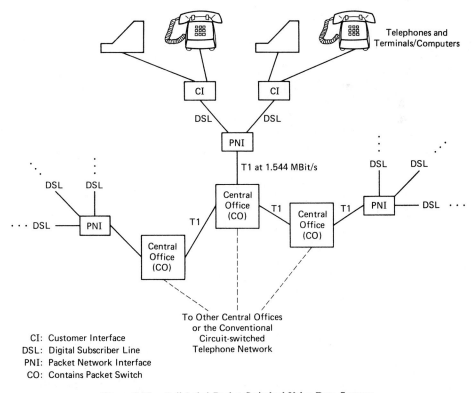

CI: Customer Interface
DSL: Digital Subscriber Line
PNI: Packet Network Interface
CO: Contains Packet Switch

Figure 9-15. Bell Labs' Packet-Switched Voice-Data Systems

BELL LABS' PACKET-SWITCHED VOICE-DATA PATENT

In contrast to the ISDN standards, which use a hybrid of circuit and packet switching, several emerging packet voice systems use only packet switching to carry both voice and data. Bell Labs has received a patent through the work of a former employee, Jonathan S. Turner (now at Washington University in St. Louis, Missouri).

The approach by Turner is shown in Figure 9-15. At the user premises, voice channels and data transmissions are packetized and digitized at the customer interface (CI) before they are sent to the telephone central office. The packets are transmitted across the customer's digital subscriber line (DSL) to the packet switch interface, then over 1.5-Mbit/s T1 channels to the packet switch residing in the central office.

Unlike conventional packet switches, Turner's system utilizes very high-speed parallel processing, in which several activities take place concurrently in the switch. The switches route the packets with self-routing algorithms, and the packets move by logical channel assignments from switch to switch to the final destination. Turner estimates a national voice-data network would experience a delay of only 100 to 200 milliseconds—certainly sufficient to diminish most of the *playout* problems discussed earlier.

SUMMARY

In the near future, a terminal or personal computer will be able to accept spoken input from its user, perform grammar and syntax corrections, and, if necessary, produce a finished, typed manuscript. Several such products are now available, offering a limited vocabulary. As the technologies of speech synthesis, artificial intelligence, packet voice, and integrated voice-data networks converge, computer networks will undergo a significant transformation. In the future, the terminal keyboard will be a thing of the past.

10

TCP/IP

INTRODUCTION

In the late 1960s and early 1970s networks were not designed to allow resource sharing among users residing in different networks. Network administrators also were reluctant to allow users to tap into their resources, due to concerns about security. In addition, they were experiencing excessive utilization of their network resources. As a result, it was difficult for a user to extend the use of an information system to another user across different networks. The networks either were incompatible with each other, or were not allowed to communicate due to administrative problems.

During this time it became increasingly acknowledged that it made good sense to share resources among user applications. But in order to do so network administrators would have to agree upon a set of common technologies and standards to allow the networks to communicate. It also followed that applications such as electronic mail and file transfer should be standardized, as well, to permit interconnections of end-user applications (not just networks). The Transmission Control Protocol and the Internet Protocol (TCP/IP) were thus developed to address these issues. This chapter provides an analysis of these protocols.

TCP/IP AND INTERNETWORKING

In order to understand the operations of TCP/IP, several terms and concepts must first be introduced. In Figure 10-1, the terms *gateway* or *router* are used to describe a machine that performs relaying functions between networks. Figure 10-1 shows a gateway placed between networks A, B, and C.

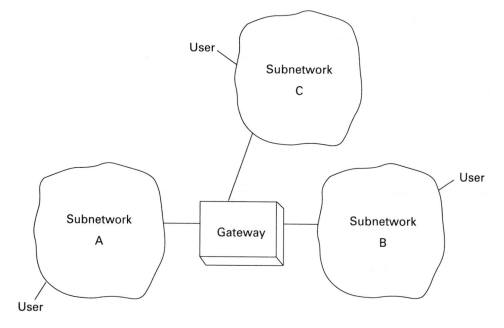

Figure 10-1. The Gateway and Subnetworks

Networks A, B, and C are often called *subnetworks*. The term does not mean that they provide fewer functions than a conventional network. Rather, it means that the three networks consist of a full logical network with the subnetworks contributing to the overall operations for internetworking. Stated another way, the subnetworks comprise an internetwork, or an internet.

An internetworking gateway is designed to remain transparent to the end-user application. Indeed, the end-user application resides in the host machines connected to the networks; rarely are user applications placed in the gateway. This approach is attractive from several standpoints. First, the gateway need not burden itself with application layer protocols. Since they are not invoked at the gateway, the gateway can dedicate itself to fewer tasks, such as managing the traffic between networks. It is not concerned with application level functions such as data base access, electronic mail, and file management.

Second, this approach allows the gateway to support any type of application, because the gateway considers the application message as nothing more than a transparent protocol data unit (PDU).

In addition to application layer transparency, most designers attempt to keep the gateway transparent to the subnetworks, and vice versa. That is, the gateway does not care what type of network is attached to it. The principal purpose of the gateway is to receive a PDU that contains adequate addressing information to enable the gateway to route the PDU to its final destination, or to the next gateway. This feature is attractive because it makes the gateway somewhat modular; it can be used on different types of networks.

Software must be written to enable communications to take place between the subnetwork protocol and the gateway. These procedures are usually proprietary in nature, and standards do not describe this interface between the gateway and the subnetwork. The exception to this statement is the publication of IEEE, OSI, and Internet service definitions that describe procedures between the host and gateway protocols (layers).

EXAMPLE OF TCP/IP OPERATIONS

Figure 10-2 shows the relationship of subnetworks and gateways to layered protocols. It is assumed that the user application in host A sends an application PDU to an application layer protocol in host B, such as a file transfer system. The file transfer software performs a variety of functions and appends a file transfer header to the user data.

As indicated by the arrows pointing downward in the protocol stack at host A, this unit is passed to TCP, which is a transport layer protocol. TCP performs several functions (discussed shortly) and adds a header to the PDU passed to it. The unit of data is now called a *segment*. The PDU from the upper layers is considered to be data to TCP.

Next, the TCP passes the segment to the network layer, which operates with IP. IP again performs specific services and appends a header. This unit (now called a *datagram* in TCP/IP terms) is passed down to the lower layers. Here, the data link layer adds its header, as well as a trailer, and the data unit (now called a *frame*) is

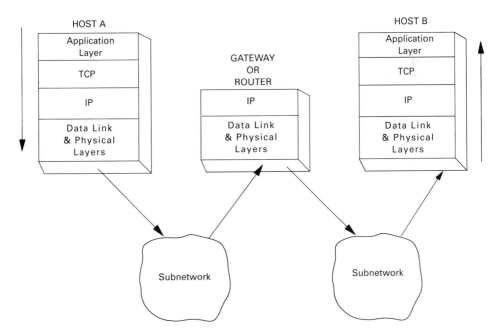

Figure 10-2. Example of TCP/IP Operations

launched into the network by the physical layer. If host B sends data to host A, the process is reversed, of course, and the direction of the arrows changes.

TCP/IP is unaware of what goes on inside the network. The network manager is free to manipulate and manage the PDU in any manner necessary. However, in most instances the Internet PDU (data and headers) remains unchanged as it is transmitted through the subnet. In Figure 10-2 we see its emergence at the gateway, where it is processed through the lower layers and passed to the IP (network) layer. Here, routing decisions are made based on the addresses provided by the host computer.

After these routing decisions have been made, the datagram is passed to the communications link that is connected to the appropriate subnetwork (consisting of the lower layers). The datagram is re-encapsulated into the data link layer PDU (usually called a *frame*) and passed to the next subnetwork. As before, this unit moves through the subnetwork transparently (usually), where finally it arrives at the destination host.

The destination (host B) receives the traffic through its lower layers and reverses the process that transpired at host A. That is, it decapsulates the headers by stripping them off in the appropriate layer. The header is used by the layer to determine the actions it is to take; the header governs the layer's operations.

The PDU created by the file transfer application is passed to the file transfer application residing at host B. If hosts A and B are large mainframe computers, this application is likely an exact duplicate of the software at the transmitting host. However, the application may perform a variety of functions, depending on the header it receives. It is conceivable that the data could be passed to another end-user application at host B, but in many instances, the user at host A merely wants to obtain the services of a server protocol, such as a file transfer or electronic mail server. If this is the case, it is not necessary for an end-user application process to be invoked at host B.

In order to return the retrieved data from the server at host B to the client at host A, the data are transferred downward through the layers in host B, through the network, through one gateway to the next gateway, then up the layers of host A to the end user.

RELATED PROTOCOLS

TCP/IP operates with a wide variety of other protocols. The protocols that rest over TCP are examples of the application layer protocols, providing services such as file transfer, electronic mail, terminal services, and so on. The lower two layers represent the data link and physical layers and, as Figure 10-2 depicts, are implemented with a wide choice of standards and protocols. Other protocols are available to perform route discovery and to build the routing tables used by IP to relay the traffic through an internet.

PORTS AND SOCKETS

Each application layer process using the TCP/IP protocols must identify itself with a *port* number. This number is used between the two host computers to identify which application program is to receive the incoming traffic.

The use of port numbers also provides a multiplexing capability by allowing multiple user programs to communicate concurrently with one application program, such as TCP. The port numbers identify these application entries. The concept is quite similar to a service application point (SAP) in the OSI Model.

In addition to the use of ports, TCP/IP-based protocols also use an abstract identifier called a *socket*. The socket was derived from the network input/output operations of the 4.3 BSD UNIX system. It is quite similar to UNIX file access procedures, in that it identifies an endpoint communications process. In TCP/IP, a socket is the concatenation of a port number and the network address (the IP address, discussed next) of the host that supports the port service.

In the Internet, some port numbers are preassigned. These are called *well-known ports,* and they are used to identify widely used applications called *well-known services.* The well-known port numbers occupy values ranging from 0 to 255. An individual organization should not use the numbers within these ranges, because they are reserved.

THE IP ADDRESS STRUCTURE

TCP/IP networks use a 32-bit address to identify a host computer and the network to which the host is attached. The structure of the IP address is depicted in Figure 10-3. Its format is *IP ADDRESS = NETWORK ADDRESS + HOST ADDRESS.*

The IP address does not identify a host, per se, but rather a host's connection to its network. Consequently, if a host machine is moved to another network, its address space must be changed.

IP addresses are classified by their formats. Four formats are permitted: class A, class B, class C, or class D. As illustrated in Figure 10-3, the first bits of the address specify the format of the remainder of the address field in relation to the network and host subfields. The host address is also called the *local address* (or the REST field).

The class A addresses provide for networks that have a large number of hosts. The host ID field is 24 bits. Therefore, 2^{24} hosts can be identified. Seven bits are devoted to the network ID, which supports an identification scheme for as many as 127 networks (bit values of 1 to 127).

Class B addresses are used for networks of intermediate size. Fourteen bits are assigned for the network ID and 16 bits are assigned for the host ID. Class C networks contain fewer than 256 hosts (2^8). Twenty-one bits are assigned to the network ID. Finally, class D addresses are reserved for multicasting, a form of broadcasting, but within a limited area.

MAJOR FEATURES OF IP

IP is quite similar to the ISO 8473 (the Connectionless Network Protocol, or CLNP) specification explained in the last section of this chapter. Many of the ISO 8473 concepts were derived from IP.

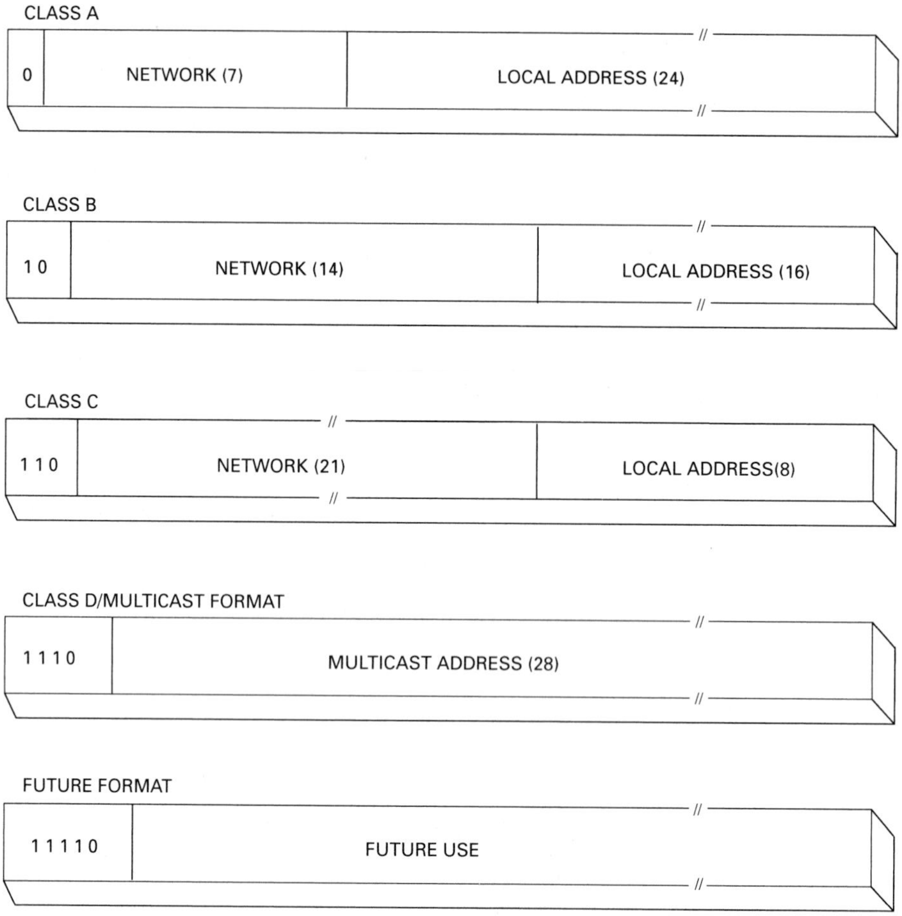

CLASS A

| 0 | NETWORK (7) | LOCAL ADDRESS (24) |

CLASS B

| 1 0 | NETWORK (14) | LOCAL ADDRESS (16) |

CLASS C

| 1 1 0 | NETWORK (21) | LOCAL ADDRESS(8) |

CLASS D/MULTICAST FORMAT

| 1 1 1 0 | MULTICAST ADDRESS (28) |

FUTURE FORMAT

| 1 1 1 1 0 | FUTURE USE |

Figure 10-3.   IP Address Formats

IP is an example of a connectionless service. It permits, without any prior call setup, the exchange of traffic between two host computers. (However, these two computers usually share a common connection-oriented transport protocol.) Since IP is connectionless, it is possible that datagrams could be lost between the two end user's stations. For example, the IP gateway enforces a maximum queue length size, and if this queue length is violated, the buffers will overflow. In this situation, additional datagrams are discarded in the network. For this reason, a higher-level transport layer protocol (such as TCP) is essential to recover from such problems.

IP hides the underlying subnetwork from the end user. In this context, it creates a virtual network for that end user. This aspect of IP is quite attractive, because it allows different types of networks to attach to an IP gateway. As a result, IP is reasonably simple to install and, because of its connectionless design, it is quite accommodating.

Since IP is an unreliable, best effort, datagram-type protocol, it has no reliability mechanisms. It provides no error recovery for the underlying subnetworks. It has no flow-control mechanisms. The user data (datagrams) may be lost, duplicated, or even arrive out of order. It is not the job of IP to deal with most of these problems. As we shall see later, most of the problems are passed to the next higher layer, TCP.

IP supports fragmentation operations. *Fragmentation* refers to an operation wherein a protocol data unit (PDU) is divided or segmented into smaller units. This feature can be quite useful, because all networks do not use the same size PDU. For example, X.25-based wide area networks (WANs) typically employ a PDU (called a *packet* in X.25) with a data field of 128 octets. Some networks allow negotiations to a smaller or larger PDU size. The Ethernet standard limits the size of a PDU to 1500 octets. Conversely, proNET-10 stipulates a PDU of 2000 octets.

Without the use of fragmentation, a gateway would be tasked with trying to resolve incompatible PDU sizes between networks. IP solves the problem by establishing the rules for fragmentation at the gateway and for reassembly at the receiving host.

IP Datagram

A productive approach to the analysis of IP is to first examine the fields in the IP datagram (PDU) depicted in Figure 10-4.

The *version* field identifies the version of IP in use. Most protocols contain this field because some network nodes may not have the latest release of the protocol available. The current version of IP is 4.

The *header length* field contains four bits which are set to a value to indicate the length of the datagram header. The length is measured in 32-bit words. Typically, a header without QOS options contains 20 octets. Therefore, the value in the length field usually is 5.

The *type of service* (TOS) field can be used to identify several QOS functions provided for in Internet. Transit delay, throughput, precedence, and reliability can be requested with this field.

The next three bits are used for other services and are described as follows: Bit 3 is the *delay bit* (D bit). When set to 1 this TOS requests a short delay through an internet. The aspect of delay is not defined in the standard, and it is up to the vendor to implement the service. The next bit is the *throughput bit* (T bit). It is set to 1 to request for high throughput through an internet. Again, its specific implementation is not defined in the standard. The last bit used is the *reliability bit* (R bit), which allows a user to request high reliability for the datagram. The next two bits, 6 and 7, are not used at this time.

The *total length* field specifies the total length of the IP datagram. It is measured in octets and includes the length of the header and the data. IP subtracts the header length field from the total length field to compute the size of the data field. The maximum possible length of a datagram is 65,535 octets (2^{16}). Gateways that service IP datagrams are required to accept any datagram that supports the maximum size of a PDU of the attached networks. Additionally, all gateways must accommodate datagrams of 576 octets in total length.

The IP protocol uses three fields in the header to control datagram fragmentation and reassembly. These are the *identifier, flags,* and the *fragmentation offset*

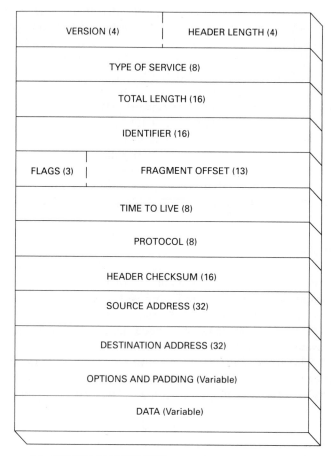

(n) = NUMBER OF BITS IN FIELD

Figure 10-4.   The IP Datagram

fields. The identifier field is used to identify uniquely all fragments from an original
datagram. It serves with the source address at the receiving host to identify the
fragment. The flags field contains bits to determine if the datagram may be fragmented, and if fragmented, one of the bits can be set to determine if this fragment
is the last fragment of the datagram. The fragmentation offset field contains a value
which specifies the relative position of the fragment to the original datagram. The
value is initialized as 0 and is subsequently set to the proper number if/when the
gateway fragments the data. The value is measured in units of eight octets. We
devote a special section later in this chapter to fragmentation/reassembly and the
use of these three fields.

The *time-to-live* (TTL) parameter is used to measure the time a datagram has
been in the internet. It is quite similar to CLNP's lifetime field. Each gateway in the
internet is required to check this field and to discard it if the TTL value equals 0. A
gateway is also required to decrement this field in each datagram it processes. In
actual implementations, the TTL field is a "number of hops" value. Therefore,
when a datagram proceeds through a gateway (hop), the value in the field is decre-

mented by a value of one. Some implementations of IP use a time counter in this field and decrement the value in one-second decrements.

The TTL field is used not only by the gateway to prevent endless loops, it can also be used by the host to limit the lifetime that segments have in an internet. Be aware that if a host is acting as a gateway, it must treat the TTL field by the gateway rules. Check with the vendor to determine when a host throws away a datagram based on the TTL value. Ideally, the TTL value could be configured and its value assigned based on observing internet performance. Additionally, network management information protocols such as those residing in SNMP might wish to set the TTL value for diagnostic purposes. Finally, if your vendor uses a fixed value that cannot be reconfigured, make certain that it is fixed initially, to allow for your internet's growth.

The *protocol* field is used to identify the next level protocol above the IP that is to receive the datagram at the final host destination. It is quite similar to the type field found in the Ethernet frame. The Internet standards groups have established a numbering system to identify the most widely used upper-layer protocols. For example, the number 6 identifies TCP, and the number 20 identifies the OSI transport layer (class 4).

The *header checksum* is used to detect a distortion that may have occurred in the header. Checks are not performed on the user data stream. Some critics of IP have stated that the provision for error detection in the user data would allow the gateway to at least notify the sending host that problems have occurred. Whatever one's view is on the issue, the current approach keeps the checksum algorithm in IP quite simple. It does not have to operate on many octets, but it does require that a higher-level protocol at the receiving host must perform some type of error check on the user data if it cares about the data integrity.

IP carries two addresses in the datagram. These are labeled *source* and *destination addresses* and remain the same value throughout the life of the datagram. These fields contain the IP addresses examined earlier in this chapter.

The *options* field is used to identify several additional services, to be discussed shortly. The options field is not used in every datagram. The majority of implementations use this field for network management and diagnostics.

The *padding* field may be used to make certain that the datagram header aligns on an exact 32-bit boundary.

Finally, the *data* field contains the user data. IP stipulates that the combination of the data field and the header cannot exceed 65,535 octets.

MAJOR IP SERVICES

This section provides an overview of the major services of IP. Be aware that vendors have different products for IP, and some may not support all the features described in this section of the book.

IP Source Routing

IP uses a mechanism called *source routing* as part of its routing algorithm. Source routing allows an upper-layer protocol (ULP) to determine how the IP gateways route the datagrams. The ULP has the option of passing a list of internet addresses to the IP module. The list contains the intermediate IP nodes that are to be transited during the routing of the datagrams to the final destination. The last address on the list is the final destination of an intermediate node.

When IP receives a datagram, it uses the addresses in the source routing field to determine the next intermediate hop. IP uses a pointer field to learn about the next IP address. If a check of the pointer and length fields indicate the list has been completed, the destination IP address field is used for routing. If the list is not exhausted, the IP module uses the IP address indicated by the pointer.

The IP module then replaces the value in the source routing list with its own address. Of course, it must then increment the pointer by one address (4 bytes) in order for the next hop to retrieve the next IP address in the route. With this approach, the datagram follows the source route dictated by the ULP and also records the route along the way.

Routing Operations.   The IP gateway makes routing decisions based on the routing list. If the destination host resides in another network, the IP gateway must decide how to route to the other network. Indeed, if multiple hops are involved in the communications process, then each gateway must be traversed, and the gateway must make decisions about the routing.

Each gateway maintains a routing table that contains the next gateway on the way to the final destination network. In effect, the table contains an entry for each reachable network. These tables could be static or dynamic, although dynamic tables are more common. The IP module makes a routing decision on all datagrams it receives.

The routing table contains an IP address for each reachable network and the address of a neighbor gateway (that is, a gateway directly attached to this network). The neighbor gateway is the shortest route to the destination network. Otherwise, the IP gateway logic establishes that the gateway is directly connected to this network.

The IP routing is based on a concept called the *distance metric*. This value is usually nothing more than the fewest number of hops between the gateway and the final destination. The gateway consults its routing table and attempts to match the destination network address contained in the IP header with a network entry contained in the routing table. If no match is found, it discards the datagram and builds an error message to send back to the IP source (by a companion protocol to IP, called the Internet Control Message Protocol [ICMP]). This message contains a "destination unreachable" code. If a match is found in the routing table, the gateway then uses it to determine the outgoing port.

Loose and Strict Routing.   IP provides two options in routing the datagram to the final destination. *Loose source routing* gives the IP modules the option of using intermediate hops to reach the addresses obtained in the source list, as long as the datagram traverses the nodes listed. Conversely, *strict source routing* requires that the datagram travel only through the networks whose addresses are indicated in the source list. If the strict source route cannot be followed, the originating host IP is notified with an error message. Both loose and strict routing require that the route-recording feature be implemented.

Route-Recording Option

The route-recording option operates in the same manner as source routing with the recording feature which was just discussed. This means that any IP module that receives a datagram must add its address to a route-recording list. In order for the route recording operation to occur, the receiving IP module uses the pointer and length fields to determine if any room is available to record the route. If the route-recording list is full, the IP module simply forwards the datagram without inserting its address. If it is not full, the pointer is used to locate the first empty full octet slot, the address is inserted, and the IP module then increments the pointer to the next IP slot.

The Timestamp Option

Another very useful option in IP is the provision for timestamping the datagram as it traverses each IP module through the internet. This idea allows a network manager to determine not only the route of the datagram through the internet, but also the time at which each IP module processed the datagram. This can be quite useful for assessing the efficiency of gateways and routing algorithms.

The time used with the timestamp is based on milliseconds (ms) using universal time (the old Greenwich mean time). Obviously, the use of the universal time does not guarantee completely accurate timestamps between machines, because machines' clocks may vary slightly. Nonetheless, in most networks the universal time in ms provides a reasonable degree of accuracy.

ICMP

The Internet Protocol is a connectionless-mode protocol, and as such, it has no error-reporting or error-correcting mechanisms. It relies on a module called the *internet control message protocol* (ICMP) to: (a) report errors in the processing of a datagram, and (b) provide for some administrative and status messages.

ICMP resides in a host computer or a gateway as a companion to the IP. The ICMP is used between hosts or gateways for a number of reasons, including: (1) when datagrams cannot be delivered; (2) when a gateway directs traffic on shorter routes; or (3) when a gateway does not have sufficient buffering capacity to hold and forward protocol data units.

The ICMP will notify the host if a destination is unreachable. ICMP is also responsible for managing or creating a time-exceeded message in the event that the lifetime of the datagram expires. ICMP also performs certain editing functions to determine if the IP header is in error or is otherwise unintelligible.

ICMP Message Format

The ICMP message format is shown in Figure 10-5. ICMP messages are carried in the user portion of the IP datagram. The protocol field in the IP header is set to 1 to signify the use of ICMP. All ICMP messages contain three fields: (a) the type field to define the type of message; (b) the code field to describe the type of error or status information; and (c) a checksum field for computing a 16-bit 1s complement on the ICMP message. The ICMP error-reporting message also carries the internet header and the first 64 bits of the user data field. These bits are quite useful for troubleshooting and problem analysis.

ICMP Error- and Status-Reporting Procedures

The error-reporting and status-reporting services as reported by ICMP are summarized below.

- Time exceeded on datagram lifetime: This service is executed by a gateway in the event that the time-to-live field in the IP datagram has expired (its value is zero) and the gateway has discarded the datagram.
- Parameter unintelligible: The destination host or gateway can invoke this service if it encounters problems processing any part of an IP header. Typically, this occurs if a field is unintelligible and it cannot process the datagram.
- Destination unreachable: This service is used by a gateway or the destination host. It is invoked if a gateway encounters problems reaching the destination network specified in the IP destination address. It also can be used by a destination host if an identified higher-level protocol is not available on the host, or if a specified port is not available (inactive).

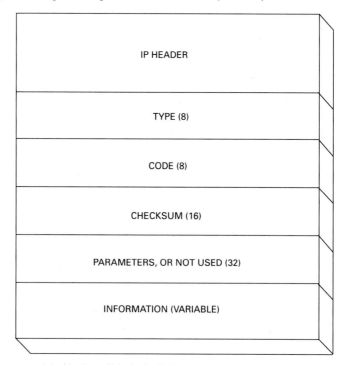

(n) = Number of bits in the field

Figure 10-5. The ICMP Message Format

- Source quench: This service is a form of flow and congestion control invoked by a router. It is invoked if the machine has insufficient buffer space for queuing incoming datagrams. If the datagram is discarded, the router may send this message to the host that originated the datagram.

- Echo and echo reply: The echo request and reply are valuable for determining the state of an internet. The echo can be sent to any IP address, such as a gateway. The gateway must return a reply to the originator. In this manner a network administrator can find out about the state of the network resources, because a reply is sent only in response to a request. If a problem exists, a reply is not returned.

- Redirect: This service, used to provide routing management information to the host, is invoked by a gateway; it sends the ICMP message to the source host. The redirect message indicates that a better route is available. Typically, this means the host should send its traffic to another gateway. Under most circumstances, the gateway generates a redirect message if its routing table indicates that the next hop—either the host or gateway—is on the same network as the network contained in the source address of the IP header.

- Timestamp and timestamp reply: This service is used by gateways and hosts to determine the delay incurred in delivering traffic through a network or networks. The ICMP data unit contains three timestamp values:
  - Originate timestamp. Time the sender last processed the message before sending it (filled in immediately before sending).
  - Receive timestamp. Time the echoer first processed the message upon receiving it (completed immediately upon receiving message).
  - Transmit timestamp. Time the echo last processed the message before sending it (filled in immediately before reply is sent).

- Information request or information reply: This service is used for a host to determine the identification of the network to which it is attached. A host sends the ICMP message with the IP header source and destination address fields coded as 0, which is used to convey "this network." A replying IP module (one designated as a server that is authorized to perform this task) will return the reply with the address fully specified in both the source and destination address fields of the IP header.

- Address mask request and reply: The use of an address mask allows the "host" part of the IP address to be divided into a subnetwork address and the host address. This technique allows a network administrator to divide a large network into more manageable, smaller subnetworks. This service is used by a host to obtain a subnet mask used on the host's network. The requesting host can send the request directly to an IP gateway, or it may broadcast it.

VALUE OF THE TRANSPORT LAYER

In previous chapters we emphasized that the Internet Protocol (IP) is not designed to recover from certain problems, nor does it guarantee the delivery of traffic. IP is designed to discard datagrams that are outdated or have exceeded the number of permissible transit hops in an internet.

Certain user applications require assurance that all datagrams have been delivered safely to the destination. Furthermore, the transmitting user may need to know that the traffic has been delivered at the receiving host. The mechanisms to achieve these important services reside in TCP (UDP is connectionless and does not provide these services).

The job of TCP may be quite complex. It must be able to satisfy a wide range of applications requirements and, equally important, it must be able to adapt to a dynamic environment within an internet. It must establish and manage sessions (logical associations) between its local users and these users' remote communicating partners. This means that TCP must maintain an awareness of the user's activities in order to support the user's data transfer through the internet. These topics are covered in more detail in this chapter.

TCP

As depicted in Figure 10-6, TCP resides in the transport layer of the conventional layered model. It is situated above IP and below the upper layers. The figure also illustrates that TCP is not loaded into the gateway. It is designed to reside in the host computer, or in a machine that is tasked with end-to-end integrity of the transfer of user data. In practice, TCP usually is placed in the user host machine.

Since IP is a connectionless network, the tasks of reliability, flow control, sequencing, opens, and closes are given to TCP. Although TCP and IP are tied together so closely that they are used in the same context "TCP/IP," TCP also can support other protocols. For example, another connectionless protocol such as the ISO 8473 (Connectionless Network Protocol or CLNP) could operate with TCP (with adjustments to the interface between the modules). In addition, the application protocols, such as the File Transfer Protocol (FTP) and the Simple Mail Transfer Protocol (SMTP), rely on many of the services of TCP.

Major Features of TCP

TCP provides a number of services to the upper layers. This section presents an overview of these services.

TCP is a *connection-oriented protocol*. This term refers to the fact that TCP maintains status and state information about each user data stream flowing into and out of the TCP module. The term used in this context also means TCP is responsible for the end-to-end transfer of data across one network or multiple networks to a receiving user application (or the next upper-layer protocol). Referring to Figure 10-2, TCP must ensure that the data are transmitted and received between the two hosts across one or more networks.

Since TCP is a connection-oriented protocol, it is responsible for the *reliable transfer* of each of the characters (bytes or octets) passed to it from an upper layer. Consequently, it uses sequence numbers and positive/negative acknowledgments.

The term associated with these aspects of a connection-oriented protocol is a *virtual circuit*.

A sequence number is assigned to each octet transmitted. The receiving TCP module uses a checksum routine to check the data for damage that may have occurred during the transmission process. If the data are acceptable, TCP returns a positive acknowledgment (ACK) to the sending TCP module. If the data are damaged, the receiving TCP discards the data and uses a sequence number to inform the sending TCP about the problem. Like many other connection-oriented protocols, TCP uses timers to ensure that the lapse of time is not excessive before remedial measures are taken for either the transmission of acknowledgments from the receiving site and/or the retransmission of data at the transmitting site.

TCP receives the data from an upper-layer protocol (ULP) in a *stream-oriented* fashion. This operation is in contrast to many protocols in the industry. Stream-oriented protocols are designed to send individual characters and *not* blocks, frames, datagrams, etc. The bytes are sent from an ULP on a stream basis, byte-by-byte. When they arrive at the TCP layer, the bytes are grouped into TCP *segments*. These segments are then passed to the IP (or another lower-layer protocol) for transmission to the next destination. The length of the segments is determined by TCP, although a system implementor can also determine how TCP makes this decision.

Implementors of TCP who have worked with block-oriented systems, such as IBM operating systems, may have to make some adjustments in their thinking regarding TCP performance. TCP allows the use of variable length segments because of its stream-oriented nature. Therefore, applications that normally work with fixed blocks of data (such as a personnel application that sends fixed employee blocks or a payroll application that transmits fixed payroll blocks) cannot rely on TCP to present this fixed block at the receiver. Actions must be taken at the application level to delineate the blocks within the TCP streams.

TCP also checks for duplicate data. In the event the sending TCP retransmits the data, the receiving TCP discards the redundant data. Redundant data might be introduced into an internet when the receiving TCP entity does not acknowledge traffic in a timely manner, in which case the sending TCP entity retransmits the data.

In consonance with the stream transfer capability, TCP also supports the concept of a *push* function. This operation is used when an application wants to make certain that all the data that it has passed to the lower-layer TCP have been transmitted. In so doing, it governs TCP's buffer management. To obtain this function, the ULP issues a send command to TCP with a push parameter flag set to 1. The operation requires TCP to forward all the buffered traffic in the form of a segment or segments to the destination.

In addition to using the sequence numbers for acknowledgment, TCP uses them to *resequence* the segments if they arrive at the final destination out of order. Because TCP rests upon a connectionless system, it is quite possible that duplicate datagrams could be created in an internet. TCP also eliminates duplicate segments.

TCP uses an inclusive acknowledgment scheme. The acknowledgment number acknowledges all octets up to and including the acknowledgment number less one. This approach provides an easy and efficient method of acknowledging traffic, but it does have a disadvantage. For example, suppose ten segments have been transmitted, yet due to routing operations, these segments arrive out of order. TCP is obligated to acknowledge only the highest contiguous byte number received without error. It is not allowed to acknowledge the highest arrived byte number until all intermediate bytes have arrived. Therefore, like any other connection-oriented protocol, the transmitting TCP entity could eventually time-out and retransmit the traffic not yet acknowledged. These retransmissions can introduce a considerable amount of overhead in a network.

The receiver's TCP module is also able to *flow control* the sender's data, which is very useful for preventing buffer overrun and a possible saturation of the receiving machine. The concept used with TCP is somewhat unusual among communications protocols. It is based on issuing a "window" value to the transmitter. The transmitter is allowed to transmit a specified number of bytes within this window, after which the window is closed and the transmitter must stop sending data.

Also, TCP has a very useful facility for *multiplexing* multiple user sessions within a single host computer onto the ULPs. This operation is performed by defining some conventions for sharing ports and sockets between users.

TCP provides *full-duplex transmission* between two TCP entities. This permits simultaneous two-way transmission without having to wait for a turnaround signal, which is required in a half-duplex situation. In addition, TCP provides the user with the capability to specify levels of *security* and *precedence* (priority level) for the connection. Even though these features are not implemented on all TCP products, they are defined in the TCP standard.

TCP provides a *graceful close* to a virtual circuit (the logical connection between the two users). A graceful close ensures that all traffic has been acknowledged before the virtual circuit is removed.

Passive and Active Opens

Two forms of connection establishment are permitted with TCP ports. The *passive open* mode allows the ULP (for example, a server) to tell the TCP and the host operating system it is to wait for the arrival of connection requests from the remote system (the foreign system), rather than issuing an active open. Upon receiving this request, the host operating system assigns a port number to this end. This feature could be used to accommodate communications from remote users without going through the delay of an active open.

The applications process requesting the passive open may accept a connection request from any user (given some profile matching requirements, explained shortly). If any call can be accepted (without profile matching), the foreign socket number is set to zeros. Unspecified foreign sockets are allowed only on passive opens.

The second form of connection establishment is the *active* open mode. In this situation, the ULP specifically designates another socket through which a connection is to be established. Typically, the active open is issued to a passive open port in order to establish a virtual circuit.

TCP supports a scenario in which two active opens are issued to each other at the same time. TCP will make the connection. This feature allows applications to issue an open at any time, without concern that another application has issued an open.

TCP provides strict conventions on how the active and passive opens may be used together. First, an active open identifies a specific socket, as well as its given precedence and security levels. TCP grants an open if the remote socket has a matching passive open, or if it has issued a matching active open.

The Transmission Control Block (TCB)

Because TCP must remember several things about each virtual connection, it stores information in a *Transmission Control Block* (TCB). Among the entries stored in the TCB are the local and remote socket numbers, pointers to the send and receive buffers, pointers to the retransmit queue, the security and precedence values for the connection, and the current segment. The TCB also contains several variables associated with the send and receive sequence numbers.

THE TCP SEGMENT

The PDUs exchanged between two TCP modules are called *segments*. Figure 10.6 illustrates the format for the segment. In this section we will examine each of the fields of the segment.

The segment is divided into two parts, the header part and the data part, with the data part following the header part. The first two fields of the segment are

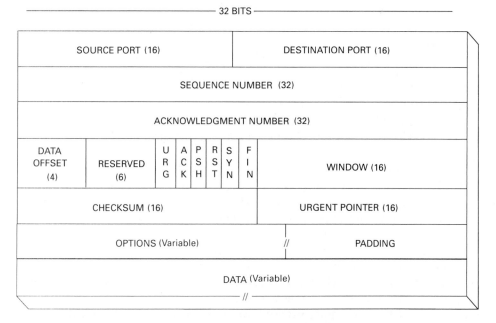

Figure 10-6. The TCP Segment (PDU)

identified as *source port* and *destination port*. These 16-bit fields identify the upper-layer application programs that are using the TCP connection.

The next field is labeled *sequence number*. This field contains the sequence number of the first octet in the user data field. Its value specifies the position of the transmitting module's byte stream. Within the segment it specifies the first user data octet in the segment.

The sequence number also is used during a connection management operation. If a connection request segment is used between two TCP entities, the sequence number specifies the *initial send sequence* (ISS) number that is to be used for the subsequent numbering of the user data.

The *acknowledgment number* is set to a value which acknowledges data previously received. The value in this field contains the value of the sequence number of the next expected octet from the transmitter. Since this number is set to the next expected octet, it provides an inclusive acknowledgment capability, in that it acknowledges all octets up to and including this number, minus 1.

The *data offset* field specifies the number of 32-bit aligned words that comprise the TCP header. This field is used to determine where the data field begins.

As you might expect, the *reserved* field is reserved. It consists of 6-bits which must be set to zero. These bits are reserved for future use.

The next six fields are called *flags*. They are labeled as control bits by TCP and are used to specify certain services and operations to be used during the session. Some of the bits determine how to interpret other fields in the header. The six bits are used to convey the following information:

- URG indicates that the urgent pointer field is significant.
- ACK signifies whether the acknowledgment field is significant.
- PSH signifies that the module is to exercise the push function.
- RST indicates that the connection is to be reset.
- SYN indicates that the sequence numbers are to be synchronized; it is used with the connection-establishment segments as a flag to indicate handshaking operations are to take place.
- FIN indicates that the sender has no more data to send. It is comparable to the end-of-transmission (EOT) signal in other protocols.

The next field, labeled *window,* is set to a value indicating how many octets the receiver is willing to accept. The value is established based on the value in the acknowledgment field (acknowledgment number). The window is established by adding the value in the window field to the value of the acknowledgment number field.

The *checksum* field performs a 16-bit 1s complement of the 1s complement sum of all the 16-bit words in the segment. This includes the header and the text. The purpose of the checksum calculation is to determine whether the segment arrived error-free from the transmitter.

The next field in the segment, the *urgent pointer,* is used only if the URG flag is set. The purpose of the urgent pointer is to signify the data octet in which urgent data follow. Urgent data also are called *out-of-band* data. TCP does not dictate what happens for urgent data. It is implementation specific; that is, it signifies *where* the urgent data are located, only. It is an offset from the sequence number and points to the octet following the urgent data.

The *options* field was conceived to provide for future enhancements to TCP. It is constructed in a manner similar to that of IP datagrams option field, in that each option specification consists of a single byte containing an option number, a field containing the length of the option, and, finally, the option values themselves.

Presently the option field is quite limited in its use, with only three options defined for the TCP standard:

0:   end-of-option list
1:   no operation
2:   maximum segment size

Finally, the *padding* field insures that the TCP header is filled to an even multiple of 32 bits. After that, as the figure illustrates, user *data* follow.

USER DATAGRAM PROTOCOL (UDP)

You may recall that the connectionless protocol provides no reliability or flow control mechanisms. It also has no error recovery procedures. The UDP is classified as a connectionless protocol. Sometimes it is used in place of TCP in situations in which the full services of TCP are not needed. For example, several application layer protocols, such as the Trivial File Transfer Protocol (TFTP) and the Remote Procedure Call (RPC), use UDP.

UDP serves as a simple application interface to the IP. Since it has no reliability, flow control, or error-recovery measures it serves principally as a multiplexer/demultiplexer for the receiving and sending of IP traffic.

UDP makes use of the port concept to direct the datagrams to the proper upper-layer applications. The UDP datagram contains a destination port number and a source port number. The destination number is used by the UDP module to deliver the traffic to the proper recipient.

Format of the UDP Message

Perhaps the best way to explain this protocol is to examine the message and the fields that reside in the message. As Figure 10-7 illustrates, the format is quite simple and includes the following fields:

Source Port: This value identifies the port of the sending application process. The field is optional. If it is not used, a value of 0 is inserted in this field.

Destination Port: This value identifies the receiving process on the destination host machine.

Figure 10-7. Format for the UDP

Length: This value indicates the length of the user datagram, including the header and the data. This value implies that the minimum length is 8 octets.

Checksum: This value is the 16-bit 1s complement of the 1s complement sum of the pseudo-IP header, the UDP header, and the data. It also performs a checksum on any padding (if it was necessary to make the message contain a multiple of two octets).

There is little more to say about UDP. It is a minimal level of service used in many transaction-based application systems. However, it is quite useful when the full services of TCP are not needed.

ROUTE DISCOVERY PROTOCOLS

Internetworking, gateways, and routers play a very important role in TCP/IP-based networks. Indeed, the IP protocol is designed around the concept of internetworking host computers with gateways and routers. IP is *not* a route discovery protocol. It makes use of the routing tables that are filled in by the protocols explained in this section.

Individual networks may be joined by a computer acting as a switch between the networks. The switch operations are programmed to route the traffic to the proper network by examining a destination address in the datagram and matching the address with entries in a routing table. Those entries indicate the best route to the next network or gateway.

Even though these individual networks may be administered by local authorities, it is common practice for a group of networks to be administered as a whole system. From the perspective of an internet, this group of networks is called an *autonomous system,* and it is administered by a single *authority.* Examples of autonomous systems are networks located on sites such as college campuses, hospital complexes, and military installations. The networks located at these sites are connected by a gateway. Since these gateways operate within an autonomous system, they often choose their own mechanisms for routing data.

The autonomous systems are identified by autonomous system numbers. The manner by which this is accomplished is up to the administrators, but the idea is to use different numbers to distinguish particular autonomous systems. Such a numbering scheme might prove helpful if a network manager does not wish to route traffic through an autonomous system which, even though it might be connected to the manager's network, may be administered by a competitor, does not have adequate or proper security services, and so on. By the use of routing protocols and numbers identifying autonomous systems, the gateways can determine how they reach each other and how they exchange routing information.

Gateways are given responsibilities for only a part of an internet. Thus, a gateway does not have to know about all other gateways of an internet, but can rely on neighbor gateways and/or gateways in other autonomous systems to reveal their routing information. Indeed, if they had insufficient knowledge to make a routing decision, they simply chose a default route. Figure 10-8 shows the relationship between external and internal gateway protocols. A number of packet-switched networks labeled autonomous system A is connected to another set of packet-switched networks labeled autonomous system B. Gateway 1 (G1) and gateway 2 (G2) use an *external gateway protocol* (EGP) to exchange data and control information. The two internets use their own *internal gateway protocols* (IGP) for route management inside each autonomous system. Therefore, it is not unusual for a gateway to support two (or more) route discovery protocols, depending on where the traffic is destined. These gateways use an IGP within each autonomous system and an EGP between autonomous systems.

The EGP and IGP systems must find the best route and construct a routing table. IP then uses the routing table to relay the datagrams through a network, between networks, or between autonomous systems.

The routing tables are changed at the gateway when another gateway discovers one of the following:

- A new network has been found.
- A better path to a network has been found.
- A "better" path must be degraded.

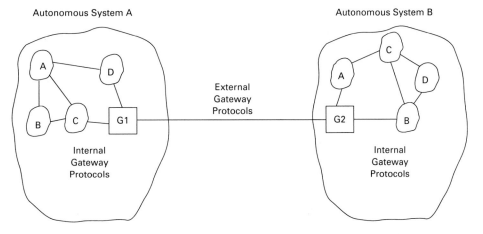

Figure 10-8. Gateway Protocols

What is a "better" path? It depends upon the choice of the network administrator. In most instances it is simply the fewest number of "hops" between the sender and the receiver. It also may be based on a variety of criteria generally referred to as *least-cost routing,* or *cost metrics.* The name does not mean that routing is based solely on obtaining the least-cost route in the literal sense, however. Other factors often are part of a network-routing algorithm:

- Capacity of the links
- Delay and throughput requirements
- Number of datagrams awaiting transmission onto a link
- Load leveling through the network
- Security requirements for the link
- Type of traffic vis-à-vis the type of link
- Number of intermediate links, networks, and gateways between the transmitting and receiving hosts
- Ability to reach (connect to) intermediate nodes and, of course, the final receiving host.

Examples of Route Discovery Protocols

The external gateway protocol (EGP) is used to provide network reachability information between neighboring gateways. Although the name of the protocol includes the term "external," these gateways may exist in the same or different autonomous systems. However, the more common approach is to use EGP between gateways not belonging to the same autonomous system.

EGP contains procedures to: (a) acquire neighbors, (b) exchange information between neighbors, and (c) monitor the reachability of neighbors. EGP uses polling procedures which allow the gateways to monitor each other and to exchange routing update messages.

EGP is restricted to advertise reachability to those networks completely within the gateway's autonomous system. Therefore, an EGP gateway has a restricted authority. One of its values is to prevent a plethora of information from being transmitted around a network. EGP messages advertise multiple gateways. The EGP gateway is able to send a sequence of reachability information blocks relative to a specified network.

EGP does not compute against the values contained in the routing update message. The software is designed only to establish that EGP can state that there is a path available. EGP is used to advertise reachability information and cannot function with elaborate topologies that include looping gateways.

The Routing Information Protocol (RIP) was developed based on research at the Xerox Palo Alto Research Center (PARC) and Xerox's PUP and XNS routing protocols. Since RIP was designed for LANs, it is based on a broadcast technology; a gateway periodically broadcasts its routing table to its neighbors. The broadcast aspect of RIP has brought forth complaints about its inefficiency.

RIP is classified as a vector-distance algorithm-routing protocol. RIP routing decisions are based on the number of intermediate "hops" to the final destination. RIP advertises only network addresses and distances (usually, a number of hops). It uses a hop count to compute the route cost, but it uses a maximum value of 16 to indicate that a network is unreachable. The hop count is a metric for the "cost" of the route. Other metrics may be used, such as delay, security, bandwidth, and so on, but most implementations use a simple hop count. Also, RIP needs information on all networks within the autonomous system, and it exchanges information only with neighbors.

Machines that participate in the RIP operations are active or passive devices. Active machines (usually gateways) advertise routes to other machines. Passive machines (usually host computers) do not advertise routes, but receive messages and update their routing tables.

RIP uses the user datagram protocol (UDP). UDP port number 520 is used by the RIP machines for sending and receiving RIP messages.

The Open Shortest-Path-First protocol (OSPF) was designed to meet the need for a high-performance gateway protocol. The purpose of a gateway protocol is to distribute routing information between routers in a network or between networks. The goal of this operation is to provide network users with reliable and efficient routes through a network or through a collection of networks. The end result, if successfully implemented, is an efficient use of the network, with the user experiencing low delay and high throughput at a reasonable cost.

OSPF is classified as a dynamic, adaptive protocol in that it adjusts automatically (without human intervention) to problems in the network (or autonomous system) and provides short convergence periods to stabilize the routing tables. In addition, it is designed to prevent looping of traffic, which is quite important in mesh networks or in LANs where multiple routers may be available to connect different LANs.

Looping occurs when a computer or network receives the traffic it originates. This problem can create throughput, delay, and congestion problems in the system. In Figure 10-9, traffic sent from network 3 to router 3 is looped back to network 3 from routers 3, 6, 5, and 4.

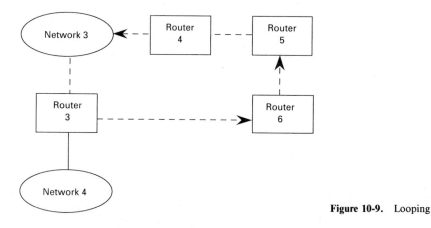

Figure 10-9. Looping

OSPF prevents looping by blocking or "pruning" the communications paths that could create this problem. Traffic transmitted from network 3 to router 4 would not be sent to router 5. Likewise, traffic sent from network 3 to router 3 would not be allowed to pass from router 5 to router 4. Despite this, all these networks and routers retain full connectivity to each other. In other words, each network and router can send and receive traffic. The OSPF spanning tree operation results in a network resembling a pruned tree, with the branches (the communications links) that could create a loop cut or pruned.

Certain networks, routers, and the host computers are organized into an autonomous system. An autonomous system is one in which a group of routers use a common routing protocol, such as OSPF, to exchange routing information. OSPF is classified as an internal gateway protocol (IGP) because it supports routing within one autonomous system only. The exchange of routing information between autonomous systems is the responsibility of another protocol—an external gateway protocol, or EGP.

Each router contains a routing directory (called a routing data base in OSPF). The data base contains information about the link interfaces at the router that are operable, as well as status information about each neighbor to a router. The data base is the same for all participating routers within an area.

The information in the routing data base focuses on the topology of the network(s) with a directed graph. Routers and networks form the vertices of the graph. Periodically, this information is broadcast (flooded) to all routers in the autonomous system. An OSPF router computes the shortest path to the other routers in the autonomous system, with itself as the working node (the working node is termed the *root* in this protocol). It then prunes away all paths except the "shortest path" to each router.

A very flexible and powerful aspect of this protocol is that separate cost metrics can be computed for various types of service (TOS), such as delay, throughput, and precedence of the datagram. If the calculations reveal that two paths are of equal value, OSPF will distribute the traffic equally on these paths.

OSPF can support one or many networks. The networks within an autonomous system can be grouped into what is termed an *area*. The design of the protocol allows an area to be hidden from other areas. Indeed, an area can be hidden from the full autonomous system. In addition, due to increasing concern about security, OSPF includes authentication procedures. Routers must go through some simple procedures to authenticate the traffic between them.

The method to determine routing information outside the autonomous system is referred to as *external routing*. Routing information pertaining to this capability is typically derived from OSPF as well as other protocols, such as the EGP. Alternately, it could be established through static routes between the autonomous systems. Routing could even be established by default routes. This information is also flooded through the autonomous system.

Each area runs its own shortest-path-first algorithm. It also has its own topological data base which differs from other areas. The purpose of the area is to isolate and partition portions of the autonomous system and to reduce the amount of information a router must maintain about the full autonomous system. Also, it means that the overhead information transmitted between routers to maintain OSPF routing tables is substantially reduced.

OSPF uses the term *backbone* to define that part of an autonomous system that conveys packets between areas. The full path of a packet proceeds as follows: (1) intra-area path to a router attached to the backbone; (b) the backbone path to the destination area router; and (c) the destination intra-area path to the destination network.

OSPF utilizes "Hello" protocol for advertising state information between neighbors. Hello packets are used to confirm agreements among routers in a common network about operations and certain timers. In effect, it is used to make certain that neighbor relationships make sense.

The purpose of OSPF is for routers to inform each other about internet paths via advertisements. These advertisements are sent to routers by update packets. Four types of advertisements are used:

- *Router links advertisement.* Contains information on a router's interfaces into an area. It is used by all routers and flooded throughout an area.
- *Networks links advertisements.* Contains a list of routers connected to a network. It is used by a broadcast network and flooded throughout an area.
- *Summary links advertisement.* Contains information on routes outside an area. It is used by border routers and flooded to the border routers' areas (but inside the autonomous system).
- *Autonomous systems (AS) extended links advertisement.* Contains information on routes in other autonomous systems. It is used by a boundary router and flooded through the autonomous system.

The Application Layer Protocols

The application layer protocols in the TCP/IP suite are some of the most widely used protocols in the industry. Some of these protocols are very rich in function—a full explanation of their operations would require an extensive discourse. Since this book is a communications book, they are not described here. The major application layer protocols are as follows:

- *TELNET* for terminal services
- *Trivial File Transfer Protocol* (TFTP) for simple file transfer services
- *File Transfer Protocol* (FTP) for more elaborate file transfer services
- *Simple Mail Transfer Protocol* (SMTP) for message transfer services (electronic mail).

SUMMARY

The Internet protocols have become one of the most widely used protocol suites in the world. They are designed to facilitate the internetworking of computer networks. While generally referred to as the TCP/IP protocols, the Internet protocols actually contain scores of protocols that are designed to support internetworking operations. Several of these protocols are called gateway protocols (more accurately, route discovery protocols) and are implemented with such widely used protocols as the external gateway protocol (EGP), the routing information protocol (RIP), and the open shortest path first (OSPF). In addition, the Internet protocols contain a wealth of application layer protocols such as TELNET, the file transfer protocol (FTP), and the simple mail transfer protocol (SMTP).

11

Personal Computer Networks

INTRODUCTION

This chapter provides an overview of the use of personal computers in data communications networks. The chapter introduces the subject by explaining how personal computers communicate with each other and handle errors. Next, the operations for linking of personal computers with mainframe computers are examined, as well as several prominent personal computer file-transfer protocols. We conclude the subject by describing the use of personal computers in local area networks, the use of network operating systems (NOSs), and prominent implementations of personal computer networks.

GROWTH IN THE PERSONAL COMPUTER INDUSTRY

The term "revolution" is often used in the computer industry to describe not only the radical transformations within the industry, but also the effect the computer has had on society. Perhaps nowhere is this more evident to the general public than in the field of personal computers (PCs). The PC has brought data processing to previously inaccessible places such as small businesses, schools, and homes. Another evidence of the extraordinary effect of the personal computer is visibly evident on television—ten years ago it would have been inconceivable to view during prime time a 15- or 30-second advertisement about a computer. The machines were somewhat mysterious and often evoked skepticism and even distrust among the general public. This writer vividly remembers seeing the first computer advertisement on prime-time TV. Today, such advertisements are commonplace, and the computer has entered into the mainstream of our lives.

The term "personal computer" typically describes a small machine that can be put to personal use, although many PCs today are powerful enough for rather extensive business applications. Prior to the advent of the name, these machines were called microcomputers to connote their smallness, not particularly in size (although that as well), but in their limited computing and input/output capacity.

The personal computer is still considered to be a machine of limited capacity, especially when compared to the maxi computers of today. Overall computing power is still a primary consideration in the purchase or acquisition of the PC. Because of these "limitations," some of the networking and communications capabilities of the PC are also limited. In this chapter we describe the data communications and networking characteristics of personal computers, describe the progress in the PC industry, and point out some opportunities that exist to utilize these machines more effectively.

PERSONAL COMPUTER COMMUNICATIONS CHARACTERISTICS

The communications characteristics of personal computers bear many similarities to larger mainframe computers. However, differences exist that must be considered when using the PC for networking and data communications. First, most personal computers are asynchronous. No technical reason exists why a PC cannot be synchronous, but many PC vendors have not built their communications board (port) with the wires necessary for carrying the timing signals required for synchronous transmission. However, more products are entering the marketplace each day that provide synchronous capabilities, such as SDLC, bisync, and even X.25.

It is possible for asynchronous PCs to communicate with synchronous systems by placing an asynchronous-to-synchronous adapter unit between the PC and its modem. The adapter also may be placed on the board. The adapter provides for signals to achieve clocking between the personal computer and the modem (pins 24, 15, and 17 of EIA-232-D, and pins 113, 114, and 115 of V.24 interfaces).

Some PC modems still use frequency modulation (FM) to carry the signal across the telephone channel. The most common approach is known as *frequency shift keying* (FSK). The concept is quite simple—two different frequency tones are used to represent either the 0 and 1 bit. Almost all PCs use full-duplex modems as well. Utilizing the FSK concept, the full-duplex modem uses four different tones: two for the transfer of 1s and 0s in one direction and the other two tones for transfer of 1s and 0s in the opposite direction.

Most PC modems use a better technology than FSK. One standard is the Bell 212A, a 1200 bit/s full-duplex *phase modulation* (PM) asynchronous device. As newer PC-oriented modems enter the market, phase modulation will be used more, due to its ability to support faster transmission rates.

With the rapidly decreasing costs of modems, most PCs today now utilize line speeds of at least 2400 bits/s, and 9.6 Kbit/s is not at all uncommon. Many PC modems today use autobaud operations which permit variable bit rates to be transmitted between the machines. These operations are usually implemented with the CCITT V.32 modem specification.

Unlike large-scale mainframe computers, many PCs house the modem within the PC cabinet. These devices are called plug-in modems and are very popular from the standpoint of relieving work space at a crowded desk and providing a modem in a portable terminal for the traveler. Their principal disadvantage lies in the fact that they cannot be used by other devices.

The high-speed modems are becoming very popular because of the decreased time required to transmit data across a channel. Anyone who has sat in front of a PC waiting for the transfer of data across a 300 bit/s modem will attest to the slow transfer rate. For example, a 300 bit/s modem can transfer a one-page document in two minutes. In contrast, a 1200 bit/s modem transfers the same document in 30 seconds. A 2400 bit/s modem is twice as fast—it transfers the document in 15 seconds. In the future, the newer modems designed for PCs will transfer a document even faster. For example, a 4800 bit/s modem transfers the same document in 7.5 seconds, and a 9.6 kbit/s modem transfers the document in 3.75 seconds.

Many PCs today use "smart" modems. These modems have built-in intelligence which allows the PC to control functions such as program-controlled dialing. The characters command the modem to perform certain functions. For instance, the Hayes smart modem uses the following command characters:

- A Places the modem in an off-hook condition and waits for a carrier from the remote modem.
- CN Turns the modem carrier on or off.
- DS Instructs the Hayes to dial a phone number; the S is the actual number.
- EN Commands the modem to perform echoplexing (discussed shortly).
- HN Instructs the modem to hang up.

Many people program the PC to perform more sophisticated functions with a smart modem. For example, some users code programs in the BASIC language to instruct the modem to perform as an automatic call unit. The BASIC program can store many telephone numbers, and the calling can be controlled by interfacing with the program from the PC keyboard.

Error Handling

Large-scale systems such as the Amdahl, IBM, Burroughs, and ICL machines perform very sophisticated error-checking techniques on the communications lines between the machines. The PC usually uses a simpler technique for performing error checking across the channel.

One of the simplest forms of error checking is called *echoplex*. The technique entails the PC sending each character across a full-duplex communications line to a remote site. In turn, the remote site sends, or echoes, each character *back* to the PC. If the PC receives the same character it sent, it assumes the transmission is correct. If not, it assumes an error has occurred and retransmits the erroneous character. Echoplex is designed for two-way, full-duplex circuits.

A new user of a PC system often confuses echoplex with *local echo*. Local echo is often used when a half-duplex modem is connected to the telephone channel.

In this situation, the data are echoed back from the *local modem,* to the PC monitor, and not from the remote site. If the device has not been set up properly, the PC may display double characters on the screen. This occurs because a modem is providing local echo and the remote site is providing remote echo (echoplex). The problem of double imaging is solved by turning off the local echo.

Parity checking is a widely used technique for detecting errors. It consists of adding a single bit (a parity bit) to each string of bits that comprise a character. For example, with a 1s odd-parity system, the bit is set to 1 or 0 to give the character bits an odd number of bits that are 1s. This parity bit is inserted at the transmitting station, sent with each character in the message, and checked at the receiver to determine if each character is the correct parity. If a transmission impairment caused a "bit flip" of 1 to 0 or 0 or 1, the parity check would so indicate.

However, a two-bit flip (for instance, a 1 flipped to a 0, and another 1 flipped to a 0) would not be detected by the single-bit parity technique, which creates a high incidence of errors in some transmissions. Multilevel modulation (where two or three bits are represented in a signal change) requires a more sophisticated technique. The single-bit parity is also unsuited to many analog voice-grade lines because of the groupings of errors that usually occur on this type of link.

The use of *double parity* is a refinement of the single-parity approach. Instead of a parity bit on each character, this technique also places a parity (odd or even) on a block of characters. The block check provides a better method to detect errors within a character and across characters. It is also called a two-dimensional parity check code. The double-parity combination provides a substantial improvement over the single method. A typical telephone line with an error rate of $1:10^5$ can be improved substantially with the two-dimensional check. However, both single and double parity reduces user throughput because of the many overhead parity bits.

Another form of error checking is the *checksum.* This is a simple technique and can provide for improved error detection over echoplex and parity checking. Essentially, the transmitting PC adds together the numeric values of all the characters in the transmission. The total is placed into a 16-bit block-check count by using the least significant 16 bits of the calculation. This value becomes the checksum and is transmitted with the user data to the receiving PC. The receiving PC performs the same calculation and compares its checksum with the transmitted checksum. If the two values are the same, the receiver assumes the block has been transmitted without errors. A slight chance exists that an erroneous block may go undetected with the checksum, but studies reveal that an erroneous block will go undetected in only one out of 1,000 transmissions. How many correct blocks are transmitted before an erroneous block is received? On a high-quality line, several thousand. Consequently, on a typical configuration an undetected block error may not occur for many months of operation.

A fairly recent entry into the PC arena for error checking is called the *cyclic redundancy check* (CRC). It is widely used with the protocols discussed in Chapter Four (HDLC, SDLC), but has found its way into the PC industry only recently.

CRC performs a division on the data before they are transmitted. The quotient for the calculation is discarded, and the remainder is transmitted as the CRC field. As in the checksum approach, the receiving device performs an identical calculation, and if the two are consistent, it is quite likely that the transmission occurred error-free. The problem of implementing a technique such as the CRC lies not in its inherent complexity, but in adapting currently existing PC boards and software to a new technique. As the PC world matures, CRC will become a common vendor offering.

Indeed, some of the new modems use a subset of HDLC called LAPM (link access procedure for modems). This specification is published as part of the CCITT's V.42 Recommendation. In effect, the use of LAPM places the data link layer protocol inside the modem and moves it outside of the user device (in this case, the personal computer). In addition to the use of a superior protocol such as HDLC, V.42 also can be implemented with V.42 *bis,* which provides for data compression features.

USING THE PERSONAL COMPUTER AS A SERVER

The concept of a *server* is based on the use of one or more personal computers to perform specific tasks for a number of other PCs. The most common functions are disk, file, and print servers. Some vendors also classify a server as one that provides an outlet (gateway) to other networks. One other classification is a 3270 server, which acts as a support mechanism to a 3270 cluster configuration.

Some confusion exists in the industry regarding the definition of a disk and file server. A disk server provides low-level support. Typically, it performs the basic read and write operations to disk sectors. In contrast, a file server is a higher-level support mechanism, performing such functions as lockout and dynamic allocation of space on the disk. As the name implies, the print server provides printing support for the PCs attached to the system.

The PC user faces two primary dilemmas when selecting a server: (1) a dedicated versus a shared server; (2) a centralized or a distributed server. The dedicated server has better performance than a shared server, since it is dedicated to one or a few specific tasks. A shared server's performance is almost always poorer because of the continuous interrupts made to its operating system to provide service to multiple users and/or multiple user applications. In addition, a shared server shares its disk with multiple users, which decreases the actual capacity available to the community. A dedicated server is usually more secure than a shared server, since measures can be concentrated to make only one machine secure. On the other hand, a dedicated server is usually more expensive, since it is dedicated to performing one task. This inefficiency is especially evident if the traffic does not warrant a dedicated personal computer server. In this case, sharing this server with other applications can reduce the cost to the user.

A workstation utilizing a disk or file server may not require hard disk. For example, tasks (in the form of software) can be downline loaded to a diskless PC, which contains optional (read only) memory on the interface card to perform the support tasks.

In summary, if the work and traffic warrant a dedicated processor, so be it. However, for a network or system in which traffic is not heavy, it may make more sense to share the server with other user applications.

The selection of servers also entails the choice of a centralized or a distributed server. A centralized server means that one PC is used to provide the service function. Distributed servers entail the use of more than one PC for the support function.

A distributed server system can be very complex. Servers with (a) large data bases, (b) multiple copies of data, and (c) short response time on updates require a complex distributed environment. If possible, complexities should be avoided because of the increased risk of system failures, data inconsistencies, and increased costs. Vendor offerings must be carefully evaluated.

LINKING THE PERSONAL COMPUTER TO MAINFRAME COMPUTERS

In today's office the PC is increasingly used as an ancillary tool to tie into the company's larger-scale computer system (mainframe computers). Several very good reasons exist for linking PCs to mainframes. First, the PC provides a valuable tool for distributing the workload onto less expensive machines to perform simple tasks. Generalized mainframe computing is quite expensive, so it is preferable that the large-scale computer be used primarily for complex functions requiring powerful computation capabilities. Second, the PC might need to use the processing power of the mainframe, to perform complex calculations such as linear regressions or involved data base manipulations, for example. Third, the PC may wish to share the software and the data bases of the mainframe computer. Today, sharing is quite common in almost all offices, as users perform certain calculations with their own PCs, but go to the mainframe to obtain support for interaction with other applications and data bases.

Several options exist for connecting a PC to the mainframe. These options are depicted in Figure 11-1. The options are not all-encompassing, but provide some practical examples of how systems are being connected today:

1. Protocol conversion software is installed in the host computer (or front-end processor, if available) [Figure 11-1(a)]. The software works with the host's operating system and telecommunications packages to allow the personal computer to communicate in its conventional asynchronous, full-duplex EIA-232-D mode. The asynchronous ports are less expensive than their synchronous counterparts. Additionally, no protocol conversion board is needed for the PCs. However, *each* PC requires a port to the host.

2. A personal computer is used to emulate a cluster controller [Figure 11-1(b)]. The other personal computers use their conventional modes to communicate with the cluster emulator. This configuration reduces the number of ports required, since the emulator has only one coaxial cable connection to the host. However, the cluster can act as a bottleneck if it is overloaded with too many personal computers.

3. A configuration similar to that discussed in option 2 is shown in Figure 11-1(c). This configuration may be useful if an organization already has a configuration with cable and wiring intact. As an example, one port of the cluster controller is connected to a personal computer.

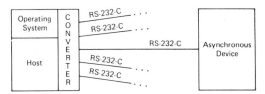

(a) Protocol Conversion Software

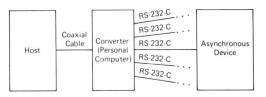

(b) Personal Computer Emulates Cluster Controller

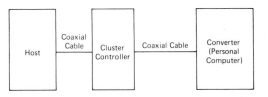

(c) Personal Computer Emulates Cluster Controller

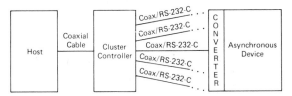

(d) Converter Boards in Personal Computer

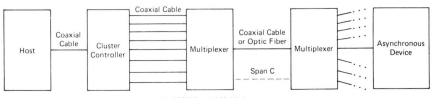

(e) 3274 Coaxial Multiplexer

Figure 11-1.   Personal Computer Link Options

4. Many organizations opt for the configuration in Figure 11-1(d). A protocol converter board is installed in each personal computer and communicates with the cluster controller through coaxial cable or EIA-232-D and the cluster's proprietary protocol. This approach is cost effective for a few personal computer connections to the host. However, over fifteen PC connections will likely sway the costs to favor the other options.

5. Another option often overlooked, but of significant merit in some installa-

tions, is the use of a 3274 coaxial multiplexer [Figure 11-1(e)]. This configuration is appropriate for connections of DTEs to the host computer which exceed 2500 feet (the maximum distance usually allowed from the terminals to the cluster controller). Some vendors claim the multiplexers become cost effective when the DTEs are located 1200 feet (and beyond) from the cluster. Moreover, the use of multiplexers has the notable advantage of pulling only one cable between the multiplexers [span C in Figure 11-1(e)].

Some personal computer literature indicates the versions of vendors' various products for linking to other computers are compatible. Unfortunately, such is not always the case. The vendor often modifies data communications packages to enable the package to run efficiently on specific hardware and operating systems. The old dictum, "let the buyer beware" is especially appropriate for PC data communications software and boards. Testing a product *before* committing to purchase it is a prudent and necessary approach to acquiring a PC data communications package.

FILE TRANSFER ON PERSONAL COMPUTERS

During the infant days of micro computing, the field was dominated primarily by hobbyists and other individuals who wished to experiment with this interesting new machine. One of the major problems during this time was exchanging data between the computers. Ward Christiansen solved this problem by writing a program which addressed the dual problems of (a) incompatible PC software and (b) incompatible telephone channel-oriented protocols. Christiansen based his program on the fact that the telephone line was usually the path to exchange data between computers, and the PC at that time almost always utilized the simple 300 bit/s modem. Most of these modems use identical modulation techniques. Christiansen wrote a file-transfer program and placed it in the public domain by donating it to various user groups. Today several versions exist of the now famous program in the public domain. Two of the better known programs are MODEM7 and XMODEM. XMODEM is described here, since it is a very widely used personal computer file transfer protocol.

The XMODEM format and data flow are depicted in Figure 11-2. The SOH field denotes the beginning of the message. The N(S) field is the sending sequence number field; it contains 8 bits, which allows for sequencing up to 255. The next field is the 1s complement of the N(S) field. It is calculated at the transmitting site and used at the receiving site to check for any damage to the sending sequence number. Next is the user data stream consisting of a maximum of 128 bytes of data. Finally, the last field is a block-check count field, which is used as a checksum on the data field.

The data flow for XMODEM is quite simple [see Figure 11-2(b)]. The transmission between the two PCs begins with the receiving computer sending a NAK control character to the transmitting site. Thereafter, the data blocks are exchanged one block at a time. The receiving site performs the checksum and sends back an ACK or NAK based on the previous transmission.

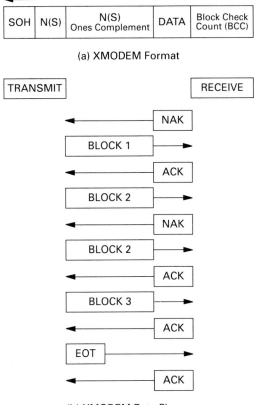

(a) XMODEM Format

(b) XMODEM Data Flow

Figure 11-2. XMODEM Personal
Computer Protocol

Like other protocols discussed in this book, personal computer protocols such as
XMODEM have additional features. For example, if a transmitting PC retransmits a
message unsuccessfully nine times, it performs a timeout and sends the *Cancel* control
character. This technique is found in the N1 (retry) and T1 (timer) functions of the
HDLC family (Chapter Four). Likewise, if the sender does not hear a receiver's response, it waits a period of ten seconds before attempting another retransmission. The
logic provides the ability for the receiving PC to ignore the duplicate message.

The XMODEM is a widely used protocol. It is simple, easy to understand, and
easy to use. Perhaps its major weakness is the use of an 8-bit field for the checksum,
which can cause some undetected errors. However, there are other versions of
XMODEM available that use the more sophisticated CRC error-checking technique,
which provides better integrity to the traffic flow.

Another popular package for the personal computer is BLAST. This product
is available for most widely sold personal computers. The BLAST protocol is more
powerful than XMODEM. It uses a two-way, full-duplex procedure with the sliding-
window concept discussed in Chapter Four. In addition, the error-checking technique utilizes CRC. BLAST allows data (binary files) as well as text files to be
transferred to another computer.

The Kermit protocol is an asynchronous protocol designed for transferring files between computers. The protocol is a very robust system providing for many options during the operations. As much as possible, Kermit remains transparent to the specific operating systems and mainframes. Indeed, Kermit can be used to support file transfer between IBM and DEC computers.

The transfer procedures for Kermit are somewhat similar to XMODEM. The process begins after the sender receives a NAK packet. It then sends a *send initiate* packet, which is used to begin the negotiation for the file transfer. After this process the sender sends a file header packet which contains the name of the file and the characteristics of the file. The successful reception of the file header enables the sender to begin sending data. Each data unit is acknowledged by the receiver. After the file transfer process is over, the sender sends an *end of file* (EOF) packet, determines whether it has more files to send, and if not, stops the process.

During the transfer operation, Kermit ensures that the characters transmitted are kept transparent to any network software or operating system by ensuring that control fields are properly identified and that control-like fields are recoded in the data field until presented in the end-user file.

One of the most attractive features of Kermit is the support of transferring any type of data, including ASCII, binary files, boolean fields, decimal fields, and so on. Before transmitting the user data, Kermit makes certain that the ASCII control characters inserted by the user are recoded during the transmission process to prevent any system from mistakenly acting upon them or absorbing them. It performs this support operation by the CHAR function, in which a control character has the value of 20 HEX added to it. The effect of this operation is to "move" this character into the printable string column of the ASCII table. The UNCHAR function reverses the process.

It is possible (likely) that control-like values could be placed in the user data field (after all, we have no control over what the user places in these fields). If actions are not taken on these values, a system could mistakenly assume these are legitimate control characters. Kermit handles this process by appending these fields with a # sign and XORing with 40 HEX. The XORing is used instead of just adding 40H because it keeps the high-order bit intact. In addition, Kermit supports several operations to ensure that seven-bit and eight-bit files operate properly.

These operations consume considerable overhead in the creation of additional control characters. Consequently, Kermit provides a simple compression scheme to reduce the amount of traffic on the communications channel.

As shown in Figure 11-3, the Kermit packet consists of six major fields. The *mark* field is coded as an ASCII SOH (value 1). This signifies the beginning of the packet. The *LEN* field is a length field that defines the number of bytes in the packet following the LEN field. The maximum total packet length is restricted to no greater than 96 bytes. The *SEQ* field is used to sequence each packet. It is a wrap-around counter in that once it reaches the maximum value of 63, it returns to 0 and continues to count. The *type* field defines the type of packet. It could contain a number of characters to define such packets types as data, ACKs, NAKs, EOTs, EOFs, etc. The *data* field contains user data, control information regarding the file

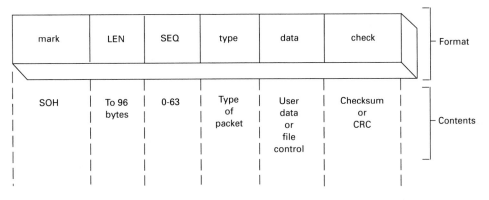

Figure 11-3. The Kermit Packet Format

transfer, or nothing. The *check* field is used to determine whether the packet was damaged on the transmission. Kermit permits several options for the use of the check field. One option uses a simple checksum, while another uses a cyclic redundancy check (CRC).

The type field in the Kermit packet is coded to provide information about end data or control fields. If coded with a *D,* this packet contains traffic from a file being transmitted. The *Y* code is used to acknowledge the successful transmission of a packet. The *Y* packet is also sent in response to a send initiate packet. The *NAK* packet is used to reject a packet which would require a retransmission from the sender. The *send initiate* packet is used to inform the receiver of this packet about the parameters to be used during the file transfer operation. The *file header* packet must contain the name of the file to be transmitted. The *error* packet is sent when an unrecoverable error (a fatal error) has been encountered. The *EOT* packet is sent when all files have been transmitted and the *EOF* is sent when one file has been completely transmitted. The *display text* on the screen is used to signify that the transmitted information is to be displayed. The *attribute* packet is used to send additional information about the file, such as administrative data (date, time, password information, security information, etc.).

Yet another popular PC package is Microcom MNP. This system operates in similar manner to the other techniques described before. It is available as a point-to-point protocol and supports a wide variety of computers.

MNP is somewhat different from the other systems in that it uses a layered protocol approach very similar to that of the OSI model. At the physical layer, it uses the 8-bit asynchronous start/stop approach. The data link level provides for error detection using a CRC 16-bit field; it also provides for Continuous ARQ error correction and for sliding-window systems, as well. It has options for half or full duplex and provides other features, such as link disconnect. In addition to these lower-level procedures, MNP provides for file-transfer capabilities similar to those of the systems discussed previously in this section. The full frame structure of MNP product is similar to the binary synchronous control protocol (BSC or bisync), except that each character within the frame is surrounded by the asynchronous start/stop bits. The start/stop bits provide the clocking signals across the interface between the devices, which enable the PCs to utilize the conventional asynchronous board.

Earlier in this section, the problem of vendor package incompatibility was discussed. While no easy answer to this problem exists, one approach would certainly ease the problem—the use of synchronous, code-transparent protocols. For example, the control fields used in word processing and data processing packages are often confused as communications protocol control fields by the communications package. However, if the I field in the synchronous frame was *not* examined or used by the synchronous communications package, the word-processing-generated or data-base-generated data could be placed into the I field without affecting the communications protocol. Such a move requires a major change to the vast majority of PCs in existence today which use asynchronous ports and protocols, but the vendors are moving toward this approach.

PERSONAL COMPUTERS AND LOCAL AREA NETWORKS

PCs are being highly touted as workstations, or even controllers, for local area networks (LANs). Rationale for the PC-oriented LAN is quite similar to the rationale for other LANs. Presently, over 40 vendors of PC LANs are in the marketplace. Unfortunately, very few of these systems are fully compatible with each other. In this section we examine some of the major PC LAN vendors and discuss some of their primary attributes.

The majority of personal computer local area networks (LAN) use one of three forms of network protocols: CSMA/CD, Star, and token passing. These systems are described in detail in Chapter Six. Consequently, they will not be discussed further here, except as they relate to specific products.

Be aware that building a PC-oriented local area network often places an individual in a world in which limited support is provided, especially in contrast to the large computer mainframe world where vendor support is rather extensive (even to the extent of having vendor systems-support personnel at the customer site 24 hours a day). The implementation of a PC LAN network often entails more individual effort and participation than does a large-scale effort. The user may be required to become familiar with the details of the system.

The performance of a vendor's product often does not live up to the sales publications' claims. This problem is one of the vexing aspects of using personal computer LANs. Several reasons exist for this situation. First, a vendor often states its local network transmission capacity is x number of megabits per second, so the customer may assume that the throughput of the application processes can obtain that speed. However, this author has seen systems which have a channel capacity stated at 10 Mbit/s, when in fact the final user throughput was below 60 kbit/s. Low throughput can often be traced to the limited capacity of the PC port (board). Some LAN PC ports have very limited buffers (perhaps even a single buffer), which creates a bottleneck between the PC and the high-capacity communications channel, often composed of broadband coaxial cable.

Other problems stem from the vendor software. The software may be inefficient, and in some instances bugs (logic errors) may still exist in the software. Even if the software works correctly, it is sometimes not up to the task of the comparable software existing on the large-scale computers. For instance, large-scale computers long ago solved the problem of multiuser access into data bases; lockouts are quite common in large-scale systems to prevent one user from writing to a data file while another user is reading it. This is not usually the case with personal computer networks—file read/write protection is fairly primitive. Moreover, the relatively straightforward mainframe task of multitasking is much more difficult with the personal computer, due to its limited CPU speed, memory size, and software. A considerable limitation exists on the amount of software that can be placed in a PC to perform the complex task of sharing software among multiple users.

It should be reemphasized that many of the PC LANs are incompatible with each other. This should come as no surprise, because most LANs and data communications packages among almost all vendors are incompatible. For example, even if a vendor states it is using the Ethernet CSMA/CD standard, it certainly does not mean that the product will communicate with another PC vendor that states it is using the Ethernet standard. The incompatibility is not due to any nefarious act on the part of the local area network vendor; rather, it stems from the facts that follow:

1. Even though a vendor may be working from a standard such as the Ethernet/ IEEE 802.3 standard, the standards must be written in excruciating detail to ensure that the designer understands the *exact* intent of each statement of the specification. This universal problem exists throughout the world of data communications.
2. A vendor often deviates from a standard to enhance a particular product. Standards often degrade a specific application in order to enhance a wider range of systems.

Another problem arises because a vendor sometimes understates the costs of a product. Costs should be examined very carefully by a potential customer. For example, let us assume the user is quoted that a LAN may be installed for $400 per node. This quote may not include additional interfaces required to make the nodes compatible; it may not even include the cable itself. It may not include other costs, such as an additional computer required to perform the duties of a file or print server.

Another potential problem may surface when an individual moves from a stand-alone PC to a configuration in which the PC ties into a LAN. The user is often chagrined to find the stand-alone system, while working very well by itself, will not work with other computers in the LAN. The solution often requires modification to the individual PC software. It may require the user to stop using particular features or particular packages that work well with the stand-alone system.

Finally, once the personal computer network is functioning, the user must be careful about adding other features. For example, the addition of another computer

board may present performance or compatibility problems with the currently existing LAN configuration. Often, this is simply a matter of trial and error until the
user finds something that actually works.

NETWORK OPERATING SYSTEMS (NOSs)

One of the important decisions an organization makes regarding PC-based LANs is
the purchase of the network operating system (NOS). The NOS is the heart and soul
of the LAN. It is responsible for managing the attached LAN stations and the
servers on the network. The NOS also provides security features, such as passwords
and access rights to software and data bases.

Administrative activities also are supported by the NOS. For example, auditing, monitoring, usage, and accounting operations are performed on network stations and server operations. Most NOSs provide for graphical user interface (GUI)
support as well as software metering. In addition, downloading software operations
fall within the responsibility of the NOS.

The NOS usually consists of many software modules for managing the LAN
resources. File backup operations, user login procedures, password aging, domain
naming, and address mapping are all common features of NOSs. Figure 11-4 summarizes the major features of the NOS.

- Manages the networking of LAN stations

- Oversees servers: users, backup, access rights

- Offers security features: passwords

- Performs naming services/directories

- Organizes users into groups with access rights

- Utilizes auditing and monitoring network resources

- Performs accounting services: correct time, disk storage, printing, . . .

- Supports application installation

- Performs software metering

- Features Login procedures

- Offers menu creation and use

Figure 11-4.   Major Features of the NOS

The major NOS vendors in the IBM and IBM clone LAN industry are Novell, Microsoft, IBM, and Banyan. The NOSs from these manufacturers contain many common operations such as directory management, naming services, and server operations. Notwithstanding, the seminar delegate should study each vendor carefully because the manner in which these NOSs provide these services varies widely.

Some NOSs have limited printer metering, others have rather awkward menu lists. The NOS should be evaluated in its ease of use and its efficiency in managing the resources on the LAN. For example, an NOS should readily accommodate to a dynamic LAN in which machines and people are relocated frequently. It should provide strong authentication and good security by supporting access rights to network resources. Without question, NOSs should have flexible and failsafe backup procedures for file servers, as well as document storage support features. Additionally, the NOS should be evaluated on the number of resources consumed to perform its management functions.

COMMON IBM PC LAN PROTOCOL STACKS

Figure 11-5 shows some of the more widely used layers for IBM PC-based LANs. IBM markets its token ring, PC broadband network, and PC baseband network as the physical and data link protocols for its products. The token ring product is aligned closely with the IEEE 802.5 standard. The PC network (both broadband and baseband) is modeled on the 802.3 standard. The logical link control (LLC) layer is usually configured as LLC type 2 on IBM LANs.

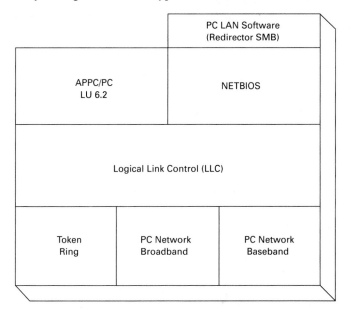

Figure 11-5. IBM PC LAN Protocol Stacks

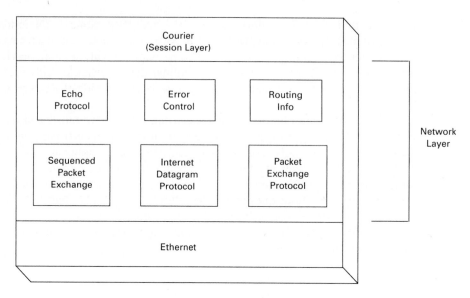

Figure 11-6. 3 COM Protocol Stack

NETBIOS or APPC/PC LU 6.2 is used to control user sessions and manage parts of the LAN. NETBIOS is a *de facto* industry standard which is used by other LAN vendors to manage the LAN resources. NETBIOS performs many functions normally associated with the network, transport, and session layers of a seven-layer model. It can be configured as connection-oriented or connectionless, and can perform source routing operations.

The upper-layer protocols that IBM supports are many. These modules perform services aligned with the presentation and application layers of a seven-layer model.

3 COM relies on the use of XNS protocols for most of its operations. Figure 11-6 shows six network layer protocols that were derived from XNS. The echo protocol is used to determine if a station is active. The error control protocol performs error reporting as well as some limited status reporting functions. The routing information protocol performs route discovery across an internetworked LAN. The sequenced packet exchange protocol is a connection-oriented protocol that works with virtual circuits. In contrast, the Internet datagram protocol is an IP-type protocol that performs for connectionless routing operations. The packet exchange protocol also provides for accountability of traffic similar to that of the sequenced packet exchange protocol, however its functions are more limited.

Novell relies principally on IPX for routing traffic on NetWare-based networks. IPX resembles the functions of IP (see Figure 11-7). NetWare has chosen not to run NETBIOS directly, but provides a NETBIOS emulator. The emulator operates with the application and DOS to mimic the functions of NETBIOS. The Net-Ware shell contains most of the control features of this NOS and also interfaces directly with the user application and DOS.

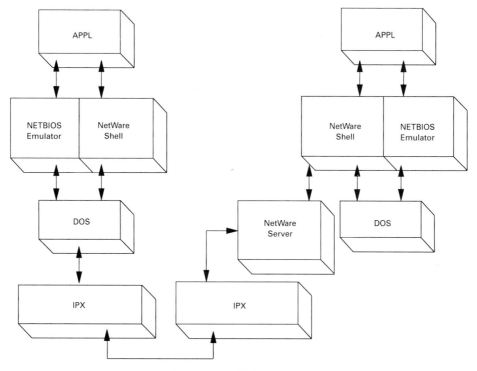

Figure 11-7. NetWare Layers

APPLETALK AND ETHERTALK

Apple Computer Company has been manufacturing local area networks (LANs) for Apple and Macintosh computers for several years. While some people in industry have stated that Apple's networks do not perform well, it should be understood that Apple's initial PC-based networks were designed to be very inexpensive, easy to implement, and as simple as possible. The personal computer product introduced by Apple when it began its networking efforts is known as AppleTalk. As stated before, the goal of AppleTalk was to provide an easy-to-implement system in which a user could almost plug-in-and-play. That is, users would not have to spend a great deal of time on configuration parameters and systems iterations. AppleTalk also provides for a peer-to-peer network in which each node is considered to be a peer to any other node, thus relieving the tiresome bottlenecks of centralized control.

As summarized in Figure 11-8, AppleTalk actually is divided into three specific types of networks—LocalTalk, EtherTalk, and TokenTalk. LocalTalk was the initial implementation of Apple's networking products. As suggested in the figure, it was designed to be inexpensive, yet still provide for modest data rates in the kilobit range. More recently, Apple also brought in the Ether-type protocol into its product line called EtherTalk. While this is more expensive technology, it does support a 10 Mbit rate and provides a large number of devices to be placed on one Apple net-

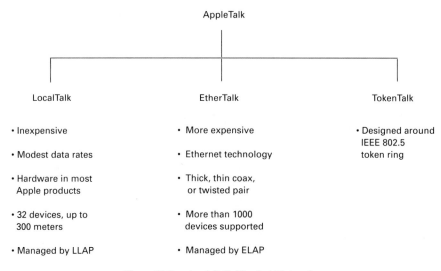

Figure 11-8. AppleTalk Physical Networks

work. A newer implementation of AppleTalk is TokenTalk, which is based on the IEEE 802.5 token ring specification.

AppleTalk contains many services other than lower-level network services. As Figure 11-9 shows, it provides upper-layer protocol services such as presentation, application, and session layer products. AppleTalk can operate at 230.4 Kbit/s for some users that do not need a large bandwidth capability, or it can be configured with a 10 Mbit/s topology.

Figure 11-9 shows the major protocols that are used in AppleTalk. The network functions are supported principally by the AppleTalk link access protocol (LLAP), which is a combination of an Ethernet system and an HDLC system. The network layer services also are provided by the datagram delivery protocol (DDP). Much of the logic of DDP is oriented toward internetworking to connect bridges and routers into an AppleTalk internet. DDP is responsible for routing datagrams within the internet and for accessing the routing table maintenance protocol (RTMP), which is a route discovery protocol. At the transport layer, AppleTalk supports a naming service called the name-binding protocol (NBP). It also supports the AppleTalk transaction protocol (ATP), which is an end-to-end reliable connection-oriented protocol.

AppleTalk supports a variety of protocols dealing with exchanging information between AppleTalk zones. The zone information protocol (ZIP) defines how information within zones is generated, managed, and deleted. The AppleTalk session protocol (ASP) is a session layer protocol responsible for managing sessions between entities, such as exchanging traffic without duplications and in the proper sequence. The printer access protocol (PAP) provides printer servers, and the echo protocol provides diagnostic services. The ADSP provides for stream protocol services similar to the ASP function.

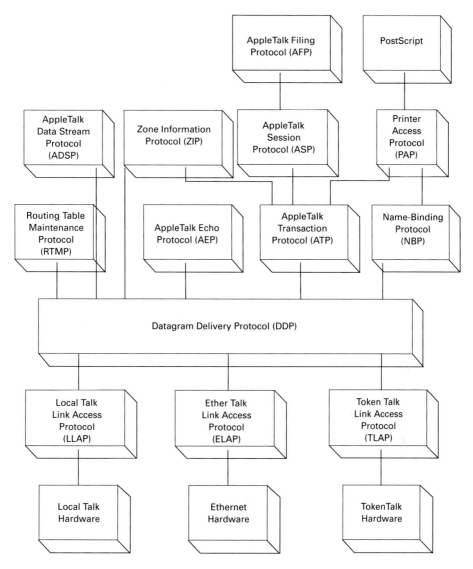

Figure 11-9. AppleTalk Layers

SUMMARY

Within a short span of ten years the personal computer has reshaped the computer industry dramatically. The PC is accelerating our movement to the information society, and with its increasing facilities and ease of use, it is becoming as familiar as the typewriter and the calculator. Yet its full potential has not yet been released. As artificial intelligence and digitized voice technologies mature, the PC will integrate these features into its architecture to create a machine of considerably more diversity and power.

12

The PBX and Data
Communications
Networks

INTRODUCTION

In the late 1970s and early 1980s the private branch exchange (PBX) was used predominantly as a telephone switching device for the office. Telephones were connected through wires into the PBX, which performed the task of switching calls between offices within an organization and trunks to the telephone central office. During this time several PBX manufacturers decided to design PBXs to handle voice and data traffic. Through a series of gradual changes, the PBX has evolved to become a powerful tool for integrated voice/data transmission and networking.

The PBX is called by other names, as well: private automated branch exchange (PABX) and computerized branch exchange (CBX). This chapter uses the generic term *PBX* to describe the device and provides a general introductory discussion of the PBX.

WHY USE A PBX IN DATA COMMUNICATIONS?

Why should the PBX be used for data communications? There are several answers to this question. First, two separate technologies have been used to support communications in the office: analog technology for voice communications and digital technology for data communications. This approach often has resulted in redundant and conflicting efforts between two separate systems. The PBX provides the opportunity to integrate these systems (as well as the personnel) to reduce redundancy, decrease costs, and take advantage of the superior aspects of digital technology. Second, since most data communications systems use the telephone system, the PBX provides a convenient conduit to the local telephone office and the telephone network.

Third, the telephone wires already installed in a building provide the paths for a local area network (LAN) without the very significant problem of pulling separate wire or cable. Fourth, for several years the PBX has had the necessary architecture to provide administrative and management support in controlling a telecommunications system. Fifth, as discussed in Chapter Nine, integration of voice and data makes good sense from many standpoints. Since the PBX is now an integrated voice/data digital device, it provides a valuable tool to accelerate the trend toward transmitting, switching, and managing all transmissions in digital images.

EVOLUTION OF THE PBX

Like many hardware and software systems, PBXs have evolved from relatively simple devices with limited functions to powerful multifunction systems. This section provides a brief description of the evolution of the PBX. Table 12-1 summarizes the central processor architecture of both early and modern PBXs.

The PBXs designed and sold in the 1970s were essentially telephone circuit-switching systems. Consequently, earlier PBXs had data capabilities "tacked" onto

TABLE 12-1. PBX PROCESSORS

Processor Type	Organization of Processor(s)	Key Points
8 BIT	Single/Central	Low horsepower; single point of failure; small memory capacity; small systems support
8 BIT	Dual/Redundant	Reliability questionable
8 BIT	Multi/Hierarchy	Higher horsepower; higher hardware cost; complicated software
8 BIT	Multi/Distributed	Reliable; very complicated software; higher-cost hardware; large memory required for operating system
16 BIT	Single/Central	Higher horsepower; single point of failure; larger memory capacity; larger systems
16 BIT	Dual/Redundant	Reliability questionable
16 BIT	Multi/Hierarchy	Higher horsepower; larger system capacity lines/trunks; complicated software; higher hardware cost; larger memory required; redundancy relatively expensive
16 BIT	Multi/Distributed	Very high horsepower; high memory capacity; very large systems capacity; very complicated software; very high cost hardware; redundancy built in; high reliability; trend of future
32 BIT	Dual/Redundant	Very powerful; very large system capacity; very large memory capacity; very high cost hardware; reliabilty questionable
32 BIT	Multi/Hierarchy	Extremely powerful; very high-cost systems; very complicated software; redundancy very expensive

the systems without much forethought, which often resulted in poor performance. In these early systems, different wires were used to accommodate voice and data traffic.

The major problem hampering early PBXs stemmed from their design. Voice-only PBXs were built with the expectation of handling connections which lasted only a short period of time, which is characteristic of most voice calls in a typical office environment. However, data calls are often of much longer duration. A terminal-to-computer session often lasts several minutes, sometimes several hours. Moreover, during the time the data calls are taking place, the communications channels and other resources are used in intermittent bursts, because many communications devices (e.g., terminals operated by humans) do not use the resources continuously. However, the earlier PBXs dedicated resources to each connection. Dedicated connections require a fixed bandwidth through the switch during the entire connection. The PBX thus wasted valuable switching and systems management capacity for extended data calls that had periodic bursts of traffic to transmit or receive.

Because of the design, the earlier systems often experienced blocking (busy or engaged signals). The problem with blocking is illustrated in Figure 12-1(a). A blocking switch is one in which a finite number of connections in a switching matrix controls the number of end-user connections through the switch. This switch shows a blocking ratio of 5:1, in which four connections can be made simultaneously through the switch to service the 20 ports coming into and out of the switch. Figure 12-1(b) illustrates a nonblocking switch, in which the switching matrix provides a path through the switch for each port. (Later PBXs adapted a nonblocking design.)

The earlier systems also supported data interfaces through a conventional EIA-232-D connection. The PBX received the data and converted them into a PBX channel format.

In the late 1970s and early 1980s the PBX manufacturers began to move away from the EIA-232-D connection (which required modems) toward a digital data interface connection (see Figure 12-2). With this approach the data bits were transmitted digitally to the PBX through the digital data interface (DDI) translation. Afterward, as in the earlier illustration, the data were switched by the PBX as if they were voice traffic. This approach was an improvement in that it did not require an associated telephone to set up data calls through the modem. Rather, the DDI provided direct communications with the user DTE, such as a terminal keyboard or a CRT monitor. However, this approach required the PBX to recognize that it was dealing with a transmission that was different from voice traffic.

More recently, PBXs provided an integration of voice and data across the same local twisted-wire pair, and while this serves as a significant improvement in eliminating an additional set of wires from each user station, the internal architecture of the PBX still provided dedicated switching facilities to a voice or data communications connection. Cabling costs were substantially reduced with this approach, but the switch itself is still worked in an inefficient mode.

Today the newer PBXs have developed full digital switching. Digital switching provides concepts quite similar to packet switching, in that a switching bandwidth is not dedicated to one particular connection. Rather, multiple users can share one physical path by the switch interleaving data or voice connections during periods of

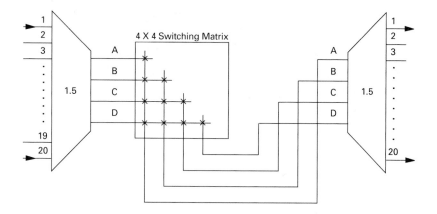

(a) A Blocking Switch

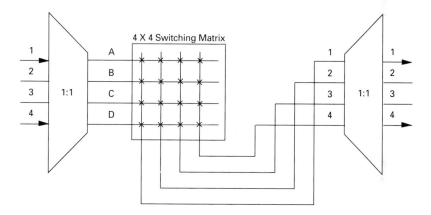

(b) A Nonblocking Switch

Figure 12-1. Switching Matrix

voice silence or during absences of transmission from the DTE. This concept (called *virtual* or *logical channels*) is integrated into most PBXs with the digital-switching concept discussed in Chapter Nine. Moreover, many of the modern PBXs today are built with nonblocking architecture.

While the earlier PBXs were relatively simple telephone circuit switches, today's PBXs are very powerful processors with provisions for such features as least-cost routing (routing the call onto the cheapest carrier connection, such as WATS, AT&T, or MCI). The new PBXs also provide such features as redial capabilities, call waiting, and call forwarding.

A significant trend in the industry is the acquisition or merger of PBX companies with conventional data processing organizations. For example, IBM has set up operations with Rolm; Wang and InteCom are operating together; and Honeywell and Ericsson have entered into cooperative agreements.

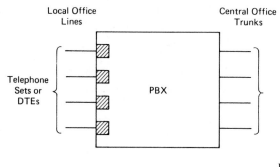

▨ : Digital Data Interface (DDI)

Figure 12-2. The PBX Digital Data Interface (DDI) Translation

    PBX architecture is rapidly evolving to the integration of voice and data and additional data communications network capabilities. Certainly, the PBXs are more powerful. For example, the major product offerings today provide small PBXs (20–30 lines), medium PBXs (200–1500 lines), and large PBXs (over 2000 lines). Some of the fourth-generation systems (discussed later) provide capabilities of over 10,000 communications lines. In addition, these systems are designed to support data communications functions such as X.25, SDLC/HDLC, the 802 IEEE local area network standards, and the emerging PBX-CPI and PBX-DMI interface standards (also discussed later).

ISSUE OF VOICE/DATA INTEGRATION

    From the previous discussion, it is evident that the early PBX industry concentrated primarily on voice transmission and voice switching. Consequently, for historical reasons and because of the large number of voice PBXs currently in existence, the problem of the integration of voice and data systems remains with us today. In most organizations, voice and data communications have evolved in separate departments. In the past a company's telephone systems were supported by a staff, as were the data communications systems—usually in the data-processing department. The segregation of voice and data transmission often resulted in a lack of continuity of services to the end user, some redundancy of services, and the certainty of political conflict between the different departments. This issue remains, even though the modern PBXs are moving to full-function, integrated voice/data systems. However, this book is intended to address data communications, not people communications, so we will focus our attention on the former.

    Presently, less than 40 percent of the line cards placed in a PBX are used for data. PBXs, although moving toward full-function capabilities, are still dominated by voice connections. To integrate voice/data or not to integrate voice/data is a question that is of major concern if an organization is using PBXs developed in the early 1980s. The new PBXs are powerful enough to obviate many (but not all) voice/data integration issues.

    Understand that even though voice and data images are all transmitted with binary 1s and 0s, these transmissions require different management. First, voice transmission cannot afford the variable delay found in practically all data communications systems. This means that voice systems must have very strict input-to-output ratios in order not to distort the voice transmission. Simply stated, one cannot afford to buffer voice packets for long periods of time because of the resulting unintelligibility of the speech. In contrast, data transmissions may be queued for long periods of time—minutes to hours in some applications.

In addition, voice communications are more tolerant of errors than data communications. If an occasional voice packet is lost, the reassembly at the receiving end does not noticeably distort the voice image. With data transmission, however, many systems cannot afford to lose any traffic.

In addition, data traffic can usually utilize long queue lengths because of the ability to compensate for variable delays. Voice transmission does not have this luxury. Typically, if voice packets are queued, they must be a short queue in order to decrease the likelihood of unacceptable delay.

Therefore, even though a PBX may support (from a mechanical/electrical viewpoint) the integration of voice and data, the PBX designer still faces the need to manage voice traffic differently from data traffic.

The basic questions about PBX use for data revolve around the DTE protocols, line speeds, data formats, throughput, and response time support capabilities of the PBX, which means a PBX evaluation for data usage is not unlike a typical evaluation for other data communications components.

ISSUE OF USING A PBX IN A LAN

One problem dealing with the PBX today is its use as a local area network (LAN) to support the automated office. Without question, the issue of office automation has come to fruition because of the intelligent workstation and the personal computer revolution in the office environment. The supporters of the PBX for office automation have cited numerous advantages to using PBXs for the LAN. In contrast, LAN vendors have cited the LAN advantages and the PBX disadvantages for use in office automation.

Certainly, the PBX will play an important role in office automation and local area networks, if for no other reason than the fact that the PBX is well entrenched (it is a pervasive tool in offices today). In addition, it connects to the ubiquitous telephone lines. To illustrate the presence of the PBX, Northern Telecom (the SL-1 PBX) has installations in over 40 countries and supports over 8,000 users (8,000 individual companies). The SL-1 supports over 3,000,000 voice-grade lines located in various offices around the world.

What are the tradeoffs of using PBXs for local area networks? First, let us cite some PBX advantages.

- As stated previously, the PBX uses the telephone lines connecting the offices to each other, as well as to the telephone company network.
- The PBX is a traffic-efficient circuit switch—its capabilities are well understood; it has been designed to be very efficient for voice traffic.

- The overall technology of the PBX is mature and well proven.
- The PBX provides long haul interfaces to communications systems around the world through the telephone system.
- The modern PBXs provide full-function integration of voice and data, thus permitting the use of voice and data transmissions in the end-user office (perhaps from a single terminal).

The critics of the PBX for use as a LAN cite these disadvantages:

- The lack of adequate data-switching capability in the PBX is still evident. (With fourth-generation systems, this is not as big a problem, but still remains.)
- Some of the architecture of the PBXs still revolves around voice technology.
- The PBX's multifunction support of the diverse world of data communications is not as extensive as equipment such as packet switches and intelligent multiplexers.
- The PBX is not fast enough to support multiple CPU-to-CPU traffic. The basic speed of a typical PBX port is 64 kbit/s—certainly fast enough to support most traffic. However, as discussed in Chapter Nine (Digital Switching), the digital switch (PBX) must be fast enough to support the switching of *all* lines attached to it. It must prevent congestion, avoid blockage, and provide high throughput and low response time.

The two technologies of the PBX and LAN are not mutually exclusive. The automated office can benefit from the use of both approaches; indeed, the office can certainly benefit from integrating the capabilities. The LAN and the PBX should coexist to support the automated office. The practical approach is not to choose one over the other, but to determine in what fashion they can be integrated to support the end-user application in the best way.

Wiring Costs

Another problem surrounding the use of a LAN or PBX for office automation focuses on the cost of wiring the building to support the system. Recent studies have focused on the cost breakdowns for average data wiring costs. The figures in Table 12-2 include the wire costs, the cost of the connector to the wire, and the labor to pull the wire and provide the connection. The figures do not relate to specific dollar

TABLE 12-2. WIRING COSTS

System Type	Wiring Mode	Cost Factor
PBX	Wire	1.0
RS-232-C	22-Gauge	1.96
Coaxial	RG58	2.25
Ethernet	Ethernet Cable	3.57
IBM Cabling System	Type 1 to closet and Type 2 to computer	3.59

values, but rather to a ratio of costs. The ratio number 1 identifies the basic costs, and the ratios above or below 1 identify the incremental or decremental cost in relation to the reference value of 1.

These wiring costs do not tell the whole story. Quality and flexibility factors are involved that must be considered. For example, at first glance the IBM cabling system appears to be prohibitively expensive, yet the high-quality shielded pair system provides considerable flexibility in moving DTEs and reconfiguring a local network. Moreover, while the Ethernet configuration is also quite costly, it provides for considerably more functions than the straight RG58 coaxial-line setup. The "ace in the hole" for the PBX is its use of *currently existing* telephone wires in the office. As we shall see in the next section, the new PBXs are exploiting this media to provide powerful voice and data communications support functions to the user. (In fairness, most other vendors are doing the same.)

THE FOURTH-GENERATION PBX

Several PBX firms have brought forth their "fourth-generation" systems, which are touted to successfully blend the functions of local area networks, PBXs, and integrated voice/data support. In this section we examine some recent PBX announcements.

There is no concise definition as to what constitutes a fourth-generation PBX. However, it is generally agreed that such a system has the following capabilities:

- The switch is all digital and integrates voice and data.
- The system provides for the use of LANs with PBXs and provides gateways to wide area networks, as well.
- The PBX is modular in its design, both from the standpoint of hardware and software. The modular design provides for growth to accommodate a larger user base. In many instances, the modules (added on) can be dedicated to specific applications, such as word processing. The modular growth allows for small or large numbers of users (from 1 to 20,000 user connections) and aggregate throughput rates to 300 kbit/s.
- The switch is nonblocking.
- The PBX supports communications with telephones and conventional terminals, as well as mainframe central processing units.
- The PBX provides for a high level of security.
- The design is built to handle an evolution to the ISDN (see Chapter Nine).
- The PBX supports a conventional PCM (pulse code modulation) transmission of 64 kbit/s, as well as higher TDM (time division multiplexed) speeds, such as 1.544 Mbit/s or 2.048 Mbit/s.

The following functions are common offerings from the new PBXs:

- Physical level support
  EIA-232-D (X.21 *bis*)

RS-449

Speeds of 1200 bit/s to 56 kbit/s

- Data link level support

  Internal or external clocking

  HDLC

  LAPB

- Network level support

  X.25 switched calls

  X.25 features such as D and Q bits

  X.25 facilities

- Protocol conversion support

  X.3 (X.28, X.29) Packet Assembly/Disassembly

EXAMPLES OF MODERN PBXs

In describing some examples of modern PBXs, understand that PBXs are designed for connection of telephone lines from one subscriber to another and to support the connection of subscriber loops to trunks. Even though the examples in this section show some very powerful data capabilities for PBXs, their principal function is still for voice/telephone traffic.

Note that the term *PBX* is used loosely with regard to machines such as the DMS-100. While it is employed as a primary branch exchange, the machine is as frequently employed as a telephone central office switch. Indeed, industry use of the term *PBX* has become blurred in the last 10 years.

The Northern Telecom DMS-100 system is highlighted in this section (principally its data communications capabilities). Even though the DMS-100, like its counterparts of AT&T, British Telecom, and other companies, provides very powerful voice switching and management capabilities, the machine also offers rather extensive data communications features, as well.

DMS-100 offers switched data capabilities for 300 bit/s through 19.2 Kbit/s with asynchronous transmissions and rates up to 64 Kbit/s for synchronous transmissions. Users can now select fractional T1 through the DMS-100 with rates in the DS1 and DS3 services.

In addition, the DMS-100 provides ISDN terminations and public packet-switched network interfaces. Figure 12-3 provides an example of the interface of a high-powered PBX-like DMS-100 into ISDN interfaces, SS7 interfaces through the signaling transfer point, and public packet network interfaces through an X.25 or X.75' interface.

Figure 12-4 shows a more detailed view of the Northern Telecom ISDN node with access through CCS #7, 2B + D (the ISDN basic rate), or a 23B + D (ISDN primary) and an X.75' connection.

The 2B + D connection provides the typical ISDN-bearer services (operating at the lower three layers of the OSI Model) consisting of the physical, data link, and network layers. The CCITT I Series and Q Series are employed for the ISDN basic rate interface. For the primary rate interface of 23B + D, the I Series and Q Series are also employed. For the common channel signaling #7 (CCS7), the CCITT Q

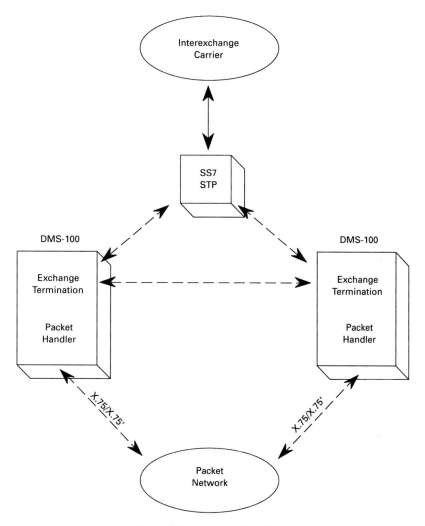

Figure 12-3. Integrated Interfaces

Series are utilized. For data packet network interfacing, the CCITT X Series are utilized, as well as several V Series Recommendations at the physical layer.

Table 12-3 lists some of the data communications capabilities in machines such as the DMS-100. This example shows the X.25 facilities that are supported by the machine (be aware that this does not include the 1988 and 1992 changes to X.25).

THE DIGITAL MULTIPLEXED INTERFACE (DMI)
AND COMPUTER-TO-PBX INTERFACE (CPI) PROPOSALS

Recently the PBX industry has attempted to develop standards for the interfacing of computers and terminals with DTEs. Two competing standards have emerged: the digital multiplexed interface (DMI) and the computer-to-PBX interface (CPI). Both

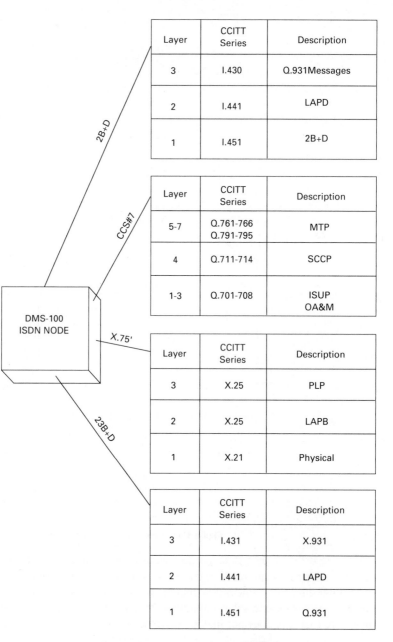

Layer	CCITT Series	Description
3	I.430	Q.931Messages
2	I.441	LAPD
1	I.451	2B+D

Layer	CCITT Series	Description
5-7	Q.761-766 Q.791-795	MTP
4	Q.711-714	SCCP
1-3	Q.701-708	ISUP OA&M

Layer	CCITT Series	Description
3	X.25	PLP
2	X.25	LAPB
1	X.21	Physical

Layer	CCITT Series	Description
3	I.431	X.931
2	I.441	LAPD
1	I.451	Q.931

Figure 12-4.   Multiple Service Offerings

standards purport to achieve four goals:

- provide a low-cost connection from DTEs through a PBX to other DTEs
- provide a nonconstraining link, which is no slower than any other link, to the PBX

TABLE 12-3. X.25 FACILITIES SUPPORTED BY THE DMS-100 ISDN NODE

CCITT 1980/1984	
• Called Line Address Modified Notification	• Interexchange Carrier Preselect
• Call Redirection	• Network User Identification
• Call Redirection Notification	• Nonstandard Default Packet Size
• Charging Information	• Nonstandard Default Window Sizes
• Closed User Group (CUG)	• One-Way Logical Channel Incoming
• Closed User Group Selection	• One-Way Logical Channel Outgoing
• Closed User Group with Incoming Access	• Outgoing Calls Barred
• Closed User Group with Outgoing Access	• Outgoing Calls Barred within a CUG
• CUG with Outgoing Access Selection	• Permanent Virtual Call Service
• Data Terminal Equipment (DTE) Facilities	• Recognized Public Operating Agency Selection
• Default Throughput Class Assignment	• Reverse Charging
• Fast Select	• Reverse Charging Acceptance
• Fast Select Acceptance	• Switched Virtual Call Service
• Flow-Control Parameter Negotiation	• Throughput Class Negotiation
• Hunt Groups	• Traffic Class
• Incoming Calls Barred	• Transit Delay Selection and Indication
• Incoming Calls Barred within a CUG	

- provide for flexible integration of voice, synchronous data, and asynchronous data
- provide a universal interface adaptable through multiple vendor products.

In the absence of these two standards, a typical communications structure through a PBX appears as in Figure 12-5(a). Each DTE connection requires a data-access module (DAM) between it and the PBX. Each of these DAMs provides for separate EIA-232-D cables, plus any line cards required for the connection between the PBX and the DTE. The DAM "conditions" the DTE to work with the PBX. The problem with this approach is the multiplicity of connections required in the office. A simple connection of only 10 DAMs and 10 terminals prevents significant wiring problems in the computer room. A connection of many of these connections produces what can best be described as a wiring mess in the building.

However, through the use of a *standard interface,* the connections to the PBX become greatly simplified [see Figure 12-5(b)]. The DMI or CPI interface permits the removal of or decrease in the connection lines in the system.

The primary differences between DMI and CPI are summarized below.

DMI

- 23 information channels are available (30 in Europe).
- Each channel has 64 kbit/s capacity.
- Signaling and control are in separate channels (24th 64 kbit/s channel).
- DMI aligns (somewhat) with ISDN standards.

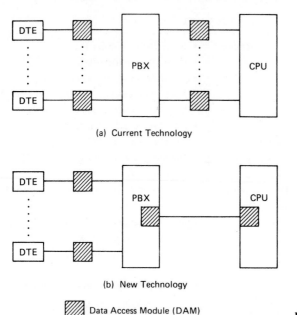

(a) Current Technology

(b) New Technology

Data Access Module (DAM)

Figure 12-5. CPI/DMI Goals

• The new approach requires new hardware and software.
• The control channel format is HDLC-oriented.

CPI

• 24 information channels are available.
• Each channel uses 56 kbit/s for traffic and 8 kbit/s for signaling.
• CPI does not align with ISDN.
• The interface requires minor adjustments to current technology.
• It has no separate control channel format.

SUMMARY

The modern PBXs now support a wide variety of integrated voice/data applications. The technologies of integrated services digital networks (ISDN), packet voice, LANs, and X.25 are finding their way into the architecture of the PBX. In the future it will be difficult to discern the difference between a PBX and some other data communications components. Voice/data integration is also propelling the industry to hardware, DTE, and DCE integration, as well.

13

Upper-Layer Protocols

INTRODUCTION

The earlier chapters of this book focused on the lower four layers of a conventional layered protocol model. The upper three layers are summarized in this chapter. Less detail is presented on the upper three layers because most of the upper-layer protocols do not deal directly with communications and networks. The chapter begins with a discussion of network security, which usually is placed in the upper layers.

You might wish to turn to Chapter Three for a review of the OSI Model and a description of the functions of the layers. Figure 13-1 is provided to assist in the review of these layers.

NETWORK SECURITY

Newspaper articles citing the breach of a computer or communications network have become almost a daily occurrence. The violations often are done to obtain financial and/or political gain; others are simply nefarious acts. Security is becoming an increasing problem in the computer and communications industry as more individuals become sophisticated in computer and network usage. The problem is exemplified in Figure 13-2, which depicts a trend in the industry toward more people who have sufficient knowledge to do damage to a computer installation in an organization. Because of this trend, increased attention and preventive measures have been devoted to network security.

Before discussing security measures, it will be beneficial to explain the major types of security violations. One of the most common and simplest security breaches is called "data diddling," which is the modifying of data prior to their

Users

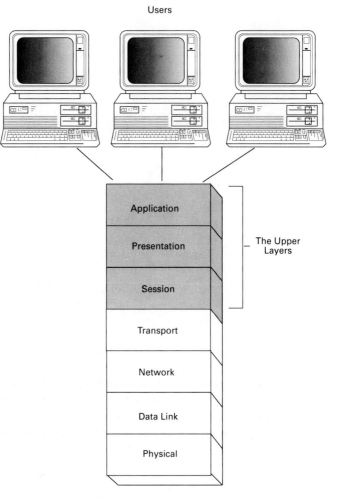

Figure 13-1. The Upper Layers

entry into the computer system and network. A famous example occurred several years ago when an individual modified a check deposit slip at the counter of a bank, resulting in illegal funds being deposited to the individual's account. Another very common security violation is called the "salami attack." This consists of small, repetitious acts, which in themselves are unnoticeable. A well-known illustration of this security violation occurred when a programmer rounded fractions of a penny and moved the fractions to the programmer's own bank account. One of the more pervasive security violations in a network is called "piggybacking" or "imperson-ation," which occurs when an individual breaks into a network through the use of unauthorized passwords or codes. The password is usually obtained directly from the authorized user of the network, often through inadvertence. Some network log-on systems can be broken by using a computer to calculate the many possible password combinations.

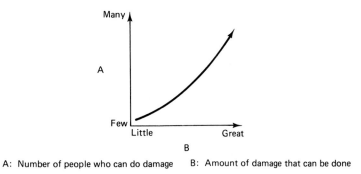

A: Number of people who can do damage   B: Amount of damage that can be done

Figure 13-2. Vulnerability Curve

One technique to combat unauthorized password use is to install a password security device between the communications channel and the computer. The device, upon receiving the password, automatically disconnects the line, consults a table for the password and its associated telephone number, then dials back the user at the designated telephone number. With this approach, the intruder must have the password *and* be physically present at the site where the authorized user is supposed to be located. (One can imagine the havoc the dial-back might create with PBX features such as automatic call-back or call-forwarding to other numbers.)

Networks also can be violated through what is known as a "trap door" breach. This problem involves network security software or hardware that is inadequate or has bugs (logic errors) in it, so that an individual finds the vulnerability of the system—in essence, goes through the "trap door" to gain access to the network. Trap door crimes often stem from naiveté on the part of the network manager, which is especially evident if a network has cryptographic capabilities. The manager assumes the cyphertext is completely immune to intelligibility, but many systems today that use simple cryptographic techniques can be breached fairly easily (more about this problem shortly).

Networks also are compromised with channel monitoring and intercepts. For example, microwave and satellite signals can be intercepted if the interloper searches and finds the proper channel frequency. Several instances of satellite signal intercepts of this nature have created significant security problems for companies transmitting secret, sensitive information.

Encryption with Private Keys

A technique widely used in computer networks to enhance security is encryption. Encryption makes plain text unintelligible by means of some type of reversible encoding scheme developed around a private key known only to the transmitter and receiver. The reverse of encryption is decryption, in which the cyphertext is reversed to the original plaintext. Encryption normally occurs at the transmitting site; decryption occurs at the receiving site. The encryption/decryption process is depicted in Figure 13.3.

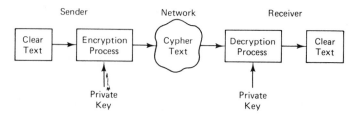

Figure 13-3. Encryption and Decryption

Encryption is classified by two methods: *substitution cyphers* and *transposition cyphers*. Substitution is the simpler form of encryption. You probably have used substitution cyphers in your own personal activities or perhaps as a youth while participating in some childhood games. Substitution cyphers entail the replacement of a letter or a group of letters for the original letter or group of letters. The simplest form of substitution cypher is called the *Caesar cypher*. With this approach, the letters of the alphabet are simply substituted with other letters of the alphabet. For example:

Plaintext: ABCDEFGHIJKLMNOPQRSTUVWXYZ
Substitution Letters: FGQRASEPTHUIBVJWKLXYZCONMD

This approach is called the *monoalphabetic* substitution cypher because each key is substituted with another letter of the full alphabet. While this approach yields 4×10^{26} possible keys, the keys themselves can reveal a considerable amount of intelligibility. If the keys are not known or the keys have no pattern, it is estimated that a computer would take 10^{13} years to try all keys by using one microsecond (.000001 second) to compute each key. However, languages exhibit certain properties which enable them to be decrypted much faster than 10^{13} years. For example, vowels occur more frequently than consonants. Other combinations such as *in, an,* and *the* (called digrams) are also quite common. Trigrams are used often in most languages as well; *the, and, ion* are examples of trigrams. The task of the cryptoanalyst is to analyze the occurrences of the individual letters, digrams and trigrams, and even words. Once the cryptoanalyst and the cryptoanalyst's computer establish the cypher of the frequently occurring letters, digrams, trigrams, or words, the cryptoanalyst can then develop a tentative plaintext based on the decoded data. The final decryption of the code then becomes a relatively simple matter, especially with the use of a high-speed computer.

Other methods improve upon the substitution cypher approach. For example, *polyalphabetic* cyphers are found in some systems. They allow for multiple cypher alphabets, which can be used in rotation. One variation of the substitution cypher approach is to make the key longer than the plaintext. A random bit stream is generated as the key, and then changed periodically.

A principal disadvantage on any type of private key structure is that all sites of the network must have knowledge of the common key. Some administrative and logistic problems arise in the distribution (and confidentiality) of the keys. Until recently, the idea of the private key has been the dominant approach for providing network cryptography. Network sites will change the key periodically; for example, every 24 hours or, if necessary, every few minutes.

A more sophisticated approach to cryptography is the use of *transposition cyphers,* in which the keys of the letter are reordered, but are not necessarily disguised. The following illustration shows an example of a transposition cypher approach. This example uses SECURITY as the key (obviously not a very good key for a security system). The key is used to number the columns. Column 1 is placed under the key whose letter is closest to the start of the alphabet; i.e., A, B, C, etc. The plaintext is then written as a series of rows underneath the key. The cyphertext is then read out by columns, starting with the column whose key letter is the lowest in the alphabet. The phrase "buy low sell high and do it today" is listed as follows:

```
S E C U R I  T Y
5 2 1 7 4 3  6 8
B U Y L O W  S E
L L H I G H  A N
D D O I T T  O D
A Y A B C D  E F
```

To produce this cyphertext: YHOAULDYWHTDOGTCBLDASAOELIIBENDF.

The Data Encryption Standard (DES)

In 1977, the Department of Commerce and the National Bureau of Standards published the DES (data encryption standard, FIPS Publication 46). The DES, a monoalphabetic system, was established in conjunction with IBM and released to the general public with the goal of providing a standardized cryptography algorithm for networks.

DES is based on developing an encryption algorithm that changes the plaintext with so many combinations that a cryptoanalyst could not figure out the plaintext even if numerous copies were available. The idea of the DES is shown in Figure 13-4. The encryption begins with the permutation function (P function); in this case 8 bits are input into the P function. As seen inside the box, the bits are changed in accordance with rules of logic. The output results in the bits changing in order. The P box can consist of wires or use programmable software to perform various kinds of permutation. The second function, the substitution function, is shown in Figure 13-4(b). In this situation, a 5-bit input (decoder) selects one of the eight possible lines into an S box. The S function performs the substitution of the lines, resulting in the encoding (encoder) of the 8 lines back to the 5 input bits.

The idea of the DES is to provide for several stages of permutation and substitution, as illustrated in 13-4(c). The DES provides a key consisting of 64 bits, of which 56 bits are used directly by the DES algorithm and 8 bits are used for error detection. There are over 70 quadrillion (70,000,000,000,000,000) possible keys of

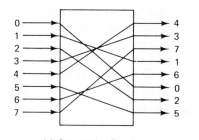

(a) Permutation Function

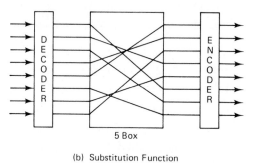

5 Box

(b) Substitution Function

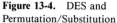

Figure 13-4. DES and Permutation/Substitution

56 bits in length. Obviously, a tremendous amount of computer power is needed to break this key. However, it can be done: high-speed computers, through the use of statistical analysis, need not cover all possible key combinations to find the key. Notwithstanding, the objective of the DES is not to provide absolute security, but rather to provide a reasonable level of security for business-oriented networks.

As shown in Figure 13-4(c), in the DES approach plaintext to be encyphered is subjected to an initial permutation (IP) with a 64-bit input block permuted as:

58	50	42	34	26	18	10	2
60	52	44	36	28	20	12	4
62	54	46	38	30	22	14	6
64	56	48	40	32	24	16	8
57	49	41	33	25	17	9	1
59	51	43	35	27	19	11	3
61	53	45	37	29	21	13	5
63	55	47	39	31	23	15	7

That is, the permuted input has bit 58 of the input as its first bit, bit 50 as its second bit, and so on, with bit 7 as its last bit. The permuted input block is then the input to a complex *key-dependent computation* consisting of 16 stages. The stages are the same in actual operation, but the cypher function uses the key (K) in different ways.

The final calculation is then subjected to the following permutation (IP^{-1}), which is the inverse of the initial permutation.

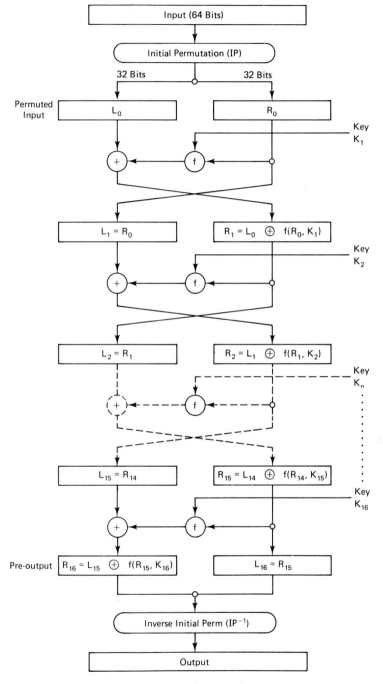

(c) The DES Approach

Figure 13-4. *(Continued)*

$$
\begin{array}{cccccccc}
40 & 8 & 48 & 16 & 56 & 24 & 64 & 32 \\
39 & 7 & 47 & 15 & 55 & 23 & 63 & 31 \\
38 & 6 & 46 & 14 & 54 & 22 & 62 & 30 \\
37 & 5 & 45 & 13 & 53 & 21 & 61 & 29 \\
36 & 4 & 44 & 12 & 52 & 20 & 60 & 28 \\
35 & 3 & 43 & 11 & 51 & 19 & 59 & 27 \\
34 & 2 & 42 & 10 & 50 & 18 & 58 & 26 \\
33 & 1 & 41 & 9 & 49 & 17 & 57 & 25 \\
\end{array}
$$

The 16 stages use the two blocks (L and R) of 32 bits to produce two 32-bit blocks of output. The left and right copies are exchanged before each stage. The function (F) performs four steps on the right output through an *exclusive or* transposition [in Figure 13-4(c), + denotes bit-by-bit addition].

1. The 32-bit R is expanded by a transposition and duplication rule to a 48-bit number E.
2. E and K are combined together by *exclusive or*. At each stage a different block K of key bits is chosen from the 64-bit key.
3. The 48 bits produced in step 2 are divided into eight 6-bit groups and input into S boxes, each of which produces 4 output bits.
4. The resulting 32 bits are input into a P box.

The DES has been a controversial issue since its inception. Part of the problem stems from the secrecy in which it was developed. IBM worked in conjunction with the National Security Agency to develop DES, and both organizations were requested to keep the design aspects of the DES secret. Its principal criticism stems from what many consider to be the short key length of 56 bits. IBM's original design provided for a 128-bit key, which would essentially eliminate a search to break the key, even on high-speed computers. Some critics believe the government does not wish an unbreakable key to be available to the public domain. As stated in previous chapters, digitized voice is now being implemented today in telephone handsets. Using semiconductor technology, it would not be too difficult to build the DES chip inside the handset of the telephone, along with the digitizing circuitry. Some critics of government oversight and surveillance believe the government wishes to have the ability to decypher any transmission from its citizens in order to protect national security and combat crime. The issue rests on political philosophies—not only on technical aspects. Encryption of telephone transmissions will become an increasingly controversial issue as voice digitization and encryption find their way into the mainstream of society.

Encryption with Public Keys

Many commercial systems use public key encryption/decryption systems. Separate keys are used to encypher and decypher data. The encyphering key and algorithm can be known to anyone; only the decyphering key is kept secret (see Figure 13-5). The logistical and administrative problems of public key distribution and management are eliminated with this approach.

The methods pioneered at Stanford University and MIT entail the generation of a pair of positive integers (E and N) which are used to encrypt the data with the formula: cleartext^E ÷ N = cyphertext. The same generation of E and N also produces D, which is used to decrypt the cyphertext with: cyphertext^D ÷ N = cleartext. Integers E, N, and D are derived by generating two large, random prime numbers (a prime number leaves a remainder when divided by any number other than itself or 1).

Public key systems also can be broken. However, as Figure 13-5 suggests, a different key could be generated with each transmission, or more realistically, at periodic or random intervals. Frequent key changes increase security of the data because a network violator must attempt to break the key every time it is changed. Another level of security can be added by the use of a private key system to encode the public keys. In other words, two levels of encryption can be used for highly sensitive data.

There are a wide variety of data-encryption units on the market today. Approximately 50 percent of these devices have opted to use the DES standard and several use the public key approach. The devices typically link to the DTE, and some operate between the DTE and the DCE. Most of the devices use the conventional EIA-232-D, RS-449, or CCITT V.35 interfaces into the DTE.

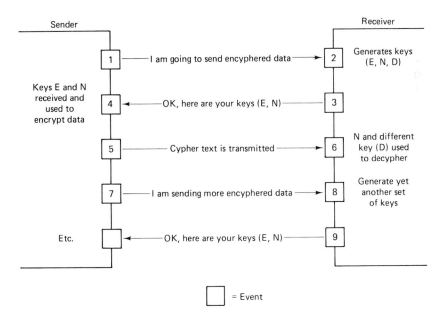

Figure 13-5. Public Keys

ISO Security Recommendations

The International Organization for Standardization (ISO) recommends that encryption be provided in the presentation layer of an OSI model implementation. The ISO explains its reasons for this recommendation:

- It is generally agreed that encryption services should be at a higher layer in a network to give an easier end-to-end encryption capability. The transport layer is the lowest possible layer where end-to-end services are provided; consequently, encryption should be performed at the fourth level or above.

- However, encryption services should be higher than the transport layer in order to minimize the amount of software that must be secure or trusted with plaintext. That is, the less software that deals with vulnerable plaintext, the better. This rationale would move encryption processes up to a higher level than the transport layer.

- Encryption must be implemented below the application layer because syntax transformations on encrypted data would be quite difficult. Moreover, if syntax transformations are performed at the presentation layer, they must be done before encryption occurs.

- Because selective protection is desirable (not all fields or records need to be encrypted), the ISO believes selection can best be done at the presentation level or higher, since knowledge of the actual fields in a user data stream is transparent below the presentation layer's level.

- While encryption can be performed at every level, the resulting overhead does not appear to be worth the additional protection given to the user data.

THE SESSION LAYER

The vast majority of application programmers are not versed in how to manage the order of their program's input/output executions *vis-à-vis* another program. The sequential execution of *puts* or *writes* from the application program does not ensure that the data in these output operations will necessarily arrive in the proper order at the other program. Additionally, the execution of *gets* or *reads* does not ensure that the data in these input operations will be properly sequenced.

Of course, the applications programmer can be trained to deal with this aspect of program-to-program communications, but most enterprises implement community software that the application programmer can execute to obtain these services.

The purpose of the session layer is to provide dialogue control between two end-user applications. It performs such activities as checkpoints (also called synchronization points) and resynchronization procedures. It allows two applications to negotiate how they will communicate by sending traffic in a half-duplex or full-duplex mode. It also uses the concept of tokens, which allow the passing of control functions back and forth between the two entities.

The session layer is puzzling to some people. It was developed largely through the impetus of the ISO, although some vendors offered services that are somewhat akin to the OSI session layer. Some organizations do not implement the session layer; and (if it is implemented) it can be done as a "thin" layer with the negotiation of just a few features.

Session Layer Operations

The session layer uses several unique terms to describe its operations. Figure 13-6 is an example of a typical session layer dialogue between two users in two different machines. The protocol permits either session entity to become the initiator of the session, wherein the other entity becomes the responder. The session layer uses various types of tokens to control the method in which traffic is exchanged, as well as several sync point options to ensure the traffic has been received correctly. This figure is largely self-explanatory by using the legend pertaining to each operation on the left- and right-hand sides of the figure.

Three possible relationships are available between the session and transport layers. One approach supports a one-to-one relationship in which there is a mapping of one session layer connection to one transport layer connection. Another approach is a one-to-many relationship, wherein a session layer connection makes use of multiple transport layer connections. In this situation, a transport layer can begin and end without discontinuing or releasing the session layer. Later, another transport layer can be initiated to support an ongoing session layer connection.

In addition, a many-to-one relationship is also supported. In this relationship, a transport layer connection can remain "up" while the session layer connections are brought up and down using the ongoing transport layer connection as necessary.

The Graceful Close

The transport layer's connection release may cause a loss of data. This is called a *destructive release* or a *destructive close*. The transport layer makes no assumptions about "rounding up" the data in the event a T-DISCONNECT indication signal is received at one of the entities. Consequently, data in the network or networks can be lost. In contrast, the session layer provides the option of a graceful close (be aware that this option must be negotiated during the session entity establishment). Upon the issuance of an S-RELEASE request, for example, data will continue to be accepted until both session entities are assured that all outstanding traffic has been accounted for. At that time, the release will occur.

Synchronization Services

The session layer provides for three types of synchronization points. Two of these "sync" points are used to confirm traffic. The third sync point is used to recover from problems.

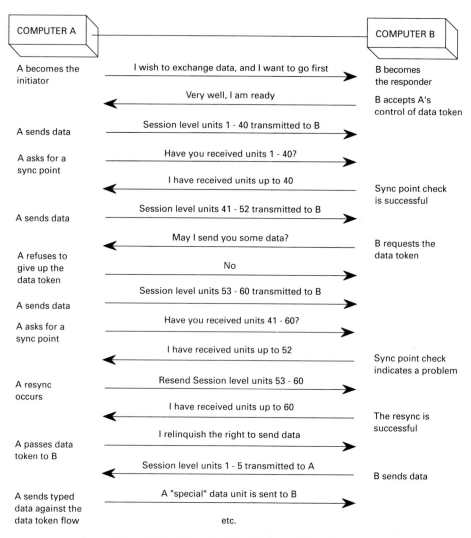

Figure 13-6.   Example of Session Layer Operations

The minor sync point is used as a "security blanket" between the two entities. The minor sync point need not be confirmed unless problems occur. During this sync point operation, the entities may continue to send data. For the minor sync point, the entities are allowed to resynchronize back to more than the last minor sync point.

In contrast, the major sync point must be confirmed, and the entities are allowed to go back only to the last major sync point.

The third type of sync point is called the *resynchronization* or *resync operation*. It provides a means for recovering from problems detected during one of the sync points. With the resync operations, the entities may choose the *abandon* operation, in which the current ongoing dialogue is discarded and the next unused session layer serial number is assigned to the session connection. As a second option for the resync, the *restart* operation permits the return of the dialogue to no earlier than the last major sync point. And, finally, with the *set* option, the dialogue is set to some sync point without affecting the unconfirmed sync points.

Session Layer Activities

The session layer makes use of activities to manage the traffic between the user entities. In its basic form, an activity is merely a procedure for splitting a job on a computer or a file or data transfer into discrete units. The provision for activities is dictated by the needs of the specific application. Each activity must be delineated with a major sync point, although the protocol does allow major sync points to exist within an activity. The activity is governed by the start and end activity, which logically enough begins and ends an activity. During the activity, the interrupt activity will allow the implementation of some other type of operation. Upon the completion of this other operation, the resume activity signal once again assumes the activity operations.

THE PRESENTATION LAYER

The presentation layer is concerned with the representation of the data in a data communications system. It provides a means to define how the bits are structured within PDUs and within the fields in the PDUs. As a simple example, it could define if the bits are positioned in a field in high or low order. It also allows two end users in two different machines to negotiate the type of syntax that will be used between two applications. For example, one user might use ASCII and the other user might use EBCDIC code. The presentation layer allows these two users to negotiate how the data will be represented and also supports the conversion of the data in a syntax that is acceptable to both programs.

The presentation layer uses ASN.1 (abstract syntax notation 1) to define the types of data, such as integer, real, octet, bit string, etc. It also employs a standard (X.209) to define the structure of the data for the communications channel.

ASN.1

ASN.1 defines a number of "built-in" types. This term means that certain types are considered an essential part of the ASN.1 standard. They are, in a sense, predefined. They are called built-in because they are defined within the standard itself. Figure 13-7 lists the built-in types.

What is a "non-built-in" type? That kind of type is not defined in the standard and is considered to be a type that is defined by an enterprise. For example, in the Internet (as published by the Internet Activities Board [IAB]) a non-built-in type is network address. This type is always identified as a 32-bit Internet Protocol (IP) address, in which the type must be coded as either *network address.host address* or *network address.subnetwork address.host address.*

The ASN.1 built-in types offer a wide array of types for the enterprise to use.

Boolean	Identifies logical data (true or false conditions)
Integer	Identifies signed whole numbers (cardinal numbers)
Bit string	Identifies binary data (ordered sequence of 1s and Os)
Octet string	Identifies text or data that can be described as a sequence or octets (bytes)
Null	A simple type consisting of a single value
Sequence	A structured type, defined by referencing an ordered list of various types
Sequence of	A structured type, defined by referencing a single type where each value in the type is an ordered list
Set	A structured type, similar to Sequence type except that Set is defined by referencing an unordered list of types, which allows data to be sent in any order
Set of	A structured type, similar to Sequence type except that Set of is defined by referencing an unordered list of types, which allows data to be sent in any order
Choice	Models a data type chosen from a collection of alternative types, which allows a data structure to hold more than one type
Selection	Models a variable whose type is that of some alternatives of a previously defined Choice
Tagged	Models a new type from an existing type, but with a different identifier
Any	Models data whose type is unrestricted and can be used with any valid type
Object Identifier	A distinguishable value associated with an object or a group of objects, like a library of rules, syntaxes, etc.
Character String	Models strings of characters for some defined character set
Enumerated	A simple type; its values are given distinct identifiers as a part of the type notation
Real	Models real values (for example: $M * B^e$, where M = the mantissa, B = the base, and e = the exponent)
Encrypted	A type whose value is a result of encrypting another type

Figure 13-7. Built-In Types

Indeed, many organizations (in order to reduce the complexity of the presentation layer) choose to implement a subset of the built-in types.

ASN.1 tags (values) are assigned to each object. Each object belongs to a class (and a class number).

Presently, four classes are defined in the standard:

- *Universal* is a class for the built-in types.
- *Application* is a class for a widely used OSI application (but not universal).
- *Private* is a class for an enterprise-specific tag.

- *Context specific* is a class that is used to tag objects in accordance with the ASN.1 code.

ASN.1 Coding Rules

Like any language, ASN.1 has coding rules. This section provides a brief summary of the major rules of ASN.1. A comment is in order, however, about the case sensitive aspects of ASN.1. Case sensitivity is determined by coded notation in one of these three forms:

- A coded notation begins with an uppercase letter: ASN.1 requires this notation to be given a type value (Integer, Boolean, etc.).
- A coded notation is "all caps": an ASN.1 reserved word.
- A coded notation begins with a lowercase letter: this notation is not acted upon by the ASN.1 compiler. It is used to enhance the readability of the code.

Some Examples of ASN.1 Coding

This section provides several examples of ASN.1 coding. Be aware that these examples are not all-inclusive of the features of ASN.1.

Figure 13-8 shows the boolean and integer types and examples of how they may be coded. The boolean type permits only two values, *true* or *false*. Its tag is *UNIVERSAL 1* and, as suggested by the name of the type, it is used to describe a boolean relationship. In this example, *employed* could be true or false, *yellow* could be true or false.

The second example in this figure is the integer type. It is *UNIVERSAL 2*. It permits whole numbers, either positive or negative values. It also permits the value of 0. Although no limits are placed on the magnitude of the type integer, the coder could place a maximum value on this through the use of a comment statement.

BOOLEAN

Tag: UNIVERSAL 1
Values: TRUE/FALSE
- *Employed* ::= BOOLEAN
- *Yellow* ::= BOOLEAN

INTEGER

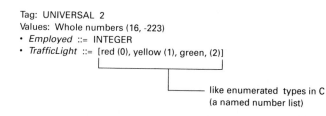

Tag: UNIVERSAL 2
Values: Whole numbers (16, -223)
- *Employed* ::= INTEGER
- *TrafficLight* ::= [red (0), yellow (1), green, (2)]

like enumerated types in C
(a named number list)

Figure 13-8. Boolean and Integer Types

In this example, *Employed* is defined as an integer (for perhaps 1 or 0 values). Another example is *TrafficLight,* which is defined as an enumerated list. This is similar to the enumerated types in C, which is simply a named number list. This allows the integer *TrafficLight* to convey a number of values.

Figure 13-9 shows examples of three more types: bit string, octet string, and null. The bit string type is used to define a string of bits. It is *UNIVERSAL 3.* The useful aspect of bit string is that it need not be aligned on an even octet (a multiple of 8-bits). The bit string also may contain a named number list like the integer type. A meaning may be assigned to each bit in the string. Bits in the bit string type are numbered from left to right, from the most significant to the least significant. Numbering begins with zero. In this example, *TelemetryData* is defined as a bit string and *Yellow* is defined as a named number list: 0 for red, 1 for yellow, 2 for green.

The octet string is used to define a string of 8-bit octets (sometimes called bytes). It is *UNIVERSAL 4* tag number. It is identical to the bit string type, except values must be aligned on an octet. The octet string is used in some installations to denote text. The programmer may define the maximum length for the octet string with the use of a comment.

The null string, as its name implies, does not provide any value. It sometimes is used to mark an empty space or to act as a placeholder. The null is *UNIVERSAL 5.* It has no values assigned to it. It is used most often as a placement holder for later use.

It is a common practice to renumber the values of the types by adding a tag. Tags assign another identifier to an existing type (see Figure 13-10). A tag is a useful tool when types must be distinguished from other similar types. For example, a

BIT STRING

Tag: UNIVERSAL 3
Values: A string of binary bits
• *Telemetry Data* ::= BIT STRING
• *Yellow* ::= [red (0), yellow (1), green, (2)]

                               A named number list
                               (Bits are numbered, left
                               to right, most significant
                               to least significant)

OCTET STRING

Tag: UNIVERSAL 4
Values: A string of 8 bit octets (bytes)
• X.21 Control ::= OCTET STRING
• X.25 Packet ::= OCTET STRING

NULL

Tag: UNIVERSAL 5
Values: None
• Reserved ::= NULL

Figure 13-9. Bit String, Octet String, and Null Types

Tagging the Types

Tag: Automatic or user defined
Values: Vary

- FtamFile ::= [APPLICATION 7] OCTET STRING
- UserID ::= [PRIVATE 3] BIT STRING
- DestPort ::= [1] IMPLICIT OCTET STRING
--or
- DestPort ::= [1] OCTET STRING

Figure 13-10.   Tags

SEQUENCE / SEQUENCE OF

Tag: UNIVERSAL 16
Values: An ordered list of types (any type for SEQUENCE
and same types for SEQUENCE OF)

--example is first part of a TCP segment

- PDU ::= SEQUENCE {

```
                destPort  OCTET String ,-- 2 octets
                sourcePort  OCTET String, -- 2 octets
                seqNumber  INTEGER, --32 bits
                --etc.
                }
```

Figure 13-11.   The Sequence Type

sequence type is used to define a collection of variables. It is useful to assign a tag to each of the variables within a sequence. As another example, the *set type* is used to define a number of variables whose order is not significant. Each variable can be further tagged to unambiguously identify it.

ASN.1 also supports a variation of the type called an *implicit type.* This is coded with the reserved word IMPLICIT. This means the type is implicitly tagged. The use of the word *IMPLICIT* is also a means to save the use of superfluous tags. Without its use, two tag values would be coded for an object.

The sequence type, whose tag is *UNIVERSAL 16,* is used to define an ordered list of types (see Figure 13-11). The *SEQUENCE* type is any type, and *SEQUENCE OF* must be all of the same type. The sequence is considered a constructed type in the sense that it has more than one variable defined. Remember that a simple type defines one variable.

Figure 13-12 shows two other ASN.1 types. The *SET/SET OF* has a *UNIVERSAL 17* tag. This type defines an unordered list of types (variables). The *SET* type can be a list of any types and the *SET OF* must contain the same types. The principle difference between *SET* and *SEQUENCE* is that *SEQUENCE* requires an ordered list of types and *SET* may have an unordered list of types.

The second type shown in this figure is *CHOICE.* This does not have a tag because the tag is coded within the chosen type.

CHOICE allows the selection of one and only one of the types between the {}. In this example, *DLSubmitPermission* is defined as a choice of one of four objects: *individual, member-of-dl, pattern-match,* or *member-of-group.*

SET/SET OF

Tag: UNIVERSAL 17
Values: An unordered list of types (any type for SET and
same types for SET OF)
• OfficeRecord ::=SET {

> • roomNumber ::= [0] IMPLICIT OCTET STRING,
> • bldgNumber ::= [1] IMPLICIT OCTET STRING,
> • rofficeType ::= [2] IMPLICIT OCTET STRING,
> • sizeSqFt ::= [3] IMPLICIT OCTET INTEGER
> }

CHOICE

Tag: None; use of the tag of the chosen type
Values: Depends on type chosen
•-- example is from X.402 and expands the use of
  -- names (user-friendly and names with types required)
DLSubmitPermission ::= CHOICE {

> individual ::= [0] ORName,
> member-of-dl ::= [1] ORName,
> pattern-match ::= [2] ORNamePattern,
> member-of-group ::= [3] Name, }

Figure 13-12. The Set and Choice Types

ASN.1 provides an array of choices to define character strings. Character strings have *UNIVERSAL* tags with values of 18, 19, 20, 21, 22, 25, 26, and 27. The character strings are really nothing more than octet strings with further rules on the values that may be used (see Figure 13-13).

The choice of how one uses character strings is simply up to the coder or the organization (if the organization chooses to use a defined subset of ASN.1). Remember, regardless of the *UNIVERSAL* tag chosen, these strings are all encoded as if they were implicit octet strings.

SET/SET OF

Tag: Universal 18, 19, 20, 21, 22, 25, 26, 27
Values: OCTET STRING with limits on the values used
Number String: Digits 0-9 and space (UNIVERSAL 18)
Printable String: All letters, digits, and punctuation marks of English alphabet (UNIVERSAL 19)
Teletex String: CCITT T.61 character set (UNIVERSAL 20)
Video String: CCITT t.100 and T.101 charcter set (UNIVERSAL 21)
Visible String: Printable (G-graph) characters from ISO 646 (S Set of ASCII) (UNIVERSAL 26)
IA5 String: Includes G and C sets (UNIVERSAL 22)
Graphic String: Any standardized G set (UNIVERSAL 25)
General String: Any G and C sets from any standardized set (UNIVERSAL 27)
--Remember   These character strings are encoded as if they were (UNIVERSAL n)
                    IMPLICIT OCTET STRING
Print It::=   (UNIVERSAL 22) IMPLICIT OCTET STRING

Figure 13-13. Character Strings

Transfer Syntax

The use of ASN.1 by itself is not useful from the standpoint of sending traffic between two machines. Another tool is needed to describe the syntax of the traffic that is sent on the circuit between these machines. The standard used to provide this tool is a transfer syntax published by both CCITT and the ISO. This transfer syntax is also known as basic encoding rules (BER). It is used to describe (a) the type of data on the channel; (b) the length of the value (in octets or bits), and (c) the data value itself (see Figure 13-14).

By the use of a common transfer syntax convention, different computers can be programmed to recognize the syntax rules and correctly decode the data units.

For example, one machine might use 2s complements in its architecture and another machine might use 1s complement. If computer A sends traffic in 2's complements representation, that traffic is so identified through the BER. The result of this operation is that computer A can translate the traffic into 1s complement for use on its own internal architecture.

The machines that communicate with the transfer syntax must be able to relate the abstract syntax coded with ASN.1 to a specific transfer syntax. This is performed through a *presentation context identifier* (PCI). The PCI can be used to identify the context needed for the transfer between the two machines. It also is used as a means to negotiate syntax between the two entities. The sum of all these contexts is called the *defined context set* (DCS).

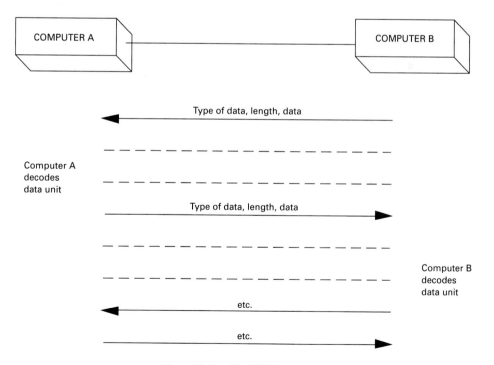

Figure 13-14. The TLV Approach

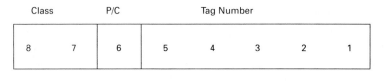

Note:
For tag numbers greater than 30, identifier is
coded with extension octets

Figure 13-15.   The Type Field

The format for the type field for the transfer syntax is based on the use of an 8-bit octet or extensions if large tag numbers are needed (see Figure 13-15).

The field consists of three "subfields." A 2-bit class value is used to identify if the class is universal, context specific, private, or application specific. The P/C bit stands for primitive/constructed. This bit is set to a 0 if the object is a simple type; it is set to a 1 if it is a structured or complex type (that is to say, consisting of more than one type).

The remaining five bits contain the value for the tag. This could be coded as a universal number, it could be coded to represent context specific, or it could be coded as application tags.

Be aware that the type field must precede *each* value. Consequently, a considerable amount of overhead can be incurred with the use of the transfer syntax.

THE APPLICATION LAYER

This section describes the architecture of the application layer. Since the application layer is complex and very diverse, this section is devoted to its structure and focuses on four major protocols (called ASEs or application service elements).

- ACSE: Association control service element
- RTSE: Reliable transfer service element
- ROSE: Remote operations service element
- CCR: Commitment, concurrency, and recovery

These protocols are called common ASEs because they are used by many applications. The best way to view these protocols is to think of them as community code.

The upper layers of the OSI Model are tightly bound to each other. This is in contrast to the lower layers, which are generally loosely coupled and are unaware of a lot of the activities within each others' entity operations.

In retrospect, one might argue that the upper three layers of the OSI Model could be one layer, because they are highly complementary in their interactions with each other. One layer cannot execute without the existence of the other two layers. Indeed, if negotiation occurs through these three layers and any entity within any of the layers fails, then none of the layers' entities will operate.

The layers communicate with each other through the PSAP and SSAP (see Figure 13-16). Some vendors do not use separate PSAP and SSAP identifiers but use one identifier to identify both. The *application service elements* (ASEs) residing in the application layer (as a composite) form the *application entity* (AE). The application process works with the AE in the application layer.

Most installations make use of several very common ASEs. These ASEs really are considered to be community software in the sense that many other applications invoke their services.

The most common and widely used ASE in the application layer is the *association control service element* (ACSE). It is used as a housekeeping function to establish association between applications and to close the association.

The *reliable transfer service element* (RTSE) is responsible for reliable transmission at the application layer and provides timing operations to ensure the receipt of data.

The *remote operations service element* (ROSE) is a remote procedure call (RPC) service which is useful for transaction-oriented activities between entities.

The *commitment, concurrency, and recovery protocol* (CCR) is used to manage traffic between files and data bases and to provide for checkpoints and backouts.

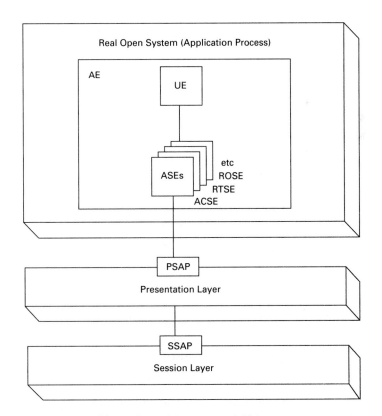

Figure 13-16.   Upper-Layer Architecture

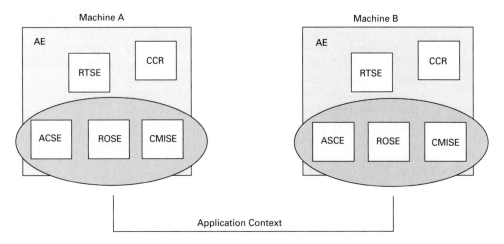

Figure 13-17. Example of an Application Context

The "bundling up" of the various application service elements needed to support an end-user application occurs at the application layer through ACSE. The composite of the upper three layers and the resources necessary to support the end-user applications is called an *application context* (see Figure 13-17).

ACSE

The *association control service element* (ACSE) manages associations between applications. In conformance with the OSI rules, all OSI applications must use ACSE. One of the principle purposes of ACSE is to allow the negotiation of options between two applications.

The ACSE module is actually concerned with beginning and ending the "connection" between the two applications. The ASE is used to bind the two users together. These users are called the *initiator* and the *responder*.

The primitives associated with this operation are shown in Figure 13-18. Each primitive has a considerable number of parameters associated with it. Many of these parameters are simply passed down to the session and presentation layers.

RTSE

The reliable transfer service element (RTSE) is responsible for the reliable transfer of data between two applications. The RTSE service must first be bound with the creation of an association. Thereafter, transfer of data is effected between two application entities (AEs). If for some reason the transfer does not occur successfully, the originating AE is informed.

The RT-TRANSFER service consists of three primitives (see Figure 13-19). The RT-TRANSFER req is used by the initiating AE to send data. This is forwarded

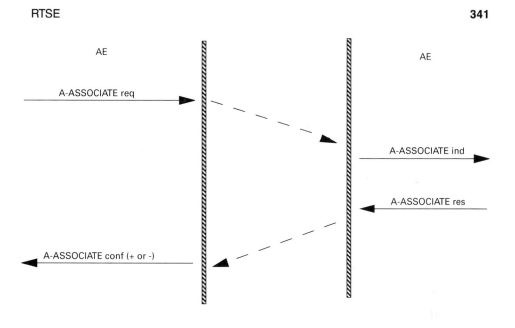

Parameters in the Operations (Not all inclusive)

- Application Context Name: Identifies ASEs to be used on this association; an OBJECT IDENTIFIER that names a collection of ASEs

- Calling AE IDs: Four fields to identify AP and AE within the AP

- Called AE IDs: Four fields to identify AP and AE within the AP

- Presentation context definition list: Entry in list for the PCI of each ASE

- Session layer requirements: Entries such as initial sync point number, token assignments, connection id

- Results and diagnostics: Responding AE-provided information

- User-data: Information from other AEs in application entity

Figure 13-18. The ACSE

in a PDU to the responding AE in the form of RT-TRANSFER ind. The responding RTSE service provider replies with an RT-TRANSFER conf to the initiator.

Interestingly, the accepting AE does not send back the confirm. Rather, RTSE establishes that the provider AE return the acknowledgment. Therefore, this service is not a complete end-to-end acknowledgment protocol. Note that this does not guarantee delivery of service to the final accepting AE. A better solution to the RTSE would be for the accepting AE (upon accepting the traffic) to send back an RT-TRANSFER res.

The PDU contains a field called the *transfer time.* This is a value which gives a maximum time that the initiator permits for the transfer of the traffic. That is, it provides a time for which the RTSE provider is required to transfer the data.

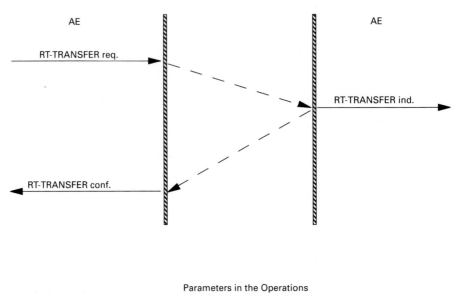

Parameters in the Operations

- AN APDU: Data

- Transfer Time: Time in which RTSE provider shall successfully transfer
  the data

- Result: Positive or negative

Figure 13-19.   RTSE Data Transfer

ROSE

The OSI Model also supports a process for remote operations and remote procedure calls. It is called the *Remote Operations Service Element* (ROSE) (see Figure 13-20). The remote procedure operation is based on a client server model which is an asymmetric type of communications. This means that a requester, such as a client, sends a request message to a process, identified as a server. It waits for an action to occur and receives a reply about the success or failure of the request. The client is not aware of the server's location (the server could be on a different machine in the network). This approach is in contrast to most of the OSI protocols and entities in which transfer is symmetric (in which traffic flows in both directions at the same time).

Many remote procedure operations are implemented in the client server through a technique called a *stub*. The stub is actually a procedure such as a *read* or *write*. A stub can be defined for each server's clients. The procedure (such as read) becomes a library procedure and the remote operation user can obtain the services through a simple *read* statement. The *read* would identify the file that is to be read, the number of bytes to be read, and a buffer to contain the result of the *read*. This operation becomes a simple message transfer to the server, after which the client waits for a reply from the server. Upon the reply arriving, the client caller is once again given control.

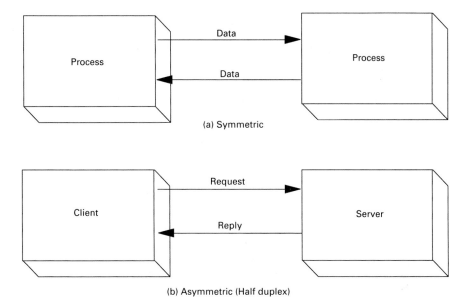

(a) Symmetric

(b) Asymmetric (Half duplex)

- Client sending a message to server = program calling a
  procedure for a result

- Client initiates action and waits for its completion and a reply

- Client is unaware that server is a different machine

Figure 13-20.   Remote Operations

These procedure calls obviate costly I/O commands such as those incurred with request primitives (or even worse, interrupts which must be implemented with indication primitives).

Implementations differ. A stub may actually be involved in transferring the data, or a stub may be a client's to server's agent (which actually pass traffic back and forth between servers).

While remote procedure calls seem to be quite simple, problems can occur if a server fails. This figure shows one case in which the request is executed successfully, but the request is not sent back to the client before the server fails. Assume the client repeats the operation and resends the traffic (once the server comes up). Then the reply is successfully executed and sent back. If no harm is done, then this type of operation is called *idempotent*. However, not all operations are idempotent. For example, harm *would* have been done if this client were sending money to another account and ended up sending the money twice.

A convenient method for approaching the problem can be categorized in one of four methods: *only once, at most once, at least once,* or *last of many.*

In the ideal world, a call is carried out only one time. This ideal world is really not achievable because it is not possible to prevent servers from crashing, software from failing, etc. The second form of handling the problem is called *at most once.* With this operation, if an error has occurred with the server, a stub will return an error call to the client. In this case, retransmission is not attempted. The client knows that the operation either has not been performed or has been performed one time. In either case, it keeps matters simple, and recovery is then the client's responsibility.

The third type of approach to this problem is called *at least once*. With this approach, the client uses a timeout and retry values to attempt the operation. When it eventually receives replies, it knows the operation has been performed at least once, and perhaps many times. For idempotent, this operation works fine. If the operation is not idempotent, it is a good idea for the client (or its stub) to uniquely identify each transaction so that it may discern which transaction is appropriate and make certain that others are either backed-out or filtered out. This approach is called the *last of many* (perhaps a better term would be *one of many*).

It is quite possible that in remote procedure operations a client can fail after issuing an RPC. This process in which a server has no waiting client (where the client is the parent) is called the *orphan*. There are a number of ways to handle this problem. With the process called *extermination,* the server or its machine recovers from the crash by determining which RPCs were in process when the problem occurred. It then takes actions to exterminate these processes. How the clients are informed would be a matter of local choice. Another term to describe the problem is the *grand-orphan*. This occurs when the orphan issues an RPC which creates a grand-orphan. The grand-orphan, in turn, could create another grand-orphan—a great-grand-orphan. The process of handling this operation is to keep bookkeeping accounts of the running processes once the system is up, and to exterminate all chains.

Another approach for killing orphans is a process called *expiration*. It requires no bookkeeping tables—it simply is a rule that a server is given a discrete amount of time to complete the process. If the process is not completed within this time, remedial action may be taken. The client may be asked for a new time, the RPC may be cancelled, etc.

Yet another approach for handling the orphan problem is called *reincarnation.* This approach may be needed in the event that extermination does not eliminate all orphans. For example, in a highly distributed network, it is possible that the grand-orphans may have been partitioned into other machines which are not reachable. In this case, the recovering client will broadcast a message out to all machines and they are requested to kill off all server operations.

A gentle reincarnation would selectively kill off server operations.

CCR

Commitment, concurrency, and recovery (CCR) protocol is widely used in the industry. Ordinarily a user may not be aware that CCR operations are being invoked, because the protocol is usually hidden behind a file transfer protocol or a data base management system.

The architecture of CCR is built on the idea of superiors controlling the operations of subordinates. In these two entities' operations on an object (which could be a file, data base, or anything that is undergoing changes), CCR provides rules for superiors and subordinates carrying out operations in a predictable manner by requiring that an object be restored to a former consistent state if all operations cannot be performed upon it. Operations on the object between the superior and the subordinate are frozen from other application processes. Nonparticipating APs are not allowed to participate in the action.

CCR is organized around a commitment tree (see Figure 13-21). The commitment tree is a hierarchical operation in which superiors inquire if subordinates are able to commit to a particular operation. In turn, subordinates can be superior to other subordinates, which convey this request down to the lowest branch of the hierarchy. After determining if the entities can participate in the operation, they forward a *yes* or *no* reply to their inquiring superior. Finally, the initiating entity (in this example, A) receives the results of the inquiry. CCR requires that all participants must agree to the action, or no action will be performed.

CCR uses several services to perform its actions. The C-BEGIN service is initiated by a superior (initiator) to begin an action. These actions are called *atomic actions* in that no one is allowed to interfere with the action until the action is complete. The C-BEGIN actually maps into a presentation layer synchronization major primitive which then, of course, is sent to the session layer for action.

The C-READY service is issued by the responder when it is ready to commit to an action. This signal is mapped to a P-TYPE-DATA service.

The C-COMMIT service is used by the initiator to actually order the commitment. Typically, this occurs after a ready has been received.

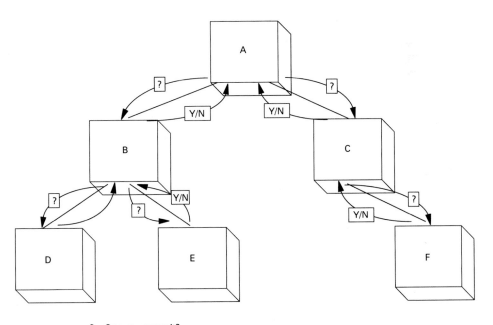

? = Can you commit?

Y/N = Yes or no

Figure 13-21. The Commitment Tree

The C-PREPARE is an optional service and is issued by a superior to determine if the subordinate is ready to commit.

The C-REFUSE service is used in the event that an entity refuses to participate in the operation. This must map to a resynchronize service, which becomes an abandon at the service layer.

A C-ROLLBACK service allows an initiator to restore the object to a previous state.

The C-RESTART is used to initiate recovery procedures.

TERMINAL SYSTEMS AND PROTOCOLS

The number of terminal- and personal-computer-based services has been increasing dramatically throughout the world. These services have a number of names attached to them: Teletext, Videotex, Teletex, public data banks, and information services.

In this section, we define these terms and focus on the technology that has gained increased interest and use throughout the world, Teletex.

Telematics

The term *telematics* is used to describe two broad ranges of service, *Teletext* and *Videotex*. Videotex describes the provision for two-way information services between a user's device and an information source. The term *Teletext* describes one-way transmission services. These two systems are illustrated in Figure 13-22. The

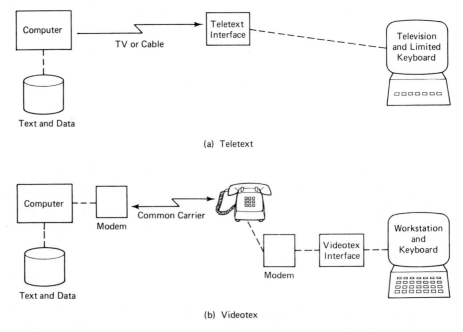

(a) Teletext

(b) Videotex

Figure 13-22. Telematics

Teletext technology uses a conventional TV broadcasting system to allow the one-way cycling of data into the user terminal. Typically, a page remains on the screen until a replacement page is automatically cycled or is requested by the user. In contrast, Videotex approaches the system with a data communications structure—a terminal keyboard can be used to interact with a remotely located data base. As seen from Figure 13-22, conventional components such as modems and telephone networks are used to provide the full two-way capability.

The basic idea of Videotex/Teletext is to provide a system with widespread dissemination capabilities for both graphic and text information. The information is disseminated by electronic means for display on low-cost terminals. The recipient of the information has selective control of the display by using easily understood procedures.

Telematics provides services which many of us may take for granted today. For example, the Teletext and Videotex uses in North America involve these major applications:

- news, weather, and sports
- shopping by terminal (teleshopping)
- advertising through Teletext broadcasts
- banking transactions through the use of a telephone or terminal
- electronic newspapers available in some cable TV areas
- financial information, such as stock market reports
- games and entertainment
- program captioning
- personal computer support
- electronic directories, such as shopping lists or mailing lists
- electronic mail
- telemetry.

Teletex

In addition to Teletext and Videotex, another technology has emerged in the last several years, and from all indications it will become the pervasive terminal-based network system standard. The term used to describe this technology is *Teletex*. This service evolved from the original TELEX and TWX (teletypewriter exchange) services.

Teletex Development. Teletex research began in the mid–1970s when the German government set up a commission to explore the possibilities of implementing a text communications service with improved capabilities over TELEX. The goal was to establish a terminal that offered text generation with communications capabilities and used the full character-set repertoire of a typewriter. Also in the mid–1970s, the Swedish PTT Televerket began work on a system to support office equipment with word processing, communications, and document filing and

TABLE 13-1.   DOCUMENT DELIVERY COSTS (GERMAN DEUTSCHE BUNDEPOST STUDY)

Number of Pages*	Postal Service	TELEX			Teletex		
		Time**	Minimum	Maximum	Time**	Minimum	Maximum
1	$0.94	3:45	$0.22	$1.02	0:08	$0.03	$0.07
2	$0.94	7:30	$0.44	$2.00	0:14	$0.04	$0.11
3	$0.94	15:00	$0.89	$4.00	0:27	$0.06	$0.19

*each page contains 1500 characters
**amount of time for document transmission (minutes and seconds)

retrieval capabilities. Studies such as these paved the way toward Teletex. Shortly thereafter, CCITT became involved in projects to improve TELEX and developed a series of detailed documents outlining recommended standards for Teletex systems. In 1980, the CCITT adopted the following recommended standards:

- F.200 Teletex service
- S.60 terminal equipment for use in the TELEX service
- S.61 character repertoire and coded character sets for Teletex
- S.62 control procedures for the Teletex service
- S.170 network-independent basic support service for Teletex.

The Deutsche Bundepost of Germany introduced its Teletex system in 1980. Since that time, several countries have implemented Teletex services, and Telecom Canada and Western Union (U.S.) have both announced Teletex systems.

One of the major reasons Teletex is gaining in use is its favorable comparison with the postal service and the older TELEX service. The German research revealed significant cost and performance differences between the postal service, TELEX, and Teletex (see Table 13-1). The postal service costs shown in the table include postage rates and other costs to handle a letter, such as the overhead of operating a mail room. The costs are based on the 1981 exchange rate between German deutsche marks and U.S. dollars. In essence, the study reveals both cost and performance advantages for the use of the improved technology of Teletex.

ELECTRONIC MAIL

Electronic mail is used extensively throughout the data communications industry. The technology offers faster delivery than conventional mail-courier service and costs are now beginning to favor some electronic document deliveries over the postal service.

The previous discussion of Teletex illustrates some aspects of an electronic mail service. However, a system such as Teletex provides only a portion of the complete protocols needed to implement electronic mail. Figure 13-23 depicts the other

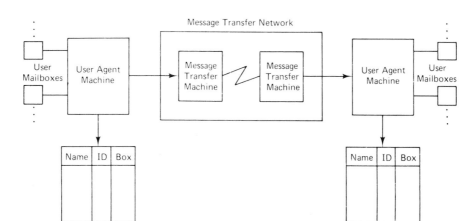

Figure 13-23. Electronic Mail Systems

major features of an electronic mail system. The *user agent* is responsible for providing text editing and proper presentation services to the end user. It provides for other activities, such as "user-friendly" interaction (for example, selective viewing on the screen), security, priority provision, delivery notification, and distribution subsets.

The *message-transfer agent* is oriented toward the actual routing of the electronic mail. This function is responsible primarily for the store-and-forward path, channel security, and the actual mail routing through the communications media.

X.400

The CCITT describes these three major functions in a series of documents entitled *Message Handling Systems* (MHS). These standards are published in the X.400 documents. The MHS series of recommendations provides electronic mail service with two options to end users: (1) message transfer (MT) supports application-independent systems, and (2) the interpersonal messaging service (IPM) supports communications with new and existing specifications and services. The message-transfer (MT) services are covered by the X.400 recommendations.

Figure 13-24 depicts the major features of an OSI electronic mail system, referred to as a *message handling system* (MHS). These terms are used in the CCITT X.400 MHS recommendations.

The *user agent* (UA) is responsible for interfacing directly with the end user. Since it is an applications process, MHS does not define how it interacts with the end user or how it performs solitary actions. In the "real world" it prepares, submits, and receives messages for the user. It also provides text editing and presentation services for the end user. It provides for other activities, such as user-friendly interaction (as examples, selective viewing, using ikons, and menus). It supports security, priority provision, delivery notification, and the distribution of subsets of documents. The user agent is the familiar electronic mailbox.

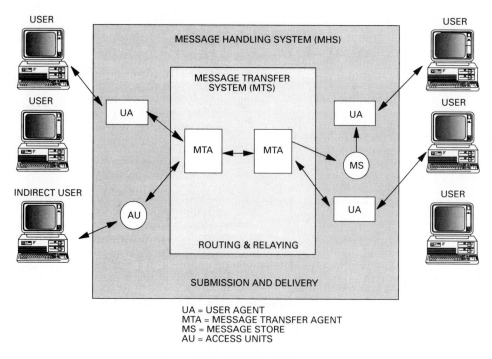

UA = USER AGENT
MTA = MESSAGE TRANSFER AGENT
MS = MESSAGE STORE
AU = ACCESS UNITS

Figure 13-24. MHS Architecture

UAs are grouped into classes by MHS based on the types of messages they can process. These UAs are then called *cooperating UAs.*

The *message transfer agent* (MTA) provides the routing and relaying of electronic mail. This function is responsible primarily for the store-and-forward path, channel security, and the actual message routing through the communications media. Upon receiving a message from a user agent, the MTA checks it for syntax problems. If the message passes the check, the message is either delivered to another local UA or forwarded to the next MTA.

A collection of MTAs is called the *message transfer system* (MTS). These functions usually are specialized to a particular vendor's product, but recent efforts have pointed the way to more standardized systems.

The *message store* (MS) provides for the storage of messages and their submission and retrieval. The MS complements the UA for machines such as personal computers and terminals that are not continuously available. The job of MS is to provide storage that is continuously available.

Finally, the *access units* (AUs) support connections to other types of communications systems, such as Telematic services, postal services, and so on.

Since X.400 is an involved and detailed specification, an overview of each recommendation is provided in this section. A comparison with the ISO MHS publications is provided in this figure.

X.400 describes the basic MHS model in accordance with the Open Systems Interconnection (OSI) Reference Model. X.400 describes in very general terms how an originator interacts with the user agent (UA) system to prepare, edit, and receive messages. It describes how the user agent interacts with the message transfer (MT) network.

X.402 describes the overall architecture of MHS, and provides examples of possible physical configurations. This specification contains some very useful definitions and rules for naming and addressing.

X.403 provides directions on conformance testing. It is a very detailed and lengthy document which defines conformance requirements, testing methodology, test structures, timers, protocol data units, and so forth.

X.407 specifies conventions used in a distributed information processing task. It describes these tasks in an abstract manner.

X.408 provides recommendations for code and format conversion; for example, conversion between International Alphabet #5 (ASCII Code) and the S.61 Teletex character set.

X.411 describes the message-transfer layer (MTL) service. This recommendation describes how the MTS user transfers messages with the MTS by defining the service definitions and the abstract syntaxes.

X.413 contains the provisions for the message store (MS). It describes how MS acts as an intermediary between the UA and the MTS.

X.419 defines the procedures for accessing the MTS and the MS, and for the message exchanges between MTAs. It describes the application contexts with three MHS protocols, known as P1, P3, and P7.

X.420 describes the interpersonal messaging service (IPM). This service defines the semantics and syntax involved in the receiving and sending of interpersonal traffic. In addition, it recommends the operations for the transfer of the protocol data units through the system.

MHS uses the principles of the OSI Reference Model. The entities and protocols reside in the application layer of the model. From the context of the OSI model, MHS appears as depicted in Figure 13-25. The application entity (AE) consists of the user element (UE) and the supporting application service elements (ASEs). The message-handling ASEs can perform two types of service. The symmetric service means a UE both supplies and consumes a service; the asymmetric service means the UE either consumes or supplies a service, but does not do both.

Access to MTS or MS is provided by a number of application service elements (ASEs), as shown in this figure.

- *Message Submission Service Element* (MSSE): Supports the services of the submission functions.
- *Message Delivery Service Element* (MDSE): Supports the services of the delivery functions.
- *Message Retrieval Service Element* (MRSE): Supports the services of the retrieval functions for MS.
- *Message Administration Service Element* (MASE): Supports the services of administrative functions among UAs, MSs, and MTAs, and controls subsequent interactions by the means of the ASEs listed directly above.

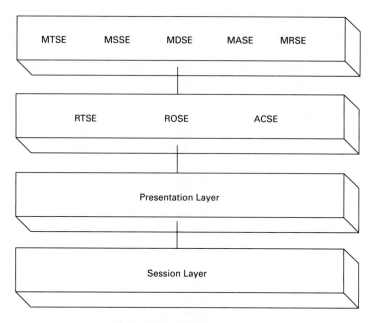

Figure 13-25. MHS Layers

Key to the management of the global MHS are the conventions for naming and addressing. Every user or distribution list (DL) must have an unambiguous *name*. MHS uses two kinds of names. A *primitive name* identifies a unique and specific entity such as an employee number or a social security number. A *descriptive name* denotes one user of the MHS, such as a job title. A descriptive name could identify different entities (in this example, people) as they move through a job. On the other hand, the primitive name is specific to the entity (a person). It may have global uniqueness (e.g., a social security number) or it may not have global uniqueness (e.g., an employee number). A name is permitted to have attributes which further identify an end user (entity) by including more detailed parameters (see Figure 13-26).

• Personal Attributes	Surname, Initials, First Name, Qualifier (II, Jr.)
• Geographical Attributes	Street name and number, Town, County, Region, State, Country
• Organizational Attributes	Name, Unit(s) within organization, Position or role with organization
• Architectural Attributes	X.121 address, Unique UA Identifier, Administration managment domain, Private managment domain

Figure 13-26. MHS Names

The MHS *address* specifies the information needed for a message delivery. It can identify the locations of the MHS entities. Typically, a name is looked up in a directory to find the corresponding address, but MHS does allow an O/R name to be a directory name, an O/R address, or both, so as to give the user considerable flexibility in this important area.

X.500 DIRECTORY SERVICES

Directories have been in use in computer installations for over a decade. Some organizations have used them for simple operations such as storing source code for software programs. Others have built data directories to store the names and attributes of the organization's data elements. Some forward-thinking companies now use directories to show the relationships of data elements to data bases, files, and programs. The Directory (also called a dictionary by some vendors) is used to check all key automated systems for accuracy and duplication, permitting an organization to access the impact of system changes to all the automated resources. The directory has become a vital component in an organization's management of its automated resources.

Typically, organizations and vendors have developed a unique and proprietary approach to the design and implementation of directories, which greatly complicates the management of resources that are stored in different machines and data bases. In the spirit of OSI, the purpose of the X.500 Directory is to provide a set of standards to govern the use of directories/dictionaries (see Figure 13-27).

The X.500 Recommendations describe the operations of the *Directory*. It is designed to support and facilitate the communication between systems of information concerning *objects* such as data, applications, hardware, people, files, distribution lists, and practically anything else that the organization deems worthy of "tracking" for management purposes. X.500 is intended to allow the communication of this information between different systems, which can include OSI applications, OSI layer entities, OSI management entities, and communications networks. X.500 actually encompasses eight recommendations, collectively known as the X.500 Recommendations (see Figure 13-28).

PROTOCOLS FOR FILE MANAGEMENT

An interesting aspect of the evolving upper-layer protocols are procedures and standards for user data base/file management. Each vendor has developed specific products and techniques to provide for this important function. Presently, the ISO is actively engaged in the development of a number of proposals for user file and data base management systems, and the File Transfer, Access, and Management (FTAM) standard is now complete.

Data usage often varies among different applications. However, a common model for all data files and data bases can provide a common foundation for file transfer, access, and management among diverse applications. This model is called the *virtual filestore*. Virtual filestore contains the file's characteristics, structure, and

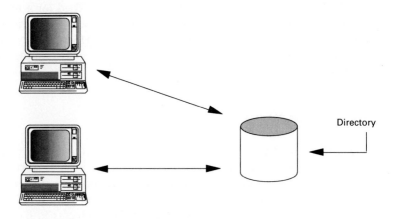

- Repository of information on many objects: applications, data bases, mail, people, etc.
- Actual information stored is not defined
- Multiple directories operate as if a single integrated directory
- Directory provides a model to guide in organizing information
- Provides ASN.1 code and macros for defining access (read, write, etc.)
- Supports a wide variety of naming services

Figure 13-27. The Directory

attributes. Its objective is to reduce the amount of detail needed to communicate with a file located in a remote part of the network.

The basic idea of virtual filestore is to provide a mapping of file definitions to/from actual files, which are called *real filestores* (see Figure 13-29). The filestore definitions form a *schema* of the file; subset descriptions of files form *subschemas*. The concepts of schemas and subschemas are very well known and understood in the data base management industry. The schema provides a map of the data, shows the names of the attributes, and establishes relationships of data elements. It pro-

CCITT	ISO
X. 500	9594/1
X. 501	9594/2
X. 509	9594/8
X. 511	9594/3
X. 518	9594/4
X. 519	9594/5
X. 520	9594/6
X. 521	9594/7

Figure 13-28. CCITT/ISO Specifications for Directories

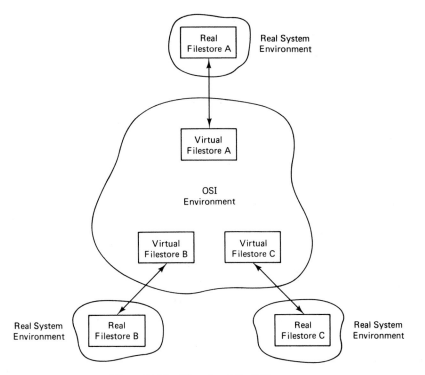

Figure 13-29.   Virtual and Real Filestore

vides the overall view of the data base. It says nothing about the physical structure of the file or the physical access method. The subschema is the specific user view of the data base, that is, the user subset of the schema.

Typically, organizations have hundreds of subschemas and individual users often have multiple subschemas to satisfy different kinds of retrieval and update requirements. This presents a challenge for the data base and network designers: They must provide for a physical design that satisfies all user subschemas at all nodes in the network. The emerging ISO standards provide methods to join different subschemas between systems at the presentation layer and additional procedures to manage file service dialogue at the session layer.

These proposals also include specifications for managing a data base activity across multiple sites in a network. This is a very ambitious undertaking, since such a system must provide for *consistent* states for all data operating in virtual filestore. A consistent state means that all data bases are accurate and correct, and any replicated copies contain the same values in the data fields. This is a very complex operation for multiple data bases that must have real-time transactions applied to them, because recovery of failed data is much more difficult. To illustrate: The efforts to achieve data reliability and consistency in a network are quite different than in a conventional centralized environment. The centralized approach assumes the availability of much information about a problem or failure. The operating system can suspend the execution of the problem program and store and query registers and control blocks, during which the problem component does not change. Moreover, the events are local and time delays in the problem analysis are very short.

In a network, the time delay in gathering data for analysis may be significant. In some cases, the data may be outdated upon receipt by the component tasked with the analysis and resolution. The problem may not be suspended as in a centralized system, since some networks have horizontal topologies and autonomous or near-autonomous components.

FTAM

FTAM is organized around the concept of the *attribute,* which describes the properties of a file. Presently, four groups of attributes are defined (see Figure 13-30):

> *Kernel group:* Properties common to all files
>
> *Storage group:* Properties of files that are stored
>
> *Security group:* Properties for access control
>
> *Private group:* Properties beyond FTAM scope

The kernel group consists of the file name, a description of the file structure (sequential, hierarchical), access restrictions (deletion, reads, etc.), location of the file user, and the identification of the application entities involved in the FTAM communications process.

The storage group describes several properties of a file. The properties are either (a) information about the ongoing characteristics of the file, or (b) information about the latest operations on the file. The following properties are included in the storage group:

- Date and time of last read, change, or attribute change.
- Identification of creator, last reader, last modifier, or last attribute modifier.
- File size and availability.
- Identification of party to be charged for file storage and file access activities.
- Description of any locks on the file.
- Identification of initiating FTAM user.

The security group includes attributes on access permission criteria, encryption procedures, and legal qualifications (trademarks, copyrights, etc.).

The private group is not defined by the FTAM standard. It is used for files beyond the virtual filestore attributes.

The FTAM model is a hierarchical structure resembling a tree. The tree can have a single root and a number of nodes below the root. Each node is identified and can have a data type associated with it. In virtual filestore, the conventional notion of a "data record" is called a *data unit* (DU), and a node may or may not have a data unit associated with it. The DUs are related to each other through a

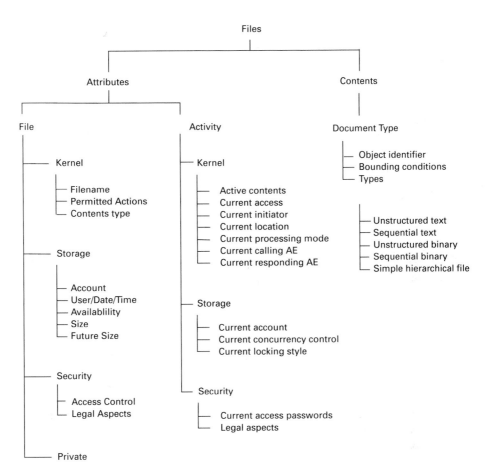

Figure 13-30. FTAM Architecture

hierarchical structure called *file access data units* (FADUs). Operations on a file are performed on a FADU through FADU identifiers (or names). The FADU is identified as a typed data unit at the presentation layer. The DU is considered to be the smallest amount that can be accessed.

The FTAM can take several forms for purposes of accessing a file or a portion of a file. For example, a file can be accessed starting from the root and traversing down through the nodes in a set order. As another example, FADUs can be accessed by "next," "last," "previous," and "beginning" signals.

The preorder tree traversal is a method to describe the structure of the tree by defining the ordering of the nodes in the following manner:

- Enter the tree through the top node.
- Go through the nodes from the top, going down and to the left.
- Go to the right in the tree when no paths remain to go down.
- Go up in the tree if the search cannot go down.

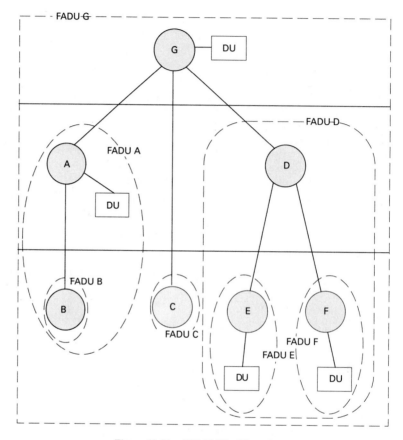

Figure 13-31. FTAM File Hierarchy

For example, the preorder traversal for the tree in Figure 13-31 is: G, A, B, C, D, E, F.

Yet another way to view FTAM is through the concept of file service regimes (see Figure 13-32). A file service is performed through a series of steps which build up a set of file contexts. The steps may include the following:

- The initiator and responder handshaking with each other to establish their identities.
- Identification of the file to be accessed.
- Establishing the file attributes.
- Providing for any file management actions.
- Locating the units in the file to be accessed.
- Operating on the units in the file.

The file service regimes define how FTAM primitives are used for the file activity. A *regime* is a period in which a common state is valid for the service users.

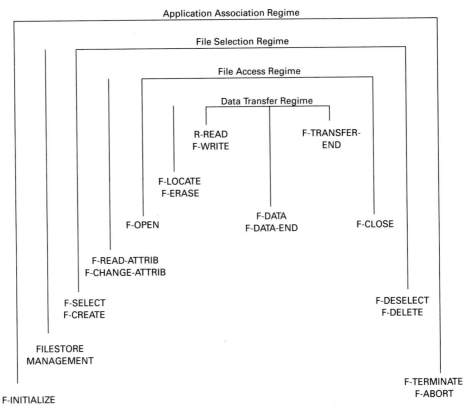

Figure 13-32. FTAM Regime

Regimes provide the protocol for file selection, file opens/closes, data transfer, and recovery operations. This figure shows the relationships of the regimes and primitives. (The primitives are explained shortly.) Four types of file service regimes are defined:

- *Application association regime:* exists during the lifetime of application association of two file service users.
- *File selection regime:* exists during the time in which a particular file is associated with the application association.
- *File access regime:* exists during a particular set of presentation contexts, concurrency controls, and commitment controls in operation for data transfer (these concepts are explained shortly).
- *Data transfer regime:* exists when a particular access context and direction of transfer are in force.

The dialogue proceeds through a series of protocol exchanges, such as the reading of a file access data unit. Specific times in which these exchanges occur are called *phases*. During a phase, FTAM imposes strict rules on state transitions and the use of primitives and state diagrams. The phases are sequential; they cannot be nested.

VIRTUAL TERMINAL PROTOCOLS

Even though you may not realize it, when you communicate in your home or office with an application through a communications network, you probably use at least a rudimentary form of the virtual terminal (VT) concept. The idea of the virtual terminal is to define the "behavior" of the terminal from the standpoint of its operating characteristics and network sessions. Ideally, the definition procedure is flexible enough to allow the terminal user (a) to readily change the behavior of the terminal, and (b) to provide a means for a terminal or a user application to access a variety of other terminals and applications.

The latter feature is especially difficult to provide, because most vendors' terminals use different upper-level protocols. While it is true that some terminals use the same codes for some functions, such as carriage return, escape, cursor movement, and so on, it remains that most vendors use their own approaches. The situation is made even more complex because the vendors also use different approaches to keyboard commands and screen control programs. IBM solves the problem by placing all terminals onto a host machine and using the same (or nearly the same) terminal protocols. However, this approach becomes unwieldy in large, distributed systems that must support a heterogeneous terminal environment.

The central concept of the virtual terminal is to isolate the terminals and applications from each other. In this manner, different terminals can access different applications running on different systems. The VT achieves this worthy goal by having one VT entity: (a) simulate a real terminal and (b) negotiate the terminal's operating characteristics with another VT entity. It becomes the task of the VTs to resolve potential differences and incompatibilities between the terminal and the application.

As with most of the OSI standards, those for VT services are not intended to blaze new technological trails, but simply to establish a standard way of connecting heterogeneous systems.

Two approaches can be used for obtaining VT services (concentrate on the latter):

Parameter Model: Use of codes and parameters to describe the terminal.

Object Model: Use of abstract objects to model the terminal characteristics and functions.

The parameter model is explained with the CCITT X.3, X.28, and X.29 protocols. The object model is explained with ISO 9040 and ISO 9041. The latter is part of the emerging OSI standards. The X.3, X.28, and X.29 protocols were developed to support non-X.25 terminals for an X.25-based network.

In a typical VT environment a terminal (say, terminal A) makes changes to an object (code, data, etc.) in accordance with vendor-specific procedures (see Figure 13-33). These changes are sent to a terminal server (say, at host B) and stored in the host's VT area. In turn, the host can reflect these changes by updating terminal C's VT area and screen. The two terminals may be different. If so, the host has the job of resolving the differences, through the use of the VT protocols.

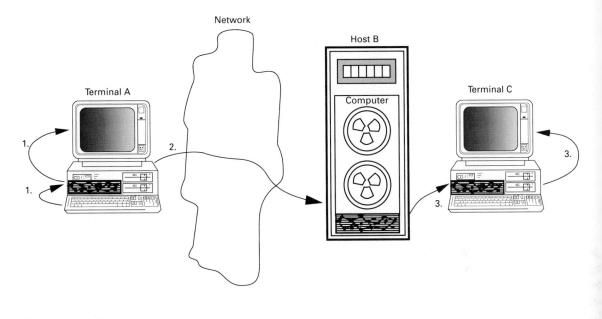

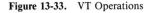

= VT areas (Contains abstract notation of the screen)

1. Keyboard entry changes terminal's copy and is reflected on the screen

2. Changes are reflected in the host's VT areas

3. Changes may be reflected on terminal C's area and screen

Figure 13-33.   VT Operations

The object model developed by the ISO uses abstract data objects to model common functions and characteristics found in terminals. The idea is that the terminals' functions can be described in an abstract notation in order to facilitate the internetworking of terminals and applications processes.

The basic idea of an object model virtual terminal is as follows. Each terminal is described by a data structure (or object) and a profile. A profile may be part of the data structure. A profile is a set of parameters which define the characteristics of the terminal. The data structure not only describes the terminal's profile, but defines the specific terminal operation. The object model differs from the parameter model in that the object model terminal (or a device acting as its agent) is considered to be much more intelligent, perhaps able to assume different profiles.

The VT negotiation process changes control tables in each of the VT entities. These control tables determine how the contents of the terminal memory will be mapped onto the display screen. However, since there is more memory than can be placed onto a screen at one time, the VT process entails using the control tables to determine how to map the *conceptual memory/display* contents onto the real display of the screen.

The mapping process is achieved with the *device object,* as seen in Figure 13-33. A device object exists for each real device used at the terminal (screen, keyboard, printer, plotter, scanner, etc.). Another term used to describe the conceptual display is the *display object.* Under the VT concept, a display object is mapped by the device object into a real display.

The VT standards also use a *control object* to define the physical aspects of the devices, such as bells, buzzers, mouse movements, lights, and other activities not related to the manipulation of text.

After the negotiation is completed, the two entities should be able to communicate with the same set of VT services.

Like the vast majority of OSI standards, the VT protocol is designed to present a number of options to the user. These options serve as a convenient means to model a standard's architecture. At the broadest level, the VT services are divided into functional units. The functional units are further classified by facilities within the functional units. Lastly, the facilities are classified by the services provided. This figure depicts the relationships of the functional units, facilities, and services.

The *kernel* functional unit is not an optional capability; it is considered the most basic set of services to be established between two VT users.

As the name suggests, the *switch profile negotiation* is used to switch the profile between the association of the two VT users. The operation entails one user proposing a VT profile by providing VT argument values in the proposal. The protocol allows the service provider and the receiving VT user to return an agreed-upon set of profile values, but only if they are within the range offered by the initial service initiator. This is quite similar to the other OSI protocols in which negotiation

- Kernel: The kernel functional unit supports the basic transaction services required to begin a dialogue, send data, signal a user- or provider-initiated error, and end the dialogue. Use of provider abort may signal abnormal terminal.

- Shared Control: In the Shared Control functional unit both TPSUIs can issue request primitives subject only to the normal sequence constraints of the primitives. For example, data can be transferred by both TPSUIs at the same time.

- Polarized Control: In the Polarized Control functional unit, only one TPSUI has control of the dialogue at any time. Many request primitives can be issued only by the TPSUI which controls the dialogue. This restriction is in addition to the normal sequence constraints for the primitives. For example, data can be transferred only by the TPSUI which has control of the dialogue.

- Handshake: The Handshake functional unit allows a pair of TPSUIs to synchronize their processing with one another.

- Commit: The Commit functional unit supports reliable commitment and rollback of provider-supported transactions.

- Unchained Transactions: The Unchained Transactions functional unit allows a superior to exclude a transaction subtree from a sequence of provider-supported transactions and to reinclude its direct subordinate in later provider-supported transactions.

Figure 13-34. TP Functional Units

begins with the initiator and can then be changed first by the service provider and next by the receiving service user.

The *multiple interaction negotiation* functional unit is used to negotiate a set of VTE parameter values which allow one VTE to ask another VTE to actually propose values for the VTE parameters. These values are proposed, and they may or may not be accepted by the inviting VTE user. It can be seen that the multiple interaction negotiation functional unit differs from the switch profile negotiation functional unit in that the inviting VTE user provides the invitation for the responding VTE user to provide its own parameters.

The *negotiated release* functional unit allows the VTE user to reject a request from its peer VTE user to release the VTE association. However, a release cannot be rejected unless the negotiated release functional unit has been established.

The *urgent data* functional unit allows the VT user to send a small amount of data to the peer VTE user, usually bypassing exchanges of lessor priority. The VT standards do not stipulate how the urgent data are to be handled.

The *break* functional unit is used to support the destructive interrupt facility.

DISTRIBUTED TRANSACTION PROCESSING

The ISO distributed processing standard (TP) is published as DP 10026. It has seen very limited use in the industry thus far because it is a relatively new standard, even though the standards groups have been working on it for a number of years.

The purpose of TP is to support distributed transaction processing. It is built on the ability to detect failures in the processing of a transaction and to notify the TP user about the nature of the failure (or success). The protocol has a number of authentication procedures and permits multipart cooperation in supporting the transaction operations.

The TP standard uses the concept of *atomicity, consistency, isolation,* and *durability* known as ACID. The idea of ACID revolves around the concurrency, commitment, and recovery (CCR) transaction tree in which all parties must coordinate in the operation against the transaction and make a commitment to fully support it.

In the event of a problem, the object that has been operated upon must be restored to its original and consistent state.

ACID also requires that a transaction be isolated from other transactions and that they must not impact each other during the actual operation. Moreover, with ACID, action must be finished before anything is revealed about it. Finally, ACID requires that all actions are performed successfully, or none are performed.

TP is organized around six functional units (see Figure 13-34). As with most OSI services, there is a *kernel functional unit* which is required as a minimal service. This functional service supports very basic TP services—the initiation of dialogue, the sending of data, certain error routines, and certain abort operations.

The *shared control functional unit* permits both TP service entities to issue primitives at any time. With *polarized control,* only one entity has control of the dialogue at any one time. This is based on the session layer control notion of having control of the token.

The *handshake functional unit* establishes rules for the TP entities to synchronize and negotiate their operations with one another. The *commit functional unit* uses the CCR protocol for proper changing and rollbacking if necessary.

Finally, the *unchained transactions functional unit* allows a TP entity (designated as superior) to exclude a transaction subtree from certain types of transactions.

RDA

The *remote data base access protocol* (RDA) is published as ISO DP 9579 and SQL specialization ISO 9075 (see Figure 13-35). This protocol is not complete and has not seen use in the industry at this time. Its purpose is to allow users to access different types of data bases without caring where these data bases might be.

The RDA protocol defines a *data manipulation language* (DML) which is used to decode the user request. This decoding is performed by an RDA server and then translated to the specific data base management system's I/O to manipulate the data.

The RDA protocol also establishes rules to cover the dialogue and messages that are passed between the user (client) and a server. The protocol is designed to operate at the application layer and invokes the services of ACSE, CCR, and ROSE.

In addition, RDA can be specialized to any specific data base type. The *structured query language* (SQL) is the working draft that ISO has been using in this endeavor.

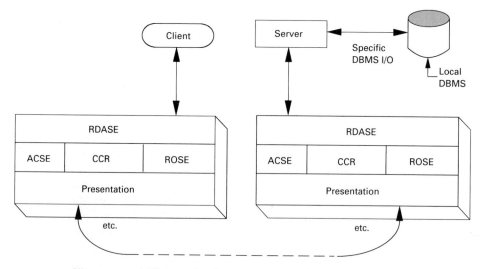

- Allows access of different types of data bases
- Defines a data manipulation language (DML) which is decoded by a server to the specific DBMS protocol
- Establishes the dialogue structure and message formats for the client/server communications process
- Generic RDA can be specialized to a specific data base type; ISO has working draft for structure query language (SQL)

Figure 13-35. The RDA Protocol

EDI

The *electronic document exchange* (EDI) standard is a very widely used specification. It is published under ANSI 12.31n and ISO's EDIFACT specification (ISO 9735). It provides rules for the creation, sending, and reception of standardized messages regarding the business environment. For example, purchase orders, customs forms, commercial invoices, insurance forms, and banking forms fall within the EDI arena. EDI operates with X.400; indeed, X.400 considers EDI its user (see Figure 13-36).

SUMMARY

This chapter can give the reader only a general idea of the many upper-layer protocols that exist or are in various stages of development. These concepts are becoming more than just ideas, and several standards on data bases and virtual files have been approved. For example, X.400 and FTAM are quite prevalent today. However, much

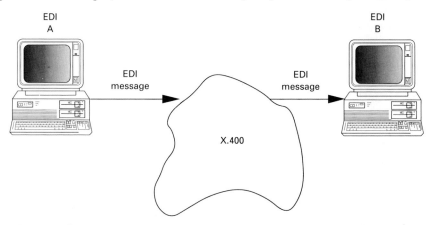

- Procedures for electronic document exchange

- Similar to EDIFACT (ISO 9735), Electronic Data Interchange for administration, commerce, and transport

- Modeled on X.400 Interpersonal Messaging (IPM) service (p2), with new contents and types
  - In CCITT drafts X.edi1 and X.edi2

- EDI header used to identify services with EDI information carried in the body of the message

  Embellishments to IPM concepts
  - EDI Responsibility Request/Indication
  - Forwarding, changed or unchanged messages

- Standardized messages for: commercial invoices, purchase orders, (response, change), dispatch service, delivery service, customs forms, banking and insurance forms, etc.

Figure 13-36. The EDI Standard

work remains to be done. Because of their number and diversity, it is doubtful that all the entities for the upper layers will ever be completed.

FINAL THOUGHTS

The protocols, standards, and interfaces at the lower levels are relatively stable and mature. They form a very solid foundation on which to build the upper layers. Moreover, most vendors and standards groups have now recognized that it is in everyone's best interest to work toward common approaches to service the end user, and the protocols, standards, and interfaces discussed in this book are now widely used. Much of this conformance has come from the insistence of members of the user community who were (and are) weary of the constant problem of interfacing different vendors' "closed systems" to service an application.

Notable progress has been made in the field of computer networks with the acceptance of protocol conventions and standards. My hope is that this book has given you an increased awareness of how computer networks function. I also hope you now have the foundation on which to build and acquire more knowledge about computer networks.

APPENDIX A

A Data Communications Tutorial

THE COMMUNICATIONS CIRCUIT

In order to understand a data communications network, we should know something about its components and how they function. Most communications systems and components are designed around electronic equipment. Consequently, it is appropriate to begin with a review of some of the basic aspects of electricity that most of us learned in science classes or physics seminars.[1]

Electricity provides the basis for storing and conveying information in the computer network (optical fibers using light sources are also used and will be discussed later). The effects of electricity can be seen in all phases of our lives; for example, in the operation of a simple automobile battery, the functioning of radio and television sets, and many other applications. All of these applications have something in common: the existence of particles of electric charge. In fact, all the materials with which we deal in our day-to-day lives—solids, liquids, and gases—are described as containing two kinds of electric charge, called *electrons* and *protons*. The electron is the smallest amount of electrical charge that concerns most engineers in the data communications world. The electron is said to have negative polarity. The proton is the basic particle that has positive polarity. The negative and positive polarities indicate two opposite characteristics that, for our purposes, are fundamental in most physical applications.

An analogy to electricity is that of the north/south poles in magnets. The opposite poles of a magnet attract each other and the like poles repel. In electricity, electrons and protons attract each other and like charges repel. Electrons repel other electrons, for example. It is the arrangement of the electrons and protons that determines the electrical characteristics of the many parts of the communications network.

Protons and electrons arrange themselves together to form an atom. The formation achieves electrical stability. For example, a hydrogen atom has one proton and one electron. Their countervailing forces compensate each other to provide stability.

Figure A-1 shows one electron in the hydrogen atom as an orbital ring around the nucleus of the atom. Also, the nucleus contains the proton, the positive charge. The stability of the atom is based on two properties: (1) the electron's attraction toward the proton, which is counterbalanced by (2) the outward mechanical force of the electron rotating around the atom. The distribution of electrons in the orbital rings determines the electrical stability. Introducing a means to make the atom unstable where the electrons move to other atoms produces energy in the form of an *electrical current*. The currents can be used to symbolize data in the data communications system.

There are many other kinds of atoms and they are usually more complex than the hydrogen atom. In fact, they usually have more than one orbital ring. One of the common atoms is the copper atom, and the copper wire is a common means of providing connections between terminals and computers in the network. We examine the copper atom in Figure A-2. This atom has more than one ring around it. Especially important is the number of electrons in the ring farthest from the nucleus. This outermost ring requires eight electrons for stability. Fewer than eight electrons creates an unstable force. (The rings vary widely among different atoms and the number of electrons actually present.) The outermost ring of the copper atom contains only one electron. When many atoms are close together in the wire, the outermost electrons (in this case, only one in the copper atom) are not sure where they belong and they wander, migrating freely and at random from atom to atom. These electrons are called *free electrons* because they move freely from one atom to the next. It is the movement of these free electrons that can provide *current* in a conductor, such as the copper wire. The electron movement creates electrical current, which can be used to convey information across the data communications channel. Due to its electrical instability, copper wire is a very good conductor of electrical signals, and consequently it is widely used in data communications systems.

A goal in communications and electrical components is to provide for a means to move the electrons in a nonrandom manner, which is in contrast to the random movement we have just discussed. The primary means to move electrons through a copper wire and hence create a *communications signal* is through a concept called the unit of *potential difference*. Simply stated, when one charge is different from another charge between two components, a difference in potential exists. Potential actually refers to the possibility of moving electrical particles such as the electrons.

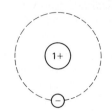

Figure A-1. The Hydrogen Atom

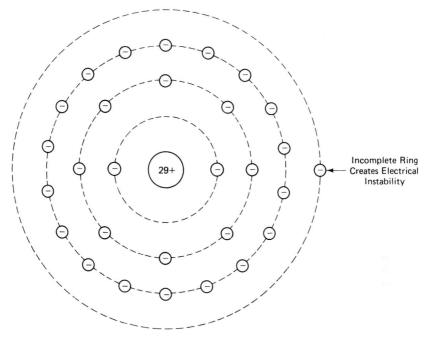

Figure A-2. The Copper Atom

Figure A-3 shows the effect of potential difference. We assume one unit of charge can move three electrons (in reality, billions of electrons are involved). The left side of the circuit has a difference potential of zero and the right side has a positive three difference in potential. This means that nine electrons can be moved, because a difference of three exists between the right and left ends of the channel.

Figure A-3(b) shows that the left side of the channel now has a potential difference of plus one. The right side of the channel has the same difference of plus

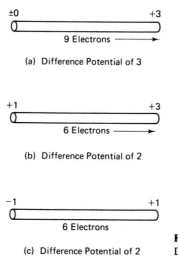

(a) Difference Potential of 3

(b) Difference Potential of 2

(c) Difference Potential of 2

Figure A-3. Effect of Potential Difference

three. The relative difference in potential is now two, which allows the movement of six units or six electrons. One last example is shown in Figure A-3(c). In this instance, the left side of the channel now has a negative potential of minus one. The right side now has a positive potential difference of plus one. The difference between these two ends of the channel (the relative difference) is two. Again, a relative difference of two exists, giving the ability to move six electrons across the channel. An important distinction should be emphasized: it is the *difference in potential* that actually determines the movement of the quantity of electrons. Moreover, electrical current consists of the movement of billions of electrons. A current of only one Ampere (Amp) moves 6.25×10^{18} electrons in one second.

In summary, current (and thereby the ability to carry information through current) occurs when the potential difference between two charges forces electrons to move through the circuit. The difference in charge is measured in a unit called the *volt*. A volt is really nothing more than what it takes in an applied charge to create a potential difference to get the free electrons moving through the circuit.

You may realize now why a battery has positive and negative charges on the terminals: to create energy within the battery, repulsing electrons at the negative terminal in order to move current through the wires connected to the poles of the battery. The higher the voltage (or stated another way, the greater the difference in potential between the terminals on the circuit), the greater the current flow will be. This means a greater intensity of free electrons moves through the circuit. We will see later how either current flow or voltage levels can be made to represent *data* and *data communications signals*.

Figure A-4 shows a picture of a simplified electrical circuit. The circuit has a positive point and a negative point where differences in voltage can be created. These points are connected through wires (in communications terms, a *channel, line, link,* or *circuit*). Placing a voltage at one end of the line will cause a disruption in electron stability, because the electrons are repulsed from the negative terminal and attracted toward the positive terminal. The charge at the negative terminal introduces excess electrons.

The simple electrical circuit shown in the figure also contains a light bulb. As the electrons flow through the wire, they enter the bulb. The tungsten filament wire in the bulb acts as a stronger resistor to the current flow than does the copper wire. This resistance—the opposition to the current—causes the filament to become white hot and the filament discharges light.

The circuit can be configured to perform the functions of a communications system by manipulating a key on the channel. By opening the key, the circuit is no longer complete and the current is halted. The difference in potential between the

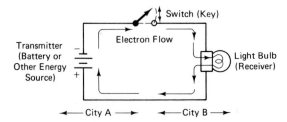

Figure A-4   An Electrical Circuit

positive and negative terminals is now irrelevant. The key is, in effect, a *switch* that is opened and closed to produce the effect of a flashing light. If a person (an operator) opens/closes the key at specific intervals, the flashing light can convey a *code*.

The *code* conveys some form of intelligence to the receiver. For example, during a five-second interval, a key operator could open and close the switch to produce: no light, light, light, light, no light. This code could represent the letter C (in fact, some codes actually use this format for C). An individual watching the light flashes would know the prearranged code and interpret the signals as a C.

Let us now extend the circuit to two different cities. The battery and key (switch) are located in city A and the light source is in city B. Thus, the system has a transmitter at city A and a receiver at city B. The wires connecting the two sites form the *communications channel* (line, link, or circuit). In order to transmit data to city B, a person enters the proper codes by closing and opening the circuit through manipulating the key. An individual at city B watches the flashing light and decodes the signals. We now have a data communications system (similar to the telegraph system developed in the 1840s).

Of course, a communications network is not quite as simple as this scenario. However, in concept networks are very similar because they are comprised of transmitters, receivers, and channels which send and receive codes conveying data and, ultimately, intelligence.

The circuit in Figure A-4 shows that two channels are involved in the system. In this instance, a circuit is connected to the negative terminal to provide for the signal propagation toward the receiver, and a return circuit is connected to the positive terminal for the current to complete the entire path.

In the early configurations of data and voice communications circuits, the return circuit was earth. This technique provided one wire for the data flow and the earth medium for the return circuit, also called the ground (or ground electrode). The grounding occurred against some piece of metal, such as pipes; it resulted in terminating the connection into the earth, the actual ground itself. In such a system, the earth or ground replaced the wire as the return path for the current flow, and the earth became the return conductor.

Figure A-5(a) illustrates how the positive terminal from the battery and the outgoing wire of the receiver are connected to ground. Instead of the light bulb, the receiver is now a communications terminal like the one you have in your office. The terminal's circuitry decodes the off/on current flow, both for transmitting and receiving. The transmitting side of the terminal uses the keyboard and switching logic to create the binary images on the channel. While this example shows current as the logic source, many devices use voltage levels to provide the binary images.

All communications channels have limitations in their capacity to transmit data between computers and terminals. One major impediment is *noise*. (Many others exist, but are beyond the scope of this tutorial.)

The noise on a line is a problem that is inherent to the line itself and cannot be eliminated. Noise (called thermal, Gaussian, white, or background noise) results from the constant, random movement of electrons on the conductor and provides a limit to the channel capacity. The hiss you hear on a telephone line is such a noise. Any electric conductor is a source of noise. The power of the noise is proportional

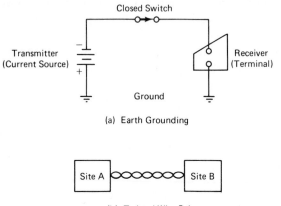

(a) Earth Grounding

(b) Twisted Wire Pair   **Figure A-5.** A Communications Circuit

to the *bandwidth* (range of frequencies contained in the channel), so an increased bandwidth also will contain increased noise.

One of the fundamental concepts in communications is Shannon's Law. Shannon demonstrated the finite limits of a transmission path with the following formula:

$$C = W \log_2 (1 + S/N)$$

where

      C   = maximum capacity in bits per second (bps)
      W   = bandwidth
      S/N = ratio of signal power (S) to noise power (N)

If you study this formula, it will be evident that increasing bandwidth, increasing signal power, or decreasing noise levels will increase the allowable bps rate. However, changing these parameters may be physically or economically prohibitive.

One method to increase the signal-to-noise ratio is to place more signal amplifiers on the line. Amplifiers strengthen the signal periodically as it travels down the communications path. Since noise is constant throughout the line, the amplifiers must be located close enough together so that the signal power does not fall below a certain level. However, while close spacing of amplifiers improves the S/N ratio, it also can be quite costly. Moreover, the amplifiers must be carefully designed to minimize the amount of noise that is amplified along with the signal.

To deal with thermal noise (as well as other types of noise, such as are caused by lightning, power fluctuations, etc.) a communications systems receiver must check for "damaged" data and ask the transmitter for a retransmission in the event of an error. These errors are classified broadly as *random, burst,* and *compound* errors. For random-error channels, each bit has a probability P of incorrect reception and a probability of P − 1 of correct reception. Errors occur randomly in the received data block. Most line-of-sight channels (as well as satellite links) are affected by random errors.

A burst-error channel exhibits an error-free state most of the time, but on occasion experiences errors that occur in groups or bursts. Radio signals are subject to burst errors, as are cable and wire links, such as twisted-pair telephone lines.

Many sections of this book describe how the data communications system attempts to deliver error-free data over error-prone communications channels.

Twisted-Pair Cable and Coaxial Cable Circuits

During the early days of *telephony,* all circuits used ground return (and some systems in remote locations may still use the technique). However, signal quality was quite poor; consequently, in 1883, a second wire was added to provide a nonground return. This approach improved the signal quality but resulted in the signals on the two wires interfering with each other. As a result, the pairs were twisted around each other to compensate for (and cancel) the effects of pair-interference. These circuits are widely used today and are called *twisted pairs* (also wire pairs) [see Figure A-5(b)]. As the telephone systems expanded, multiple wire pairs were combined in one sheath from the telephone office to the customer sites. Today, most data communications systems use these twisted pairs for transmitting data.

Figure A-6 depicts the circuit with a computer and a terminal replacing the battery and bulb. We assume one site is providing the voltage source and switching logic to create the generation of signals (the codes) to the receiving site, and vice versa. For simplicity, most data communications illustrations show the circuit as a line between the stations. The ground connections or return circuits usually are not shown.

Most cable pairs are *balanced* transmission lines. The two wires are referenced to each other regarding their relative voltage differences, so the circuit is balanced with respect to electrical ground. An *unbalanced* line uses one wire at ground potential and the other wire carries the current.

An example of an unbalanced circuit is *coaxial* cable. It consists of a shield around a conductor. The shield is held at ground potential and the center conductor carries the current. The shield prevents the signal from being radiated into space.

The balanced pair carries a stronger signal than unbalanced coaxial cable. Typically, the cable pair suffers much less signal loss at low and high transmission rates. However, coaxial line can be mounted almost anywhere. Since the outside shield is at ground potential, it can be placed against metal objects without any effect. The balanced pair must be kept clear of other conductors and stand-off insulators must be installed between some multiple cable systems.

Antenna-Oriented Channels

A transmission line, such as two wires, can be configured as an open circuit. For example, the two wires are not terminated, or are terminated such that all the power is not absorbed, and the remaining power is *reflected* back to the generator.

However, the circuit also can be designed to prevent the energy reflection and allow it to "escape" from the system and be radiated into space. The wires can be

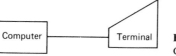

Figure A-6. A Computer-Terminal Channel

spread, and increased radiation occurs because they have less opportunity to cancel out each other's signals.

An antenna essentially converts high-frequency current into waves which are propagated into space. The antenna usually consists of a collection of wires designed to permit maximum escape and minimum reflection of the signal on an open-circuited transmission line.

Since current on a wire creates a magnetic field around it, both the magnetic and electric fields are radiated from the antenna as an *electromagnetic* wave. The wave travels outward from the antenna in various radiation patterns to receiving antenna.

Today many communications systems use electromagnetic propagation. Radio, television, and satellite systems are all designed around the principles of antennas. Chapters One and Five have additional information on these systems.

Increasingly, the industry is using optical fiber channels for the transmission of data, voice, and video images. Instead of electrical signals, optical fibers utilize light as a signal source. The light is generated by a light-emitting diode or a laser and then transmitted through a tiny reflective glasslike cable. The transmitter switches the light on and off to represent user data with binary codes. Optical transmission has several significant advantages over electrical systems: (a) greater capacity; (b) immunity to electrical interference; (c) very small and lightweight; (d) more secure.[2]

BINARY NUMBERS

Communications systems and networks transmit data in the form of binary images; that is, as a 1 or a 0. Most of us are familiar with the *decimal* number system, consisting of the numbers 0–9. However, computers and terminals are designed to represent only two signal (voltage, current, radio wave, or optic) states: a 0 or a 1. Communications networks also convey intelligence in these *binary* images.

Both decimal (base 10) and binary (base 2) systems are founded around the ideas of positional notation, a concept that originated many years ago in India. In a number system, a numeric symbol (0–9 or 0–1) has a fixed value that is one greater than the symbol to its right. A number or character is constructed by combining several symbols (digits). The magnitude of the number or the meaning of the character depends on the relative position of the individual digits and the digit values.

Let us first consider a numeric value; that is, a number. The increase of the value of each digit in a number, as one moves from right to left through the number, depends on the *base* used. In our discussion, we are using base 10 (decimal) and base 2 (binary), so the decimal system increases by a power of 10 with each relative position to the left and the binary system increases by a power of 2.

Two simple examples illustrate these concepts. First, the decimal number 394 is established by the positional notation:

$$3 \times 10^2 \quad + \quad 9 \times 10^1 \quad + \quad 4 \times 10^0$$

or $\quad$ 300 $\qquad$ + $\qquad$ 90 $\qquad$ + $\qquad$ 4

or $\quad 394_{10}$

Computers, terminals, and networks use binary notation. The binary equivalent of 394 is 110001010. Its decimal value can be established easily through positional notation.

$$1\times2^8 + 1\times2^7 + 0\times2^6 + 0\times2^5 + 0\times2^4 + 1\times2^3 + 0\times2^2 + 1\times2^1 + 0\times2^0$$

or   1   +   1   +   0   +   0   +   0   +   1   +   0   +   1   +   0

or   256   +   128   +   0   +   0   +   0   +   8   +   0   +   2   +   0

or 394_{10}

A summary of decimal to binary equivalency should help the reader in understanding the binary system.

Decimal	Binary
0	0
1	1
2	10
3	11
4	100
5	101
6	110
7	111
8	1000
9	1001
10	1010
11	1011
12	1100
13	1101
14	1110
15	1111

CODES AND PROTOCOLS

In addition to number representations, computers and networks also must represent other symbols, such as the letters of the alphabet or special characters (like the pound sign, #). The binary system is extended to represent these symbols through *codes*.

Figures A-7 and A-8 are examples of two widely used codes in data communications—the EBCDIC code, developed and sponsored by IBM, and the ASCII code, developed and sponsored by the American National Standards Institute. The ASCII code is an international standard, in conformance with the International Alphabet 5 or IA5. The EBCDIC code is quite popular primarily because of IBM's position in the industry. It was developed from the six-bit BCD (binary coded decimal) code used on the old 1400 computer series. (The six-bit code did not provide for enough combinations of bits to represent characters and control functions:

Bit Positions				7	0	0	0	0	1	1	1	1
				6	0	0	1	1	0	0	1	1
4	3	2	1	5	0	1	0	1	0	1	0	1
0	0	0	0		NUL	DLE	SP	0	@	P	\	p
0	0	0	1		SOH	DC1	!	1	A	Q	a	q
0	0	1	0		STX	DC2	''	2	B	R	b	r
0	0	1	1		ETX	DC3	#	3	C	S	c	s
0	1	0	0		EOT	DC4	$	4	D	T	d	t
0	1	0	1		ENQ	NAK	%	5	E	U	e	u
0	1	1	0		ACK	SYN	&	6	F	V	f	v
0	1	1	1		BEL	ETB	'	7	G	W	g	w
1	0	0	0		BS	CAN	(	8	H	X	h	x
1	0	0	1		HT	EM	)	9	I	Y	i	y
1	0	1	0		LF	SUB	*	:	J	Z	j	z
1	0	1	1		VT	ESC	+	;	K	[	k	{
1	1	0	0		FF	FS	'	<	L	\	l	:
1	1	0	1		CR	GS	–	=	M	]	m	}
1	1	1	0		SO	RS	.	>	N	∧	n	~
1	1	1	1		SI	US	/	?	O	–	o	DEL

Figure A-7. ASCII (IA5) by ANSI and CCITT/ISO

$2^6 = 64$.) EBCDIC is an eight-bit code. The bit positions in Figure A-8 are arranged to show the first four bits at the top of the table with the remaining four bits to the side of the table. The ASCII code is a seven-bit code, although many vendors add an eighth bit for error-checking purposes. This bit, called a parity bit, is explained in Chapter Eleven of the book.

These codes are responsible for performing three important functions:

- device control
- data representation
- protocol control.

An example of device control can be seen by the backspace (BS) function in the EBCDIC and ASCII character sets. For instance, the BS could perform a backspace function at a receiving terminal. It might backspace a cursor across a screen.

The following describe other commonly used device-control characters: The horizontal tabulation (HT) effector causes the printing device to move to the next predetermined position before printing the next character. The line feed (LF) character moves the print position to the same column position in the next line. The vertical tabulation (VT) character causes the active printing or display position to advance to the same column a predetermined number of lines down from the

Figure A-8. EBCDIC Code by IBM

Bit Positions 4321 \\ 8765	0000	0001	0010	0011	0100	0101	0110	0111	1000	1001	1010	1011	1100	1101	1110	1111
0000	NUL	DLE	DS		SP	&	-				SMM	VT	FF	CR	SO	SI
0001	SOH	DC₁	SOS				/		a	j			A	J		1
0010	STX	DC₂	FS	SYN					b	k	s		B	K	S	2
0011	ETX	DC₃							c	l	t		C	L	T	3
0100	PF	RES	BYP	PN					d	m	u		D	M	U	4
0101	HT	NL	LF	RS					e	n	v		E	N	V	5
0110	LC	BS	EOB	UC					f	o	w		F	O	W	6
0111	DEL	IL	PRE	EOT					g	p	x		G	P	X	7
1000		CAN							h	q	y		H	Q	Y	8
1001		EM							i	r	z		I	R	Z	9
1010	SMM	CC	SM		¢	!	¦	:								
1011	VT				.	$	,	#								
1100	FF	IFS	DC₄	DC₄	<	*	%	@								
1101	CR	IGS	ENQ	NAK	(	)	_	'								
1110	SO	IRS	ACK		+	;	>	=								
1111	SI	IUS	BEL	SUB	|	¬	?	"								□

Bit Positions header:

Bit Positions			
4	3	2	1
5			
6	7		
8			

377

present line being printed or displayed. The form feed (FF) code may be used to advance a print head to the next logical top of form or to a predetermined line of the next form or page. The carriage return (CR) code advances the position to the first column of the same line. Unless the carriage return is followed by a line feed, the characters that follow the carriage return will overstrike characters already printed on the line.

The second major function is actually to convey or represent data. For example, the letter C is represented as 11000011 in EBCDIC and 1000011 in IA5/ASCII. As discussed in the preceding section, levels of voltage, intensities of current, or radio signal variations are used to represent the binary states of the codes.

The ASCII/IA5 code was developed several years ago before the advent of highly intelligent terminals. These earlier terminals, with no cathode ray tube (CRT) screen, are primarily paper-oriented printers. Consequently, the device-control functions are fairly limited, such as backspace, vertical tab, line feed, and character return, depicted in Figures A-7 and A-8. As the industry moved toward much more complex terminals, the control codes were insufficient to provide all the necessary device-control commands. To address this situation, ANSI now has standards to extend the basic code. ANSI X3.41 and X3.64 use the ESC character to "arm" subsequent control characters to provide additional functions. Specifically, X3.41 defines the command set for ASCII code extension and X3.64 defines the specific actions that the codes actually initiate on the device. For example, the three symbols of ESC 6 C instruct a terminal to move its screen cursor forward by six positions.

The third major function of codes is to control the "conversation" between computers and terminals. This conversation is called a *protocol*. The term *protocol* has many and varied uses in the industry. Practically everyone versed in data communications talks about a protocol, but each person fixes a different meaning to the term. Simply stated, a protocol is an agreement on how to converse. Many levels and forms of protocol exist, which often leads to some confusion in the industry. For instance, an "agreement" can exist between two devices that they have an electrical protocol. Each device can be designed to recognize a binary one as −3 volts on the communications channel, and a binary zero as +3 volts. This agreement is one aspect of an electrical protocol.

Another form of protocol is usually software- or microcode-oriented and placed into effect with these codes. For instance, the protocol control character of EOT often signifies the end of the transmission of user data. When one device transmits to another device, it sends a block of user data and then appends the series of bits representing EOT to tell the receiving device that the receiver has received all the data. Obviously, the two devices must recognize EOT under the same format and context, or they cannot communicate with each other. This example illustrates one of the biggest problems in the industry: Vendors often build protocols that interpret code formats differently, resulting in incompatible products among vendors.

An example of the problem with protocols can be seen by examining EOT again. Some vendors establish EOT to signify the end of the transmission with the station signing off the system, similar to a "log-off" on a computer. Other vendors interpret it as end of transmission, but not as a sign-off, since at a later time the station intends to send more data. Thus, these two protocols are incompatible because of the different interpretation of the protocol control codes. The recent acceptance of international protocols discussed in several chapters of the book will play a key role in moving the industry to common standards and protocols.

We have learned from previous discussions that communications signals are subject to distortion due to noise and other problems. Several chapters in this book describe *line* or *link* protocols, and one of their principal functions is to provide the error-free delivery of user data across the communications line.

Notes

[1]An excellent reference introducing the basic concepts of electricity and electronics to beginners is *Basic Electronics* by Bernard Grob, McGraw-Hill, Inc., 1971, 3rd Edition. This book is also a well-presented text on more advanced concepts.

[2]For readers who wish more information on transmission media, see *Data Communications and Distributed Networks* by Uyless Black, Prentice Hall, 1993, 3rd Edition.

APPENDIX B

Translation Tables

The tables in Appendix B should assist the reader in understanding some jargon used throughout the book.

Appendix A explained how the binary number system is used to represent data. Large binary numbers consist of long strings of zeros and ones, which are difficult to read and interpret. The hexadecimal (hex) system is often used to provide a "shorthand" in representing large binary numbers. This technique uses 16 symbols, with each symbol representing four binary digits:

Decimal	Binary	Hexadecimal
0	0000	0
1	0001	1
2	0010	2
3	0011	3
4	0100	4
5	0101	5
6	0110	6
7	0111	7
8	1000	8
9	1001	9
10	1010	A
11	1011	B
12	1100	C
13	1101	D
14	1110	E
15	1111	F

TABLE B-1. BASE-TEN NUMBERING SYSTEM

Multiplication Factor	Prefix	Symbol	Meaning
$1\ 000\ 000\ 000\ 000\ 000\ 000 = 10^{18}$	exa	E	Quintillion
$1\ 000\ 000\ 000\ 000\ 000 = 10^{15}$	peta	P	Quadrillion
$1\ 000\ 000\ 000\ 000 = 10^{12}$	tera	T	Trillion
$1\ 000\ 000\ 000 = 10^{9}$	giga	G	Billion
$1\ 000\ 000 = 10^{6}$	mega	M	Million
$1\ 000 = 10^{3}$	kilo	k	Thousand
$100 = 10^{2}$	hecto	h	Hundred
$10 = 10^{1}$	deka	da	Ten
$0.1 = 10^{-1}$	deci	d	Tenth
$0.01 = 10^{-2}$	centi	c	Hundreth
$0.001 = 10^{-3}$	milli	m	Thousandth
$0.000\ 001 = 10^{-6}$	micro	μ	Millionth
$0.000\ 000\ 001 = 10^{-9}$	nano	n	Billionth
$0.000\ 000\ 000\ 001 = 10^{-12}$	pico	p	Trillionth
$0.000\ 000\ 000\ 000\ 001 = 10^{-15}$	femto	f	Quadrillionth
$0.000\ 000\ 000\ 000\ 000\ 001 = 10^{-18}$	atto	a	Quintillionth

The convenience of hexadecimal is evident in the following example. The decimal number 714 is represented by binary 1111100110 . . . not an easy symbol to write or read, yet many data communications situations require one to know the actual bits involved in a transmission. The decimal 714 is also awkward to relate to the specific binary bits transmitted on the channel. The hexadecimal (hex) notation is a good compromise, because we can readily translate a hex number to its decimal or binary equivalent:

	714		decimal
0011	1110	0110	binary
3	E	6	hexadecimal

Several discussions in the book use the hexadecimal notation.

OTHER SHORTHAND NOTATIONS AND TERMS

This book uses other terms to simplify otherwise lengthy explanations. Base-ten numbers are often used with terms such as *kilo, mega, milli,* and *nano.* Table B-1 provides an explanation of these terms.

Since computers and networks use binary images to convey data and information, Table B-2 should also be useful to the reader.

TABLE B-2. BINARY/DECIMAL CONVERSION

$$4,294,967,296 = 2^{32}$$
$$16,777,216 = 2^{24}$$
$$65,536 = 2^{16}$$
$$256 = 2^{8}$$
$$64 = 2^{6}$$
$$16 = 2^{4}$$
$$8 = 2^{3}$$
$$4 = 2^{2}$$

$$0.5 = 2^{-1}$$
$$0.25 = 2^{-2}$$
$$0.125 = 2^{-3}$$
$$0.0625 = 2^{-4}$$
$$0.03125 = 2^{-5}$$
$$0.015625 = 2^{-6}$$
$$0.0078125 = 2^{-7}$$
$$0.00390625 = 2^{-8}$$

APPENDIX C

Physical Level Interfaces

INTRODUCTION

Physical level interfaces are used to connect user devices into the communications circuit. To perform this important function, most physical level interfaces describe four attributes of the interface. The *electrical* attributes describe the voltage (or current) levels and the timing of the electrical changes to represent a binary 0 or 1. The *functional* attributes describe the functions to be performed by the physical interface. Many physical level protocols classify these functions as control, timing, data, and ground. The *mechanical* attributes describe the connectors and the wires of the interface. All data, signaling, and control wires usually are enclosed in one cable and connected to terminating plugs at each end of the cable. These plugs are similar in function to other power plugs (like those in residences), but they look much different and perform different functions. The procedural *attributes* describe what the connectors must do and the sequence of events required to effect actual data transfer across the interface.

This appendix provides a brief overview of physical level interfaces. More detailed information is available from other sources.[1]

RS-232-C

DTEs and DCEs usually are connected by the RS-232-C standard interface. A DTE (data terminal equipment) is typically an end-user device, such as a terminal or computer. The DCE (data circuit-terminating equipment) provides the DTE a connection into the communications circuit. (Chapter One further defines DCEs and DTEs.) The C represents the fourth version, which was approved in 1981. A newer version, EIA-232-D, has seen limited use. The CCITT standards organization has similar standards called V.24/V.28 (discussed later). RS-232-C (V.24 and V.28) describe four functions of the interface:

- defining control signals across the interface
- moving user data across the interface
- transmitting clocking signals to synchronize data flow
- forming the actual electrical characteristics of the interface.

RS-232-C conveys data across the interface by changing voltage levels. A binary 0 is represented by a range of $+3$ to $+12$ volts. A binary 1 is represented by a range of -3 to -12 volts. The actual length of the RS-232-C cable depends upon the electrical characteristics of the cable, although some vendors prohibit a length greater than 50 feet. The international standard V.28 stipulates an electrical interface similar to RS-232-C.

Figure C-1 illustrates the circuits of RS-232-C, which consists of 25 pin connections (i.e., channels). All 25 channels are not used. A DCE-to-DTE interface typically requires only four to eight channels.

The functions of the 25 pins (channels) are as follows:

Pin 1   Circuit AA Protective Ground: Conductor is electrically connected to equipment frame chassis.

Pin 7   Circuit AB Signal Ground: Common ground for all circuits. This establishes the voltage ground reference for all other lines. It actually has nothing to do with ground, but is a common reference circuit.

Pin 2   Circuit BA Transmit Data: Data signals transmitted from DTE to DCE. This usually represents the user data.

Pin 3   Circuit BB Receive Data: User data signals transmitted from DCE to DTE.

Pin 4   Circuit CA Request to Send: Signal from DTE to DCE. This circuit notifies DCE that the terminal or computer has data to transmit. Circuit CA is also used on half-duplex lines to control the direction of data transmission. The transition of OFF to ON notifies the DCE to take any necessary action to prepare for the transmission.

Pin 5   Circuit CB Clear to Send: Signal from DCE indicating the DTE can transmit the data. The Clear to Send signal may be turned ON after receiving a carrier signal from the remote modem. The timing of CB varies from modem to modem.

Pin 6   Circuit CC Data Set Ready: Signal from DCE indicating the machine is (a) off hook: connected to channel on a switched line, (b) DCE is in data transmit mode (not test, voice, etc.), (c) DCE has completed timing functions and answer tones.

Pin 20   Circuit CD Data Terminal Ready: Signal from DTE indicating terminal or computer is powered up, has no detectable malfunction, and is not in test mode. Generally, CD is ON if it is ready to transmit or receive

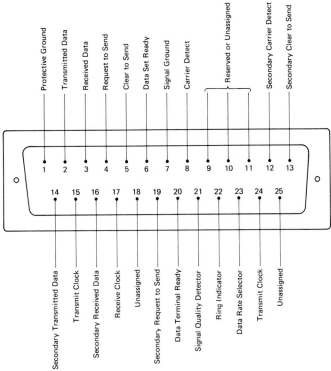

Pin	Circuit	Source	Description
1	AA	—	Protective Ground
2	BA	DTE	Transmitted Data
3	BB	DCE	Received Data
4	CA	DTE	Request to Send
5	CB	DCE	Clear to Send
6	CC	DCE	Data Set Ready
7	AB	—	Signal Ground
8	CF	DCE	Received Line Signal Detector
9	—	—	Reserved for Data Set Testing
10	—	—	Reserved for Data Set Testing
11	—	—	Unassigned
12	SCF	DCE	Secondary Received Line Signal Detector
13	SCB	DCE	Secondary Clear to Send
14	SBA	DTE	Secondary Transmitted Data
15	DB	DCE	Transmission Signal Element Timing
16	SBB	DCE	Secondary Received Data
17	DD	DCE	Receiver Signal Element Timing
18	—	—	Unassigned
19	SCA	DTE	Secondary Request to Send
20	CD	DTE	Data Terminal Ready
21	CG	DCE	Signal Quality Detector
22	CE	DTE	Ring Indicator
23	CH	DTE	Data Signal Rate Selector
23	CI	DCE	Data Signal Rate Selector
24	DA	DTE	Transmit Signal Element Timing
25	—	—	Unassigned

Figure C-1.

data. In a switched arrangement, a ring from the remote site will normally activate CD. CD holds the channel in a connected condition.

Pin 22   Circuit CE Ring Indicator: Signal from DCE indicates that a ringing signal is being received on a switched channel.

Pin 8   Circuit CF Receive Line Signal Detector: Signal from DCE indicating the DCE has detected the remote modem's carrier signal. Also called Data Carrier Detect (DCD).

Pin 21   Circuit CG Signal Qualify Detector: Signal from DCE to indicate that the received signal is of sufficient quality to believe no error has occurred.

Pin 23   Circuits CH and CI Data Signal Rate Selector: Signals from DTE and DCE, respectively, to indicate the data signaling rate for dual-rate machines. Some devices have the capability to transmit varying bit rates.

Pin 24   Circuit DA Transmitter Signal Element Timing: Signals from DTE to provide timing of the data signals being transmitted on circuit BA (Transmit Data) to the DCE. DTE provides this signal; if the DCE provides timing, then circuit DB is used.

Pin 15   Circuit DB Transmitter Signal Element Timing: Signals from DCE to provide timing of the data signals being transmitted on circuit BA (Transmit Data) to the DCE. DCE provides this signal; if the DTE provides the timing, then circuit DA is used.

Pin 17   Circuit DD Receiver Signal Element Timing: Signals from DCE to provide timing to DTE of the data signals being received on circuit BB (received data).

In addition to these circuits, RS-232-C defines five other circuits designated as secondary channels: SCA, SCB, SCF, SBA, and SBB. The remaining circuits are used for testing and other vendor-specific functions, or are not used.

Earlier discussions in this tutorial explained an unbalanced interface. RS-232 is classified as unbalanced because the voltage levels are detected at the receiver by the relative voltage difference between the signal circuit and signal ground (circuit AB). However, the transmitting and receiving stations usually have different logic ground due to different electrical characteristics of their components. As a consequence, a ground current can flow through the AB circuit. Obviously, the wire has electrical resistance, which produces a voltage drop. The voltage applied by the transmitter will be received differently by the receiver. If this potential difference is small, it will not create any errors. However, a signal of $+5$ volts with a ground potential difference of $+3$ volts means the receiver would see $+2$ volts: an undefined, transition region. A potential difference of -10 volts means the receiver mistakenly sees a 1 (MARK) instead of the intended 0 (SPACE).

Due to these problems, other interfaces are designed to be balanced (e.g., RS-422) where a circuit is referenced to another circuit and not to ground.

Figure C-2 illustrates a typical use of RS-232-C to send data from one DTE to another. DTE B could respond to DTE A later by using the same process in reverse.

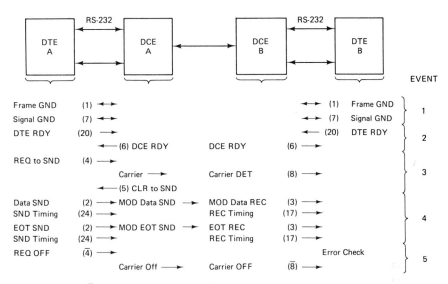

(X̄): Bar on top of pin number indicates the signal is turned off

EVENT	DESCRIPTION
1	Signal and grounding connections made.
2	DTEs and DCEs turn on pins 20 and 6 to indicate readiness.
3	DTE A requests a transmission with pin 4. DCE sends out a carrier signal to DCE B and turns on pin 5 to DTE A. DCE B detects the carrier signal and turns on pin 8 to DTE B.
4	Application data transmitted over pin 2 to DCE A. Pin 24 used to synchronize DTE A and DCE A. Data transmitted to DCE B, which transmits it to DTE B using pins 3 and 17.
5	EOT signal (end of transmission) turns pin 4 off, which instructs DCE A to turn off its carrier signal. DCE B detects carrier signal going off and turns off pin 8 to its DTE.

Figure C-2.

It is assumed by some people that a physical level interface encompasses only the *interchange circuit(s)* between the DTE and the DCE. While this view is correct for some products and standards, the physical level also includes the signals between the two DCEs. The CCITT publishes its V series physical level protocols to include (a) the DTE-to-DCE interface, and (b) the DCE-to-DCE interface. Other standards, such as RS-232, encompass only the DTE-to-DCE interface, but many vendors use the relevant portion of the CCITT V series recommendations to describe this part of the physical level interface. Other vendors use the "Bell Modem" specifications, which in many instances conform to the V series specifications (see Table C-3).

V.24

V.24 is another widely used standard in many parts of the world. Many of the products in your office are described as V.24 compatible. V.24 contains the definitions of the channels (pins) between DTEs and DCEs. RS-232-C uses different channel (or pin) identifiers, but the channels perform quite similar functions. V.24 defines more channels than does RS-232-C, because other interface standards utilize V.24 as well. In a sense, RS-232-C can be considered a subset of V.24. Table C-1 shows the V.24 interchange circuits.

The V.24 circuits perform the following functions:

Circuit 102—Signal Ground or Common Return. This conductor establishes the common return for unbalanced circuits according to Recommendation V.28 and the DC reference for circuits according to Recommendations V.10, V.11, and V.35.

Circuit 102a—DTE Common Return. This conductor is used as the reference potential for the unbalanced Recommendation V.10-type circuit receivers within the DCE.

Circuit 102b—DCE Common Return. This conductor is used as the reference potential for the unbalanced Recommendation V.10-type circuit receivers within the DTE.

Circuit 102c—Common Return. This conductor establishes the signal common return for single-current circuits with electrical characteristics according to Recommendation V.31.

Circuit 103—Transmitted Data. The data signals originated by the DTE, for transmittal to one or more stations, are transferred on this circuit to the DCE.

Circuit 104—Received Data. The data signals generated by the DCE, in response to data channel signals received from a data station, or in response to the DTE maintenance test signals, are transferred on this circuit to the DTE.

Circuit 105—Request to Send. Signals control the data channel transmit function of the DCE.

The ON condition causes the DCE to assume the data channel transmit mode. The OFF condition causes the DCE to assume the data channel nontransmit mode, when all data transferred on circuit 103 have been transmitted.

Circuit 106—Ready for Sending. Signals indicate whether the DCE is prepared to accept signals for transmission on the channel or for maintenance test purposes under control of the DTE.

The ON condition indicates that the DCE is prepared to accept data signals from the DTE. The OFF condition indicates that the DCE is not prepared to accept data signals from the DTE.

Circuit 107—Data Set Ready. Signals indicate whether the DCE is ready to operate.

TABLE C-1. V.24 CIRCUITS

Interchange Circuit Number	Interchange Circuit Name
102	Signal ground or common return
102a	DTE common return
102b	DCE common return
102c	Common return
103	Transmitted data
104	Received data
105	Request to send
106	Ready for sending
107	Data set ready
108/1	Connect data set to line
108/2	Data terminal ready
109	Data channel received line signal detector
110	Data signal quality detector
111	Data signal rate selector (DTE)
112	Data signal rate selector (DCE)
113	Transmitter signal element timing (DTE)
114	Transmitter signal element timing (DCE)
115	Receiver signal element timing (DCE)
116	Select standby
117	Standby indicator
118	Transmitted backward channel data
119	Received backward channel data
120	Transmit backward channel line signal
121	Backward channel ready
122	Backward channel received line signal detector
123	Backward channel signal quality detector
124	Select frequency groups
125	Calling indicator
126	Select transmit frequency
127	Select receive frequency
128	Receiver signal element timing (DTE)
129	Request to receive
130	Transmit backward tone
131	Received character timing
132	Return to nondata mode
133	Ready for receiving
134	Received data present
136	New signal
140	Loopback/maintenance test
141	Local loopback
142	Test indicator
191	Transmitted voice answer
192	Received voice answer

The ON condition (where circuit 142 is OFF or is not implemented) indicates that the signal converter or similar equipment is connected to the line and that the DCE is ready to exchange control signals with the DTE to initiate transfer of data.

The ON condition (with the ON condition of circuit 142) indicates the DCE is prepared to exchange data signals with the DTE for maintenance test purposes. The OFF condition indicates that the DCE is not ready to operate.

Circuit 108/1—Connect Data Set to Line.

Signals control switching of the signal-conversion or similar equipment to or from the line.

The ON condition causes the DCE to connect the signal-conversion or similar equipment to the line. The OFF condition causes the DCE to remove the signal-conversion or similar equipment from the line, after the transmission to line of all data previously transferred on circuit 103 and/or circuit 118 has been completed.

Circuit 108/2—Data Terminal Ready.

Signals control switching of the signal-conversion or similar equipment to or from the line.

The ON condition prepares the DCE to connect the signal-conversion or similar equipment to the line and maintains this connection after it has been established by supplementary means.

The DTE can preset the ON condition on circuit 108/2 when it is ready to transmit or receive data. The OFF condition causes the DCE to remove the signal-conversion or similar equipment from the line, after the transmission to line of all data previously transferred on circuit 103 and/or circuit 118 has been completed.

Circuit 109—Data Channel Received Line Signal Detector.

Signals indicate whether the received data channel line signal is within appropriate limits.

The ON condition indicates that the received signal is within appropriate limits. The OFF condition indicates that the received signal is not within appropriate limits.

Circuit 110—Data Signal Quality Detector.

Signals indicate if there is a reasonable probability of an error in the data received.

The ON condition indicates a probability of no error. The OFF condition indicates a reasonable probability of an error.

Circuit 111—Data Signaling Rate Selector (DTE Source).

Signals are used to select one of two data signaling rates of a dual-rate synchronous or asynchronous DCE.

The ON condition selects the higher rate or range of rates. The OFF condition selects the lower rate or range of rates.

Circuit 112—Data Signaling Rate Selector (DCE Source).

Signals are used to select one of the two data signaling rates in the DTE to coincide with the data signaling rate in use in a dual-rate synchronous or asynchronous DCE.

The ON condition selects the higher rate. The OFF condition selects the lower rate.

Circuit 113—Transmitter Signal Element Timing (DTE Source). Signals provide the DCE with signal element timing information.

The condition on this circuit shall be ON and OFF for equal periods of time and the transition from ON to OFF condition shall indicate the center of each signal on circuit 103.

Circuit 114—Transmitter Signal Element Timing (DCE Source). Signals provide the DTE with signal element timing information.

The condition on this circuit shall be ON and OFF for equal periods of time. The DTE shall present a signal on circuit 103 in which the transitions between signal elements occur at the time of the transitions from OFF to ON condition of circuit 114.

Circuit 115—Receiver Signal Element Timing (DCE Source). Signals provide the DTE with signal element timing information.

The condition of this circuit shall be ON and OFF for equal periods of time, and a transition from ON to OFF condition shall indicate the center of each signal element on circuit 104.

Circuit 116—Select Standby. Signals are used to select the normal or standby facilities, such as signal converters and data channels.

The ON condition selects the standby mode of operation, causing the DCE to replace predetermined facilities by their reserves. The OFF condition causes the DCE to replace the standby facilities with others. The OFF condition on this circuit shall be maintained whenever the standby facilities are not used.

Circuit 117—Standby Indicator. Signals indicate whether the DCE is conditioned to operate in standby mode with the primary facilities replaced by standbys.

The ON condition indicates that the DCE can operate in its standby mode. The OFF condition indicates that the DCE can operate in its normal mode.

Circuit 118—Transmitted Backward Channel Data. This circuit is equivalent to circuit 103 for backward (reverse) channel transmission.

Circuit 119—Received Backward Channel Data. This circuit is equivalent to circuit 104 for backward (reverse) channel transmission.

Circuit 120—Transmit Backward Channel Line Signal. This circuit is equivalent to circuit 105 for backward (reverse) transmit function of the DCE.

The ON condition causes the DCE to assume the backward channel transmit mode. The OFF condition causes the DCE to assume the backward channel nontransmit mode, after all data transferred on circuit 118 have been transmitted to line.

Circuit 121—Backward Channel Ready. This circuit is equivalent to circuit 106 for backward (reverse) channel transmission.

The ON condition indicates that the DCE can transmit data on the backward channel. The OFF condition indicates that the DCE cannot transmit data on the backward channel.

Circuit 122—Backward Channel Received Line Signal Detector. This circuit is equivalent to circuit 109, except that it is used to indicate whether the received backward channel line signal is within appropriate limits.

Circuit 123—Backward Channel Signal Quality Detector. This circuit is equivalent to circuit 110, except that it is used to indicate the signal quality of the received backward line signal.

Circuit 124—Select Frequency Groups. Signals are used to select the desired frequency groups available in the DCE.

The ON condition causes the DCE to use all frequency groups to represent data signals. The OFF condition causes the DCE to use a specified reduced number of frequency groups to represent data signals.

Circuit 125—Calling Indicator. Signals indicate whether a calling signal is being received by the DCE.

The ON condition indicates that a calling signal is being received. The OFF condition indicates no calling signal is being received.

Circuit 126—Select Transmit Frequency. Signals are used to select the required transmit frequency of the DCE.

The ON condition selects the higher transmit frequency. The OFF condition selects the lower transmit frequency.

Circuit 127—Select Receive Frequency. Signals are used to select the required receive frequency of the DCE.

The ON condition selects the lower receive frequency. The OFF condition selects the higher receive frequency.

Circuit 128—Receiver Signal Element Timing (DTE Source). Signals provide DCE with signal element timing information.

The condition of this circuit shall be ON and OFF for equal periods of time. The DCE shall present a data signal on circuit 104 in which the transitions between signal elements occur at the time of the transitions from OFF to ON condition of the signal on circuit 128.

Circuit 129—Request to Receive. Signals are used to control the receive function of the DCE.

The ON condition causes the DCE to assume the receive mode. The OFF condition causes the DCE to assume the nonreceive mode.

Circuit 130—Transmit Backward Tone. Signals control the transmission of a backward channel tone.

The ON condition causes the DCE to transmit a backward channel tone. The OFF condition causes the DCE to stop the transmission of a backward channel tone.

Circuit 131—Received Character Timing. Signals provide the DTE with character timing information.

Circuit 132—Return to Nondata Mode. Signals are used to restore the nondata mode provided with the DCE, without releasing the line connection to the remote station.

The ON condition causes the DCE to restore the nondata mode. When the nondata mode has been established, this circuit is turned OFF.

Circuit 133—Ready for Receiving. Signals control the transfer of data on circuit 104, indicating whether the DTE is capable of accepting a given amount of data as specified in the recommendation for intermediate equipment.

The ON condition must be maintained whenever the DTE is capable of accepting data and causes the intermediate equipment to transfer the received data to the DTE. The OFF condition indicates that the DTE is not able to accept data and causes the intermediate equipment to retain the data.

Circuit 134—Received Data Present. Signals are used to separate information messages from supervisory messages, transferred on circuit 104.

The ON condition indicates the data which represent information messages. The OFF condition shall be maintained at all other times.

Circuit 136—New Signal. Signals are used to control the response times of the DCE receiver.

The ON condition instructs the DCE receiver to prepare itself to detect rapidly the disappearance of the line signal (e.g., by disabling the response time circuitry associated with circuit 109). After the received line signal falls below the threshold of the received line signal detector, the DCE will turn OFF circuit 109 and prepare itself to detect rapidly the appearance of a new line signal.

Circuit 140—Loopback/Maintenance Test. Signals are used to initiate and release loopback or other maintenance test conditions in DCEs.

The ON condition causes initiation of the maintenance test condition. The OFF condition causes release of the maintenance test condition.

Circuit 141—Local Loopback. Signals are used to control the loop 3 test condition in the local DCE.

The ON condition of circuit 141 causes the establishment of the loop 3 test condition in the local DCE. The OFF condition of circuit 141 causes the release of the loop 3 test condition in the local DCE.

Circuit 142—Test Indicator. Signals indicate whether a maintenance condition exists.

The ON condition indicates that a maintenance condition exists in the DCE, precluding reception or transmission of data signals from or to a remote DTE. The OFF condition indicates that the DCE is not in a maintenance test condition.

Circuit 191—Transmitted Voice Answer. Signals generated by a voice answer unit in the DTE are transferred on this circuit to the DCE.

Circuit 192—Received Voice Answer. Received voice signals, generated by a voice answering unit at the remote DTE, are transferred on this circuit to the DTE.

V.28 specifies the electrical characteristics for unbalanced DTE/DCE interfaces. It is quite similar to RS-232-C with the ON condition (0) of more positive than 3 volts and the OFF condition (1) of more negative than minus 3 volts.

X.21

X.21 is yet another interface standard that has received considerable attention in the industry, but has not seen as extensive implementation as RS-232-C.[2] The standard was first published in 1972 and was amended in 1976, 1980, and 1984. Unlike RS-232-C, X.21 uses a 15-pin connector (a supposed replacement for RS-232-C, RS-449 provides a mapping of its circuits to that of X.21). The circuits are defined in ISO document 4903. See Figure C-3 for an illustration of the primary circuits.

The T and R circuits transmit and receive data across the interface. The data are either user or control signals. Unlike RS-232-C, X.21 uses the T and R circuits for user data *and* control. The C circuits provide an off/on signal to the network and the I circuit provides the off/on to the DTE. These two circuits serve to activate and deactivate the DCE-DTE interface session. The S and B circuits provide for

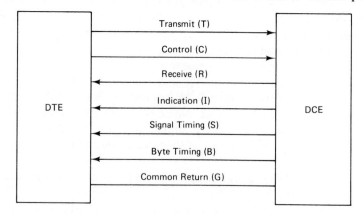

Figure C-3.

signals to synchronize the signals between the DTE and DCE. The G circuit acts as a signal ground or a common return.

This book discusses X.21 in several sections, primarily in how it is to be used in computer and terminal networks. For a variety of reasons, X.21 has not been implemented extensively. Nonetheless, it is a suitable interface option for certain applications and should be considered for situations requiring duplex, dedicated circuits operating in synchronous mode.

X.21 and other standards are designed around the concept of *states* and are explained by *state diagrams*. The allowable X.21 states are shown in Table C-2.

TABLE C-2. X.21 STATES

State Number	State Name
1	Ready
2	Call Request
3	Proceed to Select
4	Selection Signals
5	DTE Waiting
6A	DCE Waiting
6B	DCE Waiting
7	DCE Provided Information (Call Progress Signals)
8	Incoming Call
9	Call Accepted
10	DCE Provided Information (Called DTE Line Identification)
10 *bis*	DCE Provided Information (Calling DTE Line Identification)
11	Connection in Progress
12	Ready for Data
13	Data Transfer
13S	Send Data
13R	Receive Data
14	DTE Controlled Not Ready, DCE Ready
15	Call Collision
16	DTE Clear Request
17	DCE Clear Configuration
18	DTE Ready, DCE Not Ready
19	DCE Clear Indication
20	DTE Clear Confirmation
21	DCE Ready
22	DTE Uncontrolled Not Ready, DCE Not Ready
23	DTE Controlled Not Ready, DCE Not Ready
24	DTE Uncontrolled Not Ready, DCE Not Ready

Figures C-4 and C-5 explain how to read a state diagram and the call contact phase for X.21. For readers seeking a shorthand example of how X.21 works, the following explanation summarizes Figure C-5(b).

Call establishment is accomplished by the DTE and DCE both signaling Ready (State 1). From this state, the DTE enters the Call-Request state (State 2), which the DCE acknowledges by entering the Proceed-to-Select state (State 3). Next, the DTE presents its identifying digits (State 4). At the other end, the remote DCE signals its DTE by entering the Incoming-Call state (State 8) and the DTE responds with a Call-Accepted state (State 9).

Hereafter, the components pass through several optional states. The DTE and DCE can wait for the calls (States 5, 6A, 6B). An additional state, Connection in Progress (State 11) is available to allow additional network delay. The DCEs now enter the Ready-for-Data state (State 12) and then data transfer begins (State 13).

OTHER COMMON V AND X INTERFACES

Several other standards are widely used throughout the world. The majority of the standards use the basic pin arrangements of V.24 or RS-232-C. The V series stipulates recommended standards for data transmission in *telephone* networks. The X series is used for defining data transmission in public (or private) *data* networks. Several chapters in this book and Appendices D and E describe the more important X series. The prevalent V series are summarized in Table C-3.

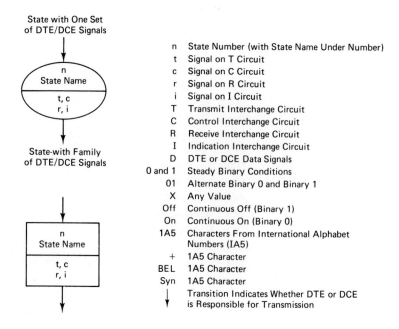

n	State Number (with State Name Under Number)
t	Signal on T Circuit
c	Signal on C Circuit
r	Signal on R Circuit
i	Signal on I Circuit
T	Transmit Interchange Circuit
C	Control Interchange Circuit
R	Receive Interchange Circuit
I	Indication Interchange Circuit
D	DTE or DCE Data Signals
0 and 1	Steady Binary Conditions
01	Alternate Binary 0 and Binary 1
X	Any Value
Off	Continuous Off (Binary 1)
On	Continuous On (Binary 0)
1A5	Characters From International Alphabet Numbers (IA5)
+	1A5 Character
BEL	1A5 Character
Syn	1A5 Character
↓	Transition Indicates Whether DTE or DCE is Responsible for Transmission

Figure C-4.

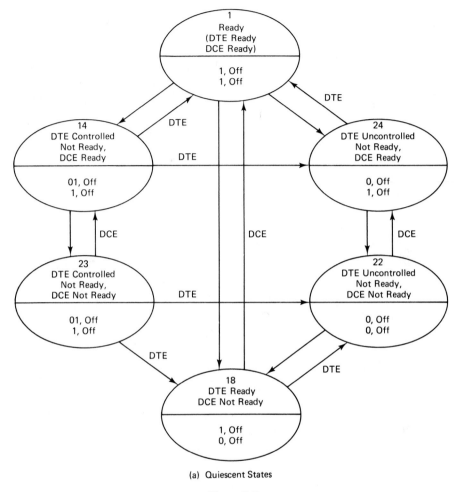

(a) Quiescent States

Figure C-5.

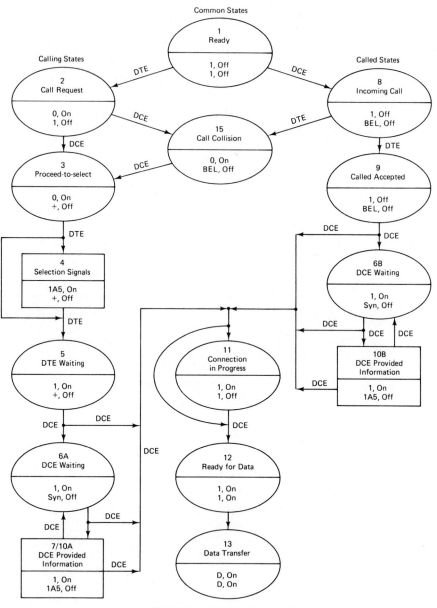

(b) X.21 Circuit Switched Call Control Phase

Figure C-5. *(Continued)*

TABLE C-3.　V SERIES INTERFACES

Series Number	Line Speed	FDX or HDX	Synchronous or Asynchronous	Modulation Technique	Switched Lines	Leased Lines
V.21	300	FDX	Either	FS	Yes	O
V.22	1200	FDX	Either	PS	Yes	PP 2W
V.22	600	FDX	Either	PS	Yes	PP 2W
V.22bis	2400	FDX	Either	QAM	Yes	PP 2W
V.22bis	1200	FDX	Either	QAM	Yes	PP 2W
V.23	600	HDX	Either	FM	Yes	O
V.23	1200	HDX	Either	FM	Yes	O
V.26	2400	FDX	Synchronous	PS	No	PP MP 2W
V.26bis	2400	HDX	Synchronous	PS	Yes	No
V.26bis	1200	HDX	Synchronous	PS	Yes	No
V.26ter	2400	FDX	Either	PS	Yes	PP 2W
V.26ter	1200	FDX	Either	PS	Yes	PP 2W
V.27	4800	Either	Synchronous	PS	No	4W
V.27bis	4800	Either	Synchronous	PS	No	2W 4W
V.27bis	2400	Either	Synchronous	PS	No	2W 4W
V.27ter	4800	HDX	Synchronous	PS	Yes	No
V.27ter	2400	HDX	Synchronous	PS	Yes	No
V.29	9600	Either	Synchronous	QAM	No	PP 4W
V.29	7200	Either	Synchronous	PS	No	PP 4W
V.29	4800	Either	Synchronous	PS	No	PP 4W
V.32	9600	FDX	Synchronous	QAM	Yes	PP 2W
V.32	9600	FDX	Synchronous	TCM	Yes	PP 2W
V.32	4800	FDX	Synchronous	QAM	Yes	PP 2W
V.35	48000	FDX	Synchronous	AM-FM	No	Yes

LEGEND

Line Speed:	In bit/s	FM:	Frequency modulation
FDX:	Full duplex	AM:	Amplitude modulation
HDX:	Half duplex	O:	Optional
FS:	Frequency shift	PP:	Point-to-point
PS:	Phase shift	MP:	Multipoint
QAM:	Quadrature amplitude modulation	2W:	Two-wire
TCM:	Trellis coded modulation	4W:	Four-wire

Notes

[1]Black, Uyless D., *Physical Level Interfaces,* Arlington VA: Information Engineering, Inc., 1985.

[2]CCITT Recommendation X.21, "Interface Between Data Terminal Equipment (DTE) and Data Circuit Terminating Equipment (DCE) for Synchronous Operation on Public Data Networks," Geneva, 1980.

APPENDIX D

Commonly Used
Standards

STANDARDS ORGANIZATIONS' ADDRESSES

Chapter Three describes the functions of the organizations responsible for developing and publishing standards for computer/terminal communications. The major
organizations are listed below.

ANSI   American National Standards Institute
       1430 Broadway, New York, NY 10018
       Telephone (212) 354-3300

EIA   Electronic Industries Association
       2001 Eye St., Washington, DC 20006
       Telephone (202) 457-4966

FED-STD General Services Administration
       Specification Distribution Branch
       Building 197, Washington Navy Yard, Washington, DC 20407
       Telephone (202) 472-1082

FIPS   U.S. Department of Commerce
       National Technical Information Service
       5285 Port Royal Road, Springfield, VA 22161
       Telephone (703) 487-4650

CCITT *Outside USA*
       General Secretariat
       International Telecommunications Union
       Place des Nations, 1121 Geneva 20, Switzerland
       Telephone +41 22 995111

        In the USA
United States Department of Commerce
National Technical Information Service
5285 Port Royal Road, Springfield, VA 22161
Telephone (703) 487-4650

ISO   *Outside USA*
International Organization for Standardization
Central Secretariat
1 rue de Varembe, CH-1211 Geneva, Switzerland
Telephone +41 22 34-12-40

      In the USA
American National Standards Institute (Address above)

ECMA   European Computer Manufacturers Association
114 rue du Rhone, CH-1204 Geneva, Switzerland
Telephone +41 22 35-36-34

IEEE   Institute of Electronic and Electrical Engineers
345 East 47th St., New York, NY 10017
Telephone (212) 705-7900

National Institute of Standards and Technology
Technology Building, Rm. B-253
Gaithersburg, Maryland 20899
Telephone (301) 921-2731

PREVALENT STANDARDS

The more widely used communications standards are listed here for your convenience. CCITT publishes revisions to its standards every four years. In its Plenary Assembly (October 8–19, 1984), CCITT approved new and revised recommendations for the ensuing four years. These recommended standards are now available in the "Red Book" series and can be obtained from CCITT, the United Nations Book Shop, or Omnicom, a reader service in Vienna, Virginia.

CCITT V-SERIES RECOMMENDATIONS

Number	Title
V.1	Equivalence between binary notation symbols and the significant conditions of a two-condition code
V.2	Power levels for data transmission over telephone lines
V.3	International Alphabet No. 5
V.4	General structure of signals of International Alphabet No. 5 code for data transmission over public telephone networks
V.5	Standardization of data signaling rates for synchronous data transmission in the general switched telephone network

V.6	Standardization of data signaling rates for synchronous data transmission on leased telephone-type circuits
V.7	Definitions of terms concerning data communications over the telephone network
V.10 (X.26)	Electrical characteristics for unbalanced double-current interchange circuits for general use with integrated circuit equipment in data communications
V.11 (X.27)	Electrical characteristics for balanced double-current interchange circuits for general use with integrated circuit equipment in data communications
V.15	Use of acoustic coupling for data transmission
V.16	Medical analog data transmission modems
V.19	Modems for parallel data transmission using telephone signaling frequencies
V.20	Parallel data transmission modems for use in the general switched telephone network
V.21	300 bits per second duplex modem for use on general switched telephone network
V.22	1200 bits per second duplex modem for use on general switched telephone network and on leased circuits
V.23 bis	2400 bits per second duplex modem standardized for use on general switched telephone network and on leased circuits
V.23	600/1200-baud modem for use in the general switched telephone network
V.24	List of definitions for interchange circuits between data terminal equipment (DTE) and data circuit-terminating equipment (DCE)
V.25	Automatic calling and/or answering equipment on the general switched telephone network, including disabling of echo suppressors on manually established calls
V.26	2400 bits per second modem for use on four-wire leased circuits
V.26 bis	2400/1200 bits per second modem for use in the general switched telephone network
V.27	4800 bits per second modem with manual equalizer telephone-type circuits for use on leased circuits
V.27 bis	4800/2400 bits per second modem with automatic equalizer for use on leased telephone-type circuits
V.27 ter	4800/2400 bits per second modem for use in the general switched telephone network
V.28	Electrical characteristics for unbalanced double-current interchange circuits
V.29	9600 bits per second modem for use on point-to-point four-wire leased telephone-type circuits
V.31	Electrical characteristics for single-current interchange circuits controlled by contact closure
V.35	Data transmission at 48 kilobits per second using 60–180 kHz group band circuits
V.36	Modems for synchronous data transmission using 60–180 kHz group band circuits
V.37	Synchronous data transmission at a data signaling rate higher than 72 kbits using 60–180 kHz group band circuits
V.40	Error indication with electromechanical equipment
V.41	Code-independent error-control system
V.50	Standard limits for transmission quality of data transmission
V.51	Organization of maintenance of international telephone-type circuits used for data transmission
V.52	Characteristics of distortion and error-rate measuring apparatus for data transmission
V.53	Limits for the maintenance of telephone-type circuits used for data transmission
V.54	Loop-test devices for modems
V.55	Specification for impulse noise measuring instrument for telephone-type circuits

V.56	Comparative tests of modems for use over telephone-type circuits
V.57	Comprehensive data test set for high data signaling rates

CCITT X-SERIES RECOMMENDATIONS
(Several of these recommended standards are explained in more detail in Appendices D
and E and in several chapters in the book.)

Number	Title
X.1	International user classes of service in public data networks
X.2	International user services and facilities in public data networks
X.3	Packet assembly/disassembly facility (PAD) in a public data network
X.4	General structure of signals of International Alphabet No. 5 (IA5) code for data transmission over public data networks
X.15	Definitions of terms concerning public data networks
X.20	Interface between data terminal equipment (DTE) and data circuit-terminating equipment (DCE) for start/stop transmission services on public data networks
X.20 bis	Use on public data networks of data terminal equipment (DTE) which is designed for interfacing to asynchronous duplex V-series modems
X.21	Interface between data terminal equipment (DTE) and data circuit-terminating equipment (DCE) for synchronous operation on public data networks
X.21 bis	Use on public data networks of data terminal equipment which is designed for interfacing to synchronous V-series modems (similar to RS-232-C)
X.22	Multiplex DTE/DCE interface for user classes 3–6 (see X.1 in Appendix E)
X.24	List of definitions for interchange circuits between data terminal equipment (DTE) and data circuit-terminating equipment (DCE) on public data networks
X.25	Interface between data terminal equipment (DTE) and data circuit-terminating equipment (DCE) for terminals operating in the packet mode on public data networks
X.26 (V.10)	Electrical characteristics for unbalanced double-current interchange circuits for general use with integrated circuit equipment of data communications
X.27 (V.11)	Electrical characteristics for balanced double-current interchange circuits for general use with integrated circuit equipment in data communications
X.28	DTE/DCE interface for a start/stop mode data terminal equipment accessing the packet assembly/disassembly facility (PAD) in a public data network situated in the same country
X.29	Procedures for the exchange of control information and user data between a packet assembly/disassembly facility (PAD) and a packet mode DTE or another PAD
X.40	Standardization of frequency-shift and modulated transmission systems for the provision of telegraph and data channels by frequency division of a group
X.50	Parameters of a multiplexing scheme for the international interface between synchronous data networks
X.50 bis	Parameters of a 48 kbit/s user data signaling rate transmission scheme for the international interface between synchronous data networks
X.51	Parameters of a multiplexing scheme for the international interface between synchronous data networks
X.51 bis	Parameters of a 48 kbit/s user data signaling rate transmission scheme for the international interface between synchronous data networks using 10-bit envelope structure

X.53	Numbering of channels on international multiplex links at 64 kbit/s
X.54	Allocation of channels on international multiplex links at 64 kbit/s
X.60	Common channel signaling for circuit-switched data applications
X.61	Signaling system No. 7
X.70	Terminal and transit control signaling system for start/stop services on international circuits
X.71	Decentralized terminal and transit control signaling system on international circuits between synchronous data networks
X.75	Terminal and transit call control procedures and data-transfer system on international circuits between packet-switched data networks
X.80	Interworking of interexchange signaling systems for circuit-switched data services
X.87	Principles and procedures for realization of international user facilities and network utilities in public data networks
X.92	Hypothetical reference connections for public synchronous data networks
X.96	Call-progress signals in public data networks
X.110	Routing principles for international public data services through switched public data networks of the same type
X.121	International numbering plan for public data networks
X.130	Provisional objectives for call setup and clear-down times in public synchronous data networks (circuit switching)
X.132	Provisional objectives for grade of service in international data communications over circuit-switched public data networks
X.150	DTE and DCE test loops in public data networks
X.180	Administrative arrangements for international closed user groups (CUGs)

INTERNATIONAL ORGANIZATION FOR STANDARDIZATION (ISO)
(Several other ISO specifications are referenced in Chapter 13.)

Number	Title
ISO 646	7-bit character set for information processing interchange—1973, confirmed 1979
ISO 1155	Information processing—Use of longitudinal parity to detect errors in information messages
ISO 1177	Information processing—Character structure for start/stop and synchronous transmission
ISO 1745	Information processing—Basic mode control procedures for data communications systems
ISO 2022	Code extension techniques for use with ISO 7-bit coded character set
ISO 2110	Data communication—25-pin DTE/DCE interface connector and pin assignments
ISO 2111	Data communication—Basic mode control procedures—Code independent information transfer
ISO 2593	Connector pin allocations for use with high-speed data terminal equipment
ISO 2628	Basic mode control procedures—Complements
ISO 2629	Basic mode control procedures—Conversational information message transfer
ISO 3309	Data communication—High-level data link control procedures—frame structure
ISO 4335	Data communication—High-level data link control procedures—Elements of procedures 1979—Addendum I, 1979—Addendum II, 1981
ISO 4902	Data communication—37-pin DTE/DCE interface connector and pin assignments

ISO 4903	Data communication—15-pin DTE/DCE interface connector and pin assignments
ISO 6159	Data communication—HDLC unbalanced classes of procedures
ISO 6256	Data communication—HDLC balanced class of procedures

EUROPEAN COMPUTER MANUFACTURERS ASSOCIATION (ECMA)

Number	Title
ECMA-40	HDLC Frame Structure
ECMA-49	HDLC Elements of Procedure
ECMA-60	HDLC Unbalanced Class of Procedures
ECMA-61	HDLC Balanced Class of Procedures
ECMA-71	HDLC Selected Procedures
ECMA-72	Transport Protocol
ECMA-75	Session Protocol
ECMA-80	Local Area Networks, Coaxial Cable System (CSMA-CD Baseband)
ECMA-81	Local Area Networks, Physical Layer (CSMA-CD Baseband)
ECMA-82	Local Area Networks, Link Layer (CSMA-CD Baseband)
ECMA-84	Data Presentation Protocol
ECMA-85	Virtual File Protocol (File Transfer)
	TECHNICAL REPORTS
TR-13	Network Layer Principles
TR-14	Local Area Networks, Layers 1 to 4 Architecture and Protocols

CCITT TELEMATICS RECOMMENDATIONS
(Chapter Thirteen discusses Telematics, Teletex, and TELEX.)

Number	Title
F.60	Operational provisions for the international TELEX service
F.61	Measurement of the chargeable duration of an international TELEX call for charging and accounting purposes
F.62	Duplex operation in the TELEX service
F.63	Additional facilities in the international TELEX service
F.64	Determination of the number of international TELEX circuits required to carry a given volume of traffic
F.65	Time-to-answer by operators at international TELEX positions
F.66	Regional tariff recommendations for the international TELEX service
F.67	Charging and accounting in the international TELEX service
F.68	Establishment of the automatic intercontinental TELEX network
F.69	Plan for TELEX destination codes
F.70	Observations on the quality of service in the international TELEX service
F.71	Interconnection of private teleprinter networks with the TELEX network
F.72	International TELEX store and forward—general principles and operational aspects
F.79	Instructions for the international TELEX service
F.200	Teletex service
F.201	Internetworking between Teletex and TELEX Service

F.300	Videotex service
T.0	Classification of facsimile apparatus for document transmission over the public networks
T.2	Standardization of Group 1 facsimile apparatus for document transmission
T.3	Standardization of Group 2 facsimile apparatus for document transmission
T.4	Standardization of Group 3 facsimile apparatus for document transmission
T.5	General aspects of Group 4 facsimile apparatus
T.6	Facsimile coding schemes and coding control functions for Group 4 facsimile apparatus
T.10	Document facsimile transmissions on leased telephone-type circuits
T.10	Document facsimile transmissions in the general switched telephone network
T.11	Phototelegraphic transmissions on telephone-type circuit
T.12	Range of phototelegraphic transmissions on a telephone-type circuit
T.15	Phototelegraphic transmission over combined radio and metallic circuits
T.20	Standardized test chart for facsimile transmissions
T.21	Standardized test charts for document facsimile transmissions
T.30	Procedures for document facsimile transmission in the general switched telephone network
T.35	Procedure for the allocation of CCITT members' codes
T.50	International Alphabet No. 5
T.51	Coded character sets for telematic services
T.60	Terminal equipment for use in the Teletex service
T.61	Character repertoire and coded character sets for the international Teletex service
T.62	Control procedures for Teletex and Group 4 facsimile services
T.63	Provisions for verification of Teletex terminal compliance
T.70	Network-independent basic transport service for the telematic services
T.71	LAPB extended for half-duplex physical level facility
T.72	Terminal capabilities for mixed mode of operation

CROSS REFERENCE OF STANDARDS

Many of the standards of the organizations listed in the previous section are duplicates or near-duplicates of each other. This section provides cross references of these standards.[1] Be aware that some differences do exist between these standards. The *specific* document should be read (or the vendor queried) to properly judge the true compatibility of the standards. In many instances, the differences are minor, but can affect communications significantly.

ISO

Series	Description	Related Standards
ISO 646	7-bit character set for information processing interchange	CCITT V.3; ANSI X3.4; FIPS 1-1, 7, 15
ISO 1155	Information processing—Use of longitudinal parity to detect errors in information messages	CCITT V.4, X.4; ANSI X3.15, X3.16; FED-STD 1010, 1011; FIPS 16-1, 17-1

ISO 1177	Information processing—Character structure for start/stop synchronous transmission	CCITT V.4, X.4; ANSI X3.15, X3.16; FED-STD 1010, 1011; FIPS 16-1, 17-1
ISO 1745	Information processing—Basic mode-control procedures for data communications systems	ANSI X3.28
ISO 2022	Code extension techniques for use with ISO 7-bit coded character set	ANSI X3.41; FIPS 35
ISO 2110	Data communication—25-pin DTE/DCE interface connector and pin assignments	EIA RS-232-C
ISO 2111	Data communication—Basic mode-control procedures—Code independent information transfer	ANSI X3.28
ISO 2593	Connector pin allocations for use with high-speed data terminal equipment	None
ISO 2628	Basic mode-control procedures—Complements	ANSI X3.28
ISO 2629	Basic mode-control procedures—Conversational information message transfer	ANSI X3.28
ISO 3309	Data communication—High-level data link control procedures—Frame structure	CCITT X.25, X.75; ECMA 40; ANSI X3.66; FED-STD 1003; FIPS 71
ISO 4335	Data communication—High-level data link control procedures—Elements of procedures Addendum I, 1979	CCITT X.25, X.75; ECMA 49; ANSI X3.66; FED-STD 1003; FIPS 71
ISO 4902	Data communication—37-pin and 9-pin DTE/DCE interface connector and pin assignments	EIA RS-449
ISO 4903	Data communication—15-pin DTE/DCE interface connector and pin assignments	None
ISO 6159	Data communication—HDLC unbalanced classes of procedures	CCITT X.25; ECMA 60, 71; ANSI X3.66; FED-STD 1003; FIPS 71
ISO 6256	Data communication—HDLC balanced class of procedures	CCITT X.25, X.75; ECMA 61, 71; ANSI X3.66; FED-STD 1003; FIPS 71

EIA

Series	Description	Related Standards
RS-232-C	Interface between data terminal equipment and data communications equipment employing serial binary data interchange	CCITT V.24, V.28; ISO 2110
RS-269-B	Synchronous signaling rates for data transmission	CCITT V.5, V.6, X.1; ANSI X3.1; FED-STD 1013; FIPS 22-1
RS-334-A	Signal quality at interface between data terminal equipment and synchronous data communication equipment for serial data transmission	ANSI X3.24

RS-363	Standard for specifying signal quality for transmitting and receiving data processing terminal equipment using serial data transmission at the interface with nonsynchronous data communication equipment	None
RS-366-A	Interface between data terminal equipment and automatic calling equipment for data communication	CCITT V.25
RS-404	Standard for start/stop signal quality between data terminal equipment and synchronous data communication equipment	None
RS-410	Standard for the electrical characteristics of Class A closure interchange circuits	None
RS-422-A	Electrical characteristics of balanced voltage digital interface circuits	CCITT V.11, X.27; FED-STD 1020A
RS-423-A	Electrical characteristics of unbalanced voltage digital interface circuits	CCITT V.10, X.26; FED-STD 1030A
RS-449	General-purpose 37-position and 9-position interface for data terminal equipment and data circuit-terminating equipment employing serial binary data interchange	CCITT V.24, V.54, X.21 bis

ECMA

Series	Description	Related Standards
ECMA-40	HDLC Frame Structure	CCITT X.25, X.75; ISO 3309; ANSI X3.66; FED-STD 1003; FIPS 71
ECMA-49	HDLC Elements of Procedure	CCITT X.25, X.75; ISO 4335; ANSI X3.66; FTD-STD 1002; FIPS 71
ECMA-60	HDLC Unbalanced Class of Procedures	CCITT X.25, ISO 6159; ANSI X3.66; FED-STD 1003; FIPS 71
ECMA-61	HDLC Balanced Class of Procedures	CCITT X.25, X.75; ISO 6256; ANSI X3.66; FED-STD 1003; FIPS 71
ECMA-71	HDLC Selected Procedures (HDLC Subset)	CCITT X.26, X.75
ECMA-72	Transport Protocol	None

CCITT

Series	Description	Related Standards
V.3	International Alphabet No. 5	ISO 646; ANSI X3.4; FIPS 1-1
V.4	Structure of signals of International Alphabet No. 5 code for data transmission over public telephone networks	CCITT X.4; ISO 1155, 1177; ANSI X3.15, X3.16; FED-STD 1010, 1011; FIPS 16-1, 17-1

V.5	Standardization of data signaling rates for synchronous data transmission in the general switched telephone network	ANSI X3.1; EIA RS-269-B; FED-STD 1013; FIPS 22-1
V.6	Standardization of data signaling rates for synchronous data transmission of leased telephone-type circuits	ANSI X3.1; EIA RS-269-B; FED-STD 1013; FIPS 22-1
V.10	Electrical characteristics for unbalanced double-current interchange circuits for general use with integrated circuit equipment in the field of data communications	CCITT X.26; EIA RS-423-A; FED-STD 1030A
V.11	Electrical characteristics for balanced double-current interchange circuits for general use with integrated circuit equipment in the field of data communications	CCITT X.27; EIA RS-422-A; FED-STD 1020A
V.22	1200 bits per second duplex modem standardized for use on the general switched telephone network and on leased circuits	FED-STD 1008
V.24	List of definitions for interchange circuits between data terminal equipment and data circuit-terminating equipment	EIA RS-232-C, RS-449, RS-449.1, RS-266-A
V.25	Automatic calling and/or answering equipment on the general switched telephone network, including disabling of echo suppressors on manually established calls	EIA RS-366-A
V.26 bis	2400/1200 bits per second modem standardized for use in the general switched telephone network	FED-STD 1005
V.27 bis	4800/2400 bits per second modem with automatic equalizer standardized for use on leased telephone-type circuits	FED-STD 1006
V.27 ter	4800/2400 bits per second modem standardized for use in the generalized switched telephone network	FED-STD 1006
V.28	Electrical characteristics for unbalanced double-current interchange circuits	EIA RS-232-C
V.29	9600 bits per second modem standardized for use on point-to-point leased telephone-type circuits	FED-STD 1007
V.54	Loop-test devices for modems	EIA RS-449
X.1	International user classes of service in public data networks	ANSI X3.1, X3.36; EIA RS-269-B; FED-STD 1001, 1013; FIPS 22-1, 37
X.2	International user services and facilities in public data networks	INT-FED-STD 001041
X.4	General structure of signals of International Alphabet No. 5 code for data transmission over public data networks	CCITT V.4; ISO 1155, 1177; ANSI X3.15; X3.16; FED-STD 1010, 1011; FIPS 16-1, 17-1
X.20 bis	Use on public data networks of data terminal equipment (DTE) which is designed for interfacing to asynchronous duplex V-Series modems	EIA RS-232-C

X.21 bis	Use on public data networks of data terminal equipment (DTE) which is designed for interfacing to synchronous duplex V-Series modems	EIA RS-232-C, RS-449
X.25	Interface between data terminal equipment (DTE) and data circuit-terminating equipment (DCE) for terminals operating in the packet mode on public data networks	INT-FED-STD 001041
X.26	Electrical characteristics for unbalanced double-circuit interchange circuits for general use with integrated circuit equipment in the field of data communications	CCITT V.10; EIA RS-423-A; FED-STD 1030A
X.27	Electrical characteristics for balanced double-current interchange circuits for general use with integrated circuit equipment in the field of data communications	CCITT V.11; EIA RS-422-A; FED-STD 1020A
X.96	Call-progress signals in public data networks	INT-FED-STD 001041

ANSI

Series	Description	Related Standards
X3.1	Synchronous signaling rates for data transmission	CCITT V.5, V.6, X.1; EIA RS-269-B; FED-STD 1013; FIPS 22-1
X3.4	Code for information interchange	CCITT V.3; ISO 646; FIPS 1-1, 7, 15
X3.15	Bit sequencing of the American National Standard Code for Information Interchange in serial-by-bit data transmission	CCITT V.4, X.4; ISO 1155, 1177; FED-STD 1010; FIPS 16-1
X3.16	Character structure and character parity sense for serial-by-bit data communication in the American National Standard Code for Information Interchange	CCITT V.4, X.4; ISO 1155, 1177; FED-STD 1011; FIPS 17-1
X3.24	Signal quality at interface between data terminal equipment and synchronous data communication equipment for serial data transmission	EIA RS-334-A
X3.25	Character structure and character parity sense for parallel-by-bit communication in the American National Standard Code for Information Interchange	FED-STD 1012; FIPS 18-1
X3.28	Procedures for the use of communication control characters of American National Standard Code for Information Interchange in specified data communication links	ISO 1745, 2111, 2628, 2629
X3.36	Synchronous high-speed data signaling rates between data terminal equipment and data communication equipment	CCITT X.1; FED-STD 1001; FIPS 37

X3.41	Code extension techniques for use with 7-bit coded character set of American National Standard Code for Information Interchange	ISO 2022; FIPS 35
X3.44	Determination of the performance of data communication systems	None
X3.57	Structure for formatting headings for information interchange using the American National Standard Code for Information Interchange for data communication system control	None
X3.66	For advanced data communications control procedures (ADCCP)	CCITT X.25, X.75; ISO 3309, 4335, 6159, 6256; ECMA 40, 49, 60, 61, 71; FED-STD 1003; FIPS 71, 78
X3.79	Determination of performance of data communication systems that use bit-oriented control procedures	None
X3.92	Data encryption algorithm	FIPS 46

Notes

[1]An option to the somewhat onerous and expensive task of obtaining and maintaining the many documents is to obtain McGraw-Hill's *Compilation of Data Communications Standards,* a hardcover book of over 1900 pages. You will probably receive documents in which you have little or no interest, and the bound document precludes updating of the standards, but the documents do not change often, so the book has a reasonable shelf life. The cross-reference tables were extracted from this publication. (Data Communications Information Systems, 1221 Avenue of the Americas, New York, NY 10020. Reprinted from McGraw-Hill's *Compilation of Data Communications Standards,* Edition 11. Copyright 1982. *Data Communications.* McGraw-Hill, Inc., all rights reserved.)

APPENDIX E

Supporting Standards to X.25/X.75 Networks

This appendix is provided for readers who wish more detail about the supporting standards to X.25 and X.75. However, the chapter on X.25 networks is written without requiring knowledge of the X series in this appendix.

RECOMMENDATION X.1: INTERNATIONAL USER CLASSES OF SERVICE IN PUBLIC DATA NETWORKS

For several years, the CCITT has published recommendations for the V series (which standardize data signaling rates on the telephone network and modulation rates for modems). X.1 provides a standard for the signaling rates on public data networks.

X.1 defines 16 classes of service. The classes of service depend on whether the DTE operates as (a) an asynchronous start/stop device, (b) a synchronous device, or (c) a packet-mode device. The user classes of service and the data signaling rates are:

User Class of Service	Data Signaling Rate	Terminal Operating Mode
1	300 bit/s	Start/Stop Asynchronous
2	50–200 bit/s	Start/Stop Asynchronous
3	600 bit/s	Synchronous
4	2400 bit/s	Synchronous
5	4800 bit/s	Synchronous
6	9600 bit/s	Synchronous
7	48000 bit/s	Synchronous

8	2400 bit/s	X.25
9	4800 bit/s	X.25
10	9600 bit/s	X.25
11	48000 bit/s	X.25
12	1200 bit/s	X.25
20	50–300 bit/s	Terminals in Start/Stop mode using X.28 interface
21	75–200 bit/s	Terminals in Start/Stop mode using X.28 interface
22	200 bit/s	Terminals in Start/Stop mode using X.28 interface
30	64 kbit/s	ISDN terminals for reference S interface (as an interim measure, X.21 and X.21 bis can be used at reference point R)

Each carrier in a country or an administration (PTT) may or may not support all these classes of service.

RECOMMENDATION X.2: INTERNATIONAL DATA TRANSMISSION SERVICES AND OPTIONAL USER FACILITIES IN PUBLIC DATA NETWORKS

The chapter on the packet-switching recommended standard X.25 (Chapter Eight) discusses at some length user facilities for X.25 networks. Recommendation X.2 describes these facilities and indicates if they are an essential facility that must be made with the network, an additional facility (which is optional), and if they are applicable for a switched call (VC) or permanent virtual circuit (PVC). The recommendation also stipulates the facilities that are to be used with a circuit-switched network or a packet-switched network. Tables E-1 and E-2 summarize the X.2 facilities for circuit- and packet-switched systems.

RECOMMENDATION X.10: CATEGORIES OF ACCESS FOR DATA TERMINAL EQUIPMENT (DTE) TO PUBLIC DATA TRANSMISSION SERVICES PROVIDED BY PDNS AND/OR ISDNS THROUGH TERMINAL ADAPTERS

This recommendation was adopted at the 1984 CCITT session in Spain. X.10 defines the different categories of access for DTEs into different kinds of networks. Specifically, the standard defines how DTEs interface into (a) circuit-switched networks, (b) packet-switched networks, and (c) leased circuit networks. In addition, the standard defines how terminals interface into the ISDN network (described in Chapter Nine).

This recommendation has been used by many vendors and organizations in the past. However, to clear up any possible misunderstanding, the standards groups published this recommendation to codify what many people were already doing. Moreover, the recent release of the ISDN standards necessitated some additions to handle the digital network interface.

TABLE E-1. RECOMMENDATION X.2 CIRCUIT-SWITCHED DATA TRANSMISSION SERVICE

1. Optional User Facilities Assigned for an Agreed Contractual Period		Category*
1.1	Direct call	A
1.2	Closed user group	E
1.3	Closed user group with outgoing access	A
1.4	Closed user group with incoming access	A
1.5	Incoming calls barred within a closed user group	A
1.6	Outgoing calls barred within a closed user group	A
1.7	Calling line identification	A
1.8	Called line identification	A
1.9	Bilateral closed user group	A
1.10	Bilateral closed user group with outgoing access	A
1.11	Incoming calls barred	A
1.12	Reverse charging acceptance	A
1.13	Connect when free	A
1.14	Waiting allowed	A
1.15	Redirection of calls	A
1.16	On-line facility parameter registration/cancellation	A
1.17	DTE inactive registration/cancellation	A
1.18	Date and time indication	A
1.19	Hunt group	A

2. Optional User Facilities Requested by the DTE on a Per-Call Basis		Category*
2.1	Direct call	A
2.2	Abbreviated address calling	A
2.3	Multiaddress calling	A
2.4	Reverse charging	A
2.5	RPOA selection	A
2.6	Charging information	A
2.7	Called line identification	A

*E = Essential Service or Facility   A = Additional Service or Facility

TABLE E-2. RECOMMENDATION X.2 PACKET-SWITCHED DATA TRANSMISSION SERVICE

1. Optional User Facilities Assigned for an Agreed Contractual Period	Category*			
	8-11**		20-22**	
	VC	PVC	VC	PVC
1.1 Extended packet sequence numbering (modula 128)	A	A	—	—
1.2 Nonstandard default window sizes	A	A	—	—
1.3 Nonstandard default packet sizes 16, 32, 64, 256, 512, 1024, 2048, 4096	A	A	FS	FS
1.4 Default throughput classes assignment	A	A	FS	FS
1.5 Flow control parameter negotiation	E	—	FS	—
1.6 Throughput class negotiation	E	—	FS	—
1.7 Packet retransmission	A	A	—	—
1.8 Incoming calls barred	E	—	A	—
1.9 Outgoing calls barred	E	—	A	—
1.10 One-way logical channel outgoing	E	—	—	—
1.11 One-way logical channel incoming	A	—	—	—
1.12 Closed user group	E	—	E	—
1.13 Closed user group with outgoing access	A	—	A	—
1.14 Closed user group with incoming access	A	—	A	—
1.15 Incoming calls barred within a closed user group	A	—	A	—
1.16 Outgoing calls barred within a closed user group	A	—	A	—
1.17 Bilateral closed user group	A	—	A	—
1.18 Bilateral closed user group with outgoing access	A	—	A	—
1.19 Reverse charging acceptance	A	—	A	—
1.20 Fast select acceptance	E	—	FS	—
1.21 Multilink procedure	A	A	—	—
1.22 Charging information	A	—	A	—
1.23 Direct call	FS	—	A	—
1.24 Hunt group	A	—	A	—
1.25 On-line facility registration	A	—	FS	—
1.26 D-bit modification	A	A	FS	—
1.27 Local charging prevention	A	—	FS	—
1.28 Call redirection	A	—	FS	—
1.29 Network user identification	A	—	A	—
1.30 Extended frame sequence numbering	A	A	—	—
1.31 RPOA selection	A	—	A	—

(Continued)

TABLE E-2. *(Continued)*

2. Optional User Facilities on a Per-Call Basis		Category*			
		8-11**		20-22**	
		VC	PVC	VC	PVC
2.1	Closed user group selection	E	—	E	—
2.2	Bilateral closed user group selection	A	—	FS	—
2.3	Reverse charging	A	—	A	—
2.4	RPOA selection	A	—	A	—
2.5	Flow control parameter negotiation	E	—	—	—
2.6	Fast select	E	—	FS	—
2.7	Throughput class negotiation	E	—	—	—
2.8	Abbreviated address calling	FS	—	A	—
2.9	Charging information	A	—	A	—
2.10	Transit delay selection and indication	E	—	—	—
2.11	Call redirection notification	A	—	FS	—
2.12	Called line address modified notification	A	—	FS	—
2.13	Network user identification	A	—	A	—
2.14	Closed user group with outgoing access selection	A	—	FS	—

*E = Essential Service or Facility; FS = For Further Study; A = Additional Service or Facility;
— = Not Applicable
VC: Virtual Call (Switched)
PVC: Permanent Virtual Circuit
**User Classes of Service (Recommendation X.1)

The following categories of access are provided by X.10:

START/STOP DIRECT CONNECTION TO A CIRCUIT-SWITCHED DATA TRANSMISSION SERVICE

Category of Access	Data Signaling Rate	DTE/DCE Interface Requirements
A1	50–200 bit/s	Recommendations X.20 and X.20 bis
A2	300 bit/s	Recommendations X.20 and X.20 bis

SYNCHRONOUS DIRECT CONNECTION TO A CIRCUIT-SWITCHED DATA TRANSMISSION SERVICE

Category of Access	Data Signaling Rate	DTE/DCE Interface Requirements
B1	600 bit/s	Recommendations X.21 and X.21 bis
B2	2400 bit/s	Recommendations X.21 and X.21 bis
B3	4800 bit/s	Recommendations X.21 and X.21 bis
B4	9600 bit/s	Recommendations X.21 and X.21 bis
B5	48000 bit/s	Recommendations X.21 and X.21 bis

START/STOP DIRECT CONNECTION TO A PACKET-SWITCHED DATA TRANSMISSION SERVICE

Category of Access	Data Signaling Rate	DTE/DCE Interface Requirements
C1	110 bit/s	Recommendation X.28
C2	200 bit/s	Recommendation X.28
C3	300 bit/s	Recommendation X.28
C4	1200 bit/s	Recommendation X.28
C5	75/1200 bit/s	Recommendation X.28

SYNCHRONOUS DIRECT CONNECTION TO A PACKET-SWITCHED DATA TRANSMISSION SERVICE

Category of Access	Data Signaling Rate	DTE/DCE Interface Requirements
D1	2400 bit/s	Recommendation X.25
D2	4800 bit/s	Recommendation X.25
D3	9600 bit/s	Recommendation X.25
D4	48000 bit/s	Recommendation X.25

START/STOP DIRECT CONNECTION TO A LEASED CIRCUIT DATA TRANSMISSION SERVICE

Category of Access	Data Signaling Rate	DTE/DCE Interface Requirements
E1	50–200 bit/s	Recommendations X.20 and X.20 bis
E2	300 bit/s	Recommendations X.20 and X.20 bis

SYNCHRONOUS DIRECT CONNECTION TO A LEASED CIRCUIT DATA TRANSMISSION SERVICE

Category of Access	Data Signaling Rate	DTE/DCE Interface Requirements
F1	600 bit/s	Recommendations X.21 and X.21 bis
F2	2400 bit/s	Recommendations X.21 and X.21 bis
F3	4800 bit/s	Recommendations X.21 and X.21 bis
F4	9600 bit/s	Recommendations X.21 and X.21 bis
F5	48000 bit/s	Recommendations X.21 and X.21 bis

START/STOP SWITCHED CONNECTION BY MEANS OF THE PSTN TO A CIRCUIT-SWITCHED DATA TRANSMISSION SERVICE

Category of Access	Data Signaling Rate	DTE/DCE Interface Requirements
G1	300 bit/s	Further Study

SYNCHRONOUS SWITCHED CONNECTION BY MEANS OF THE PSTN TO A CIRCUIT-SWITCHED DATA TRANSMISSION SERVICE

Category of Access	Data Signaling Rate	DTE/DCE Interface Requirements
I1	600 bit/s	Further Study
I2	2400 bit/s	Further Study
I3	4800 bit/s	Further Study
I4	9600 bit/s	Further Study

SYNCHRONOUS SWITCHED CONNECTION BY MEANS OF AN ISDN D CHANNEL TO A CIRCUIT-SWITCHED DATA TRANSMISSION SERVICE

Category of Access	Data Signaling Rate	DTE/DCE Interface Requirements
J1	600 bit/s	Recommendations X.21, X.21 bis and X.30
J2	2400 bit/s	Recommendations X.21, X.21 bis and X.30
J3	4800 bit/s	Recommendations X.21, X.21 bis and X.30
J4	9600 bit/s	Recommendations X.21, X.21 bis and X.30
J5	48000 bit/s	Recommendations X.21, X.21 bis and X.30

START/STOP CONNECTION BY MEANS OF A CSPDN TO A PACKET-SWITCHED DATA TRANSMISSION SERVICE

Category of Access	Data Signaling Rate	DTE/DCE Interface Requirements
K1	300 bit/s	Recommendation X.28

START/STOP SWITCHED CONNECTION BY MEANS OF THE PSTN TO A PACKET-SWITCHED DATA TRANSMISSION SERVICE

Category of Access	Data Signaling Rate	DTE/DCE Interface Requirements
L1	110 bit/s	Recommendation X.28
L2	200 bit/s	Recommendation X.28
L3	300 bit/s	Recommendation X.28
L4	1200 bit/s	Recommendation X.28
L5	75/1200 bit/s	Recommendation X.28

SYNCHRONOUS SWITCHED CONNECTION BY MEANS OF A CSPDN TO A PACKET-SWITCHED DATA TRANSMISSION SERVICE

Category of Access	Data Signaling Rate	DTE/DCE Interface Requirements
O1	2400 bit/s	Recommendation X.32
O2	4800 bit/s	Recommendation X.32
O3	9600 bit/s	Recommendation X.32
O4	4800 bit/s	Recommendation X.32

SYNCHRONOUS SWITCHED CONNECTION BY MEANS OF THE PSTN TO A
PACKET-SWITCHED DATA TRANSMISSION SERVICE

Category of Access	Data Signaling Rate	DTE/DCE Interface Requirements
P1	4800 bit/s	Recommendation X.32
P2	2400 bit/s	Recommendation X.32
P3	4800 bit/s	Recommendation X.32
P4	9600 bit/s	Recommendation X.32

SYNCHRONOUS SWITCHED ACCESS BY MEANS OF AN ISDN B CHANNEL TO A
PACKET-SWITCHED DATA TRANSMISSION SERVICE

Category of Access	Data Signaling Rate	DTE/DCE Interface Requirements
Q1	2400 bit/s	Recommendations X.25 and X.31
Q2	4800 bit/s	Recommendations X.25 and X.31
Q3	9600 bit/s	Recommendations X.25 and X.31
Q4	48000 bit/s	Recommendations X.25 and X.31

SYNCHRONOUS DIRECT CONNECTION TO A CIRCUIT-SWITCHED DATA
TRANSMISSION SERVICE

Category of Access	Data Signaling Rate	DTE/DCE Interface Requirements
S1	600 bit/s	Recommendations X.21, X.21 bis and X.30
S2	2400 bit/s	Recommendations X.21, X.21 bis and X.30
S3	4800 bit/s	Recommendations X.21, X.21 bis and X.30
S4	9600 bit/s	Recommendations X.21, X.21 bis and X.30
S5	48000 bit/s	Recommendations X.21, X.21 bis and X.30
S6	64000 bit/s	Recommendations X.21, X.21 bis and X.30

SYNCHRONOUS DIRECT CONNECTION VIA THE B CHANNEL TO A PACKET-SWITCHED
DATA TRANSMISSION SERVICE

Category of Access	Data Signaling Rate	DTE/DCE Interface Requirements
T1	2400 bit/s	Recommendations X.25 and X.31
T2	4800 bit/s	Recommendations X.25 and X.31
T3	9600 bit/s	Recommendations X.25 and X.31
T4	48000 bit/s	Recommendations X.25 and X.31

SYNCHRONOUS DIRECT CONNECTION VIA THE D CHANNEL TO A PACKET-SWITCHED
DATA TRANSMISSION SERVICE

Category of Access	Data Signaling Rate	DTE/DCE Interface Requirements
U1	2400 bit/s	Recommendations X.25 and X.31
U2	4800 bit/s	Recommendations X.25 and X.31
U3	9600 bit/s	Recommendations X.25 and X.31
U4	48000 bit/s	Recommendations X.25 and X.31
U5	64000 bit/s	Recommendations X.25 and X.31

SYNCHRONOUS SWITCHED CONNECTION BY MEANS OF AN ISDN B CHANNEL TO A
PACKET-SWITCHED DATA TRANSMISSION SERVICE

Category of Access	Data Signaling Rate	DTE/DCE Interface Requirements
Y1	2400 bit/s	Recommendations X.25 and X.31
Y2	4800 bit/s	Recommendations X.25 and X.31
Y3	9600 bit/s	Recommendations X.25 and X.31
Y4	48000 bit/s	Recommendations X.25 and X.31
Y5	64000 bit/s	Recommendations X.25 and X.31

RECOMMENDATION X.92: HYPOTHETICAL REFERENCE CONNECTIONS FOR A PUBLIC SYNCHRONOUS DATA NETWORK

This recommendation establishes the specific connections available for DTEs, DSEs, and DCEs into data networks. X.92 is referenced in many of the other data network standards, such as X.25 and X.75. Consequently, like the other standards in this appendix, it serves as a foundation for higher-level standards. The reference connections are illustrated in Figure E-1. The legends in the figure explain the various options for connections. The following links are permitted within the standard:

Link A   data link between two adjacent data-switching exchanges in a national network

Link A1   data link between two adjacent gateway data-switching exchanges in an international connection

Link B   data link between a source DSE and a destination DSE

Link B1   data link between a local DSE and a gateway DSE

Link G1   data link between a source gateway DSE and a destination gateway DSE in an international connection

Link C   data link between source DTE and destination DTE

Link D   data link between source DTE and the source local DSE or the data link between destination DTE and destination local DSE

Link E   data link between communicating processes

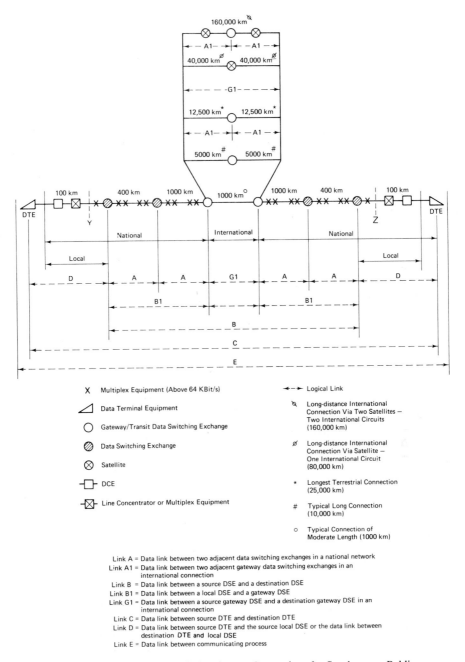

Figure E-1. X.92: Hypothetical Reference Connections for Synchronous Public Data Networks

RECOMMENDATION X.96: CALL PROGRESS SIGNALS IN PUBLIC DATA NETWORKS

This standard establishes the signals that may be used to inform DTEs (such as calling DTEs) of the progress of a connection call or connection request through a public network. X.96 defines the signals to be returned to the caller to indicate connections that were not made (and why) and to indicate circumstances regarding the progress of a call through a network. It can be very valuable for a calling DTE to know if (a) there is a problem detected at the DTE/DCE interface, (b) if a virtual call has been reset or cleared, or (c) if a permanent virtual circuit has been reset. These services can be provided by the X.96 standard. The call-progress signals within this standard are:

A	Call not cleared. Calling DTE is expected to wait.
B	Call cleared because the procedure is complete.
C1/C2	Call cleared. The calling DTE should call again soon; the next attempt may be successful. The interval between successive attempts and the maximum number of attempts will depend on a number of circumstances including: —nature of the call-progress signal —user's traffic pattern —tariffs —possible regulations by the Administrations, or reset (for packet-switched services only).
D1/D2	Call cleared. The calling DTE should take other action to clarify when the call attempt might be successful, or reset (for permanent virtual circuit only). The DTE should cease data transmission and take other action as appropriate.
C1/D1	Due to subscriber condition.
C2/D2	Due to network condition.

RECOMMENDATION X.121: INTERNATIONAL NUMBERING PLAN FOR PUBLIC DATA NETWORKS

This recommendation has received considerable attention throughout the world because its intent is to provide a universal addressing scheme, allowing users to communicate with each other through multiple networks. X.121 establishes a standard numbering scheme for all countries' networks and individual users within those networks.

A DTE within a public data network is addressed by an international data network address. The international data network address consists of a data network identification code (DNIC) plus a network terminal number (NTN). Another option is to provide the international data number as the data country code (DCC) plus a national number (NN).

DATA NETWORK IDENTIFICATION CODE (DNIC)
FOUR DIGIT CODE: **XXX Y**

XXX = WORLD ZONES (Europe, North America, etc.) and
an escape to link with Telex and telephone networks.

Y = Specific Network

XXX also called a Data Country Code (DCC)

INTERNATIONAL DATA NUMBER
TWO APPROACHES:

ONE   P + DNIC + Network Terminal Number
        (1)   (4)   (10)

TWO   P + DCC + National Number
        (1)   (3)   (11)

PRIVATE DATA NETWORKS:
INTERNATIONAL NUMBERING PLAN
CCITT X.121

P + DNIC + Network Terminal Number (NTN)

Where NTN: Private Network Identification Code (PNIC) (6)
And End Terminal Number (ETN) (4)   **Figure E-2.**

The four codes consist of the following identifiers: the DNIC consists of four digits—the first three digits identify the country and can be regarded as a data country code (DCC). The fourth digit identifies a specific data network within a country. The network terminal number can consist of 10 digits or, if in place of the NTN, a national number (NN) is used; 11 digits are allowed. Figure E-2 shows the configurations allowed under X.121.

RECOMMENDATION X.213: NETWORK SERVICE DEFINITION FOR OPEN SYSTEMS INTERCONNECTION FOR CCITT APPLICATIONS

This standard is used by several higher-level standards in the OSI model. It defines the service provided by the network layer to the transport layer at the boundary between the two layers. The recommendation of the recently released transport layer standard (discussed in Chapter Eight) covers many of the X.213 specifications. Consequently, it will not be discussed in detail here, since it was covered in the earlier chapter. In summary, the recommendation defines the network services in terms of the primitive actions and events provided between the layers, the parameters associated with each action, and the interrelationships of the events.

Index

A

Abandon operation, 330
A bit, 194
Abort signal, 82
Access, categories of, for data terminal
  equipment to public data transmission
  services, 413, 416-20
Access control machine, 134
Access right, 54
Access token, 54
Access units, 350
ACK, 29, 278
ACK0/ACK1 technique, 75
Acknowledgment number, 278
Active open mode, 276
Adaptive differential PCM, 237
Adaptive directory, 162
Adaptive routing, 168
Address field, 80-81, 250
ALOHA, 108-10
Alternate mark inversion code, 21, 233
Amdahl, 289
American National Standards Institute (ANSI),
  47, 64, 117, 145-48, 365, 378, 400, 410-11
American Telephones and Telegraph
  Corporation (AT&T), 118, 138-39, 152, 154,
  170, 171, 232, 233, 234, 258, 309, 314
Amplitude, 14
Analog signal, 14, 228-29, 236
Analog-to-digital techniques, 234-38, 258
Analog waveforms, 14
Analysis synthesis, 237
Antenna-oriented channels, 373-74
A packets, 193
APPC/PC LU 6.2, 302
AppleTalk, 303-4
Application association regime, 359
Application context, 340
Application entities, 339, 340, 351
Application layer, 285, 338-40
Application process, 2
Application service elements, 339, 351
Arbiter, 54
ARPANET, 163, 167-68
ASCII code, 375-76, 378

ASN.1, 331-33
  coding rules, 333
  examples of, 333-37
Association control service element, 339, 340
Asynchronous balanced mode, 78
Asynchronous disconnected mode, 77-78
Asynchronous formatting, 22-23
Asynchronous response mode, 78
Asynchronous transmission, 23
At least once approach, 343
At most once approach, 343
Atomic actions, 345
Atomicity, consistency, isolation, and durability,
  363
Atoms, 368
Attribute, 356
Attribute packet, 297
Automatic call-back, 321
Automatic Electric Company, 152
Automatic intercept system, 155
Automatic ring-down, 150
Autonomous system, 280
Autonomous systems extended links
  advertisement, 285

B

Backbone, 285
Balanced configuration, 79
Balanced transmission lines, 373
Bandwidth, 15, 17, 372
Base, 374
Baseband network, 119
Baseband signal, 18
Base-ten numbering system, 381
Basic encoding rules, 337
BASIC language, 289
Baud, 14
B channels, 246-47
Bearer services, 243, 247
Bell Laboratories, 22, 228, 230, 234, 260, 288
Bidirectional transmission, 256-57
Binary code, 21
Binary coded decimal code, 378-79
Binary/decimal conversion, 382
Binary numbers, 374-75

Binary synchronous control, 73-76
  formats and control codes, 73-74
  line control, 75-76
  line modes, 74-75
  problems with BSC, 76
Binary synchronous control protocol, 105, 297-98
Bipolar code, 21
Bit protocols, 72
Bit rate, 13-14
Bits per second, 13
BLAST, 295
Block check, 290
B packets, 193
Break functional unit, 363
British Telecommunications, 252, 314
Broadband network, 118-19
Broadcast capability, 103
Broadcasting, 108, 162
4.3 BSD UNIX system, 265
Burroughs, 289
Burst error, 372
Burst-error channel, 372
Bus interface units, 50
Bypass, 116

C

Caesar cypher, 322
Call-forwarding, 321
Call progress signals in public data networks, 422
Carriage return code, 378
Carrier frequency, 18
Carrier sense (collision) systems, 50-52
Carrier sense (collision-free) systems, 54-55
Cathode ray tube, 378
C-BEGIN service, 345
CCITT. *See* International Telegraph & Telephone Consultative Committee (CCITT)
C-COMMIT service, 345
Centralized routing network, 161
Central office, 10-11
Channel, 370
Channel access, 127-30
Channel banks, 230
Channel service unit, 234
Channel speed, 13-14
Character protocols, 72
CHAR function, 296
Check field, 297
Checkpoint, 85
Checksum, 278, 290-91
Christiansen, Ward, 294
Circuit, 370
Circuit switching, 149-50, 252
Circuit-switching networks
  components of, 150, 152

packet-switching support to, 170-72
Classification tree, 36
Class-of-service option, 136, 164
Clear packet, 184-85
Cluster controller, 27
Coaxial cable, 373
Code, 371, 375-79
Code book, 238
Collisions, 128-30
Collision window, 51-52, 128
Combined station, 77
Command frames, 77
Command/response field, 250
Command/response field bits, 252
Commit functional unit, 364
Commitment, concurrence, and recovery protocol, 339, 344-46
Commitment tree, 345
Common Channel Interoffice Signalling system, 170-71
Common control devices, 153
Common IBM PC LAN protocol stacks, 301-2
Communication
  classification of protocols, 36, 38
  connection-oriented and connectionless networks, 34-36
  nonpolling systems, 46-47
    request to send/clear to send, 47
    time division multiple access, 48-49
    xon/xoff, 47-48
  peer-to-peer nonpriority systems, 49-54
  peer-to-peer priority systems, 54-55
  polling/selection systems, 38-40
    continuous ARQ (sliding windows), 43-46
    selective and group polling, 40-41
    stop-and-wait polling/selection, 41-43
  using satellites for, 104-14
  traffic control and accountability, 28-30
  wide area and local networks, 30-31, 33-34
Communications channel, 371
Communications circuit, 367-74
Communications port, 24-25
Communications protocols, classification of, 36, 38
Communications signal, 368
Communications theory
  bandwidth and the frequency spectrum, 14-15, 17
  channel speed and bit rate, 13-14
  voice communications and analog waveforms, 14
Companded delta modulation scheme, 239
Companding, 230, 232
Compound error, 372
Computerized branch exchange, 306
Computer networks
  advantages of, 2-3

definition of, 1
structure of, 2-6
Computer-to-PBX interface proposals, 315-18
Conceptual memory/display, 361
Concurrence, commitment, and recovery, 363
Connectionless-mode networks, 211
Connectionless networks, 34-36
Connection-oriented networks, 34-36
Connection-oriented protocol, 274
Consistent state, 356
Contention operation, 75
Continuous ARQ, 43-46, 106, 297
Continuously variable slope delta modulation, 237
Control field, 81
Control mode, 74
Control object, 362
Control packet, 170
Conventional multiplexing, 104
Cooperating user agents, 350
Cost metrics, 282
C-PREPARE, 346
C-READY, 345
C-REFUSE, 346
C-RESTART, 346
C-ROLLBACK, 346
Crossbar switches, 153
Crossbar tandem, 153
CSMA/CD, 125-26, 298
Current, 368
Customer interface, 260
Customer premises equipment, 234
Continuously variable slope delta modulation, 258
Cycle, 14
Cyclic redundancy checking, 24, 30, 81, 125, 290-91, 297
Cyphers, 322

D

Data, 279, 370
Data activity compression, 241
Data circuit-termination equipment, 3, 383
Data communications, reasons for using PBX in, 306-7
Data communications channel, speed of, 13-14
Data communications signals, 370
Data country code, 422, 423
Data diddling, 319-20
Data encapsulation decapsulation, 126-27
Data encoding/decoding, 127
Data encryption standard, 323-26
Data field, 269, 296
Data flow, 4-5
Datagram, 24, 34, 263
Datagram delivery protocol, 304

Datagram routing, 168
Data length field, 125
Data link controls, 28, 36
Data link layer, 126, 176-77
Data manipulation language, 364
Data network identification code, 422
Data offset field, 278
Data packet networks, 258-59
Dataphone Digital Service, 139
Data service unit, 25-26, 234
Data switching equipment, 5, 27
Data terminal equipment, 2-3, 155, 181, 247, 383
Data transfer regime, 359
Data unit, 356
D bit, 192, 267
D channel, 246, 247
Decimal number, 374
Defense Advanced Research Projects Agency, 258
Defined context set, 337
Delay bit, 192, 267
Delta modulation, 237
Descriptive name, 352
Destination addresses, 124, 269
Destination port, 278, 279
Destination subarea, 165
Destructive close, 329
Destructive release, 329
Device object, 362
Diagnostic packet, 185
Difference in potential, 370
Differential pulse code modulation, 234, 236
Digital carrier systems, 232-34
Digital data interface translation, 308
Digital data port, 241
Digital Equipment Corporation, 125
Digital multiplexed interface, 315-18
Digital networks, 228
  advantages of, 228-29
  analog-to-digital techniques, 234-38
  Bell Labs' packet-switched voice-data patent, 260
  channel and data service units, 234
  digital carrier systems, 232-34
  future, 238-39
  integrated, 239-55
  integrated services digital network, 241-55
  SBS integrated network, 239-41
  signal conversion, 230-32
  voice transmission by packet, 257-59
Digital signals, 18
Digital subscriber line, 260
Digital switching, 255-57, 308
Digital-to-analog converter, 230
Digits, 374
Direct distance dialing, 153
Directory, 355
Directory routing, 163-68

Direct progressive control system, 152
DISC (Disconnect), 87
Display object, 362
Display text, 297
Distance metric, 270
Distributed routing, 161
Distributed transaction processing, 363-64
Distribution list, 352
DL Submit Permission, 335
Double parity, 290
DP 10026, 363
DQDB operations, 137
Dual queue dual bus, 137
Duplicate packets, 170
Durability, 366
Dynamic directory, 162
Dynamic nonhierarchical routing, 12
Dynamic polling/selection tables, 40

E

Early Bird, 104
EBCDIC code, 58, 331, 375-79
E channel, 246, 247
Echoplex, 289-90
Elastic buffer, 241
Electrical attributes, 383
Electrical current, 368
Electromagnetic wave, 374
Electromechanical program control, 150
Electromechanical systems, 152-53
Electronic document exchange, 367-68
Electronic Industries Association, 64
EIA-232-D, 14, 19, 47, 64, 139, 176, 244, 288,
    292, 293, 308, 317, 327, 400, 407-8
Electronic mail, 348-49
Electrons, 367-68
Encryption
    with private keys, 321-23
    with public keys, 326-27
End of file packet, 296
End-of-transmission code, 39, 378
End-to-end protocols, 30
ENQ code, 75
Ericsson, 309
Error checking, 30, 290
Error-detecting modems, 96
Error handling, 289-91
Error packet, 297
ESC character, 378
Ethernet CSMA/CD standard, 299
EtherTalk, 303
European Computer Manufacturers
    Association, 64, 117, 119, 120, 205, 401,
    405, 408

European Telecommunications Satellite
    Organization, 111
Exchange Station Identification, 88
Expiration, 344
Explicit routes, 164, 165
Explicit token system, 54
Extermination, 344
External gateway protocol, 281, 282
External routing, 284

F

Fast select, 181-82
Fast select call, 181
Fast select with immediate clear, 181
Federal Communications Commission rulings,
    234
FED-STD, 400
Fiber distributed data interface, 145-48
File access data units, 357
File header packet, 297
File management, protocols for, 353-56
File open regime, 359
File selection regime, 359
File service regimes, 358-59
File transfer, 356
    on personal computers, 294-98
File Transfer, Access, and Management
    standard, 353, 356-59
File Transfer Protocol, 274, 285
FIN, 278
FIPS, 400
Fixed directory, 162
Flag fields, 80, 267
Flags, 23, 278
Flow control, 170, 173, 276
Form feed code, 378
Fourth-generation PBX, 313-14
Four-wire circuit, 5
Fragmentation, 267
Fragmentation offset field, 267-68
Frame, 23, 24, 263-64
Frame check-sequence field, 24, 81
Frame Reject command, 88, 227
Frame relay, 224-26
Free electrons, 368
Frequency, 14
Frequency division multiplexing, 104-5, 118-19
Frequency modulation, 288
Frequency shift keying, 288
Frequency spectrum, 16
Front-end processor, 25
FT-4E-432, 232
Full-duplex transmission, 4-5, 276
Full-path directory, 162

Functional attributes, 383
Functional groupings, 243

G

Gateway, 261
General broadcast, 144
Go-Back-N technique, 106, 108
Government Open Systems Interconnection
    Profile, 67-71
Graceful close, 276
Grand-orphan, 344
Granular noise, 237
Graphical user interface, 300
Ground, 371
Group polling, 40-41
GTE Corp., 258
Guardband, 105

H

Half-duplex, 4-5
Handshake, 34, 43
Handshake functional unit, 364
H channels, 246
High-level data link control, 40, 77, 120, 177,
    291, 295
  code transparency and synchronization,
    81-83
  commands and responses, 85-89
  control field, 83-85
  frame format, 79-81
  options, 77-79
  subsets, 95-96
  synchronous data link control, 97-99
  transmission process, 89-94
HDLC/LAPB standard, 194
Header checksum, 269
Header length field, 267
Headers, 61
Hertz, 14
Hexadecimal system, 380
Hierarchical topology, 7-9
Higher-level protocol, 35
High-usage trunks, 11-12
Honeywell, 309
Horizontal tabulation effector, 376
Horizontal topology, 9
Host address, 333

I

ICL machines, 289
Idempotent, 343
Identification field, 24

Identifier field, 267
Idle channel condition, 80
Idle signal, 82
Implicit token system, 53
Implicit type, 335
Inclusive acknowledgment, 45
Information field, 81
Information format frame, 79
Information System Network, 138-39
Information transfer, 38, 78, 87, 133-34
Initialization state, 78
Initial send sequence number, 278
Initiator, 340
Institute of Electrical and Electronic Engineers
    (IEEE), 64
  802 standards, 68, 117, 137-38, 181
  802.3 standard, 125-26, 147
  802.4, 134-37
  802.5 standard, 130, 132-34, 140, 143, 301
  standards, 119-25
InteCom, 309
Integrated services digital network, 239, 241-55
Intel Corporation, 125
Interchange circuit(s), 387
Interface control information, 60
Interface data unit, 60
Interface machine, 134-35
Interframe time, 82
Internal gateway protocols, 281, 283
International Business Machines (IBM), 139-45,
    289, 309, 326, 360
International data transmission services in
    public data networks, 413, 414, 415-16
International numbering plan, 422-23
International Organization for Standardization,
    63-64, 76, 117, 204, 205, 328, 401, 404-5, 406-7
  ISO 8473, 265, 274
  ISO 8802, 68
  ISO 9075, 364
  ISO 9735, 365
  ISO/CCITT Model, relationship of the 802
    standards to, 120
  ISO DP 9579, 364
  ISO network model, 120
International Telecommunications Union, 63
International Telegraph & Telephone
    Consultative Committee (CCITT), 63, 173,
    205, 243, 348, 400, 401, 408-10, 412
  network service definition for open systems
    interconnection for, 423
  standards, 247, 384
  telematics recommendations, 405-6
  v.32 modem specification, 288
  v.35, 327
  X series, 315

International user classes of service in public
data networks, 412-14
International X.25 networks, 226-27
Internet Activities Board, 332
Internet Control Message Protocol, 270, 271-73
Internet Protocol, 273-74, 332
Internetworking, 209-10, 261-63
Internetwork Protocol, 211
    address structure, 265
    datagram, 267-69
    source routing, 269-70
Interpersonal messaging service, 349, 351
Interrupt procedure, 182
IPX, 302

K

Kermit packet, 296-97
Kermit protocol, 296
Kernel, 362
Kernel functional unit, 363
Kernel group, 356
Key-dependent computation, 324

L

LAN/WAN-carrier network, 224-25
LAPB, 95-96, 221
LAPD, 96, 247-52
LAPX (LAPB extended), 96
Large-scale integration circuitry, 228
Last of many approach, 344
Layered protocols
    communication between layers, 58-60
    goals of, 56-57
    pragmatic illustration, 61-62
Least-cost routing, 282
Least once approach, 346
LEN field, 296
Limited broadcast, 144
Line, 370
Linear coding, 232
Linear predictive coding, 237, 258
Line feed character, 376
Line protocol, 28, 36
Link, 370
Link access procedure, 95, 291
Link-access protocol, 304
Link establishment, 36
Link protocol, 28
Link termination, 38
Local address, 265
Local area network (LAN), 31, 33, 34, 35-36,
    68, 243
    broadband and baseband, 118-19

connection options with, 120-23
control of operations through packet
    flooding, 162-63
IEEE standards, 119-25
issue of using PBX in, 311-13
personal computers and, 298-300
primary attributes of, 118-19
reasons for, 117-18
topologies and protocols, 125-38
Local echo, 289-90
Local loop, 10
Local modem, 290
LocalTalk, 303
Logarithmic companded delta modulation, 239
Logical channel numbers, 174, 175, 178, 179
Logical channels, 167, 309
Logical link control, 68, 96, 120, 123, 144
Logical link control layer, 301
Logically disconnected state, 77
Logical units, 163, 164
London International Data Centre, 226
Looping, 283
Loose source routing, 270

M

MAC/LLC split, 120
MAC protocol data unit, 124-25
Mainframe computer, linking personal
    computer to, 292-93
Major sync point, 330
Manchester code, 22, 23, 127, 128, 147
Mark field, 296
Master/slave protocol, 38
M bit, 192
MCI, 309
Mechanical attributes, 383
Media-access management, 127
Medium access control, 120
Mesh topology, 10
Message Administration Service Element, 351
Message Delivery Service Element, 351
Message formats, 24
Message Handling Systems, 349, 353
Message mode, 74
Message Retrieval Service Element, 351
Message store, 350, 351
Message Submission Service Element, 351
Message switching, 156-57
Message transfer, 349
Message transfer agent, 349, 350
Message-transfer layer service, 353
Message transfer system, 350
Metropolitan area network standard, 119
Metropolitan Area Networks, 137

Microcom MNP, 297
Microcomputers, 288
Minor sync point, 330
Miscellaneous commands, 87
MIT, 258
Modeling, 237
Modem, 18-19, 25, 289
  error-detecting, 96
MODEM7, 294
Mode-setting commands, 83, 87
Modulation/demodulation, 18
Modulo 8, 188
Modulo 128 operation, 128, 188, 194, 250
Monoalphabetic substitution, 322
Mu law, 232
Multidrip configuration, 4
Multilevel modulation, 290
Multilink procedure, 213-14
Multiple interaction negotiation, 363
Multiplexing, 25, 276

N

Name-binding protocol, 304
Narrowcasting, 108
National Bureau of Standards, 64
National Communications System, 64
National Institute of Standards and Technology, 67
National number, 422, 423
National Security Agency, 326
Negative acknowledgment, 29, 39-40
  packet, 296, 297
Negotiated release functional unit, 363
NETBIOS, 302
Network
  address, 333
  and design goals, 6-7
  hierarchical topology, 7-9
  horizontal topology, 9
  mesh topology, 10
  ring topology, 9-10
  security on, 319-28
  star topology, 9
  topologies, 6
Network addressable units, 163, 164
Network components, synchronizing, 19-23
Network design problems, 57
Network interface card, 25
Network operating systems, 300-1
Network purge, 170
Network reliability, 6-7
Networks links advertisements, 285
Network terminal number, 422, 423
Node "route-around," 161
Noise, 17, 229, 371-72

Nonlinear coding, 232
Nonpersistent carrier sense technique, 50
Nonpolling systems, 46-47
  peer/peer systems, 108-10
  primary/secondary systems, 111-14
Non-return-to-zero code, 22
Non-self-clocking codes, 20
Normal disconnected mode, 77
Normal response mode, 78
Northern Telecom, 311
Northern Telecom DMS-100 system, 314
Novell, 302
N(S) field, 294
NT1 (network termination 1), 243
NT12 (network termination 1, 2), 244
Nyquist sampling theory, 230

O

Object model, 360, 361
One-bit error, 30
One of many approach, 344
1-persistent carrier, 50
Only once approach, 343
Open Shortest-Path-First protocol, 283-85
Open Systems Interconnection model, 56, 63, 247
  application layer, 66
  attachment unit interface, 66
  data link layer, 65
  goals of, 64-65
  layers of, 64-66
  medium dependent interface, 66
  network layer, 66
  network service definition for open systems
    interconnection for, 423
  physical layer, 65
  presentation layer, 66
  session layer, 66
  status, 66-67
  transport layer, 66
Optical fiber channels, 374
Optical transmission, 374
Options field, 269, 279
Orphan, 344
Out-of-band data, 279

P

Packet, 24, 267
  voice transmission by, 257-59
Packet assembly/disassembly, 31, 198, 200-2
Packet choking, 170
Packet die-out, 161
Packet flooding, 144, 162-63
Packet flow, 204

Packet formats, 188-94, 204
Packet loss, 184
Packet routing, 161-70
Packet-switch connections, 252
Packet switching, 157-59, 256
   determining when to use, 159-61
   packet routing, 161-70
   support to circuit-switching networks, 170-72
Packet voice terminal, 158
Padding field, 269, 279
Parameter coding, 237-38
Parameter model, 360
Parity checking, 290
Partial-path directory, 162
Passive open mode, 276
Path information unit, 165
P/C bit, 338
Peer-to-peer nonpriority systems, 49-54
Peer-to-peer priority systems, 54-55
Peer-to-peer protocol, 38
Permanent virtual circuit, 178
Personal computer
   communications characteristics of, 288-91
   file transfer on, 294-98
   growth in industry, 287-88
   linking to mainframe computers, 292-94
   and local area networks, 298-300
   using as a server, 291-93
Phase modulation, 288
Phases, 14, 359
Physical circuits, 4-5
Physical level interfaces, 383-99
Physical units, 163
Piggybacking, 41, 53, 320
Playout, 259, 260
Point-to-point routing, 4, 144
Polar code, 21
Polarized control, 363
Poll command, 38-40
Polling/selection, 105-8
   binary synchronous control, 73-76
      formats and control codes, 73-74
      line control, 75-76
      line modes, 74-75
      problems with, 76
   character and bit protocols, 72
   code transparency and synchronization, 81-83
   High-level data link control, 77-96
   protocol conversion, 100
Polling/selection systems, 38-40
Polyalphabetic cyphers, 322
Ports, 264-65, 288
Positive acknowledgment, 275
Postal and Telegraph Ministries, 226-27
   Televerket, 349-50
Potential difference, 368-69

P-persistent carrier sense, 50
Preamble, 23, 127
Pre-arbitrated services, 137
Precedence, 276
Prenegotiated target time, 148
Preorder tree traversal, 357
Presentation, context identifier, 337
Presentation layer, 331
Primary/secondary protocol, 38
Primary station, 77
Primitive name, 352
Primitives, 58
Printer access protocol, 304
Priority bits, 132
Priority slot, 54
Private automated branch exchange, 306
Private branch exchange, 27, 243, 257, 306
   computer-to-PBX interface proposals, 315-18
   digital multiplexed interface, 315-18
   evolution of, 307-10
   examples of modern, 314
   fourth-generation, 313-14
   issue of using in a LAN, 311-13
   issue of voice/data integration, 310-11
   PBX-CPI, 310
   PBX-DMI, 310
   processors, 307
   reasons for using in data communications,
      306-7
   switchboards, 152
Private group, 356
Private keys, excryption with, 321-23
Profile, 361
Progressive control system, 152
Protocol control information, 60
Protocol conversion, 100, 115, 198, 292
Protocol data unit, 60, 61, 123, 211, 262, 263-64,
   267
Protocol field, 269
Protocols, 3, 28, 375-79
   for file management, 353-56
   higher-level, 35
   line, 28
   link, 28
   routing, 28
   switching, 28
Protons, 367-68
PSH, 278
PTT Televerket, 347-48
P-TYPE-DATA service, 345
Public data networks
   call progress signals in, 422
   international data transmission services and
      optional user facilities in, 413, 414, 415-16
   international numbering plan for, 422-27
   international user classes of service in, 412-14

Public data transmission services, categories of access for data terminal equipment to, 413, 416-20
Public keys, encryption with, 326-27
Public synchronous data network, hypothetical reference connections for, 420-21
Pulse amplitude modulation, 230, 232
Pulse code modulation, 230, 234
Push function, 275

Q

Q.722, 172
Q bit, 193
Quality of service, 205, 207
Quantization noise, 237
Quantizing, 230
  errors, 232
Queued arbitrated service, 137

R

Random ALOHA, 108, 109-10
Random error, 372
Random routing, 163
R bit, 267
Read, 342
Read request, 3
Real filestores, 354
Receive machine, 134-35
Receive Not Ready, 40, 85, 87, 91, 182-84, 194
Receiver, 82-83
Receive Ready, 40, 85, 91, 93, 182, 194
Receiver sampling, 21
Receive state variable, 43
Recognized private operating agencies, 63
Recovery commands, 87
Reeves, A. H., 230
Reference points, 243
Reference, 111-12
Reference station, 48, 113
Regenerative repeaters, 229
Regime, 358-59
Regional Bell Operating Companies, 137
Register insertion, 50
Register-progressive control, 152
Registration packets, 186
Reincarnation, 344
Reject command, 45-46, 85, 87, 184, 221
Reliability bit (R bit), 267
Reliable transfer, 274
Reliable transfer service element, 339, 340-41
Remote data base access protocol, 364
Remote job entry, 182
Remote operations service element, 339, 343-44
Remote Procedure Call, 279

Repeaters, 229
Request Disconnect, 88
Request Initialization Mode, 87
Request for proposals, 67
Request to send/clear to send, 47
Reservation bits, 132
Reserved field, 278
Reset, 89
Reset packet, 184
Responder, 340
Response windows, 136
Restart operations, 184, 331
Resynchronization, 330
Return-to-zero code, 22, 23
Ring, 152
Ring interface unit, 141
Ring segment broadcast, 144
Ring topology, 9-10
RNR packet, 183
Rolm, 309
Route discovery protocols, 280-85
Route-recording option, 271
Router, 261
Router links advertisement, 285
Routing, loose and strict, 270
Routing data base, 284
Routing Information Protocol, 282-83
Routing operations, 270
Routing protocol, 28
Routing table maintenance protocol, 304
RS-232-C standard interface, 383-87
RS-449, 327
RST, 278

S

Salami attack, 320
Satellite Business Systems', 239-41, 252
Satellite communications controller, 113
Satellite delay compensation unit, 114-15
Satellite delay units, 108, 114-15
Satellite networks
  brief history, 103-4
  for communication, 104-14
    conventional multiplexing, 104-5
    nonpolling peer/peer systems, 108-10
    nonpolling primary/secondary systems, 111-14
    polling/selection, 105-8
  components, 101-2
  orbits of, 104
  pros and cons of, 102-3
Schema, 354
SDLC/HDLC, 310
Secondary station acts, 77
Security, 276, 323

Security blanket, 330
Security group, 356
Segment, 24, 263, 277-79
Select command, 38-40
Select-hold mode, 75
Selective polling, 40-41
Selective Reject, 85, 87, 93
Selective repeat, 45-46
Self-clocking code, 20
Send initiate packet, 296, 297
Send state variable, 43
SEQ field, 296
Sequence number, 275, 278
Sequence type, 334
Server, using personal computer as, 291-93
Service access point identifier, 250
Service access points, 58, 59, 120
Service application point, 265
Service data unit, 60
Session layer, 328-31
Session-oriented directory, 162, 163
Set Asynchronous Balanced Mode command,
    89, 95, 177, 215, 227
Set Asynchronous Balanced Mode Extended, 89
Set Initialization Mode, 87
Set Normal Response Mode, 87
Set Normal Response Mode Extended, 89
Set-successor frame, 136
Set type, 335
Shannon's Law, 372
Shared control functional unit, 363
Signal conversion, 230-32
Signal to distortion ratio, 232
Signalling terminal exchange, 212-13
Signal-to-noise ratio, 372
Signal transfer point, 171
Signal units, 171
Simple Mail Transfer Protocol, 274, 285
Simplex, 4
Sliding windows, 43-46
Slope overload, 237
Slotted ALOHA, 108, 110
SNA/APPC, 140
Sockets, 264-65
Solar eclipse, 103
Solicit-successor frame, 136
Source address, 124, 269
Source port, 278, 279
Source routing, 143, 269-70
Source service access point, 123
Space switching, 255-56
Speech segments, 237-38
S-RELEASE request, 329
Stacking station, 132
Standard interface, 317

Standards
    cross reference of, 406-11
    prevalent, 401-6
    supporting, to X.25/X.75 networks, 412-23
Standards organizations, 63-64
    addresses of, 400-1
Start frame delimiter, 124-25
Star topology, 9, 298
State diagrams, 395
State variables, 43
Static directory, 162
Step-by-step system, 152
Stop-and-wait polling/selection, 41-43
Storage group, 356
Store-and-forward technology, 156
Stored program control systems, 150, 153-55
Stream-oriented fashion, 275
Strict source routing, 270
Structured query language, 364
Stub, 342
Stuffing, 82
Subchannels, 17
Subnetwork access function, 209
Subnetwork address, 333
Subnetwork dependent convergence function,
    209
Subnetwork independence convergence
    function, 209, 210
Subnetworks, 262
Subschemas, 354
Subscriber loop, 10
Substitution cyphers, 322
Summary links advertisement, 285
Sun transient, 103
Supervisory format, 79, 85
Switch, 371
Switchboard, 152
Switched Multi-megabit Data Service, 137
Switching protocol, 28
Switch profile negotiation, 362-63
Symmetrical configuration, 78-79
SYN, 278
Synchronization, 20, 329-31
Synchronization codes, 20-22
Synchronization points, 328
Synchronous data-link control, 97-99
Synchronous transmission, 23
System Network Architecture, 163-65
System Services Control Point, 163-64

T

T1 carrier system, 232
Tandem center, 10
T bit, 267

T-DISCONNECT indication, 329
Telematics, 346-47
Telephone channel, speed of, 14
Telephone network, 10-12
  switched and nonswitched options, 12-13
Telephone switching systems, 149-52
  electromechanical, 152-53
  stored program control, 153-55
Telephony, 373
Teleport, 115-16
Teleservices, 243, 247
Teletext, 346, 347-48
TELNET, 285
Terminal adaptors, 243
Terminal end-point identifier, 250
Terminal equipment, 244
Terminal systems and protocols, 346-48
TEST, 88
Text mode, 74
Throughput bit (T bit), 267
Time division multiple access, 48-49, 111-14, 138
Time division multiplexed data stream, 230
Time/division multiplexing, 49, 105, 114, 119,
    230, 232, 233, 244
Time division switching, 255-56
Timed token approach, 148
Time multiplexed switch, 256
Timeout, 42-43
Timer, 54
Time slot interchange facility, 256
Timestamp option, 271
Time-to-live parameter, 268-69
Time varying model, 237
Tip, 152
Token bus, 53-54, 134-37
Token-holding station, 137
Token passing, 52-54, 55, 298
Token ring, 52-53, 130-34, 139-45, 301
Token rotation time, 148
TokenTalk, 303, 304
Total length field, 267
Traffic multiplication effect, 161, 162, 163
Traffic service position system, 155
Transfer Syntax, 337-40
Transfer time, 341
Transit machine, 134-35
Transit routing table, 164
Translation tables, 380-82
Transmission control block, 277
Transmission Control Protocol, 274-77
Transmission Control Protocol and the Internet
    Protocol, 261
  example of operations, 263-64
  and internetworking, 261-63
  IP address structure, 265

major IP services, 269-73
  ports and sockets, 264-65
  related protocols, 264
  segments, 275, 277-79
  value of the transport layer, 273-74
Transmission groups, 164-65
Transmit media-access management, 129
Transmitter, 374
Transparent text mode, 73-74
Transponder, 102
Transport layer, 36, 204-9
Transposition cyphers, 322, 323
Trap door breach, 321
Tree network, 8
Trigrams, 322
Trivial File Transfer Protocol, 279, 285
Truncated binary exponential back-off, 129
Tungsten filament wire, 370
Turner, Jonathan S., 260
Twisted pairs, 373
Two-wire circuit, 5
TYMNET, 166-67, 170, 258
Type field, 296
Type of service field, 267

U

Unbalanced configuration, 78
Unbalanced line, 373
Unchained transactions functional unit, 364
UNCHAR function, 296
Unipolar code, 21
Universal synchronous/asynchronous receiver
    transmitter, 25
Unnumbered acknowledgment, 215
Unnumbered commands and responses, 87
Unnumbered format frame, 79
Unnumbered Information, 87
Unnumbered polls, 88, 89
Upper-layer protocol, 269-70, 275
  applications layer, 338-40
  ASN.1, 331-38
  association control service element, 340
  commitment, concurrency, and recovery, 344-46
  distributed transaction processing, 363-64
  electronic mail, 348-53
  for file management, 353-56
  file transfer, access, and management, 356-60
  network security, 319-28
  presentation layer, 331
  reliable transfer service element, 340-42
  remote data base access, 364-65
  remote operations service element, 342-44
  terminal systems and protocols, 346-48
  virtual terminal, 360-63

X.500 directory services, 353
URG, 278
Urgent data functional unit, 363
Urgent pointer, 278
User agent, 349
User data, 61
User Datagram protocol, 279-80, 283
User element, 353
User facilities, in public data networks, 413, 414, 415-16
User-to-user connections, 252

V

V series
  interfaces, 400-3, 405-7
  V.24, 19, 244, 387-94
  V.25, 224-26
  V.42, 96, 291
Value-added carriers, 160
Version field, 267
Vertical network, 8
Vertical tabulation character, 376
Videotex, 346-47
Virtual call, 178-81
Virtual channels, 158, 309
Virtual circuit, 158, 275
Virtual filestore, 353-54
Virtual routes, 164
Virtual terminal protocols, 360-63
Vocoding, 237
Voice activity compression, 240-41
Voice communications, 14
Voice/data integration, 310-11
Voice digitalization rate, 236
Voice transmission by packet, 257-59
Volt, 370

W

Wang, 309
WATS, 309
Waveform analysis, 234-37
Wellknown ports, 265
Wellknown services, 265
Wide area networks (WANs), 31, 32, 33, 35, 45, 68, 267
Windows, 43-46, 278
Wire pairs, 373
Wiring, costs of, 312-13
Write, 342

X

X series
  X.1, 412-13

X.2, 413, 414, 415-16
X.3, 198-99
X.10, 413, 416-20
X.21, 175, 177, 244, 394-396
X.25, 68, 181, 186, 195-97, 213, 256, 258, 310, 315
X.25 network
  communications between the layers, 214-24
  companion standards to, 177-78
  features of, 173-75
    channel options, 178-82
  flow control and windows, 194-95
  flow-control principles, 182
  and the frame relay and X.25, 224-26
  international, 226-27
  layers of, 175-77
  packet formats, 188-94
  packet mode device, 247
  reasons for, 175
  supporting standards to, 412-23
  timeouts and time limits, 187
  X.25 facilities, 195-97
  X.25 logical channel states, 186
  X.28, 199, 202, 213
  X.29, 193, 202-4
  X.29 protocol, 189
  X.75, 211-14, 412-23
  X.92, 213, 420-21
  X.121, 188
  X.209, 331
  X.213, 423
  X.400, 349-53, 365
  X.402, 351
  X.403, 351
  X.407, 351
  X.408, 351
  X.411, 351
  X.413, 351
  X.419, 351
  X.420, 351
  X.500, 353
Xerox Corporation, 125, 282
Xerox's PUP, 282
XMODEM, 294-96
XNS, 282, 302
Xon/Xoff, 47-48
XORing, 296
X-series recommendations, 403-4
X standard interfaces, 396-99

Z

Zone information protocol, 304